80°N

Greenland Sea

GREENLAND

MANITOBA

Hudson Bay

Fort Severn

Severn River

Big Trout Lake

James Bay

Deer Lake

Albany River

Red Lake

Moosonee

Kenora

ONTARIO

Lake Nipigon

QUÉBEC

Missinaibi River

Abitibi River

Nipigon

Lake of the Woods

Rainy River

Thunder Bay

Timmins

Kirkland Lake

Lake Superior

Sudbury

Ottawa River

Sault Ste. Marie

North Bay

Georgian Bay

Ottawa-Gatineau

Lake Huron

Kingston

St. Lawrence Seaway

Lake Michigan

Toronto

Lake Ontario

Hamilton

Niagara

London

Falls

Windsor

Lake Erie

0   200 km

Projection:
Lambert Conformal Conic

tarjuaq

Davis Strait

Iqaluit

Labrador Sea

NEWFOUNDLAND AND LABRADOR

Nain

Happy Valley-Goose Bay

QUÉBEC

Corner Brook

St John's

Gulf of St. Lawrence

PRINCE EDWARD ISLAND

50°W

Sydney

onee

Saguenay

NEW BRUNSWICK

Charlottetown

Chicoutimi-Jonquière

Moncton

Kirkland Lake

Quebec

Saint John

40°N

Trois-Rivières

Fredericton

Halifax

Montreal

NOVA SCOTIA

bury

Ottawa Gatineau

St. Lawrence Seaway

Bay of Fundy

oronto

Lake Ontario

ton

Lake Erie

ATLANTIC OCEAN

80°W   70°W   60°W

KEY

✪ National capital

★ Provincial or Territorial capital

◉ CMA (city)

● Other important city, town, or settlement

0   500 km

Projection:
Lambert's Equal Area

The Canada map was adapted from Mountain High Maps®
Copyright © 1993
Digital Wisdom®, Inc.

W9-AMU-618

Making Connections

ISSUES IN CANADIAN GEOGRAPHY

THIRD EDITION

Authors

Bruce W. Clark

John K. Wallace

PEARSON

Copyright © 2015 Pearson Canada Inc., Toronto, Ontario.

All rights reserved. This publication is protected by copyright and permission should be obtained from the publisher prior to any prohibited reproduction, storage in a retrieval system, or transmission in any form or by any means, electronic, mechanical, photocopying, recording, or likewise.

Portions of this publication may be reproduced under licence from Access Copyright, or with the express written permission of Pearson Canada Inc., or as permitted by law. Permission to reproduce material from this resource is restricted to the purchasing school.

Permission to reprint copyright material is gratefully acknowledged. Every effort was made to trace ownership of copyright material, secure permission, and accurately acknowledge its use. For information regarding permissions, please contact the Permissions Department through www.pearsoncanada.ca.

The information and activities presented in this work have been carefully edited and reviewed. However, the publisher shall not be liable for any damages resulting, in whole or in part, from the reader's use of this material.

Brand names and logos that appear in photographs provide students with a sense of real-world application and are in no way intended to endorse specific products.

Feedback on this publication can be sent to editorialfeedback@pearsoned.com

Pearson Canada Inc.
26 Prince Andrew Place
Don Mills, ON   M3C 2T8
Customer Service: 1-800-361-6128

1 2 3 4 5   TC   18 17 16 15 14
Printed and bound in Canada

Publisher: Susan Cox
Research and Communications Manager: Mark Cressman
Senior Marketing Specialist: Barbara Mlotek
Managing Editor: Lee Ensor
Developmental Editors: Cathy Fraccaro, Jessica Fung, Cara James, Jessica Pegis, Laurie Thomas,
    Yvonne Van Ruskenveld
Editorial Assistants: Kristiana Kang, Megan Watcher
Project Managers, Editorial: Lisa Dimson, Sheila Stephenson
Copy Editor: Linda Jenkins
Proofreader: Paula Pettitt-Townsend
Fact Checker: Tracy Westell
Indexer: Noeline Bridge
Photo Researcher and Permissions Editor: MRM Associates
Manager, Project Management K–12: Alison Dale
Project Manager, Production: Louise Avery
Art Director: Zena Denchik
Cover Design, Interior Design: Alex Li
Composition: ArtPlus Ltd.
Vice-President, Publishing: Mark Cobham

ISBN: 978-0-13-378998-0

©P

Acknowledgements

CONTRIBUTING WRITERS

Becky Cheung

Tom Conklin

Kim M. Earle

Ivan Ius

Mark Lowry

Craig Parkinson

TEACHER REVIEWERS

Tom Conklin
St. Patrick's High School
Ottawa Catholic School Board

Brian Gallagher
Sacred Heart Catholic High School
York Catholic District School Board

Aaron Liscum
L'Amoreaux Collegiate Institute
Toronto District School Board

Lou Maida
Blessed Trinity Catholic Secondary School
Niagara Catholic District School Board

Lucy Nguyen
Martingrove Collegiate Institute
Toronto District School Board

Nicole Shipowick
Sandalwood Heights Secondary School
Peel District School Board

EXPERT REVIEWERS

BIAS CONSULTANT

Sherida Sherry Hassanali
Mount Saint Vincent University

ABORIGINAL STUDIES CONSULTANT

Kevin Reed
Limestone District School Board

MAP CONSULTANT

Al Friesen

SUBJECT MATTER CONSULTANTS

Lesley Hymers, M.Sc.
Environment and Education Specialist
Ontario Mining Association

Laura-Belle Robinson
Design Consultant
Strategies for PlaceShaping

Janice Williams
Manager, Teacher Training and School Programs
Mining Matters

Contents

Contents

©P

Exploring Geography

BIG QUESTION

How can geographic inquiry and geotechnologies help us ask and answer important questions about the world around us?

▲ Geographic issues can range from large academic and public-policy issues to everyday issues. These issues can prompt a wide variety of geographic questions. This photograph shows scientists from the University of Northern British Columbia installing a GPS device designed to measure changes in thickness in the Castle Creek Glacier. What questions do you think this type of study is meant to answer?

LET'S GO!

- What does geography have to do with your life?
- What are key geographic concepts that can help you think like a geographer?
- How can you use critical thinking and geographic inquiry to answer questions?
- How can geotechnologies help you solve problems?

KEY CONCEPTS

- interrelationships
- spatial significance
- patterns
- trends
- geographic perspective
- geographic inquiry
- geotechnology

©P

What Does Geography Have to Do with Your Life?

If someone told you that "everything has to do with geography," would this seem like an exaggeration? Geography is all around us, and geographic issues directly affect almost every part of our lives. Successful geographers are always curious about the world around them. They want to know more about the things they see, read, or hear about. But curiosity is just the start. Once an important question has been asked, a geographer needs to know how to find the best answer.

Seeing What There Is to See

Each photo in Figure A–1 has a question. These are not the only questions that could be asked about the photos. They may not even be the most important questions. But questions such as these will help you make the kinds of connections that are key to thinking like a geographer.

▼ **Figure A–1** What questions would you ask about the geographic issues in these images? How might they relate to your life?

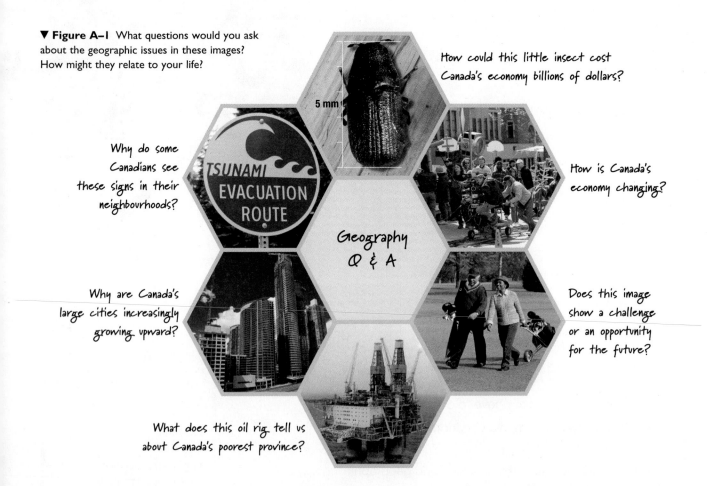

How could this little insect cost Canada's economy billions of dollars?

5 mm

Why do some Canadians see these signs in their neighbourhoods?

TSUNAMI EVACUATION ROUTE

Geography Q & A

How is Canada's economy changing?

Why are Canada's large cities increasingly growing upward?

Does this image show a challenge or an opportunity for the future?

What does this oil rig tell us about Canada's poorest province?

©P

Developing a Sense of Place: Three Key Questions

Imagine a particular place that holds some meaning for you. What was it about the landscape, buildings, history, or people that created a sense of place for you?

A "sense of place" is what makes a place special or unique. It involves not only our knowledge of the place, but our understanding of how humans interact with that place. Geographers develop a sense of place by asking three key geographic questions. Let's see how this works using the example of the mountain pine beetle.

absolute location where something is located in terms of latitude and longitude

relative location where something is located in relation to other geographic features

ecosystem a community of living things and the physical environment in which they live

WHAT IS WHERE?

Geography is all about location. You need to know the location of something before you can move on to more complex questions. There are two types of location in geography: **absolute location** and **relative location**.

Answers

- *What?* This is a mountain pine beetle. It lives most of its life inside the bark of pine trees. If enough beetles infest a tree, they will kill the tree.
- *Where?* The mountain pine beetle is native to western North America, from northern Mexico to central British Columbia. In the last 20 years, its range has expanded into parts of northern British Columbia and Alberta.

WHY THERE?

There are both simple and complex reasons why things are located where they are. In some cases, the natural environment, such as landforms or climate patterns, provide an explanation. In other cases, human actions affect the natural environment.

Answer

Mountain pine beetles have been around for thousands of years without causing too much damage. Why has this changed? Scientists have linked their increase in numbers and range to warmer weather caused by global climate change. In the past, cold winter temperatures limited the number and spread of the beetles. Recent winters have been warmer, so more beetles are surviving. The spread of the mountain pine beetle can therefore show links between human actions and the natural environment.

WHY CARE?

The importance of this question becomes clearer if we expand it a bit and say, "Why *should we* care?"

Answer

There are two reasons why we should care about the mountain pine beetle. The first is economic. Forestry is a key source of wealth and employment. Mountain pine beetles are spreading eastward, threatening the forest industry across Canada. The second reason is environmental. The beetles are disrupting an important **ecosystem**. It may be many years before we know their full impact. The final task is to decide what can and should be done about this problem.

Four Important Geographic Concepts

When geographers ask questions about a particular topic or issue, they must keep in mind four important geographic concepts, or ways of thinking. You will apply these concepts throughout this course (Figure A–2).

INTERRELATIONSHIPS

Geographers try to identify the relationships that exist within and between natural and human environments. If you can identify interrelationships, it is easier to see how things affect each other, and to answer the question "Why care?"

SPATIAL SIGNIFICANCE

Spatial significance is directly related to the key questions "What is where?" and "Why there?" The location of something can be important (or unimportant) for many reasons. The significance of a place can also be different for people, animals, and plants. This way of thinking can help you explore connections between natural and human environments.

PATTERNS AND TRENDS

Geographers are always on the lookout for patterns and trends. Being able to identify patterns and trends can help you understand why something is where it is, and why this matters.

GEOGRAPHIC PERSPECTIVE

A perspective is a way of looking at the world. Geography is a unique subject that has connections with many other fields, such as economics, geophysics, urban planning, and history. This allows geographers to consider multiple perspectives while studying an issue in geography. Developing the skill to understand a variety of perspectives can help you solve problems and make judgements. Looking at things from a geographic perspective is central to all geographic analysis.

---

interrelationship a relationship that exists between different patterns and trends

spatial significance the importance of a particular location in geography

pattern the arrangement of objects on Earth's surface in relationship to each other

trend a noticeable change in a pattern over time

GEOGRAPHIC THINKING

- Interrelationships
- Spatial Significance
- Patterns and Trends
- Geographic Perspective

▲ **Figure A–2** These concepts will appear with questions and activities throughout this book. They will help you keep in mind which geographic concepts are being explored.

geographic perspective a way of looking at the world that includes environmental, political, and social implications

---

APPLY IT!

1. How can a sense of place help you identify an issue and understand why it is important?

2. Describe at least one geographic pattern and one geographic trend that you have noticed where you live.

3. Choose one of the photographs in Figure A–1 (other than the mountain pine beetle). Suggest, with specific examples, how the three key questions and four ways of thinking could be used to answer the question posed with the photograph.

©P

Aboriginal Peoples and Geographic Thinking

Aboriginal peoples—First Nations, Métis, and Inuit—have a special connection to the geography of Canada. They and their ancestors have lived here for thousands of years. Over hundreds of generations, they learned how to survive in this challenging land: where and how to catch fish and hunt animals, where to search for plants and animals in each season, how to prepare food and clothing to survive the winters, and how to travel across land and water (Figure A–3). They learned about the ecology and natural rhythms of the areas in which they lived. They saw the interrelationships between all living things.

What Aboriginal peoples learned, they passed from one generation to another. Over time, their lifestyles and cultures became intimately connected with the specific places in Canada where they lived (Figure A–4). They named the places in their territories and told stories about them. These cultures endure, even though many Aboriginal people now live in towns and cities.

In this book, you will discover many ways in which First Nations, Métis, and Inuit peoples still maintain a deep knowledge of and respect for the land. You will also discover how they react to resource development, climate change, population trends, and the need to find a job—challenges faced by all Canadians.

▲ **Figure A–3** A detail from Métis artist Christi Belcourt's *Good Land*. Many Aboriginal peoples are working to reclaim the original, Aboriginal names for places in Canada. How can a map or a name change our perspective of a place?

WHAT QUESTIONS MIGHT GEOGRAPHERS ASK ABOUT ABORIGINAL PEOPLES AND THEIR RELATIONSHIPS TO THE LAND?

You have seen how the geographic thinking concepts help shape our understanding of the world around us. Let's consider how geographers might think about Aboriginal peoples' relationship to the land. They might ask the following questions:

- How did access to natural resources, such as plants and animals, affect the lifestyles of Aboriginal peoples? (Interrelationships)

- Why did Aboriginal peoples choose to live where they did? (Spatial Significance)

- Do Aboriginal peoples still live as their ancestors did? (Patterns and Trends)

- In light of their traditional connection to the land, why might Aboriginal peoples view resource development differently from other Canadians? (Geographic Perspective)

▲ **Figure A–4** Mary Simon is an Inuk from the northern part of Québec. She has spent much of her life fostering links between Canada's Arctic residents and the residents of other polar regions, including Alaska, Greenland, and Russia.

©P

1. Use the images in Figure A–5 to create questions that reflect the four concepts of geographic thinking.

2. What sources would you consider to be the best places to find perspectives on life in Northern Canada? Explain.

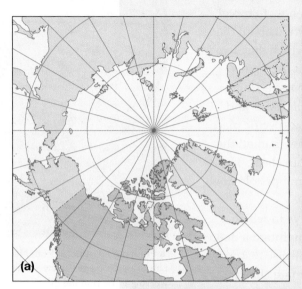

▲ **Figure A–5** (a) Inuit live in the northern areas of Canada, near other polar regions in Alaska, Greenland, and Russia. (b) Traditional knowledge about the land helped Inuit survive in a challenging environment. This knowledge is shared with geographers and scientists today. (c) Many Inuit communities, such as Mittimatalik (Pond Inlet), are isolated. However, populations are steadily growing.

Critical Thinking in Geography

To a greater or lesser extent, you have been doing critical thinking for years. *Critical thinking* means thinking seriously about an issue and making sound judgements based on reliable sources of information. It is important to remember that the word *critical* has several different meanings (Figure A–6). Make sure that you have the correct meaning in mind as we proceed.

crit·i·cal *adjective*
1. inclined to criticize severely and unfavourably
2. being in or approaching a state of crisis
3. using or involving careful judgement
4. being or relating to an illness or condition involving danger of death

This is the one!

◀ **Figure A–6** Remember to use definition number 3 when you think about critical thinking!

Critical thinking is a vital part of **geographic inquiry**, which is really what thinking like a geographer is all about. Geographers gather data and information when they study an issue, but they also consider perspectives, study patterns and trends, make connections, and make judgements.

geographic inquiry an active, questioning approach to learning about the world from a geographic perspective

Geographic Inquiry

You will use geographic inquiry throughout this course to investigate issues and events in Canadian geography. In order to do good inquiry, you need to develop the following skills.

Keep in mind that inquiry is not a linear process. The following steps are meant to be a guide to good inquiry, but you should use them in the order that is most appropriate for you and the task at hand.

FORMULATE QUESTIONS

Focus your research and analysis on one important question—something we will call the "big question" in this textbook. You might do this by writing a number of questions about the issue, then narrowing it down to one clearly stated and important big question. Good questions raise more questions and start debate. There can be several, or even many, big questions for most topics (Figure A–7).

Formulating questions can help you identify the focus of your inquiry. You can also review the four concepts of geographic thinking (page 4) to determine which one is relevant to your inquiry. This can help you develop the criteria you will use when you start to gather and analyze data and evidence.

▲ **Figure A–7** Most documentary films start with big questions created by filmmakers. The documentary film *Maidentrip* tells the story of a Dutch teenager who sailed around the world by herself (see page 13). What geographic inquiry questions could you pose about this story?

Table A–1 Some sources of information

field studies	studies in local neighbourhoods, school grounds, and various sites
primary sources	census data, letters, photographs, speeches, and works of art
secondary sources	documentaries and other films, news articles, reference books, and most websites
visuals	satellite images, maps, globes, models, graphs, and diagrams
community resources	local conservation areas, resources from community groups and associations, government resources, and local plans

▲ Primary sources are sources of information that were created during an investigation or event. Secondary sources are ones created later. Both categories can include visuals and community resources. Field studies can be used to create primary sources of information.

GATHER AND ORGANIZE INFORMATION

There are many sources of information available to you (Table A-1). Part of the inquiry process is determining not only what information you need to answer your question, but whether or not the information is reliable. When you consider a source, keep these questions in mind.

- Does the source focus on fact or on opinion?
- Is the source accurate and reliable?
- Is the source biased?
- Is the information up to date?

It is helpful to organize your search from the beginning. Keep a record of where you have searched, and flag sources of information you might want to revisit later. For example, you might bookmark websites you have found. This will also help you keep a record of your sources. You might also keep a record by using an organizer to detail the source, the author, and key points of information.

You will need to decide when you have enough data. It takes experience to know when enough is enough, or when you need to do additional research. You may even have more questions.

INTERPRET AND ANALYZE THE INFORMATION

Determine if you have the right data as you read articles or decipher data and maps. Remember that the importance of any piece of information is directly related to the inquiry question. Identify the key points and ideas. Look again to identify any bias and to determine if you have included all points of view. You might also consider how the information affects different groups.

EVALUATE AND DRAW CONCLUSIONS

Once you are happy with and understand your data, it is time to work toward a conclusion—the answer to your big question. Look at the information you have gathered and organized. What does it tell you about your question? What conclusions can you make based on your data, evidence, and information?

COMMUNICATE YOUR CONCLUSION TO OTHERS

There are many ways in which a conclusion can be presented. It is important to communicate your findings in a way that suits your purpose and your audience. Your ideas can be communicated in many different ways, such as essays, blog posts, posters, or videos. These presentations can be supported by maps, photos, graphs, and charts.

Remember to use appropriate geographic terminology during your presentation, and clearly cite your sources.

©P

An Inquiry Project: The Geography of Your Lunch

*Knowledge is of
two kinds. We know a subject
ourselves, or we know where we
can find information upon it.*

–Samuel Johnson, 1775

You might wonder what a lunch has to do with geography. In fact, there is a whole world of geography in any lunch. To learn more about the lunch shown on the next two pages, we can use the geographic inquiry process.

The following pages will take you through a geographic inquiry exercise. Our big question will be, How does this lunch demonstrate the geographic connections that are part of our lives?

To save time in this exercise, we will provide some data for you on the following pages. By the end of this course, you should be very skilled at finding your own data. The data here came from a variety of sources—company websites, environmental groups, and even package labels. Finding data is generally not very hard. The challenge is to determine which data are relevant and which can be safely ignored. Table A–2 will give you some useful ideas on how to do this.

Steps to Inquiry

Formulate your big question.

Gather and organize information.

Interpret and analyze the information.

Evaluate and draw conclusions.

Communicate your conclusion to others.

Table A–2 Analyzing information

	Interesting	**Not Interesting**
Important	Material that is *important* and *interesting* is not a problem, since you will be drawn to it by its high interest factor.	Material that is *important* but *not interesting* is a problem, since it is easy to miss. It takes practice to be able to recognize this type of information.
Not Important	Material that is *not important* but *interesting* is a problem. You will be attracted to it, but you have to be careful not to be distracted by it.	Material that is *not important* and *not interesting* is not a problem, since you will probably not even notice it.

▲ Information can be important or not important. It can also be interesting or not interesting. When you combine these two ideas, you get four possible kinds of information.

TUNA

- Several species of tuna are caught commercially (Figure A–8). Some species are threatened by overfishing.
- A DNA analysis of "tuna" being served in sushi restaurants in New York City found that none of the fish was actually tuna. A similar analysis of canned tuna indicated that almost all of it was tuna.

▲ **Figure A–8** Fishing boats, like this one, are used to catch tuna in the Pacific and Indian Oceans using a technique called long lining. How could you determine if the tuna you eat is caught in an environmentally sensitive way?

BREAD

- The bread you eat is made from hard spring wheat that was almost certainly grown in the Prairie provinces, most likely Saskatchewan.
- Winter wheat is grown in Southern Ontario. It is planted in the fall and grows a few centimetres tall before lying dormant for the winter. This soft wheat is best used to make pasta and pastries.
- Bakeries are typically built near stores where the bread is sold to ensure freshness.

LETTUCE

- During the summer, lettuce may come from local farms.
- Year round, it may come from greenhouses in Southern Ontario. The lettuce is grown hydroponically, in what is called a *soilless mixture*. Nutrients are provided in the water.
- Depending on the season, lettuce may be imported from warmer areas, such as Mexico, California, or Florida.

APPLE

- The apple could come from many countries, depending on the type of apple and the time of year. The sticker on the apple will show its origin (Figure A–9).

◄ **Figure A–9**

DRINK

- Pepsi is produced by an American-based multinational corporation called PepsiCo.
- Although it is the world's number two beverage company, 52 percent of PepsiCo's revenue comes from food products and the rest from beverages.
- Many years ago, Pepsi was much cheaper (5¢ vs. 10¢) than Coca-Cola, and it was more popular in poorer regions, including parts of Québec. English Canadians sometimes insultingly called French Canadians "Pepsis" as a result.

©P

SNACK BAR

- Snack bars were invented by cereal companies so they could sell their products (grains, nuts, and sugar) to people who were not having a sit-down breakfast.
- Quaker is a PepsiCo brand and part of the company's business that is not beverages.

CONTAINERS

- A student may start the year with a new lunch bag and a couple of different plastic boxes. Assuming that they are not lost, they may be used for the entire school year.
- These bags and boxes are manufactured in many countries around the world.

CHIPS

- Frito-Lay is another PepsiCo product. If you had Aunt Jemima pancakes, Quaker cereals, or Tropicana orange juice for breakfast, your family was contributing to PepsiCo's annual sales of US$66 billion in 2013.

APPLY IT!

1. How does the lunch in this inquiry project demonstrate the geographic connections that are part of our lives? Consider the four ways of thinking like a geographer (page 4) when formulating your answer.

2. What questions came to mind as you analyzed the information provided about the sample lunch?

3. Of the information provided, what was most important? What information was not useful to support your conclusion? Using Table A–2 on page 9 as a model, organize the information in a table to show what was interesting, important, not interesting, and not important.

4. Analyze the lunch you had (or will have) today.

   a) Write a number of questions you have about the lunch. Narrow your questions down to one clearly stated big question.

   b) What areas would you have to research to answer your big question? Suggest three or four resources. Where might you find various viewpoints?

   c) Use your notes to take a position and suggest a conclusion.

   d) List four different ways you could communicate your conclusion.

The Role of Geotechnologies in Geographic Thinking

You have seen that geographers develop a sense of place by asking questions such as "What is where?" "Why there?" "Why care?" How can technology help answer these questions?

Consider Figure A–10 below. This device allows drivers to see the state of traffic on their route as they are driving. This is a simple yet powerful example of geotechnology in action.

geotechnology the use of advanced technology in the study of geography and in everyday use

This information exists because of a unique combination of technologies and geographic thinking skills. Only 25 years ago, the technologies used here did not yet exist. We can only guess at how we might be using geotechnologies in another 25 years, as our needs change and new technologies develop.

▲ **Figure A–10** What other information can be derived from geotechnologies?

Before and After the Geotechnology Revolution

Geographers have used technology for as long as there have been geographers. The Greek scholar Eratosthenes (276 BCE–195 BCE), perhaps the first geographer, made the first near-accurate estimate of Earth's size in an attempt to make greater sense of the world he lived in. He did this using the geotechnology tools that existed 2200 years ago.

Over time, geographers have continued to seek answers to their questions about the world. The only thing that has changed is the quality of the tools they have to work with. Advances in electronic and satellite technologies have meant that geographers like you have a much more powerful toolbox to use than your parents did at your age.

©P

Kinds of Geotechnologies

There are several kinds of geotechnologies. These have become very familiar parts of modern life and have many different applications. Sometimes only one of these technologies is used. More often, more than one is combined in the devices we rely on.

GPS

Laura Dekker (Figure A–11) was able to rely on several modern geotechnologies during her solo voyage around the world. The first of these was a reliable and inexpensive **GPS (Global Positioning System)**. Dekker used an electronic chartplotter with a built-in GPS sensor for navigation.

GPS (Global Positioning System) a satellite-based system that provides location data

◀ **Figure A–11**
Dutch teenager Laura Dekker onboard *Guppy*. She sailed around the world by herself between 2010 and 2012 using modern geotechnology tools for navigation. She was 14 years old when she left on her voyage and 16 when she returned.

go online

Watch the trailer for *Maidentrip*, a documentary made about Laura Dekker's journey (2:08 minutes).

GIS

A **GIS (Geographic Information System)** is a computer system designed to gather and analyze particular kinds of data. It can be used, for example, to create a map showing changes to a community over time. GIS can allow a user to do a complex analysis of an issue. For example, it can be used to examine water quality in a particular area.

GIS and GPS are combined in navigation systems such as the one that Laura Dekker used to sail around the world. They are also combined in most smartphones. The GPS part of the system provides location and movement data. The GIS part is a database of information. All of these data have gone through a process called **georeferencing**. This means that a precise location was linked to each item. The device's control software combines the GPS and GIS data in a user-friendly fashion.

GIS (Geographic Information System) computer system that manages and analyzes geographic information

georeferencing linking geographic data to a particular location

APPLY IT!

1. Describe one specific way in which GPS and GIS could be used in each of the following industries:

   a) farming   **b)** mining   **c)** forestry

2. You want to invent a GPS-enabled device for a specific use. Choose a problem you would like to solve, and work with a partner to answer these questions.

   a) What kind of geographic information would you need to meet the purpose of the device?

   b) How could GPS and GIS be used to give you that information?

   c) Explain how your invention would use GPS (and possibly GIS) technology and why it is different than what already exists.

REMOTE SENSING

remote sensing seeing or measuring something from a considerable distance, often from a satellite

Remote sensing is essentially a one-way process. A satellite does the sensing and sends the results to a ground station for analysis and use. Various satellite technologies are used. Figure A–12 shows the type of remote sensing that most of us are familiar with. Images of weather events are a common feature on television and the Internet.

Canada is the world leader in one particular aspect of remote sensing. Figure A–13 shows flooding in New Brunswick in 2008. The image comes from a Canadian satellite called Radarsat-2. This satellite uses radar energy (long-wavelength, low-frequency radiation) rather than any of the forms of light energy that are used by most satellites. Radar beams are able to capture images through clouds, rain, snow, and haze, and at night. Note that the image is a false-colour image. This means that the satellite captures digital data only, not a picture of what it is seeing. The colours are added on the ground.

▼ **Figure A–12** We are used to seeing images of tropical cyclones (hurricanes in North America) on news and in weather broadcasts. What is unusual in this image for people used to seeing hurricane images in North America?

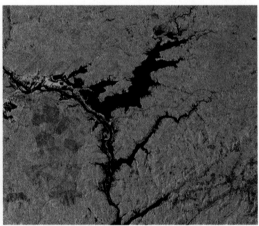

◄ **Figure A–13** On this Radarsat-2 image, black areas are lakes and rivers. The light purple colour shows flooded areas.

©P

Look at Figure A–14. In geography, we always want to work toward the simplicity that comes from solving a problem or from answering a question. What clues can you use to decipher this image?

◀ **Figure A–14** This image was taken from the International Space Station and shows part of the United States and Canada. What is the green, uneven line along the top of the image?

1. What are light areas and dark areas?

2. Where is this? What evidence did you use to identify the location?

3. What specific natural and human features can you identify here? It will help a lot if you can refer to a map showing the location you identified in question 2.

TELEMATICS

The word **telematics** is short for **tele**communications infor**matics**. Telematics are an important part of what is called the Internet of Things— a network that exists to link machines rather than people. It is growing so rapidly that experts suggest there will be 50 billion M2M (machine-to-machine) connections by 2020. You are already familiar with some of these links. For example, your family car may have a navigation system.

M2M connections are becoming common in environmental management. For example, a traditional weather station needs a trained observer to take readings of temperature, humidity, precipitation, and other measures. Robot stations are now being used. These stations take measurements throughout the day and transmit them every few minutes to a central location using cellular service or satellite communication. This allows weather stations to be positioned in remote locations. Similar systems can be used to monitor air and water quality, as well as the operation of landfills and wastewater treatment systems.

telematics any technology that involves the long-distance transmission of digital information

What Is the Future of Geotechnology?

No one can predict with any certainty what will come in the world of geotechnology in the next 10 to 20 years. Two separate but related factors will influence the developments that do occur.

- The first is the ongoing development of existing technologies, such as smaller and cheaper GPS computer chips.

- The second is the potential of human imagination. What new technologies might emerge? What new uses will be found for existing technologies?

You will learn more about the use of Google Earth and ArcGIS as you proceed through the book. Just to give you a sample of what is in store, however, take **GeoFlight A.1** for a quick tour of Canada.

▲ **Figure A–15** Google cars have driven more than 644 000 kilometres without an accident. Many aspects of driverless cars have already appeared in production cars. Can you name any? Where do you think this technology may lead?

One prediction is pretty certain, though. We are not too many years away from having cars that are self-driving. Strangely enough, the company most responsible for this is not an automaker. It is Google, a company famous for encouraging its employees to search for innovations far beyond the company's core business (Figure A–15). Remember that Google started as an Internet search engine company before becoming the world leader in bringing important and useful GIS products, such as Google Maps and Google Earth, to the general public. Which geotechnologies are fundamental to the driverless car?

Geotechnologies at School and Beyond

Geotechnologies have now become a routine part of studying geography. In this course, you may be using Google Earth or ArcGIS Online (or both), along with remote sensing images to study Canada and the world. Each application provides you with capabilities that only a generation ago would have seemed like something out of a sci-fi movie. Outside school, geotechnology applications are becoming so common that we may not even think about them. Can you suggest some examples? As for the future—only time and human imagination will tell us.

APPLY IT!

1. Create four big questions that explore the possible benefits and problems that M2M might have.

2. How will driverless cars integrate the following geotechnologies?

   a) GPS   **b)** GIS   **c)** telematics

3. What are the advantages and disadvantages of driverless cars?

4. Time to let loose your imagination. What innovations in geotechnology would you like to be able to use 25 years from now?

Interactions with the Physical Environment

©P

BIG QUESTION

How does the physical environment affect where Canadians live?

▲ How does the rapid growth of Calgary illustrate the intimate relationships between Canada's physical geography and its people?

LET'S GO!

- In what ways is the physical geography of the area in which you live typical of all of Canada? In what ways is it different?

- How does Canada's physical geography make Canada unique in the world?

- How do our patterns of physical geography contribute to where people live in Canada?

KEY CONCEPTS

- regions
- plate tectonics
- glaciation
- climate factors
- soil-forming processes
- natural vegetation
- population patterns and landform types

Canada's Population Patterns

KEY TERMS

census metropolitan area (CMA)

community

continuous ecumene

discontinuous ecumene

survey system

dispersed population

concentrated population

linear population

? **Where in our vast country do Canadians live—and not live?**

Oh! Canada?

China is Canada's fourth largest, and fastest-growing, source of tourists after the United States, the United Kingdom, and France. This poster promotes 10-day trips to Canada from China, starting at about $4400. The trips offered generally include outdoor or wilderness activities such as skiing, aurora viewing, wildlife viewing, and dogsled trips. Similar imagery is found in Canadian travel ads all over the world. The British Airways website recently encouraged British tourists to Canada to

Hire a canoe to explore Canada's Great Lakes—
the biggest freshwater bodies in the world.

Tourism ads about Canada typically show the wilder parts of the country with pictures of moose, mountains, bears (of all types, from cuddly polar bear cubs to fierce grizzlies), canoes, the northern lights, and Mounties.

THINKING CRITICALLY

Is this image typical of the part of Canada where you live? Do you think it is typical of where most Canadians live? In what ways is this image typical of Canada? Why do travel companies use images like this to attract tourists to Canada? Do campaigns with this type of image work?

©P

Big Country, Small Population

In many ways, there are two Canadas. One is the "True North" of our national anthem, the wild and thinly populated land that is so attractive to foreign tourists. The other Canada is the largely urban place where tens of millions of people live in relatively small areas of the country. In this chapter, we will look in detail at this odd distribution of population.

Canada has a remarkable range of landscapes, both natural and those that human beings have modified significantly or even completely. Examples of modified landscapes include land used for cities or for farming. In this unit, you will learn about the physical geography of Canada—landforms, climate, soils, and natural vegetation. You will come to understand why Canadians live where they do and, at the same time, why there are huge areas of the country where few people live. As you think about this, consider both the natural factors and human choices that influence where people live.

As we begin our study of Canada's population, it is critical to remember that Canada does not have many people for such a large country. Canada's area is very similar to (and just slightly larger than) the areas of China and the United States. The three countries are very different, however, when we start talking about people. The population of the United States is about nine times that of Canada, while China's population, remarkably, is almost 40 times as much. You can "see" this difference in Figure 1–1, which represents the population densities of the three countries. **Population density** is generally expressed as the number of people per square kilometre.

Canada's relatively small population is dramatically shown by what is called an *isodemographic map* (Figure 1–2 on the next page). (In Greek, *iso* means "equal" and *demos* means "people.") Most world maps are drawn so that the size of the country on the map is based on its area. On an isodemographic map, a country's population determines its size on the map. You will notice that the shape of each country on an isodemographic map is the same as its shape on a regular map, but the boundaries may be deformed. The result is that some parts of the world look pretty much as they do on a map based on area, while other parts look very distorted — either much too big or much too small.

GeoCareers

Aurora Viewing Is Best in the Winter

Amy Snowdon Isalkina is the manager of Blachford Lake Lodge, a resort near Yellowknife that is a leader in environmental adventure tourism in the North. About 60 percent of the lodge's visitors come to view the aurora borealis. The remainder participate in a wide range of activities from fishing to conferences. Visitors come from all over the world—mainly the United States, China, Australia, and Japan. Only 15 percent come from Canada. Amy's post-secondary education was in natural resources and environmental management. She also has training in wilderness first aid, firearm use, boat operation, forestry, and business management.

Geo ⚙ Inquiry

Gather and Organize

Canada is a huge country. Brainstorm a list of advantages and disadvantages of a large country like Canada.

population density the average number of people living in a particular place. It is calculated by dividing the population of a place (e.g., country, province, or city) by the area of the place.

United States: 35

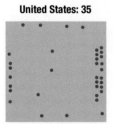

Canada: 4

China: 146

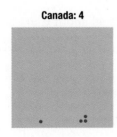

Source: United Nations

◀ **Figure 1–1** Each square represents one square kilometre. The dots represent the average number of people in that country per square kilometre. In most countries, the population is actually concentrated in cities or other settled areas. Where is Canada's population concentrated?

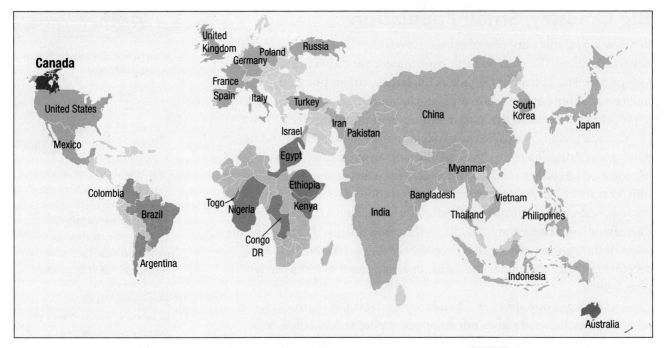

▲ **Figure 1–2 Isodemographic map of the world.** `OSSLT` The colours identify the different continents. In some ways, this looks like the world maps we are used to seeing; in others ways, it is very different. Why does it look different?

Geo✿Inquiry

Communicate

Colour choice is important in the creation of any map. Why? Look at a selection of maps in this book and suggest at least two factors that contribute to an effective choice of colour.

APPLY IT!

1. Identify two continents on the isodemographic map that look similar to those on a regular map. What does this say about the relative populations of the countries on these continents?

2. Which two countries stand out because they are so large?

3. How does Canada appear on this map? Why?

4. Name another country that has a similar appearance to Canada's on this kind of map.

5. What important geographic relationship is shown graphically on this type of map?

6. Why is this map so powerful?

7. How does this map make you feel about Canada?

8. ■ **Patterns and Trends** Imagine that you were looking at a version of this map drawn in 2040.

   a) In what ways would it be similar?

   b) In what ways would it be different?

Population Concentrations in Canada

Isodemographic maps can also be used to show population distribution within a country. Figure 1–3 is an isodemographic map of Canada drawn using slightly different logic than the world isodemographic map. Instead of shapes staying the same and the boundaries changing, as in Figure 1–2, boundaries on this map are kept the same but the shapes are distorted. The effect is dramatic—you can see that most Canadians live in just a small part of the country. In fact, more than 80 percent of the population lives in cities and towns. Most of these people live in cities with more than 100 000 people. Geographers call the population concentrations centred around these large cities **census metropolitan areas** or **CMAs**. The CMA that includes the City of Toronto also includes the adjacent regional municipalities of York, Peel, Halton, and Durham. The CMA that includes the City of Ottawa includes the City of Gatineau in Québec.

go online

Statistics Canada has created a profile of each of Canada's CMAs.

census metropolitan area (CMA) an urban area in Canada with a population over 100 000. A CMA is centred around a city and generally extends beyond the borders of the city.

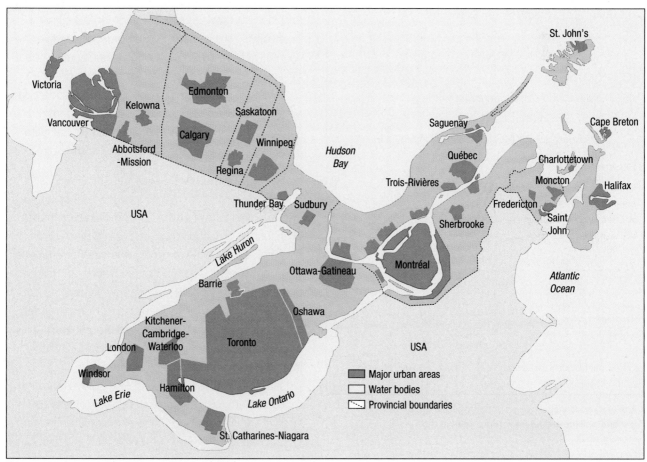

Sources: University of British Columbia; Statistics Canada

▲ **Figure 1–3 Isodemographic map of Canada.** On this map, the areas of provinces and cities are drawn in proportion to their populations. Describe the pattern you see.

Identifying Canadian Communities Using Census Data

community a group of people who share common characteristics, such as their history, culture, beliefs, or simply the space where they live. You belong to more than one community (e.g., your neighbourhood, town, ethnic group, school, country, or even the world).

Table 1–1 Communities for you to research

A. Neighbourhood in central Mississauga, ON
B. City of Fort McMurray, AB
C. Hochelaga-Maisonneuve neighbourhood in Montréal, QC
D. Rural area in southeastern Saskatchewan
E. Town of Burgeo, NL
F. Town of Palmerston, ON
G. Village of Carcross, YT
H. Rural area in northern Nunavut*
I. City of Edmundston, NB
J. Neighbourhood of New Edinburgh-Lindenlea in Ottawa, ON
K. City of Penticton, BC
L. Town of Cochrane, ON
M. Neighbourhood in northeastern Québec City, QC
N. Hamlet of Gjoa Haven, NU*
O. Neighbourhood in Markham, ON
P. Rural area in Grey County, Ontario
Q. City of Surrey, BC
R. Moose Lake 31A Indian Reserve, MB*
S. Fashion District neighbourhood in Toronto, ON
T. Neighbourhood adjacent to the two universities in Waterloo, ON

* Google *Street View* images are not available for these locations. A second oblique (angle) view is provided in the GeoFlight feature instead.

Take **GeoFlight 1.1** to visit the 20 communities before you start your community–data matching.

So far, we have looked at the big picture—comparing Canada with other countries and looking at the distribution of urban areas across Canada. Now it is time to focus on the characteristics of specific **communities** in Canada. Some of these communities are in large cities, some are individual towns and small cities, and others are in rural areas. In this activity, you will use data from the census of Canada. The census publishes data for the whole country, for provinces, for cities and towns, and even for individual neighbourhoods. The census is conducted every five years. That is why you will often see Canadian data for years ending in 1 or 6 (such as 2011 or 1956).

You will start with a list of 20 communities from all over Canada—from coast to coast to coast (Table 1–1). You will then be given 20 sets of data. Your job is to match the data to the community.

The 20 Communities

You may live in one of the 20 communities. If not, chances are very good that you live in a place similar to one of them. Before we go on, it is time for a unique geographic perspective on these places—a perspective that was impossible only a few years ago. You can take a "field trip" to them from your computer, tablet, or even smartphone using Google Earth. You will be able to "fly" over each community (using imagery from various satellites) and zoom in for a closer look. You will also be able to "drive" through most of them, using imagery Google collects using special vehicles that combine videos with precise GPS locations (Figure 1–4). Enjoy your journey!

On to the Data

Your teacher will give you a handout that contains 21 data sets—one for Canada and one for each of the 20 communities. Data Set 4 in your handout has some comments to help you with your matching.

▲ **Figure 1–4** If you were lucky, you may have seen or will see one of these vehicles driving on your street. It was taking images that are geo-referenced in Google Earth to produce a feature called *Street View*. Check Google Earth to see if your home and school have street views. Note that if you are new to Google Earth, you have to download the free program first.

To get you started with your matching, Data Set 4 goes with community A, a neighbourhood in Mississauga.

Work like a detective to match communities and data sets. Look for the important clues and do not be distracted by other data that do not tell you very much.

A good way to start is to compare each community's values to the overall Canadian values. Look at the data again and see why such a comparison makes sense.

1. Start matching. A few of the communities are very easy to identify because something in the data stands out. Look for these places first.

2. Next, use simple graphic organizers to group communities that share one characteristic. (Venn diagrams may help.) Here are a few suggestions:
   - Group large cities, smaller urban places, and rural areas. (How would you know this?)
   - Group communities that are dominantly French speaking or English speaking.
   - Group communities with substantial First Nation or Inuit populations.
   - Group communities with older populations, younger populations, and "average" populations.
   - Group communities with higher population densities, lower population densities, and very low population densities.

APPLY IT!

1. Compare your matches to those of classmates. Discuss any differences between the matches until you have a consensus.

2. **a)** Once you have successfully done the matching (your teacher will tell you when you are correct), it is time to identify the characteristics that make different communities distinct. List five to seven important characteristics.

   b) For each characteristic, identify the range of possible values that exist in different communities across Canada. For example, population densities can range from thousands of people per square kilometre to less than one person per square kilometre.

3. **a)** Finally, group communities that are similar because they share two or more characteristics. Give each group a descriptive name based on the characteristics that those communities share.

   b) Briefly describe the characteristics that make each group of communities distinct.

4. **a)** On page 19, two distinct Canadas were mentioned—the one that foreign tourists come to visit and the other in which most Canadians live. Divide the 20 communities into two lists, one for the "touristy" parts of Canada and the other for the parts where most people live.

   b) What similarities do the communities in each list have? What differences are there within each list?

   c) How are physical characteristics of the land related to the density and distribution of the population of the communities in each list?

People Patterns and Terminology

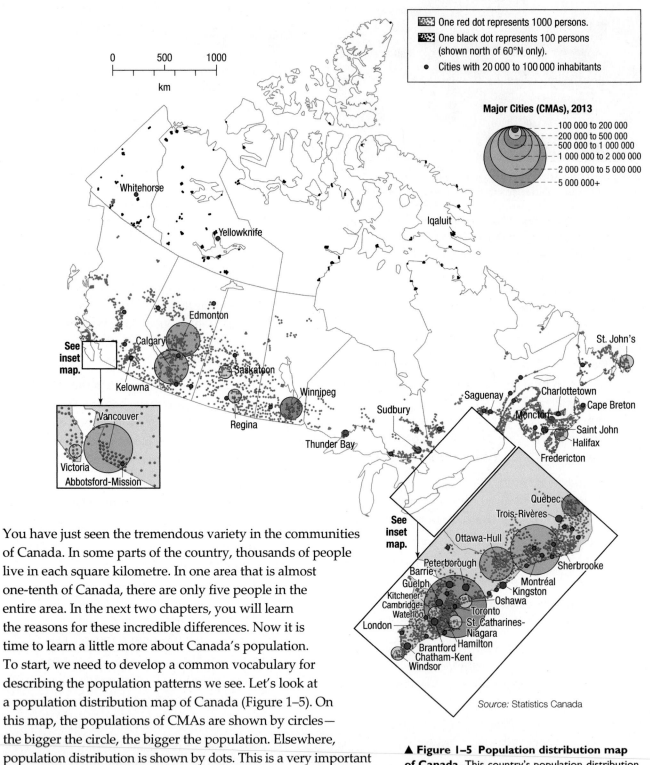

One red dot represents 1000 persons.

One black dot represents 100 persons (shown north of 60°N only).

• Cities with 20 000 to 100 000 inhabitants

Major Cities (CMAs), 2013

- 100 000 to 200 000
- 200 000 to 500 000
- 500 000 to 1 000 000
- 1 000 000 to 2 000 000
- 2 000 000 to 5 000 000
- 5 000 000+

You have just seen the tremendous variety in the communities of Canada. In some parts of the country, thousands of people live in each square kilometre. In one area that is almost one-tenth of Canada, there are only five people in the entire area. In the next two chapters, you will learn the reasons for these incredible differences. Now it is time to learn a little more about Canada's population. To start, we need to develop a common vocabulary for describing the population patterns we see. Let's look at a population distribution map of Canada (Figure 1–5). On this map, the populations of CMAs are shown by circles— the bigger the circle, the bigger the population. Elsewhere, population distribution is shown by dots. This is a very important map. You will be referring back to it often to see the connections among population, physical geography, and economic geography.

Source: Statistics Canada

▲ **Figure 1–5 Population distribution map of Canada.** This country's population distribution is remarkably uneven. In the remainder of this unit, you can learn why.

1. Use Figure 1–5 to answer these questions.

   a) Which CMA has a population greater than five million?

   b) Which CMAs have populations between two million and five million?

   c) Which CMAs have populations between one million and two million?

   d) Which CMAs have populations between 500 000 and one million?

   e) In a table, list the number of CMAs in each province and territory.

   f) Name, in order of population from highest to lowest, the four parts of Canada that have the most people. This ranking is based on both the number of CMAs of different sizes and the overall population density of each region.

2. a) On a base map, outline and shade the areas of continuous settlement in Canada. Label these areas **continuous ecumene**. Hint: Consider the red dots as well as the CMA circles.

   b) Next, outline and shade (in a lighter shade of the same colour) areas where there are patches of population near the continuous ecumene. Label those areas **discontinuous ecumene**.

   c) Why are there gaps in the continuous ecumene?

   d) As Canada's population grows, is the continuous ecumene likely to get larger? Explain your answer.

   e) What patterns of physical and economic geography explain the existence of the various patches of population that make up the discontinuous ecumene?

3. How is Canada's transportation system (roads, railways, ships, and planes used for moving people and freight) related to the ecumene and non-ecumene areas of the country?

4. Figure 1–6 shows signs on a road leaving Kenora, Ontario. Find Kenora on a map and identify where it would be in Figure 1–5. Why might Kenora be seen as the crossroads of the Canadian ecumene?

5. Most Canadians live in cities. What are the costs and benefits of having so many cities?

Geo Inquiry

Evaluate and Draw Conclusions

Canadian cities and towns are often twinned with cities and towns in other countries. Who are the "twins" for your community (or another Canadian community)? In what ways are the population patterns of the twinned communities similar? In what ways are they different? How is this related to fundamental differences in the countries involved?

go online

Find out what communities Canadian cities and towns are twinned with.

continuous ecumene the part of the country where there is continuous, permanent settlement

discontinuous ecumene the part of the country where there are significant patches of settlement

▼ **Figure 1–6** Road signs at Kenora, Ontario

Does It Matter If Areas Far from Large Cities Lose Population?

Table 1–2 shows the population changes between 2006 and 2011 in some small Canadian communities from coast to coast. They share a number of important characteristics:

💬 Perhaps most important is that they are losing population at a time when Canada's population is slowly but steadily growing (Figure 1–7).

💬 Another is that they are far from Canada's economic (and population) growth centres— the CMAs and booming resource towns and cities.

There are several reasons why rural areas like these are losing population. The most important is poor job prospects. This is a particular problem for young people who are finishing school. Two related questions emerge about communities that are losing people. Can we do anything about it? Should we even be trying?

▲ **Figure 1–7** "Ghost towns" (towns that have been completely abandoned) do exist in Canada but they are relatively rare. Much more common are towns, villages, and rural areas that are constantly losing population.

Table 1–2   Examples of small communities with decreasing populations

Community	Population change 2006–2011 (%)	Median age of residents*
Canada	+5.9	40.6
Buchans, NL	−8.5	54.9
Bas-Caraquet, NB	−6.2	49.0
Baie-Comeau, QC	−2.0	45.2
North Frontenac, ON	−3.3	57.6
Lorne, MB	−5.9	41.2
Barrier Valley, SK	−13.5	47.7
Coutts, AB	−9.2	47.2
Harrison Hot Springs, BC	−6.7	54.0

Source: Statistics Canada

*"Median" means that 50% of the residents are older than that age and 50% are younger.
Why is the median age significant in understanding what is happening in communities like these?

Geo ⚙ Inquiry

Gather and Organize

Are any settlements in your area losing population and the services that go with a larger population? How would you know? Consider both statistical sources on the Internet and evidence you can see in the area.

We must find ways to protect small towns and help them survive.

🗩 Rural communities, and the villages and towns that support them, are an important part of our history and help make Canada the special place it is. Without them, Canada is a less varied and interesting place. We need to find ways to help these communities survive.

🗩 It is not fair that young people from these communities need to leave home to find a job after they finish their education.

🗩 Companies could move operations to these communities and find willing workers and lower costs.

🗩 These communities provide a lifestyle alternative for people who want to move out of the big cities.

Viewpoint 2

It may be sad that these places are declining, but there is nothing that can or should be done about it.

🗩 Canada's population pattern today is different because of basic changes in our economy and technology.

🗩 In the past, economic activities in rural areas (forestry, agriculture, mining, and fishing) required more workers. Mechanization means that these workers are no longer needed. We can't go back in time.

🗩 The cost of providing services, such as roads and schools, to these communities is too high.

🗩 Companies locate where it makes the most sense for them. If it made sense to move away from CMAs, they would have already done so.

APPLY IT!

1. **a)** Give three specific examples of how technology is reducing the number of jobs in rural areas.

   b) How might the Internet help the survival of small communities by allowing more people to work there?

2. **a)** What options do young people in these parts of Canada have when they finish high school and post-secondary education?

   b) Why is this stressful for both the young people and their families?

3. Why is population loss not a problem in rural communities that are reasonably close to large cities (less than 200 kilometres)?

4. **a)** What could governments do to help rural communities survive?

   b) **OSSLT** Should governments be involved in this situation? Why or why not?

5. What is your view on the issue? Should we be worrying about rural population loss? If so, what should we do about it?

Rural Settlement Patterns

CONNECTING

Chapter 2 describes Canada's physical features and how they affect where people live.

survey system a grid system used to locate and identify parcels of land and roads

dispersed population a population spread evenly across the land; common in agricultural areas

concentrated population a population focused in patches with specific resource industries, such as mines or paper mills

linear population a population settled along a line, such as a coastline, river, or highway

▶ **Figure 1–8** What factors do you think influenced each of these settlement patterns?

▼ **Figure 1–9**
■ **Spatial Significance** What settlement pattern or patterns do you see in these photos?

Three important factors affect the pattern of rural settlement in a particular area:

- The *nature of the resources* that attracted people to the area in the first place. For example, the settlement pattern in a rich agricultural region will be quite different from the pattern in an area based on commercial fishing.

- The *transportation methods* that were in use when the area was settled. If people travelled by water (or in winter by sled on frozen rivers and lakes), the pattern will be different from that in areas settled later when travel was by railway or on roads.

- The *role of government* in determining the pattern. In some areas of Canada, settlement occurred with little, if any, influence by government. People pretty much settled where they wanted, keeping in mind the two factors mentioned above. In other areas, such as Southern Ontario and the southern Prairies, the government imposed a survey system before settlement occurred. The survey system included a pattern of roads and lots that still exist.

As a result of these patterns, populations in rural areas can be described as being **dispersed**, **concentrated**, or **linear** (Figures 1–8 and 1–9).

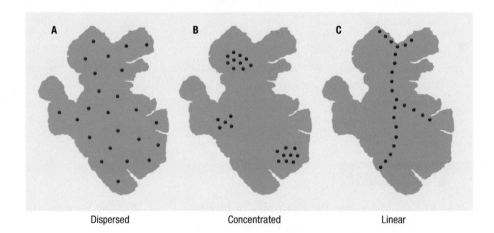

| A | B | C |
| Dispersed | Concentrated | Linear |

1. If you live in a city in Ontario south of the Canadian Shield, the grid of major roads you use is the product of the survey system that was imposed in the first half of the 1800s. Most commonly, the roads are located 2 kilometres apart, although various patterns were used. Name some of these roads in your community.

2. Examine the four maps in Figure 1–10.

   a) For each, decide which settlement pattern exists (see Figure 1–8).

   b) Analyze the relative importance of each factor described on the previous page in creating the patterns you see.

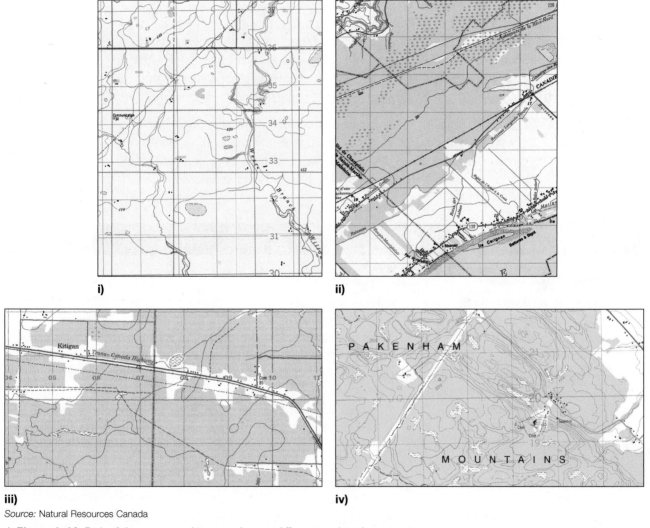

i)

ii)

iii)

iv)

Source: Natural Resources Canada

▲ **Figure 1–10** Each of these topographic maps shows a different rural settlement pattern. Note that houses are shown as tiny black squares. Barns and similar buildings are slightly larger black rectangles. The scale of these maps is 1:50 000.

Canada's Population Patterns

? **Where in our vast country do Canadians live—and not live?**

By now, you should have a good sense of Canada's population distribution. As you worked your way through this chapter, you were probably asking yourself (or your teacher) why the pattern is so uneven. Perhaps you even started to answer this important question. In the next chapter and in the rest of the book, you will discover why people live and work where they do. You will also see how our population is changing in many ways, including its total number, distribution, growth rate, age structure, and ethnic composition.

Think back to our initial issue about where foreign tourists want to go in Canada. Most tourists would pick a European holiday if they want to see cities. If they want to see wilderness—remote spaces, interesting wildlife, beautiful scenery—the "True North" part of Canada, the part without a significant population, is the most attractive destination.

1. **OSSLT** Use a graphic organizer of your choice to describe where in this vast country Canadians live. In your description, consider the location of a) CMAs, b) smaller cities and towns, c) the remainder of the continuous ecumene, d) the discontinuous ecumene, and e) population outside the ecumene.

Geo ⚙ Inquiry

Interpret and Analyze

2. a) What advantages does Canada's settlement pattern provide to Canadians?

b) What problems are created by the settlement pattern? How do we experience these problems in everyday life?

Evaluate and Draw Conclusions

3. What factors do you think contribute to Canada's population being distributed so unevenly? Consider both physical and human geography factors.

Analyze an Issue

4. Think about issues related to Canada's population patterns that you have read about or that affect your everyday life. Pick one of these issues.

a) Write a number of questions about the issue. Narrow your questions down to one clearly stated and important big question. Good questions raise more questions and start debate.

b) What areas would you have to research to answer your big question? Find three or four resources and collect information to answer it.

Be sure to analyze the information and consider various viewpoints.

c) Use your notes to take a position and answer your question. Support your answer with facts from your research.

d) Create a product that communicates the answer to your question. This could be an opinion paper, a blog post, a poster, or a letter to the editor. Be creative!

e) If you had to complete another inquiry like this one, what would you do differently?

©P

Exploring Connections: Landforms, Geology, and Human Activities

? **How do different landforms and geologic processes contribute to where and how people live?**

KEY TERMS

plate tectonics
weathering
erosion
deposition
glaciation

Why Do Cities Sprawl over the Best Farmland?

You eat a variety of foods every day—probably including dairy products, various meats, fruits, vegetables, and grain products. You may not think very much about the farmland where your food is produced, but you should. The government published maps in the late 1960s rating the quality of Canada's land for farming. The map below shows parts of Peel and Halton regions from one of these maps. A quick look will give you a good sense of the high quality of the farmland in the area. When you look at this map, remember a couple of important points. Excellent farmland (called Class 1 on this map) is very rare (only 0.5 percent of all of Canada's land). Good farmland (Classes 2 and 3) makes up only another 4.5 percent of Canada's land. The dashed white line on this map shows the extent of the land that a 2006 report predicted would become urbanized by 2031. In fact, most of it has already been built on.

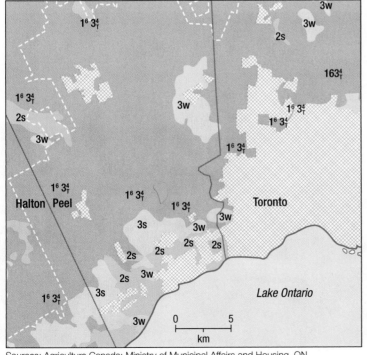

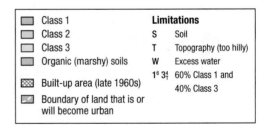

		Limitations	
▢	Class 1		
▢	Class 2	S	Soil
▢	Class 3	T	Topography (too hilly)
▣	Organic (marshy) soils	W	Excess water
▨	Built-up area (late 1960s)	$1^6 \, 3^4_T$	60% Class 1 and 40% Class 3
▨	Boundary of land that is or will become urban		

Sources: Agriculture Canada; Ministry of Municipal Affairs and Housing, ON

◀ **Agricultural land and urban growth.** This map shows agricultural land quality and the extent of the built-up urban area in 1968. The dashed white line shows how much of this area has been or will be built on.

THINKING CRITICALLY

What is more important, farmland or land for housing? Carefully explain your position.

Patterns and Processes

In this chapter and the next, we will look at four interrelated aspects of physical geography that affect where people live and work in Canada—landforms, climate, natural vegetation, and soils. For each aspect, we will look not only at the *patterns* that exist, but also at underlying *processes* that cause the patterns. Which of the four aspects do you think has the biggest impact on where people locate? Why?

Landform Processes

Let's start our study of landforms by looking at a specific part of the country. Coastal British Columbia is a very beautiful part of Canada (Figure 2–1). It also has Canada's mildest climate. You may live there some day. You might go home from school today to learn that your family is moving there as a result of a parent's new job offer. In a few years, you might choose to move there for university or to take advantage of the mild winters and great recreational activities. (Vancouverites can choose among snowboarding, golf, or sailing—all on the same day.)

Not everything about Vancouver is quite so rosy, however. One of the effects of Vancouver's popularity for Canadian and foreign migrants is that an average house costs almost $1 million. In addition, Vancouver and other areas of coastal British Columbia face a potentially devastating natural hazard. How would you feel about living where the risk of a catastrophic earthquake and **tsunami** is very high?

GeoCareers

Emergency Preparedness Coordinator

Jackie Kloosterboer is an emergency preparedness coordinator for the City of Vancouver. She leads more than 100 earthquake preparedness workshops each year. She also coordinates the efforts of 500 volunteers who have been trained to help people in a variety of emergency situations. After completing a general studies degree at Simon Fraser University, she received a certificate in emergency management from the Justice Institute of British Columbia. She has also written a book, *My Earthquake Preparedness Guide*, to help BC residents prepare for an earthquake.

tsunami a set of large ocean waves caused by an earthquake or other powerful disturbance under the sea. A tsunami can cause great destruction when it reaches land.

go online

Canada experiences hundreds of earthquakes in a typical month. Find out where and when they have occurred or are occurring.

▶ **Figure 2–1** OSSLT Why is Vancouver an attractive place to live for both Canadians and new immigrants?

Drop, Cover, and Hold On!

Imagine your teacher suddenly shouting these words in the middle of a lesson. What would you do? If you were a student in British Columbia, you would know exactly what to do, since you had practised the correct response to this order (Figure 2–2). You would instantly drop to the floor, get under your desk, and hold onto it, because you would know that an earthquake was starting. You would know that "Drop, cover, and hold on!" was the best way to survive a serious quake.

While small earthquakes are a common feature of life in coastal British Columbia, people were shocked when scientists discovered that a massive earthquake with a magnitude estimated between 8.7 and 9.2 had occurred in 1700 under the ocean near Vancouver Island. To understand why this matters, we need to look at the mathematics of the scale used to measure quakes. It is not a linear scale. A magnitude 9.0 quake does not have 50 percent more power than a magnitude 6.0 quake—remember that a 6.0 earthquake is still strong enough to damage buildings and kill people. A 9.0 quake is *more than 30 000 times as powerful* as a 6.0 quake!

Earthquakes this strong are relatively rare. One of these mega-quakes hit Japan in 2011. That earthquake, along with the tsunami it caused, killed 16 000 people, caused tens of billions of dollars in damage, and left a broken nuclear plant leaking radioactivity into the sea. Further research in British Columbia suggested that magnitude 9.0 quakes should occur roughly every 300 to 800 years. Consider 1700 + 300 years—you can do the math. Suddenly British Columbians were taking the earthquake risk very seriously.

▲ **Figure 2–2** BC students during an earthquake drill

Use **ArcGIS Online** to create a map of Canada showing where settlements are in relation to fault lines and earthquake intensities.

go online

You can learn more about earthquakes from a short National Geographic video (2:30 minutes).

APPLY IT!

1. Assume you are considering a move to coastal British Columbia. What concerns should you have about the earthquake risk? What factors might make you less worried about the earthquake risk?

2. **OSSLT** What would make you more reluctant to move to British Columbia—the risk of a devastating earthquake or the high cost of housing? Explain your answer.

3. "Canadians must constantly make compromises with the natural environment." Explain how this applies to British Columbia.

4. Who would be important in preparedness planning for a massive earthquake? Describe the roles of government officials and others. Describe each person's point of view.

Forces that Shape Earth

The earthquake risk in British Columbia, along with the landforms that we see in all parts of Canada, are the result of the interplay of a number of powerful natural processes. Some of these processes build up the land, while others wear it down (Figure 2–3). When the building-up processes are more powerful, the land gets higher. When the wearing-down processes are stronger, the land gets lower. Most importantly, if you want to understand the interplay and power of these forces, you must remember that the time spans involved are far beyond anything related to human experience. Figure 2–4 shows a geological time scale and compares it to one year to show the relative lengths of the time periods.

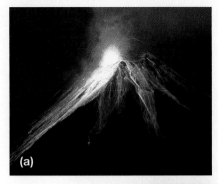

▲ **Figure 2–3** Most processes that (a) build up the land or (b) wear it down happen very slowly and involve vast areas. Sometimes, as these photos show, the processes happen more quickly, affect smaller areas, and can be directly observed. What is happening in each photo that causes the land to be built up or worn down?

Date and time of the year	Millions of years ago: key event
December 31 @ 11:59:59.996 p.m.	You were born.
December 31 @ 11:59 p.m.	0.001: Last ice age ends.
December 31 @ 11:48 p.m.	0.1: Modern humans appear.
December 31 @10:05 p.m.	1: First ice age begins.
December 31 @ 5:20 p.m.	4: Oldest human-like ancestors appear.
December 26	65: *Cenozoic Era* ("recent time") begins—dinosaurs are extinct.
December 22	115: First flowering plants appear.
December 19	150: First birds appear.
December 12	220: First mammals appear.
December 12	245: *Mesozoic Era* ("middle time") begins.
December 1	400: First insects appear.
November 11	544: *Paleozoic Era* ("old time") begins.
November 11	550: First animals with hard shells appear.
March 20	3600: Oldest organisms (a type of algae) appear.
March 4	3800: Oldest rocks begin to form.
January 1	4600: Earth formed: *Precambrian Era* ("before the Cambrian," the first part of the Paleozoic Era) begins.

▲ **Figure 2–4** Evidence of the Precambrian Era exists in only nine places in the world, such as the Canadian Shield. Most of the world was formed and shaped in more recent times.

PLATE TECTONICS

The theory of **plate tectonics** is one of the most important theories ever to result from scientific research. It explains why we have high mountain ranges, majestic plains, and the deepest parts of the ocean. Here is how it works. Earth's crust may seem solid and unyielding—we live on it and build massive buildings and other structures on it. But the theory of plate tectonics tells us that the crust is actually floating on molten rocks inside Earth. Furthermore, the crust is not a single piece. It is made of dozens of pieces called *plates*. There are seven major plates, eight secondary plates, and more than 60 minor plates (Figure 2–5). A good way to imagine the plates is to picture the cracked shell of a hard-boiled egg, with the cracks being the plate boundaries.

The movement of Earth's plates has shaped Canada in many ways. For example, the mountain chains on the east and west coasts grew as a result of plates colliding. The movement of plates has also played a role in the formation of Canada's fossil fuels. Oil, gas, and coal formed when Canada's land mass was located in a warmer, tropical climate. Where will Canada be located in the next few hundred million years? Time—and data on plate direction and speed—will tell.

plate tectonics the theory that Earth's outer shell is made up of individual plates that move, causing earthquakes, volcanoes, mountains, and the formation and destruction of areas of the crust

go online

Find out more about mid-ocean ridges and see new crust forming at a mid-ocean ridge (2:53 minutes).

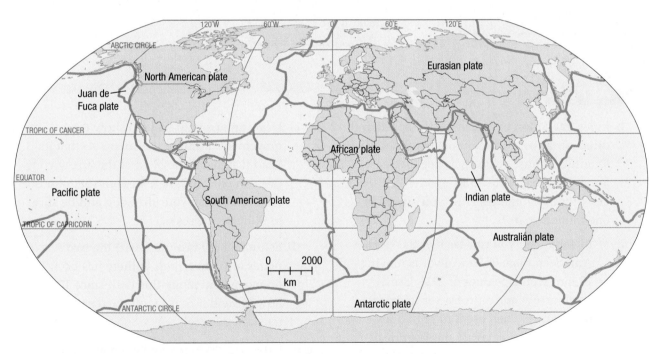

▲ **Figure 2–5 Earth's major tectonic plates.** This map names the seven major plates. The minor plates are shown, but not named, except for the Juan de Fuca and Indian plates.

Plate Motion Calculator

go online

You can check the movement of any place with a plate motion calculator.

Use the website given in the Go Online feature to check the amount of plate movement at a specific location. Simply enter a place's latitude (lat) and longitude (lon). Table 2–1 shows the result for Vancouver. We can round the speed and azimuth (bearing) to the nearest whole number. So at Vancouver, the North American plate is moving 20 millimetres per year (mm/y) on a bearing of 221°.

Table 2–1 Example of plate motion calculator data table

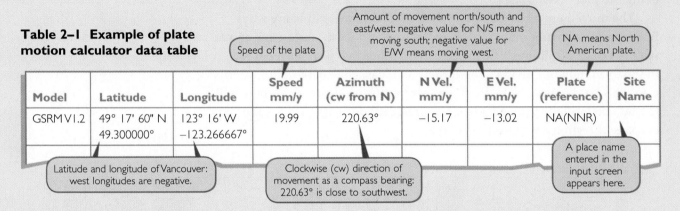

Speed of the plate

Amount of movement north/south and east/west: negative value for N/S means moving south; negative value for E/W means moving west.

NA means North American plate.

Model	Latitude	Longitude	Speed mm/y	Azimuth (cw from N)	N Vel. mm/y	E Vel. mm/y	Plate (reference)	Site Name
GSRM V1.2	49° 17' 60" N 49.300000°	123° 16' W −123.266667°	19.99	220.63°	−15.17	−13.02	NA(NNR)	

Latitude and longitude of Vancouver: west longitudes are negative.

Clockwise (cw) direction of movement as a compass bearing: 220.63° is close to southwest.

A place name entered in the input screen appears here.

APPLY IT!

1. Enter the lat/lon to determine the speed and direction of your plate. Remember that west longitudes must be given as negative east longitudes (e.g., 078° 23′W = −078° 23′E). How far in kilometres will "you" move in one million years?

2. a) In Table 2–1, you can see that the North American plate at Vancouver is moving 20 mm/y on a bearing of 221°. Use a north arrow and a protractor to draw the bearing. Then use a ruler to draw an arrow to scale along this bearing (1 centimetre to 2 millimetres per year works well).

   b) Next determine the movement of the Juan de Fuca plate. Use a location of 45°N 128°W.

   c) Draw an arrow to scale to show the movement. Position this arrow so that its head just meets the head of the arrow you drew in part a). Where in your diagram is the fault? Label your drawing and be sure to indicate the scale.

   d) Estimate how fast (per year) the two plates are converging. If there has been no movement along this fault since 1700, how far will it move if all the tension is released at once?

   e) How would this event be felt along the coast of British Columbia, Washington, and Oregon, and in Japan and other places on the other side of the Pacific?

Types of Plate Movement

Plates are not joined to each other—they are only touching. They move because the molten rock below them moves. There are three possible directions of movement.

- **Divergent:** This occurs when two plates move apart (Figure 2–6). Most commonly this happens along a **mid-ocean ridge**, although it does happen on land too (Figure 2–7). When this happens, both plates get larger. New areas of Earth's crust are constantly being created in that way along 70 000 kilometres of mid-ocean ridges. Most of the world's volcanoes occur along divergent plate boundaries.

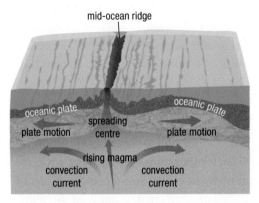

◀ **Figure 2–6** Divergent plates: oceanic plate ⟵ ⟶ oceanic plate

- **Convergent:** Two plates move toward each other. There are two types of convergence, depending on the kinds of plates that are colliding.

  1. *Continental plate meets oceanic plate:* The rocks that make up deep-ocean plates are denser than those that make up continental plates. As a result, a heavier oceanic plate slides underneath a continental plate (Figure 2–8). This process is called **subduction**. Note that existing crust is "recycled" by subduction. The crust being melted here balances the new crust forming at a divergent plate boundary.

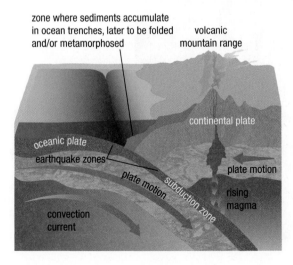

◀ **Figure 2–8** Convergent plates 1: oceanic plate ⟶⟵ continental plate

mid-ocean ridge a feature created by the spreading of the sea floor where two plates are diverging. The best-known example runs through the Atlantic Ocean from north to south.

▲ **Figure 2–7** This man in Iceland is standing with one foot on the Eurasian plate and the other on the North American plate. The gap is increasing at slightly less than one centimetre per year.

subduction the process in which one plate slides underneath another. The subducted plate moves into Earth's interior and is "recycled" (it melts).

go online

Mount St. Helens in Washington state, not far from the Canadian border, is a volcano caused by subduction along a plate boundary. You can learn more about its 1980 eruption through the words of the scientists who observed it (7 minutes).

go online

Find out more about plate boundaries in a National Geographic video (6 minutes).

Subduction can happen fairly smoothly when the oceanic plate moves slowly and continuously under the continental plate. As it does, there are many small earthquakes that cause no damage, and might not even be felt by people. However, in some places, the plates do not move. They push against one another and tension builds up for centuries. Eventually this tension is released in only a few seconds. The result can be a catastrophic 8.0 to 9.0+ quake. This is the situation that concerns officials in British Columbia, since they know the plates there have been locked since 1700.

Most of history's most devastating earthquakes (often accompanied by tsunamis) are of this type. These include the 1700 earthquake off the BC coast (estimated intensity 8.7 to 9.2), the 1964 Alaska earthquake (9.2), the 2004 Indian Ocean earthquake and tsunami (9.0), and the 2011 Japan earthquake and tsunami (9.0). The destructiveness of these mega-quakes is sadly demonstrated by the fact that the Indian Ocean earthquake and tsunamis killed over 275 000 people in 11 countries. People were killed by the tsunami as far away as Africa, nearly 5000 kilometres from the centre of the quake.

2. *Continental plate meets continental plate* (Figure 2–9): When two continental plates run into each other, massive layers of rock are folded, broken, and forced upward by the immense pressures of the collision (Figure 2–10). This process created many of the world's most important mountain ranges. The Himalayas (including Mount Everest, the world's tallest mountain) began forming when the Indian secondary plate collided with the Eurasian plate. This process started about 55 million years ago and continues today as Mount Everest rises higher and higher above sea level.

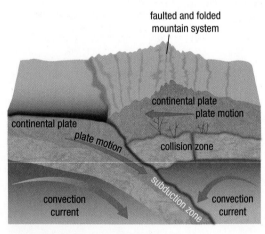

▲ **Figure 2–9** Convergent plates 2: continental plate —→←— continental plate

◀ **Figure 2–10** These rocks were created in horizontal layers at the bottom of the ocean. You can still see the layers, but they are no longer flat. The incredible power of plates colliding folded them into this shape in Canada's Rocky Mountains.

- **Transform:** Along a transform plate boundary (also called a conservative boundary), plates are made neither larger nor smaller. In these locations, plates move in roughly parallel, but opposite, directions (Figure 2–11). As with subduction, this process often happens fairly smoothly, with many small earthquakes but no catastrophic damage. But sometimes, again like in subduction zones, the plates lock up for many years until an enormous release of energy occurs, resulting in a damaging earthquake. These quakes tend to be much less severe than the worst ones along subduction zones. Major quakes at transform boundaries are generally in the intensity range of 5.5 to 7.5.

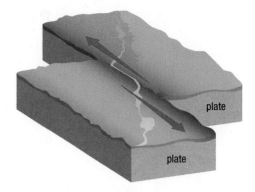

▲ **Figure 2–11** Plates move along a transform plate boundary in opposite directions. The 2010 Haiti earthquake was a magnitude 7.0 quake along a transform boundary.

APPLY IT!

1. a) What is happening to the size of the Atlantic Ocean? How do you know?

   b) Something about a map of the Atlantic Ocean helped early geologists consider the possibility that the continents were moving. What was this?

2. a) What does *subduction* mean?

   b) We know that the North American plate and the Juan de Fuca plate are converging, but which one is subducting under the other? How do you know?

   c) What will eventually happen to the plate that is subducting?

3. a) With your classmates, answer this question without doing research. You know that students in British Columbia are taught how to react to an earthquake if they are at school. Assume that you are the BC government official in charge of earthquake preparedness. What additional preparations should people make to minimize the impact of a major earthquake and tsunami? Note: Nothing can be done to stop an earthquake and tsunami from happening.

   b) Now go online to see how well you did in being prepared for an earthquake.

4. ■ **Geographic Perspective** Debate this question: Government should spend tax dollars on reinforcing buildings, roads, and bridges instead of building tourist facilities (e.g., for the Olympics).

5. The first person to observe that the shapes of Africa and the Americas fit together well was the famous geographer and mapmaker Abraham Ortellius in 1596. In spite of his early insight, the theory of plate tectonics was not generally accepted until the second half of the 20th century. Imagine you are someone writing a newspaper column in 1900 about the idea of continental drift. Why would you have been unwilling to support the ideas of Ortellius?

Rock Cycle

To understand how landforms affect where people live, we need to know about the major types of rocks and how one type can eventually become another (Figure 2–12). Below Figure 2–12 is a handy summary of important points about the rock cycle. Note that the letters beside each description in the summary relate to the letters in the diagram. They do not indicate an order. This is a *cycle*, so there is no beginning or end. Geologic time is so long that there has been enough time for many cycles of rock formation and destruction.

▶ **Figure 2–12** The rock cycle illustrates that rocks are constantly being created and destroyed. Most of these processes happen far too slowly for people to see in their lifetime. What is an exception to this?

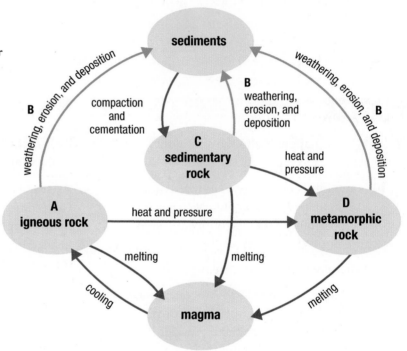

A. *Igneous rocks* form when magma or lava cools. We are familiar with this process in films about spectacular volcanic eruptions, but most cooling happens out of sight, either at the bottom of the ocean or inside Earth's crust. You can tell where an igneous rock cooled by the structure of its crystals. The granite in Figure 2–13 formed from magma that cooled very slowly deep inside Earth, giving time for large crystals to form. Igneous rocks that cool below Earth's surface are called *intrusive* rocks. Igneous rocks formed from molten rock called *lava* that cools on the surface are called *extrusive* rocks. These usually have tiny crystals that are barely visible to the naked eye. An extreme example of extrusive rock is called obsidian. It is blown explosively out of a volcano and cools almost instantly. Crystals do not have time to form, so the rock looks like black glass.

▲ **Figure 2–13** Granite is a common intrusive rock.

©P

B. *Weathering, erosion, and deposition* are related processes that break down all types of rock into small particles and then move the particles to a new location. Weathering is the process of breaking down rocks by water, wind, chemicals, and living things. For example, rocks can be broken by water freezing and thawing in cracks. Erosion is the process of moving the broken-up pieces of rock. For example, rivers move rock and soil particles. Deposition is the process of the eroded materials building up in a new location. An example is the creation of a delta in the sea at the mouth of a river.

weathering the breaking down of rocks

erosion the moving of broken-up pieces of rock

deposition the building up of eroded materials in a new location

C. *Most sedimentary rocks* are created after millions of years of *compaction* and *cementation* of loose sediments. Compaction occurs as loose sediments become tightly packed from drying or the weight of more layers of sediments on top. Eventually the sediments become cemented together by minerals deposited between them. The type of sedimentary rock that forms, not surprisingly, depends on the type of sediment. For example, shale is made up of fine silt and clay particles, and sandstone is made up of sand. Not all sedimentary rocks come from eroded sediments. Limestone, the rock in Figure 2–14, is formed from the shells of tiny marine animals.

▲ **Figure 2–14** Limestone is a common sedimentary rock. Limestone beds often contain fossils.

The most important location for the formation of sedimentary rocks is in the ocean next to continents. Three things can typically happen to this sedimentary rock on the bottom of the ocean.

- The first is that the rock layers just sit on the bottom of the ocean. In many places in the world, sedimentary rocks on the seabed contain deposits of crude oil and natural gas. These deposits are critical sources of the world's energy supply. Examples include Canada's Atlantic Coast, the Gulf of Mexico, the North Sea, and the Persian Gulf.

- The second possibility is that the sedimentary rocks become the "bumper" when two continental plate collide. Canada's Rocky Mountains (and Mount Everest and many other high mountains) are composed of rocks that formed in the sea and were folded and forced up by plates colliding. As a result, it is common to see fossils of sea creatures thousands of metres above sea level.

- The third possibility is that tectonic forces lift layers of sedimentary rocks out of the sea while keeping them more or less horizontal. The result is the creation of plains, on which most of the world's people live. If you live in Ontario, south of the Canadian Shield, the rock beneath you was lifted from the sea in this way.

Some sedimentary rocks contain deposits of fossil fuels (oil, natural gas, and coal) and are the geologic base of most agricultural regions. Aside from these two benefits, the economic importance of sedimentary rocks is often underestimated. It is hard to imagine what our society would be like without concrete, whose ingredients (lime, sand, crushed stone, and gravel) come from sedimentary deposits.

▲ **Figure 2–15** Gneiss (pronounced "nice") is a common metamorphic rock. It is formed from rock that was originally either igneous or sedimentary.

D. *Metamorphic rocks* are "changed" versions of igneous, sedimentary, and other metamorphic rocks (Figure 2–15). The changes occur when the rocks are exposed to great amounts of heat and pressure, such as when molten rock intrudes into existing rock layers. Metamorphic versions of sedimentary rock are much harder than the original. Shale changes into slate, for example, and limestone becomes marble. (*Metamorphosis* means "change form." You may have heard this word used in science class to describe the change of a caterpillar into a butterfly.)

Metamorphism in igneous rocks is hugely important in the creation of mineral deposits. The great heat and pressure involved can cause minerals to concentrate in relatively small areas. Sometimes, the concentrations of iron ore, gold, nickel, and other minerals are rich enough to make mining worthwhile.

CONNECTING

You can learn more about mineral resources in **Chapter 7 (pages 154–166)**.

APPLY IT!

1. **a)** The strange word *mnemonic* refers to a phrase that you can use to help you remember something. For example, you could remember magma and the three rock types with *m*any *I*rish singing *m*en for *m*agma, *i*gneous, *s*edimentary, *m*etamorphic. Create another mnemonic for these four words. Why does it make sense to have the words in this order?

   b) Create a mnemonic to help you remember the various processes that transform one rock type into another. You will need to start by making a list of the processes in a logical order.

2. **a)** *Weathering* breaks down existing rock. Briefly describe any three physical or chemical forces that act as weathering agents.

   b) *Erosion* is the movement of weathered rock. Briefly describe any three ways in which weathered rock materials are moved.

   c) *Deposition* is the placement of eroded rock materials in a location different from where they formed. Briefly describe two examples of deposition.

3. **a)** Various igneous and metamorphic rocks are used for kitchen counters and floors, as well as walls in office buildings. Name some of the rocks that are used for these purposes.

   b) What characteristics of those rocks make them desirable for these purposes?

   c) Would people tend to choose intrusive or extrusive rocks for these purposes? Why?

Glaciation

Massive glaciers cover Antarctica, Greenland, and some mountainous areas. At times in the past, when global temperatures were cooler, ice sheets covered much larger areas of land. This advance and coverage by ice is called **glaciation**. Although glaciation is a much less powerful force than plate tectonics, it is still fundamentally important to the creation of the Canadian landforms that we see. The reason is simple: glaciation ended only "one minute ago" in our geological year (Figure 2–4 on page 34). In geologic terms, there has been no time for the effects of glaciation to be wiped away by other landform processes. Here are some glaciation facts to consider:

glaciation the process of ice advancing and covering large areas of land

- Glaciers advanced across Canada four separate times in the last 2.5 million years (Figure 2–16). After each advance, there was a retreat as the glaciers melted.

- Assuming you are in Canada, the place where you are sitting right now was covered by as much as three kilometres of ice only 15 000 years ago. As you can see in Figure 2–16, there is one exception to this—one small part of Canada was not glaciated.

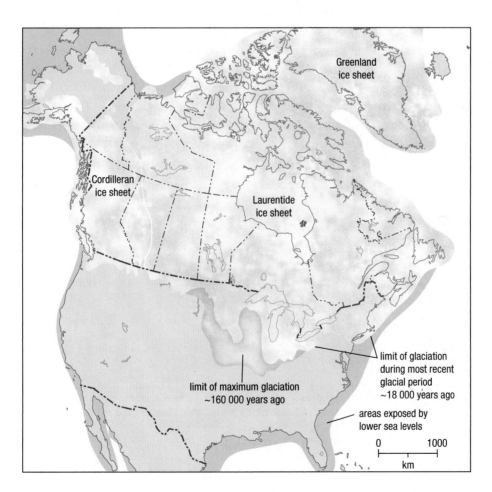

◀ **Figure 2–16 The most recent glaciation of North America.**
■ **Patterns and Trends** Glaciers covered almost all of Canada and part of the northern United States until 11:59 p.m. on December 31 of our geological history year.

Greenland ice sheet

Cordilleran ice sheet

Laurentide ice sheet

limit of glaciation during most recent glacial period
~18 000 years ago

limit of maximum glaciation
~160 000 years ago

areas exposed by lower sea levels

0   1000
km

Geo ⚙ Inquiry

Evaluate and Draw Conclusions

In Figure 2–16, what small part of Canada was not glaciated? Why did the glaciers miss this area, considering how far north it is? How might the landforms of this small area look different from those of neighbouring areas that were glaciated?

- The first three glacial advances are not important in Canada today because the fourth one wiped away evidence of them. Geographers in North America call the fourth glacial advance the *Wisconsin glaciation* because the ice advanced as far south as that American state.

- Glaciers remain in a few mountainous areas of Canada. Western Canada has remnants of the Cordilleran ice sheet, and glaciers still exist in the extreme north on Ellesmere and Axel Heiberg Islands.

- Some Earth scientists think that glaciation may not be over. They suggest that we are only in the interglacial period between the fourth and a possible fifth glacial advance. But there is no immediate threat—another advance might not happen for 100 000 years or more. Climate change resulting from human activities is a much more immediate threat.

go online

Find out more about glaciers.

Use **ArcGIS Online** to create a journal map that starts with physical features like lakes and rivers, and adds landforms and population information.

Glaciation and Canada's Landforms

Everywhere you look in Canada, you will see the many effects of glaciation. Often these are not very obvious because, when we look at the land, we see a prosperous farming area, a great city, a gravel pit, or an attractive, rugged holiday destination. We do not see how glaciation contributed to the existence of the feature. Glaciers affected the land in many different ways. It is beyond the scope of this book, however, to examine these effects in detail. You will have to take a physical geography course to learn about them. Instead, we will focus on the most important forces involved and how these forces produced the landscapes we live in (Figure 2–17).

Glacial effects fall into two broad categories: *erosional* and *depositional*. The descriptions on the next two pages are numbered so that you can match them with the photos in Apply It! question 1 on page 46.

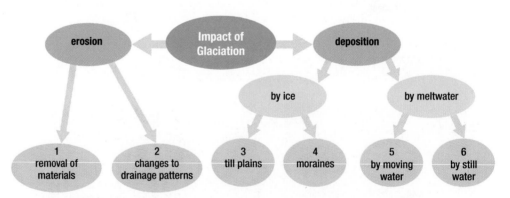

▲ **Figure 2–17** The impact of glaciation in any particular location is often related to how close that place was to both the centre and edge of the glacier. Why? See the text for details.

EROSIONAL EFFECTS

1. Glaciers acted as giant earth-moving machines, scraping away the soil and rocks that covered much of Canada. The result is that much of the country has little or no soil today. While most of this eroded land is far north and away from population centres, you can find some as far south as a line from the southern tip of Georgian Bay to Kingston.

2. Glaciers also completely changed the drainage patterns of rivers, streams, and lakes. In particular, lakes and rivers that had existed in low areas of loose earth materials were destroyed. New lakes formed in rock basins that filled with water as the glaciers melted away. The result is that northern Canada has more lakes than it is possible to count (partly because it is often impossible to say which small water bodies are lakes and which are ponds, swamps, and other kinds of wetlands).

DEPOSITIONAL EFFECTS

Deposition as a result of glaciation also falls into two categories: eroded materials deposited directly by ice and those deposited by massive amounts of meltwater.

Deposition by ice: The key thing to remember is that materials deposited directly by ice are *not sorted* by size. These unsorted materials, a mixture of loose sediments and rocks of all sizes, are called *till*. If you see a mix of particle sizes, for example, at a road cut, you can assume that you are looking at a feature made by ice.

3. A common feature formed by deposition is a till plain. Till plains are generally rather featureless, with small hills and valleys. They are formed from rock and sediment released from the glaciers as they melt.

4. A very common feature formed directly by ice is a moraine (Figure 2–18). Moraines are deposits of till that form at the edges (nose and/or sides) of a glacier. The Oak Ridges Moraine, which extends from the Orangeville area to north of Trenton, is an excellent example of the rolling hills and small lakes typical of a moraine.

Geo ☼ Inquiry

Communicate

Choose an area of Canada to research. Use diagrams, photos, and maps to explain how that area has been affected by glaciation.

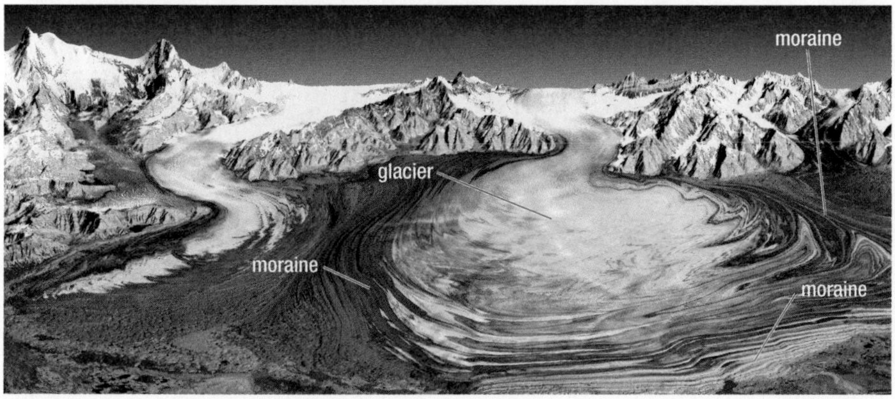

◀ **Figure 2–18** Moraines being formed at the edges and nose of a glacier in Antarctica. The materials being deposited here were weathered a considerable distance "up-ice" and transported by the ice to be deposited here.

Deposition by water: If you start with an immense amount of ice and it warms, either in the summer or as a glacier is melting, you get an immense amount of meltwater.

5. Meltwater moves glacial debris as any river would, but on a much more massive scale. Fast-moving water can move heavy particles like gravel and rocks. As the water slows, it deposits these particles based on weight. First the rocks drop out, then the gravel, and then the sand. The result is that we see materials that have been *sorted* by size.

6. Meltwater rivers flow into meltwater lakes. In these lakes, where there is very little movement of the water, the lightest materials—silt and clay particles—are deposited. Glacial lakes were much larger than today's lakes (even the Great Lakes), so glacial lake deposits are a common feature in many parts of Ontario and the southern Prairies. These areas tend to be very flat, have deep, rich soils, and are often prime farmland.

APPLY IT!

1. **a)** Each of the photos in Figure 2–19 corresponds to one of the numbered descriptions on pages 45 to 46. Match each photo to the correct description. In your notebook, record your findings like this:

   A = [short written description]

   b) What evidence did you use to decide which photo shows which glacial feature?

2. **OSSLT** Some of the areas shown in the photographs support larger populations than other areas do. Apply one of the descriptors below to each photo. Next to the descriptor, indicate the reasons why your choice makes sense. Hints: Remember that a population, of whatever size, only exists if people can find work. You can use each descriptor more than once, and you do not have to use all the descriptors.
   - **i)** very high population potential
   - **ii)** high population potential
   - **iii)** moderate population potential
   - **iv)** low population potential
   - **v)** very low population potential

▲ **Figure 2–19** The effects of glaciation can be seen everywhere in Canada, if you know what to look for.

Landform Patterns

While tectonic forces painted the big picture, glaciation filled in the details on the many "portraits" of Canada. Keeping with this artistic approach, let's look at Canada through the eyes of artists (Figures 2–20 to 2–23). It should not be a surprise that many Canadian artists have been inspired by the land. What is a surprise is that this focus in relatively new. Until the emergence of the famous *Group of Seven* after World War I, Canadians artists (and average Canadians) thought that art was something that came from Europe. This changed when young artists travelled north and discovered the fascinating, and often stark, beauty of Canada. They could not have guessed that they were producing an interesting body of work for geographers to analyze a century later.

Paintings go beyond what photographs are capable of showing because the artist *interprets* the landscape for the viewer. This means that the artist paints in a way that conveys personal ideas or feelings about the subject. In this section, we will look at four well-known landscape paintings. In particular, we will look for the role played by plate tectonics and glaciation in creating these landscapes.

SKILL FOCUS

Here are some things to keep in mind when "reading" these paintings:

- How is the painting different from a photo?
- Where does the artist want you to focus your attention?
- For our purposes, what geographic information can be gathered from the painting? Think about the physical features of the land and also about human activities in these areas.

▶ **Figure 2–20** *White Pine* by A. J. Casson

Where: La Cloche Mountains in what is now Killarney Provincial Park, north of Georgian Bay, Ontario

Background: This is one of the most famous pieces of Canadian art. You can see the real thing at the McMichael Canadian Art Collection, in Kleinburg, Ontario.

Glaciation: Two effects of glaciers can be seen. First, bare rocks were exposed by glacial erosion. The dark patches are lichen, a plant-like combination of fungus and algae that grows on rocks. Lichens weather the rock and help to form new soil. Secondly, the lake is typical of the vast number of lakes left behind by the glaciers.

Plate tectonics: The painting shows the very worn-down remains of once-high mountains that were pushed out of the sea in the Precambrian Era. They are mainly white quartzite, a metamorphic rock.

▲ **Figure 2–21**
Hillside, Lake Alphonse
by William Goodridge
Roberts

Where: Southern Québec

Glaciation: The low, rounded hills and the scattered large rocks suggest direct deposition by ice. Because we see only a small area, we cannot know whether it is a moraine or till plain.

Background: This could have been painted in many places across southern Canada that have similar geography. The land has been cleared for farming. After so much back-breaking work, the poor quality of the land must have been very discouraging for the farmer.

Plate tectonics: The thick layer of glacial surface deposits hides the underlying geology. Horizontal layers of sedimentary rock were laid down under the sea in the Paleozoic Era and later lifted above the sea.

Where: Rocky Mountains in Alberta

Plate tectonics: These are newer mountains (Cenozoic Era) than the ancient mountains in *White Pine*. They were produced by the collision of the North American and Pacific plates.

Background: Lismer, like Casson, was a member of the Group of Seven. He painted this scene when he visited the Rockies in 1928. To own a Lismer or a Casson, you would probably have to settle for a reproduction on a T-shirt or a coffee mug. Some of their paintings have sold for more than $1 million.

Glaciation: Mountain glaciers are different from glaciers on flatter land. Mountain glaciers carve out deep U-shaped valleys (under the glacier in the left front corner) and sharpen mountain peaks. Farther downhill, there are moraines and various meltwater features.

▲ **Figure 2–22** *The Glacier* by Arthur Lismer

Background: The artist "tricks" the viewer's eye by making the horizon seem farther away than it really is, which exaggerates the flatness of the land. This painting is part of a series that the artist called *Big Lonely*. It expresses his feelings about growing up in the area.

Plate tectonics: Relatively horizontal sedimentary rock, from the Cenozoic Era, contributes to this area being quite flat. These are much younger rocks than those in the previous painting.

Where: Southern Prairies, likely southwestern Manitoba

Glaciation: The sorted deposits of a vast glacial lake helped make the land very flat. Many people who have never been to the Prairies think that the whole region is like this. In fact, such extreme flatness is only found where there were large glacial lakes.

◀ **Figure 2–23** *No Grass Grows on the Beaten Path* by William Kurelek

Only rarely do geographers use paintings rather than photographs in their studies. You could probably suggest reasons why. In any case, it is interesting to compare a painting with a photograph of the same area (Figure 2–24).

Geo ⚙ Inquiry

Interpret and Analyze

Canada's longest-serving prime minister, William Lyon Mackenzie King, once commented, "If some countries have too much history, we have too much geography." What did he mean in the latter part of his comment? How have our landforms contributed to this?

◀ **Figure 2–24** This is also southern Manitoba. In what ways did the artist capture this landscape accurately in his painting (Figure 2–23)?

CHAPTER 2 EXPLORING CONNECTIONS: LANDFORMS, GEOLOGY, AND HUMAN ACTIVITIES

1. If you look at the paintings in the following order, you are seeing a geological time line from oldest to most recent: Figure 2–20, Figure 2–21, Figure 2–23, Figure 2–22. What evidence of the age differences do you see?

2. In which paintings is plate tectonics the more powerful force? In which is glaciation more significant? How can you tell the difference?

3. **OSSLT** How each of us reacts to a piece of art is very personal. What emotional reaction did you have to each painting? Why?

4. How could humans use each of the landscapes shown in the paintings? Explain your answers.

5. What are the advantages and disadvantages of doing geographic analysis using artwork?

Landform Regions of Canada

Take **GeoFlight 2.1** to see all of Canada's landform regions.

Canada's landforms can be divided into three types (Figure 2–25):

- the Canadian Shield, an immense area of ancient, worn-down mountains
- areas of lowlands that surround the Shield
- areas of highlands that surround the lowlands

Geo ⚙ Inquiry

Formulate Questions

Skim the next three pages about Canada's landform regions. List questions you have about all the regions (e.g., about topography, population, resources). As you learn about each region, record answers to your questions. Make sure to use headings under each question to identify the regions.

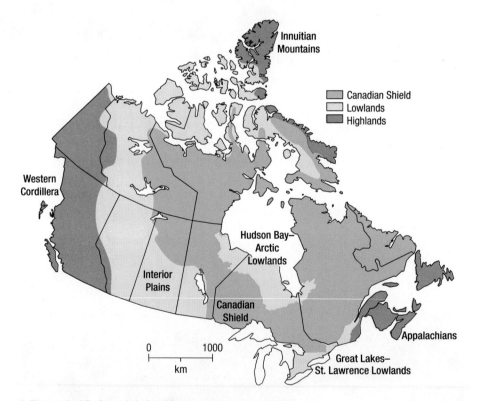

▲ Figure 2–25 Canada's landform types and regions

Seven Things You Should Know About the Canadian Shield

✓ The Canadian Shield (Figure 2–26) is the geologic foundation of Canada and is, by far, its oldest and largest landform region.

✓ It is of Precambrian age. More than one billion years ago, it had many huge mountains, but most of these have eroded away over the years.

✓ It covers more than half of Canada, most of Greenland, and two small areas of the United States. It is almost completely uninhabited except for places in the south and near mineral and forest resources. Aboriginal people are the majority of the population on much of the Shield.

✓ It is one of the world's important sources of metallic minerals and diamonds.

✓ Most of the Shield is not good for farming because of rock and poor soil.

✓ Unlike most of the world, it has an abundant supply of fresh water.

✓ Most of its many rivers flow into Hudson Bay. Rivers in the southern part of the Shield are used to generate hydroelectricity.

▲ **Figure 2–26** The Canadian Shield. Do you think the population density of this area of the Shield is high or low? Why?

Seven Things You Should Know About Canada's Lowland Regions

✓ Canada has three lowland areas: the Interior Plains (IP), the Great Lakes–St. Lawrence Lowlands (GL-SL), and the Hudson Bay–Arctic Lowlands (HB-A) (Figure 2–27).

✓ Almost 60 percent of Canadians live in the GL-SL, even though this area is only slightly less than 2 percent of the country. Another 17 percent of the population lives in the southernmost part of the IP. In contrast, the HB-A has a population of slightly more than 10 000 (about 0.03 percent of the total population). Aboriginal people are the majority of the population in the HB-A.

Geo ⚙ Inquiry

Evaluate and Draw Conclusions

For each region, describe how its physical features affect the number of people living there, where in the region they live, and other population-related factors such as transportation.

▲ **Figure 2–27** All three landforms share a similar geologic structure, but different climate and soil characteristics have resulted in a very different pattern of human settlement in the Hudson Bay–Arctic Lowlands (a) compared to the Great Lakes–St. Lawrence Lowlands (b) and the Interior Plains (c).

Take **GeoFlight 2.2** to visit the Niagara Escarpment, one of the most distinctive landform features of the GL-SL.

✓ The GL-SL and IP (southern part) are, by far, the most important agricultural areas in Canada. They account for about 75 percent of Canada's total farm production. Much of the farm production from the IP is exported, while most of the production in the GL-SL is used within Canada.

✓ The sedimentary rock underlying the IP is enormously important for the production of oil and natural gas—Canada's most important export products. This region is also the world leader in the production of potash, a major ingredient in fertilizer.

✓ A narrow band of the Canadian Shield, which extends into the United States just east of Kingston, separates the GL and SL into two parts.

✓ Two escarpments break the IP into three distinct levels, from east to west, with the lowest section being in Manitoba.

✓ The HB-A consists of two parts. The HB (Hudson Bay) part of the region is on the mainland south of Hudson Bay, while the A (Arctic) part is several islands in Hudson Bay.

Seven Things You Should Know About Canada's Highland Regions

go online

View photos showing the variety of landscapes in the Western Cordillera.

✓ Two of these regions (the Western Cordillera and the Innuitian Mountains) are much younger, and hence higher, than the third (the Appalachian Mountains) (Figure 2–28).

✓ The Western Cordillera (WC) and Appalachian regions extend far south into the United States. The WC also extends north and west into Alaska.

✓ The Innuitian is Canada's most remote region and has no full-time population. Because of its location, and in spite of its rugged beauty, it attracts few visitors.

✓ It is *wrong* to call all of the highlands west of Calgary and Edmonton "The Rockies." The Rockies are, in fact, just the easternmost section of the WC (Figure 2–29).

▼ **Figure 2–28** Western Cordillera (a), Appalachian Mountains (b), and Innuitian Mountains (c). How can you tell from these photos that the Appalachian Mountains are much older than the mountains in the other two regions?

✓ The WC in southern British Columbia has a large population in valleys (the lower Fraser Valley, which includes Vancouver, and interior valleys like the Okanagan) and coastal plains (the southeastern side of Vancouver Island, which includes Victoria).

✓ Not all of the Appalachian region has a high elevation. Most of the population lives on narrow coastal plains (in cities such as Halifax, Saint John, and St. John's) and in a few river valleys (in cities such as Fredericton).

✓ The complex geology of these regions means that valuable mineral resources are found in some locations.

Geo✿Inquiry

Gather and Organize

Identify three different parts of Canada that were settled because of the minerals found there. How has this affected all aspects of the lives of the people who live there? Use a graphic organizer to display your information.

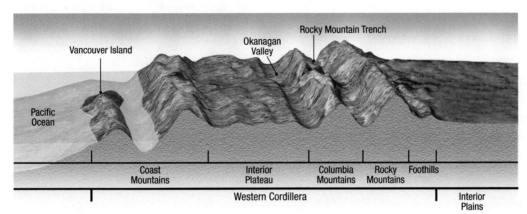

◀ **Figure 2–29** A profile of the Western Cordillera from Vancouver Island to the Interior Plains. Note that the Rockies are just one part of this large, complex region.

APPLY IT!

1. **a)** The Great Lakes–St. Lawrence Lowlands is actually divided into two parts. How?

   b) Why is this considered to be one region even though it is divided?

2. **a)** Name six very large lakes in Canada that are just parts of larger lakes that existed as the glaciers were retreating slightly more than 10 000 years ago.

   b) ■ **Spatial Significance** What evidence of a large glacial lake is there in northeastern Ontario?

3. While the Appalachian region experiences the odd small earthquake, there is no fear of the "Big One" as there is in British Columbia. Why does this difference exist?

4. It is time to compare the landform regions map (Figure 2–25, on page 50) to our population distribution map (Figure 1–5, on page 24).

   a) In what landform region(s) are there CMAs of more than one million people?

   b) In what region(s) are there significant areas of *continuous ecumene*?

   c) In what region(s) are there significant areas of *discontinuous ecumene*?

   d) In what region(s) do very few people live?

   e) What are five ways that Canada's landforms affect population? Give specific examples to support each way. Consider factors such as the effects of geology, plate tectonics, glaciation, height and shape of the land, and features like lakes and rivers.

Exploring Connections: Landforms, Geology, and Human Activities

? **How do different landforms and geologic processes contribute to where and how people live?**

We can look at Canada's landforms in different ways. We can focus on the processes involved in their creation. We can also look at them to appreciate their beauty and majesty. Finally, we can look at them from a practical perspective—what opportunities and challenges do the landforms present?

▲ **Figure 2–30** Avalanche sheds over railway tracks. When you look at this photo, what questions come to mind?

1. The best kind of graphic organizer for the material in this chapter is a blank map of Canada—either a full-page one you draw or a printed one from your teacher. On it, summarize the important information in this chapter. Be neat; there is a lot of information to show.

2. Figure 2–30 shows the Canadian Pacific rail line through the Fraser River Canyon in British Columbia. Compare this photo to Figure 5–2 (page 103). What do these very different images tell us about the relationships that Canadians have with their landforms?

Geo ☼ Inquiry

Interpret and Analyze

3. Review this chapter and discuss the following quotation: "Canada is an east-west country trying to survive in a north-south continent." Hint: Look at a landform regions map and population distributions map.

Evaluate and Draw Conclusions

4. a) Consider the landforms in the area where you live. First, define the size of the area you want to consider. Then answer this question: How important have plate tectonics and glaciation been in creating your local landscape? Discuss both the positive and negative features of the landforms for human settlement.

   b) What have people done over the years to deal with any of the difficulties presented by the landforms?

Analyze an Issue

5. Think about issues related to the connections between landforms, geology, and human activities that you have read about or that affect your everyday life. Pick one of these issues.

   a) Write a number of questions about the issue. Select one clearly stated and important big question.

   b) What areas would you have to research to answer your big question? Find three or four resources and collect information to answer your question. Be sure to analyze the information and consider various viewpoints.

   c) Use your notes to take a position and answer your question. Support your answer with facts from your research.

   d) Create a product that communicates the answer to your question. This could be an opinion paper, a blog post, a poster, or a letter to the editor. Be creative!

Exploring Connections: Climate, Soil, and Natural Vegetation and Human Activities

Climate Change Up Close

When we think about climate change, we may worry more about the big picture than about the individuals and small communities that will be affected. They have to be prepared to adjust how they live and earn a living. You may have driven through the Holland Marsh, a relatively small, unique farming area on Highway 400 between Toronto and Barrie. The Marsh, which originally was a marsh, was drained for agriculture starting in 1925. Earlier in its history, the Marsh specialized in the production of lettuce, carrots, onions, and celery. More recently, production has been diversified to include dozens of different vegetables. These include vegetables used by the many diverse ethnic groups that have moved to Southern Ontario in recent decades.

The agricultural ecosystem of the Marsh is very specialized and involves the right amount of heat during the day and cooler air at night, along with the right amount of moisture during each part of the growing season. Marsh farmers are worried that climate change will upset the delicate balance of climate conditions that they have relied on for generations.

KEY TERMS

natural vegetation

maritime climate

annual temperature range

continental climate

climate graph

soil profile

wet-climate soils

dry-climate soils

go online

You can learn about the Holland Marsh and the farmers' concerns about climate change in a video (4:05 minutes).

THINKING CRITICALLY

What environmental and human factors have contributed to the agricultural importance of the Holland Marsh? How might climate change upset the balance of the marsh? What could the farmers do about this? What impact might this have on the food you eat?

Climate Processes

As in Chapter 2, we will focus in on *processes* and *patterns* in this chapter. Here we will look at three other important aspects of Canada's physical geography: climate, soils, and **natural vegetation**.

natural vegetation the plants that would grow in an area with no human interference

Climate refers to long-term patterns of weather. To understand Canada's climate, it helps to remember three things:

- Canada is a very large country, which means there is a lot of room for widely varying climates.
- Northern parts of Canada have different climates than southern parts.
- Coastal areas have very different climate conditions than inland areas.

Factors That Determine Climate

Six major factors determine the climate that exists in any particular location. The first letter of five factors, along with the last factor, can be combined to make this simple phrase to help you remember them: LOWER Near Water.

- **L**atitude
- **O**cean currents
- **W**inds, air masses, and jet streams
- **E**levation
- **R**elief
- **Near Water**

LATITUDE

As Figure 3–1 shows, latitude is an important factor in determining how warm a climate is. This is not surprising if we remember how much Canadians enjoy winter vacations to places with latitudes in the 10°N to 30°N range. The reason is quite simple: the farther you are from the equator, the less direct sunlight you receive (Figure 3–2).

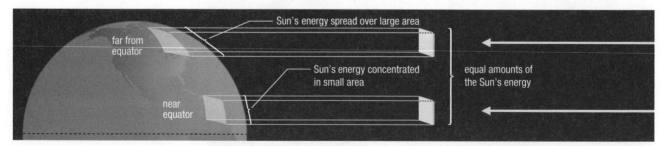

▲ **Figure 3–1** Earth's curvature causes the Sun's energy to be less concentrated at the poles than near the equator.

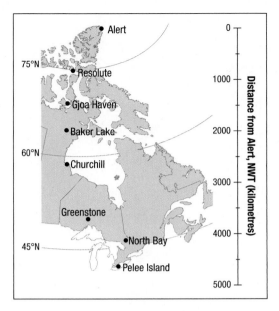
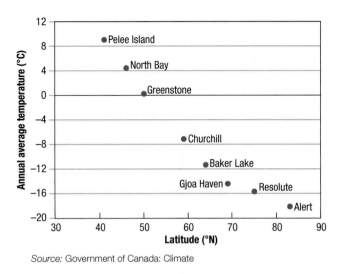

Source: Government of Canada: Climate

▲ **Figure 3–2** Generally, the farther north you go, the cooler it gets. In contrast, Miami Beach at 25°N has an annual average temperature of 25.0°C. Match the place names on the map to the names on the graph. Why do the names on the graph appear in reverse order to those on the map?

OCEAN CURRENTS

An ocean current moving away from the equator is relatively warmer than the surrounding water. An ocean current flowing toward the equator is cooler (Figure 3–3 on the next page). For example, on the east coast, the Gulf Stream brings warm water from the tropics to the coast of Atlantic Canada. On the west coast, a relatively warm current crosses the Pacific Ocean from Japan. When it hits North America, it splits into two parts. The North Pacific Current moves north up the coast of British Columbia and Alaska, while the California Current flows southward. Note that it is the same water, but—in relative terms—it is warm as it flows north and cold as it flows south. For example, if the water in the current has a temperature of 15°C and the surrounding water is 12°C, then the current is considered warm. On the other hand, if the surrounding water is 18°C, the current is considered cold.

Winds moving across an ocean current are warmed or cooled, again depending on the relative temperature of the water. The winds bring that temperature to land areas they cross. The impact of this can be seen with a simple comparison. Prince Rupert, BC, and Cartwright, NL, are both at about 54°N. The average annual temperature for Prince Rupert, which is affected by a warm current, is 7.5°C. Cartwright, which is affected by a cold current, has an average annual temperature of 0.0°C.

Use **ArcGIS Online** to create a world map showing ocean currents and where they affect Canadian shores.

► **Figure 3–3 Ocean currents and air masses.**

■ **Interrelationships** Air masses take on the moisture and temperature characteristics of their source areas. Each air mass has a two-letter code that describes its characteristics. For example, a **cP** (continental polar) air mass is dry and cold. When a **cP** air mass covers Ontario in the middle of winter, you get a cold, sunny day.

- Moisture:
  - **m** = maritime (moist: formed over water)
  - **c** = continental (dry: formed over land)
- Temperature:
  - **T** = tropical (hot: formed in or near the tropics)
  - **P** = polar (cool to cold: formed between 55°N and 65°N)
  - **A** = arctic (very cold)

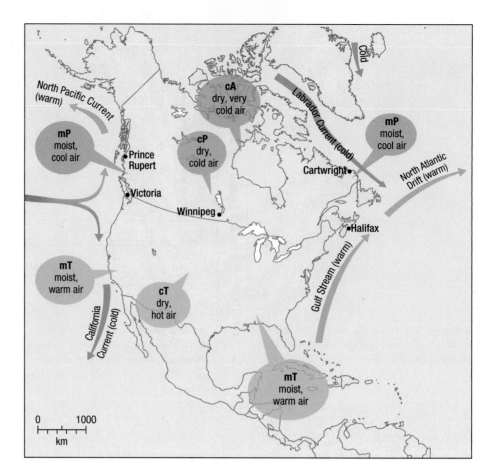

AIR MASSES AND WINDS

(OSSLT)

Geo✿Inquiry

Communicate

Using the map in Figure 3–3, describe the climate of Victoria, British Columbia, Winnipeg, Manitoba, and Halifax, Nova Scotia. You can do this in complete sentences, pictures, drawings, or even a video report.

An air mass is a large volume of air that takes on the climatic conditions of the area in which it forms. For example, an air mass forming over an ocean contains moist air, while one forming far from the ocean has very dry air. Figure 3–3 outlines the various air masses that affect Canada's climate.

It is important to understand that air masses move depending on the particular weather patterns that exist at any given time. This means that the area where you live may experience one air mass for several days, followed by several days with an air mass that has completely different characteristics. Think of a hot, humid spell in the middle of the summer when the temperature exceeds 30°C, followed by a cool, sunny spell during which the thermometer might reach only 20°C. This would mean that a moist, hot air mass (mT in Figure 3–3) that pushed north from the Gulf of Mexico was replaced by a cold and dry air mass (cP) that moved south from northern Canada. When you look at the influence of different air masses over many years, you can see how local climates are affected by air masses.

58   INTERACTIONS WITH THE PHYSICAL ENVIRONMENT   ©P

Air moves over Earth's surface from areas of higher air pressure to areas of lower air pressure. This moving air is, of course, wind. Earth has a well-established pattern of low- and high-pressure areas, which create wind belts (Figure 3–4). The most important wind belt for most of Canada is the westerlies. The westerlies are named after the direction they come from—the winds move from the west toward the east. A general pattern of westerly movement gives us most of our weather and changes the air masses that affect us.

go online

Find out more about wind.

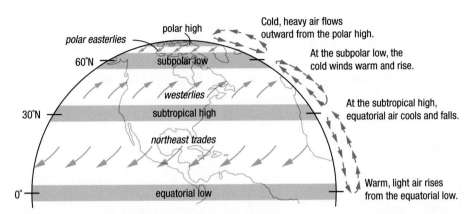

▲ **Figure 3–4** Wind belts are created when air rises high into the atmosphere above low-pressure zones and then descends into high-pressure zones. Air then moves on the surface from high pressure to low pressure, creating wind. Note that the pressure and wind patterns of the southern hemisphere are similar to those in the northern hemisphere. Also note that pressure zones and wind belts move north and south with the seasons.

ELEVATION

When you travel from sea level to the top of a nearby mountain, it gets colder the higher you go. But why does it get colder if you are getting closer to the Sun? It is simple physics at work. Picture air moving eastward from the Pacific Ocean and being forced to rise over the Coast Mountains. At a higher elevation, there is less air sitting on top of the air, so there is less pressure.

So, as air rises, the pressure decreases. As a result, the air expands and cools.

- If the expansion occurs without condensation happening, then the air will cool by 1.0°C for every 100 metres of elevation change. This happens because there is less air for the Sun's radiation to heat.

- Cooler air cannot hold as much moisture, so condensation eventually starts to happen. Condensation gives off heat so that the rate of cooling drops to 0.6°C for every 100 metres.

- The result is that on a warm summer day in Vancouver at sea level, the temperature might be 26°C. At the top of a nearby mountain, at 1400 metres, the temperature might be only 14°C. Hikers would need a jacket!

Geo ☼ Inquiry

Interpret and Analyze

Explain why going up a tall mountain can be like travelling a considerable distance northward in Canada in terms of the climate patterns that you will experience.

RELIEF

Geo ⚙ Inquiry

Evaluate and Draw Conclusions

What is the purpose of Figure 3–5? Does it achieve its purpose? Why or why not? Is a diagram like this more or less helpful in providing geographical information than a map that shows relief? Explain your answer.

Relief in geography means the shape of the surface of the land. The relief in an area is an important factor in determining the amount of precipitation that the area gets. Places on the *windward* side of a height of land (the side facing the wind) get substantially more rain and snow than places on the *leeward* side (the opposite side, away from the wind's direction). The leeward side can also be called the *rain shadow*. This is demonstrated well if you look at a profile of Canada from the Pacific Ocean to Calgary (Figure 3–5). The effect can even be seen in Southern Ontario, although the relief there is much less dramatic than the relief in British Columbia. Hanover, near Lake Huron, receives an average of 271 centimetres of snow a year. Bradford, 115 kilometres directly to the east, receives only 125 centimetres. The difference between these two towns is that Hanover is on the windward side of an area of relatively small glacial moraines and low hills, while Bradford is on the leeward side.

Relief Precipitation in the Western Cordillera

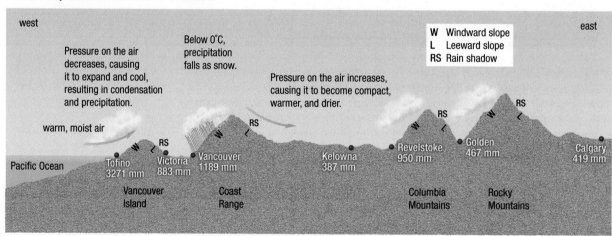

▲ **Figure 3–5** ■ **Spatial Significance** What is the relationship between precipitation amounts and relief in this part of western Canada?

NEAR WATER

maritime climate climate in areas near an ocean. The annual temperature range (summer to winter) is small and precipitation is high.

annual temperature range temperature of the warmest month minus the temperature of the coldest month

One of the most important climate factors is closeness to water. Places that are close to an ocean have what is called a **maritime climate**. Winter temperatures are relatively mild, while summers never get too hot. As a result, the **annual temperature range** is quite small. For example, Vancouver, which has a maritime climate, has a range of only 14.4°C (July temperature – December temperature = 18.0°C – 3.6°C = 14.4°C). The proximity to a major body of water means, however, that precipitation is quite high. Vancouver receives 1189 millimetres of precipitation per year, which is fairly typical for a maritime location.

Climate conditions for places far from the ocean are quite different. Such places have a **continental climate**. Land heats (and cools) much more quickly than water, so extreme temperatures are the norm. Regina has a continental climate. It has an annual temperature range of 31.3°C (July temperature – December temperature = 18.9°C – [–12.4]°C = 31.3°C), which is more than twice that of Vancouver. No nearby source of moisture is available, so precipitation is low—only 390 millimetres.

continental climate climate in areas far from an ocean. The annual temperature range is large and precipitation is low.

Areas near the Great Lakes are a special case. They are far enough away from the ocean that they should be continental, but because they are so large, the Great Lakes provide a partial maritime influence. They moderate the temperatures somewhat and provide a source of moisture, as long as they are not frozen. Once they are frozen, they act just like land. The climate here can be called *modified continental.*

APPLY IT!

1. What is the difference between weather and climate?

2. Why is it important to understand the difference between maritime climate and continental climate if we are to understand Canadian climate patterns?

3. a) When the cold water of the Labrador Current meets the warm water of the Gulf Stream off the southeast corner of Newfoundland, the result is the foggiest place on Earth. What causes all the fog?

   b) The Labrador Current not only brings cold water south—it brings icebergs from the Greenland ice sheet. Perhaps the most famous marine tragedy of all time happened because of this. What happened? When did it happen?

4. In this chapter, you have learned what happens to the temperature of a body of air that moves from sea level at Vancouver to the top of a 1400 metre mountain.

   a) Which side of the mountain would you like to live on? Give three well-explained reasons for your choice.

   b) What would the temperature be if the air returned to sea level on the leeward side of the mountain?

   c) How much precipitation would there be on the leeward slope?

   d) How would this pattern affect the climate of places like Victoria, Kelowna, and Calgary?

5. a) What letter grade would you give the climate where you live? Explain your grade using the good and bad points of your climate.

   b) To what world climate would you give an A+? What are the advantages of this climate compared with your climate?

6. Research the impact of global climate change on Canadian climates. How will climates improve? How will they get worse?

Reading Climate Graphs

climate graph (also called a *climograph*) a graph that summarizes climate data for a particular location

Before we start looking at climate patterns, let's look at a **climate graph**, a handy tool that summarizes a lot of information in a compact, easily understood way.

Figure 3–6 shows the location of some critical data on a climate graph for Regina. Figure 3–7 provides climate graphs for seven other cities in Canada, as well as Regina. Together, these graphs provide a good overview of the range of climates from coast to coast to coast.

▶ **Figure 3–6** The four pieces of data shown will help you describe and understand any climate. How does Regina's climate compare with the climate where you live? You may also want to think about the varying lengths of the growing seasons in different parts of Canada. Recall that most plants that grow in Canada need a minimum temperature of at least 6°C.

▼ **Figure 3–7** Canada's climates are very variable. None of them are particularly warm compared to climates in most of the world.

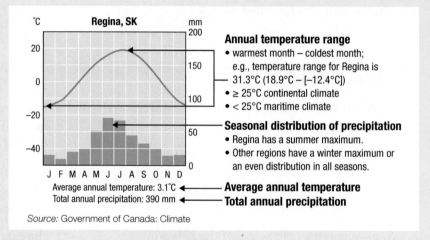

Annual temperature range
- warmest month − coldest month; e.g., temperature range for Regina is 31.3°C (18.9°C − [−12.4°C])
- ≥ 25°C continental climate
- < 25°C maritime climate

Seasonal distribution of precipitation
- Regina has a summer maximum.
- Other regions have a winter maximum or an even distribution in all seasons.

Average annual temperature: 3.1°C ◄——— **Average annual temperature**
Total annual precipitation: 390 mm ◄——— **Total annual precipitation**

Source: Government of Canada: Climate

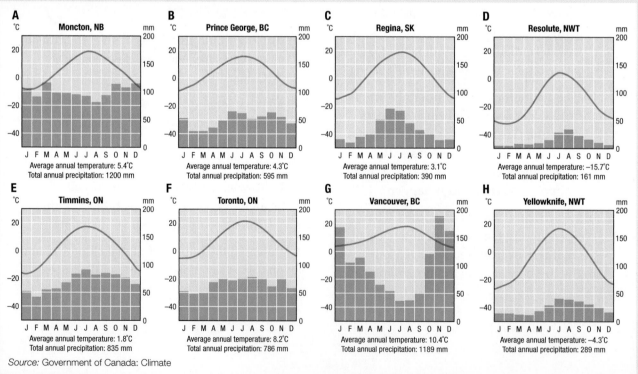

Source: Government of Canada: Climate

1. Start by locating and naming the eight places on a blank map of Canada. Do this neatly since you will be adding a lot of data to the map.

2. Make some comparisons among the four types of data using graphic organizers. The first one, for *average annual temperature*, has been done for you (Figure 3–8). Design similar organizers for *total annual precipitation*, *annual temperature range*, and *seasonal distribution of precipitation*.

3. Now that your data are organized, it is time to do your analysis.

   a) Draw fine, double-headed arrows linking these pairs of places on your map from question 1:
      • Moncton to Toronto and Moncton to Timmins
      • Timmins to Regina, Timmins to Toronto, and Timmins to Yellowknife
      • Yellowknife to Regina and Yellowknife to Resolute (Note that Yellowknife and Timmins are already linked.)

   b) Each of the seven arrows on your map links a pair of cities with different climates. You are now going to show the differences between each pair. Neatly, and in small print, indicate the differences you see. The information in your organizers from question 2 will be a big help in doing this.

   c) You will also have noticed that there are similarities in adjacent climates. In a different colour than you used in part b), note on your map the similarities you see in adjacent climates.

   d) Although Vancouver and Moncton are very far apart, they are both in coastal locations at similar latitudes. In what ways are their climates similar? In what ways are they different?

   e) We have not yet mentioned Prince George, BC. Prince George is in a valley in the middle of the Western Cordillera. Why does this mean that comparing the climate of Prince George with the climates of its neighbours is not very useful?

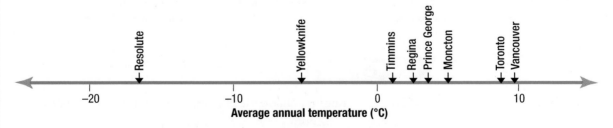

▲ **Figure 3–8** Organizing your data like this makes comparisons easier.

Climate Regions of Canada

Identifying the landform regions in Chapter 2 was fairly straightforward. For example, the Western Cordillera looks quite different and has different geology than the Interior Plains. The Canadian Shield is obviously different from the Great Lakes–St. Lawrence Lowlands. Defining climate regions is not quite so simple. For example, the climate in Toronto is noticeably different from the climate in Timmins. They should be placed in different climate regions, but where should we put the regional boundary? Figure 3–9 shows one common way in which climate regions have been laid out.

Geo ✹ Inquiry

Communicate

How does the climate in each region affect the people who live there? Use the climate graphs in Figure 3–7 on page 62, this map (Figure 3–9), and other information from this chapter to help you write a short paragraph for each region.

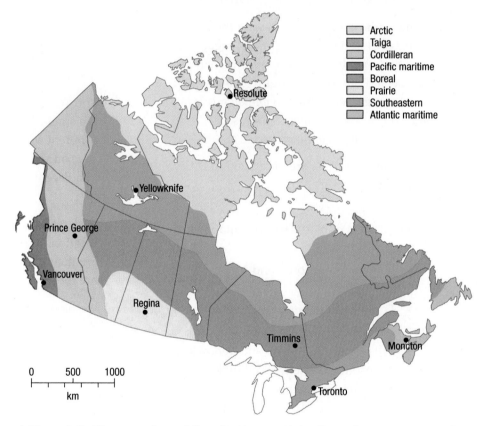

Legend:
- Arctic
- Taiga
- Cordilleran
- Pacific maritime
- Boreal
- Prairie
- Southeastern
- Atlantic maritime

▲ **Figure 3–9 Climate regions of Canada.** How would the climate change as you crossed the country from Moncton to Vancouver? What if you went from Resolute to Toronto?

APPLY IT!

1. Locate and lightly shade the climate regions on the map you started in the Zoom In on pages 62 and 63.

2. For answering parts a) to c), on the next page, keep in mind that each of the climate graph cities and towns is in a different region. You can use the data for each city or town to represent a region.

a) Describe in words the major climate characteristics of each region, except the Cordilleran region. Base your description on comparisons to other regions and to all of Canada. Remember to use the correct technical terms, such as *continental climate* and *average annual temperature* in your descriptions.

b) Explain why each region has these characteristics. Use information from earlier in this chapter about factors that affect climate.

c) Why can you not do a simple description of the Cordilleran climate region?

3. ⬭OSSLT It is time to compare the climate regions map (Figure 3–9) with the population distribution map (Figure 1–5 on page 24).

a) In what climate region(s) are there CMAs of more than one million people?

b) What region(s) have significant areas of *continuous ecumene?*

c) What region(s) have significant areas of *discontinuous ecumene?*

d) In what region(s) do very few people live? Why?

e) How does climate affect where people live (Figure 3–10)?

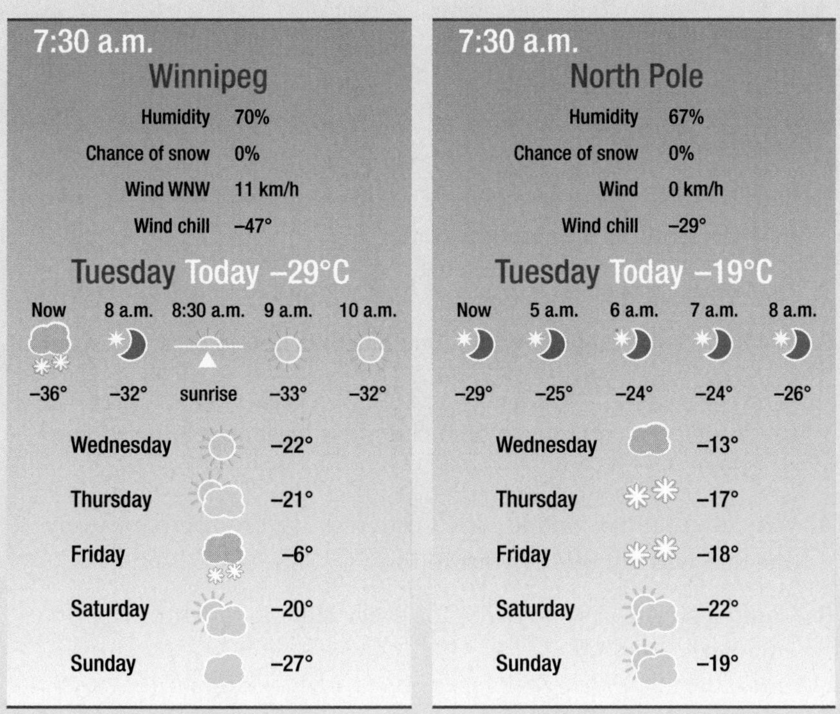

Geo ☼ Inquiry

Interpret and Analyze

Find a world climate map. Choose two places in Canada that are at different latitudes. Compare their climates with two places at the same latitudes elsewhere in the world. Explain the similarities and differences in temperature.

7:30 a.m. **Winnipeg**				
Humidity	70%			
Chance of snow	0%			
Wind WNW	11 km/h			
Wind chill	−47°			

Tuesday Today −29°C

Now	8 a.m.	8:30 a.m.	9 a.m.	10 a.m.
−36°	−32°	sunrise	−33°	−32°

Wednesday	−22°
Thursday	−21°
Friday	−6°
Saturday	−20°
Sunday	−27°

7:30 a.m. **North Pole**				
Humidity	67%			
Chance of snow	0%			
Wind	0 km/h			
Wind chill	−29°			

Tuesday Today −19°C

Now	5 a.m.	6 a.m.	7 a.m.	8 a.m.
−29°	−25°	−24°	−24°	−26°

Wednesday	−13°
Thursday	−17°
Friday	−18°
Saturday	−22°
Sunday	−19°

Source: Government of Canada: Weather

◀ **Figure 3–10** People who live in Winnipeg often call their city "Winterpeg" for good reason. It is one of the coldest major cities in the world. But its latitude is only 50°N, very much in the southern part of Canada. Why is "Winterpeg" so cold?

Which Part of Canada Has the "Nicest" Climate?

In most of the other Viewpoints on an Issue in *Making Connections*, you are given the viewpoints to consider. You only have to assess the conflicting views and decide which one makes more sense to you. This Viewpoint is a bit different. You will choose the two sides for the debate and defend both sides.

▲ **Figure 3–11** What factors do you consider important when choosing the "nicest" weather?

SKILL FOCUS

You likely know the difference between a fact and an opinion. For example, climate graphs are factual. They are the result of decades of weather observations. On the other hand, different people have different opinions about climate conditions. Some people like hot, sunny weather; others hate it.

This brings us to *inference*, which can be defined as a conclusion based on evidence and reasoning. Look over your answers to questions 1 to 5. In each case, identify the facts, opinions, and inferences that make up each answer.

APPLY IT!

1. Start by picking the two climate regions (of the eight possibilities) that *you* would find most pleasant.

2. Provide arguments in support of each region's climate (Figure 3–11).

3. **a)** Of the two finalists, which one has the climate that you would most enjoy? Why?

   b) Of the other regions, which climate is least appealing to you? Why?

4. Why might other people pick a different region—perhaps even one that was not one of your top two?

5. Could a strong case be made for every climate region? Why or why not?

Why Do We Treat Our Soil Like Dirt?

Figure 3–12 is probably the least interesting photo in this book—and very possibly the most important. It shows a soil profile: a cross section of the layers of the soil. This particular soil is quite fertile, which means that it has a good stock of the nutrients that plants need to grow. You can tell this because it has a thick, dark *A horizon* or *topsoil* layer. The dark colour is a result of the large quantity of nutrient-rich organic (plant) material present.

Why is this photo so important? Fertile soils are nothing less than the basis of human civilization. A society cannot exist unless it has the reliable food supply that rich soils provide. This was true 1000 years ago when rich empires existed in places like China and Peru, and it remains true today when the world has more than seven billion mouths to feed. Regions with rich soils support many billions of people, while parts of the world with poor-quality soils have low (or, in extreme cases, even no) population. Yet most people take soils entirely for granted, knowing little about them.

Soil Processes

Let's first consider how soils are formed. In Figure 3–12, you see the soil profile of a very well-developed, fertile soil. Such rich soils exist in areas where the right combination of geology, climate, and vegetation are found.

Geology: There has to be a thick layer of loose parent material available from which a fertile soil can develop. In much of Canada, the parent material is unsorted or sorted glacial deposits. In the rest of the country, where glacial erosion was the more powerful force, the parent material is often bare rock (Figure 2–26 on page 51). If you have 100 000 years to wait while the rock is weathered into loose mineral materials, this is not a problem. Unfortunately, the ice has only been gone for 11 000 years or so. The soil formation process has barely begun in these areas.

Climate: Two climatic processes are important. The growing season has to be long enough for rich plant growth in the summer. This plant growth adds nutrient-rich organic material to the soil. As well, you need just the right amount of precipitation. If there is too much rainfall, water is constantly moving downward through the soil. This process, called *leaching*, removes nutrients that are important for plant growth. These nutrients are mineral compounds of nitrogen, phosphorus, potassium, and other chemical elements that dissolve in water. They must be water-soluble so the plant roots can absorb them with water.

If leaching occurs, the soil loses fertility. You can identify these severely leached soils easily because they lack the dark brown, fertile topsoil horizon shown in Figure 3–12. Instead, leached soils tend to be greyish. While there are many technical terms to describe these soils, we will call them **wet-climate soils** (Figure 3–13 on the next page).

soil profile the three different layers that exist in the soil beneath the surface of the ground. Each layer has a particular combination of physical, biological, and chemical characteristics.

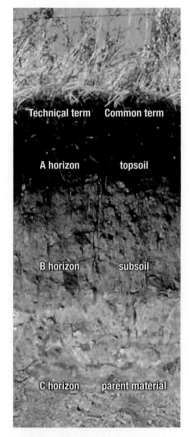

Technical term	Common term
A horizon	topsoil
B horizon	subsoil
C horizon	parent material

▲ **Figure 3–12** This soil from the southern Prairies is extremely good for growing crops. Which horizon is most important in making this soil so valuable for farming? How could people reduce this soil's fertility?

CONNECTING

In Casson's *White Pine* painting (Figure 2–20 on **page 47**), it is possible to see patches of lichen on the bare rock. Lichen is a plant-like combination of fungus and algae. It is an important agent for weathering the surface of rock.

wet-climate soils soils that develop where leaching is the dominant soil-forming process

dry-climate soils soils that develop where calcification is the dominant soil-forming process

In areas that are drier, moisture tends to move upward from the parent material and subsoil, bringing valuable plant nutrients with it. The rich, dark topsoil layer, where plants grow, stands out. These are dry-climate soils (Figure 3–14). However, if the climate is too dry, the soil will be infertile—there is little plant growth, so the amount of organic material in the soil is low. The soils of southern Saskatchewan provide good examples of dry-climate soils. In the southeastern part of the province, slightly higher precipitation has produced the exceptionally rich soils that are the basis of the region's productive grain and oilseed farms. Farther west, where rainfall amounts are lower, the soil does not contain a rich layer of organic material.

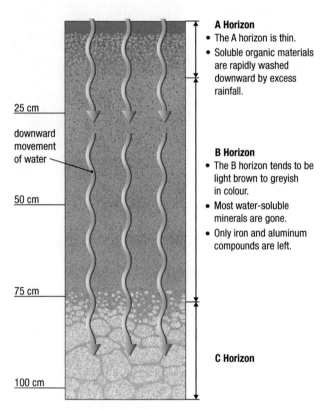

25 cm

downward movement of water

50 cm

75 cm

100 cm

A Horizon
- The A horizon is thin.
- Soluble organic materials are rapidly washed downward by excess rainfall.

B Horizon
- The B horizon tends to be light brown to greyish in colour.
- Most water-soluble minerals are gone.
- Only iron and aluminum compounds are left.

C Horizon

▲ **Figure 3–13** Profile of a typical wet-climate soil. The abundance of rainfall means that leaching is the dominant soil-forming process.

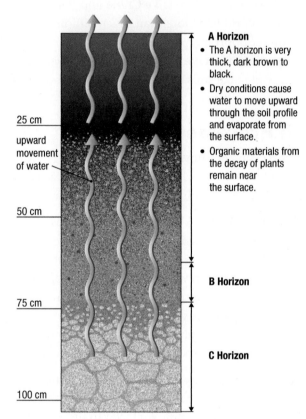

25 cm

upward movement of water

50 cm

75 cm

100 cm

A Horizon
- The A horizon is very thick, dark brown to black.
- Dry conditions cause water to move upward through the soil profile and evaporate from the surface.
- Organic materials from the decay of plants remain near the surface.

B Horizon

C Horizon

▲ **Figure 3–14** Profile of a typical dry-climate soil. The relatively dry climate means that calcification is the dominant soil process.

Soil Patterns

Figure 3–15 shows Canada's soil regions. In the Western Cordillera, a wide range of soils exist because of that region's varied relief and climate patterns. The characteristics of the soil there can change over very short distances. In contrast, the harsh climate of the tundra soils region makes the formation of proper soil horizons difficult. You will learn more about tundra soils in the Zoom In feature on pages 70 and 71.

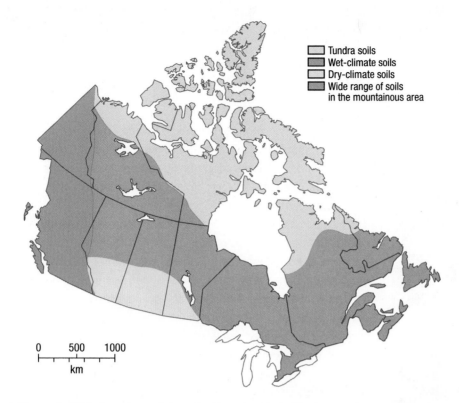

Tundra soils
Wet-climate soils
Dry-climate soils
Wide range of soils in the mountainous area

0   500   1000
         km

▲ **Figure 3–15 Soil regions of Canada.** Note that the highlands area of western Canada has all three types of soil, depending on local conditions. These conditions include elevation, relief, temperature, and precipitation.

APPLY IT!

1. Why do most people ignore the importance of soil? Which people understand and value soil?

2. How is it possible to damage soil? Explain.

3. What relationship would you expect between Canada's soils and its population distribution?

4. Think about how humans rely on soil. From a human point of view, how has glaciation had a good and bad effect on Canada's soils?

5. Use a graphic organizer to summarize the information you have learned about soils and soil regions.

6. a) Formulate at least two questions about how farmers can damage their soil.

   b) Research answers to your questions.

   c) Using this information, produce a poster, public service announcement, blog post, or video to encourage farming practices that protect soil quality.

GeoCareers

Looking for Climate Change in Forest Soils

Kara Webster is a research scientist at the Great Lakes Forestry Centre in Sault Ste. Marie, Ontario. She is a soil ecologist. This means that she studies the interrelationships that exist between the living and non-living parts of the soil. In particular, she is interested in the role that forest soils play in both releasing and absorbing carbon and how climate change is affecting the balance of these processes. To do this, she uses ecosystem models that describe both the chemistry and biological activity of these soils, which are found in much of Canada. Dr. Webster uses GIS mapping software to organize and present her findings.

Geo ⚙ Inquiry

Communicate

The Haudenosaunee traditionally grew what they called "the Three Sisters": corn, beans, and squash. The three crops were planted together. Find out why planting them this way helped to maintain the soil quality. On a poster or in a blog post, use illustrations and photos to help explain the planting system and its benefits.

Tundra and Climate Change

(a)

(b)

▲ **Figure 3–16** (a) Permafrost, near the mouth of the Mackenzie River, was exposed by river erosion. Normally the frozen layer is well below the surface. If you look carefully, you can see the darkish, active layer just below the surface of the ground. The permafrost layer here extends downward 400 metres. (b) In this photo, you can see the active layer near the surface, with a few "lenses" of ice that have not yet melted. The darker permafrost layer is visible at the bottom of the picture. It does not melt in summer.

Tundra soils cover most of northern Canada. They are found in areas with extremely cold climates. These soils do not develop distinct horizons like the soils mentioned previously. Instead, they tend to be very rich in old plant material that cannot decompose because it is too cold.

In these areas, an unusual soil condition called *permafrost* exists. To understand permafrost, we need to think about what happens to soils in southern Canada each winter and spring. In southern Canadian winters, the top metre or so of the soil freezes. In the spring, the frozen soil quickly thaws. In the far north though, only the top metre or so of the soil thaws in the summer. This is called the *active layer*. Farther down, the soil remains permanently frozen (Figure 3–16). The frozen lower layer prevents water from draining away. The result is that land becomes waterlogged, with many swampy areas. Permafrost makes construction and travel difficult. In fact, travel is much easier in the winter (other than having to deal with temperatures of –40°C).

When you first think about it, rising temperatures caused by climate change might seem to be a good thing for the northernmost parts of Canada. The northern polar and subpolar regions of the world will probably warm at about twice the rate of places farther south. Forests will spread northward and trees will grow more each year. This plant growth will actually help reduce the rate of future warming, since it will absorb carbon dioxide from the air. But a warmer climate will also melt the permafrost.

On the positive side, this would allow the ground to drain and make the land less swampy. On the other hand, it would allow the organic material that has been frozen in the soil, in many cases for thousands of years, to decompose. Since this decomposition would happen below the surface of the ground, where there is little oxygen, the result would be the release of a chemical called methane (chemical formula CH_4). Unfortunately, methane is a much more powerful greenhouse gas than carbon dioxide.

Feedback Loops

Permafrost melting introduces the idea of a **feedback loop**. With a feedback loop, change happens that causes even more change of the same type. Figure 3–17(a) shows how this idea applies to climate change. Figure 3–17(b) shows the feedback loop for permafrost.

Inuit and Climate Change

Climate change is having, and will have, its greatest impact on our Arctic region. Permafrost is melting. Sea ice is disappearing. Animal migration patterns are being affected. All of these changes have a profound impact on the ability of Inuit to live according to their traditions. If they cannot hunt, it means that their culture will be destroyed. According to Sheila Watt-Cloutier, Chair of the Inuit Circumpolar Conference, this makes it a human rights issue. She has argued that

> *It is because climate change is a human story that we have connected climate change and human rights... We need to capture the attention and conscience of the world, for climate change is a threat to our entire way of life, and to yours... As our hunting culture is based on the cold, being frozen with lots of snow and ice, we thrive on it. We are in essence fighting for our right to be cold.*

feedback loop a cycle in which the output of a process becomes an input back into the process

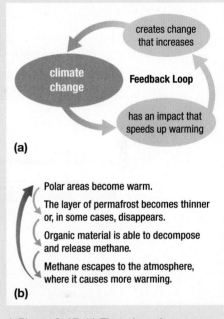

(a)

(b)

▲ **Figure 3–17** (a) This is how the output of the process of warming caused by climate change becomes an input back into the process. (b) What two conditions would stop the permafrost loop?

APPLY IT!

1. Explain in your own words how the process of permafrost melting is an example of a feedback loop.

2. Climate change is causing Arctic ice to melt. Explain how this is another example of a feed-back loop. Use a labelled diagram for your answer. Hint: Think about the colour of the ice and the colour of the water or land that will be exposed when the ice melts.

3. Why are the consequences of climate change much greater for Inuit than for urban Canadians?

4. a) In your own words, define the term "human rights." Briefly describe three generally accepted human rights.

   b) Explain how the fight against climate change could be called a fight to protect the human rights of Inuit.

Natural Vegetation Processes

Geo ⚙ Inquiry

Communicate

Summarize each of the transects in Figures 3–18 and 3–19 in words. Begin your summaries with "As you move east from west..." and "As you move south from north..."

The natural vegetation in any given location is mainly a product of the particular combination of temperature and precipitation. Figure 3–18 shows the transition in vegetation types as these two factors change.

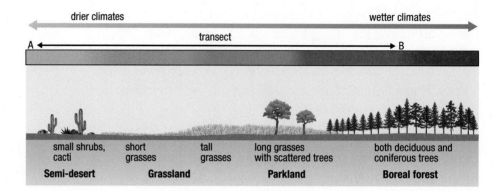

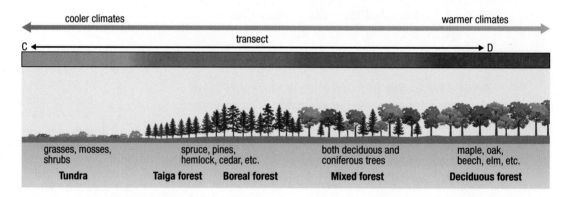

▲ **Figure 3–18** The location of the transects A-B and C-D can be seen in Figure 3–19. Where do you live in relation to these transects? Note that where you live may or may not be on a transect.

Vegetation Patterns

Visit Canada's vegetation regions with **GeoFlight 3.1**.

Canada has three main types of vegetation: tundra, forest, and grassland. Since there are four different subtypes of forest, this means that there are six natural vegetation regions, not including the Cordilleran region (Figure 3–19).

It is a mistake to think that, at a regional boundary, there is an abrupt change from one type of vegetation to another. Instead there is a *transition zone*, an area where the vegetation changes gradually.

The Cordilleran vegetation zone is not included in the descriptions below because, like the Cordilleran climate and soil regions, it is not uniform. This is not surprising since conditions can change dramatically from one place to another, even if the two places are only a few kilometres apart. A windward slope can have lush forest while a nearby valley can be a dry grassland area. Also, temperature and rainfall change as you go up a mountain, so the types of vegetation can change from a lush rainforest to a barren, treeless slope.

Geo✿Inquiry

Gather and Organize

The natural vegetation of a region is generally quite different from the plants that humans choose to grow in that region. Why? What do farmers or gardeners grow in your region? How do they decide what they will plant?

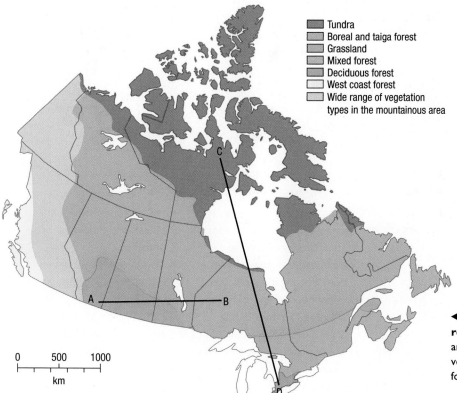

Tundra
Boreal and taiga forest
Grassland
Mixed forest
Deciduous forest
West coast forest
Wide range of vegetation types in the mountainous area

0   500   1000
km

◀ **Figure 3–19 Natural vegetation regions of Canada.** The mountainous area of western Canada has every vegetation zone, except for deciduous forest and mixed forest.

Tundra

As you might expect, based on its Arctic climate, conditions in the tundra region are incredibly harsh for plant growth.

- Only a few, very small trees grow here.
- Small shrubs, flowering plants, mosses, and lichens grow close to the surface, where they soak up as much heat as possible in the very short growing season (Figure 3–20).

▶ **Figure 3–20** Summer on the tundra is short, and plants have evolved to flower and produce their seeds very quickly. What evidence of glaciation do you see here? What evidence of soil formation do you see?

Forests

Before we look at Canada's forests, let's review the two main types of trees: coniferous and deciduous (Table 3–1).

Table 3–1 The two types of trees in Canada

go online

Find out more about individual tree species.

	Coniferous (also called evergreen, needle-leaved, softwood)	Deciduous (also called broadleaf, broad-leaved, hardwood)
Typical tree shapes		
Typical leaf shapes		
Canadian examples	white spruce, black spruce, balsam fir, red pine, white pine	sugar maple, beech, hickory, poplar, red oak
Special features	• They are able to survive in areas with poor-quality soils. • Their sticky sap acts like antifreeze, stopping needles from freezing in cold winters. • Waxy needles and thick bark preserve moisture during dry conditions. • Needles and flexible branches shed snow, preventing damage to the tree.	• Having no leaves in winter lessens the snow load on branches. • They are dormant in winter, but sap flows strongly as spring warms. • Most deciduous species need at least five months with average temperatures above 10°C.

▼ **Figure 3–21** The boreal forest stretches for thousands of kilometres across Canada.

BOREAL FOREST

As we move south from the tundra, we cross the tree line and move into the largest vegetation region in Canada, the *boreal forest* (Figure 3–21).

- Canada's boreal forest is one of the largest forest regions in the world.
- The growing season gets longer the farther south we go, while precipitation levels are generally higher. The result is more lush forests and a wider range of species farther south in the boreal forest.

- Winters are long and cold; summers are warm and short. Soil conditions in the boreal forest are generally not very good, with thin, acidic soils, and poor fertility caused by large amounts of leaching.
- Hardy species of deciduous trees, such as white birch and poplar, are common in the southern part of the boreal forest. Farther north, only the hardiest coniferous trees, like black spruce and balsam fir, can survive.

DECIDUOUS FOREST

For a moment, we will skip over the mixed forest on our journey south and move very far south to the *deciduous forest region*.

- Canada's tiny deciduous forest region in southwestern Ontario is the northernmost tip of the very large deciduous belt in the United States (Figure 3–22).
- The hot summers and relatively mild winters, at least by Canadian standards, allow a wide range of species to exist. These include various kinds of maple, beech, and oak, and even exotic types (for Canada), such as tulip trees and butternut.
- Almost the entire forest region has been cleared for farming and urban growth.
- Soils are fertile. They are not as acidic as the soils farther north, which develop under coniferous trees.

▲ **Figure 3–22** This deciduous forest may have been cleared or partially logged at one time but has regrown.

MIXED FOREST

You have seen what the boreal forest is like and what the deciduous forest is like. The *mixed forest* is the very wide transition zone between the two (Figure 3–23).

- Not surprisingly, when we go south in this region, the mixed forest is mainly deciduous; farther north, it is more boreal.
- Winters are cool and summers are warm.
- Since climate and vegetation conditions are transitional, so are the soils. They are not as rich as those farther south, but much more fertile than those in the boreal forest. Much of the southern part of the mixed forest has been cleared for agriculture or growing towns and cities.

▲ **Figure 3–23** As you would expect, the mixed forest region combines the characteristics of the regions to the north and south of it. What are these?

WEST COAST FOREST

Geo ✿ Inquiry

**Evaluate and
Draw Conclusions**

Canada's forests are under pressure. In some areas, forest companies harvest large areas. In populated areas, expanding towns and cities remove whole forests to free land for construction. What are the negative impacts of these actions? What can we do to protect our forests?

When you visit the *west coast forest*, what stands out most is the enormous size of trees. Some trees are more than 50 metres tall (Figure 3–24). They are able to grow so large because of the mild temperatures and abundant precipitation of this region.

- While the west coast forest could be seen as part of the diverse Cordilleran region, its distinct appearance and importance for forestry make it worth looking at as a separate region.

- This region receives so much precipitation that it is called a *temperate rainforest*. A temperate rainforest has mild temperatures in comparison to the hot temperatures of a tropical rainforest.

- Large coniferous species, such as Douglas fir, Sitka spruce, red cedar, and western hemlock, dominate in the west coast forest.

▶ **Figure 3–24** OSSLT This is an *old-growth* temperate rainforest on the windward side of Vancouver Island. *Old-growth* means it has never been logged. Why would trees of this size be valued greatly by both forest products companies and environmentalists?

Grasslands

Some parts of southern Canada are just too dry for significant tree growth. These areas are called *grasslands* because the natural vegetation is grasses of various types and sizes (Figure 3–25).

- Some trees, such as trembling aspen, willow, and spruce, grow in wetter areas of the grasslands region and in river valleys in drier areas.

- The natural grasses grow taller in the wetter areas of the region than in the drier areas. These two areas are called the *tall-grass prairie* and the *short-grass prairie*, respectively.

- A transition zone, called *parkland*, exists between the tall grasses and the adjoining boreal forest. This area has a mix of trees and grasslands.

▲ **Figure 3–25** This is an example of the *short-grass prairie*. In the wetter *tall-grass prairie*, the grasses would be taller.

1. Why are the Cordilleran climate region, soil region, and vegetation region fundamentally different from all the other regions?

2. ■ **Patterns and Trends**

   a) A soil can include particles ranging in size from very fine clay to coarse sand. Why is neither of these soils ideal for plant growth, including agriculture?

   b) What size of soil particles is best for agriculture? What advantages does this size of particles have? What is the type of soil with this size of particles called? Hint: The name is not in the chapter. You will have to check outside sources, perhaps including a family member who gardens.

3. On a per-square-kilometre basis, which three vegetation regions have the most value economically? How is this value determined?

4. ■ **Patterns and Trends** Rank the vegetation regions' potential for agriculture, from best to useless.

5. It is time to compare the soil regions map (Figure 3–15 on page 69) with the population distribution map (Figure 1–5 on page 24).

   a) In what soil region(s) are there CMAs of more than one million people?

   b) In what region(s) are there significant areas of *continuous ecumene?*

   c) In what region(s) are there significant areas of *discontinuous ecumene?*

   d) In what region(s) do very few people live?

6. It is also time to compare the natural vegetation regions map (Figure 3–19 on page 73) with the population distribution map (Figure 1–5 on page 24).

   a) In what vegetation region(s) are there CMAs of more than one million people?

   b) In what region(s) are there significant areas of *continuous ecumene?*

   c) In what region(s) are there significant areas of *discontinuous ecumene?*

   d) In what region(s) do very few people live?

7. State how climate, soils, and vegetation affect the population of each of the following four areas of Canada: the Maritimes, Prairies, Southern Ontario and Québec, and the North.

> **go online**
>
> Find pictures from each of the vegetation regions. Add your own descriptions as to how these pictures are representative of that region.

Exploring Connections: Climate, Soil, and Natural Vegetation and Human Activities

> **?** How do different climate, soil, and natural vegetation regions contribute to where and how people live?

Climate, soils, and natural vegetation are members of an interesting, interrelated trio. While most people pay almost no attention to the soils and natural vegetation, climate and its short-term cousin, weather, are never far from our attention. The emergence of climate change as a critical issue has made us even more aware of the importance of climate. Yet, all three of these parts of the natural world are of great importance to our security and happiness.

1. Climate, soils, and natural vegetation do not exist in isolation from each other. Use a graphic organizer to explain how the three are closely linked. A concept map format makes sense for these kinds of data.

2. Look around the place where you live and consult maps that show climate, vegetation, and soils. List the climate, vegetation, and soil characteristics of your community. Then jot down as many ways as you can think of that these characteristics have affected the population. Choose three important effects and explain them in written paragraphs, diagrams and/or charts, collections of pictures, or a short video report.

Geo Inquiry

Interpret and Analyze

3. How will climate change affect Canada's climate, soil, and natural vegetation patterns, positively and negatively?

Evaluate and Draw Conclusions

4. a) Why are climate, soils, and vegetation each important to Canadians?

   b) Which do you think has more influence on Canada's population pattern—landforms or the combination of climate, soils, and natural vegetation? Explain your answer.

Analyze an Issue

5. Think about issues related to the connections between climate, soil, and natural vegetation and human activities that you have read about or that affect your everyday life. Pick one of these issues.

   a) Write a number of questions about the issue. Narrow your questions down to one clearly stated and important big question.

   b) What areas would you have to research to answer your big question? Find three or four resources and collect information to answer your question. Be sure to analyze the information and consider various viewpoints.

   c) Use your notes to take a position and answer your question. Support your answer with facts from your research.

   d) Create a product that communicates the answer to your question. This could be an opinion paper, a blog post, a poster, or a letter to the editor. Be creative!

   e) If you had to complete another inquiry like this one, what would you do differently?

Creating Your Own Multi-Factor Regional Map of Canada

In this exercise, you will create a map of Canadian regions that will help you answer the Big Question from the beginning of this unit: How does the physical environment affect where Canadians live? Regions in geography allow us to organize our knowledge of Canada into smaller chunks that are easier to remember and understand. Each region has characteristics that make it different from other regions.

Chapters 2 and 3 focused on single-factor regions. The regional maps in those chapters are based on only one factor—soil characteristics, for example. The map you create will have multi-factor regions—that is, regions based on a combination of factors. The factors that you will consider in your analysis are the regions from Chapters 2 and 3, along with the population distribution that you learned about in Chapter 1.

ACTIVITY

1. The process of choosing regional borders is easy to describe, but it can be a challenge to do at times. Let's see how it works in one part of Canada—the southern part of the Prairie provinces (Alberta, Saskatchewan, and Manitoba). The first step is to get all of your single-factor regional map data in one place. An example has been done for you in Figure 1 on the next page.

2. Draw the region from step 1 on a base map of Canada. Begin by drawing the border lightly in pencil in case you want to make changes. Note that your border may be slightly different from those created by others. There is more than one "right" answer.

3. Next, decide on the best name for the region. In this case, *Prairies* seems obvious. Note: It is not the Prairie provinces—that would be a political region subdivision.

4. Repeat the process of creating regions until the entire country is done. Hints:
   • Note that as you create the boundary for one region, you are also creating parts of boundaries for neighbouring regions.
   • Choose an appropriate number of regions—not too many, but not too few. Let the data guide you to a reasonable number. Aim for between 5 and 12 regions.
   • When you are satisfied with all the borders, you can add colours and labels to make your finished copy.

CONNECTING

In particular, you should look at these maps:

• population distribution: page 24
• landforms: page 50
• climate: page 64
• soils: page 69
• natural vegetation: page 73

THINKING CRITICALLY

Your Regions and Canada's Ecumene

Which of your regions are in the continuous ecumene? the discontinuous ecumene? outside the ecumene? Is this distribution likely to change in the decades to come? Why or why not?

How Many Regions?

What is the problem if you have too many regions? What is the problem if you have too few? If you were to add one additional region to your map, where would it be? Why choose this one? If you decided to have one fewer region, would you combine two regions or redraw the entire map with one less region? Explain your reasoning.

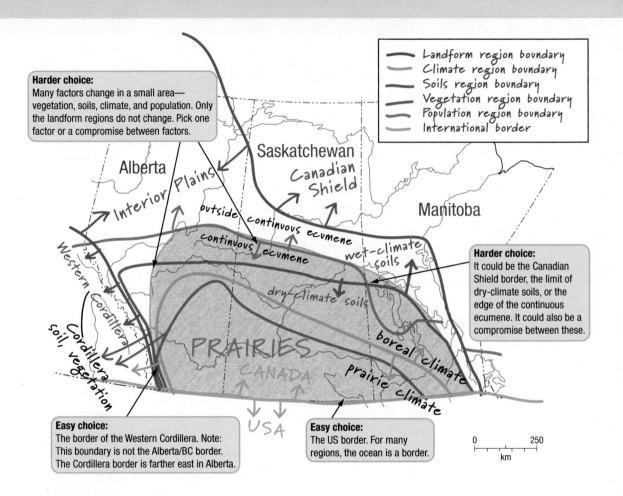

Legend:
- Landform region boundary
- Climate region boundary
- Soils region boundary
- Vegetation region boundary
- Population region boundary
- International border

Harder choice: Many factors change in a small area—vegetation, soils, climate, and population. Only the landform regions do not change. Pick one factor or a compromise between factors.

Alberta

Saskatchewan

Canadian Shield

Manitoba

Interior Plains

outside continuous ecumene

continuous ecumene

wet-climate soils

Western Cordillera

dry-climate soils

Harder choice: It could be the Canadian Shield border, the limit of dry-climate soils, or the edge of the continuous ecumene. It could also be a compromise between these.

Cordillera soil, vegetation

PRAIRIES

CANADA

boreal climate

prairie climate

Easy choice: The border of the Western Cordillera. Note: This boundary is not the Alberta/BC border. The Cordillera border is farther east in Alberta.

USA

Easy choice: The US border. For many regions, the ocean is a border.

0   250
km

▲ **Figure 1 Example map.** Can you see the border of a multi-factor region emerging here?

5. The final step is to describe each region in paragraph form or in a table. Make sure to explain how the physical environment in your regions affects where Canadians live.

Criteria for Success

Your map and description will

❏ show an appropriate number of regions for the entire country, and give a logical explanation of why you chose this number of regions

❏ have an appropriate title and legend

❏ clearly describe each of your regions

❏ be well-organized, easy to read, and neat

❏ demonstrate a clear understanding of how the physical environment affects where Canadians live

Resources and Industries

How is our future tied to our ability to manage our resources and economic activities effectively?

▲ Oil sands mining in northern Alberta: The oil sands are taken from here to a processing plant, where the oil is separated from the sand.

LET'S GO!

- How is your quality of life related to Canada's abundant resources?

- Is your lifestyle good for the environment? Is it harmful?

- How would you feel about living and working in another part of Canada in the future?

KEY CONCEPTS

- renewable and non-renewable resources
- resource management
- sectors of the economy
- jobs and economic growth
- globalization and international trade

KEY TERMS

total stock

resource

natural resources

renewable resources

non-renewable resources

flow resources

other resources

waste diversion

conservation

? **Should we rethink how we perceive and use our natural resources?**

New Cars for New Times   OSSLT

BMW built its reputation by making cars that combine performance, innovation, and style. Even BMW's cheapest cars have powerful engines. BMW Canada sells cars with engines ranging from 180 horsepower (hp) in the 320i to 560 hp in the M6. In spite of careful engineering, such powerful engines use a lot of fuel and produce high carbon emissions.

Times are changing in the auto world. Individuals, companies, and governments are all rethinking ways we can use less resources or use them more effectively. Consumers are looking to save money on fuel and protect the planet. Companies are developing cars that are environmentally friendly without sacrificing performance, safety, or comfort. Governments are imposing more demanding fuel economy standards on automakers.

BMW's response has been the release of its first electric and hybrid (electric and gasoline-powered) cars. The i3 is an all-electric family sedan that has excellent performance, similar to that of the 320i, which uses 7.1 litres of gas per 100 kilometres (L/100 km). The i8 is a hybrid sports car that uses only 2.5 L/100 km. In comparison, BMW's most powerful car, the M6, is only slightly faster but uses 11.2 L/100 km.

THINKING CRITICALLY

What comes first in the production of cars like the BMW i3: consumer demand, government regulation, or an innovative company wanting to lead the marketplace? What factors would encourage someone to buy an electric car rather than a car with a conventional engine? What factors would discourage someone from buying an electric car?

What Are Natural Resources?

All the components of the environment taken together are called the total stock. The total stock includes energy, living organisms such as plants and animals, and non-living materials such as water and minerals. Any part of the total stock that becomes useful to human beings is called a resource. Most of us understand that a resource is something that is of value in some way. For example, this book could be called a learning resource. In geography, we tend to use a narrower definition, focusing our attention on resources that are found in the natural environment. These are called natural resources.

A famous geographer, Erich Zimmermann, beautifully summarized an important characteristic of natural resources in just a few words:

"Resources are not, they become."

What he meant was that something in the natural environment is seen as a resource only when people can find a use for it and have the technology needed to exploit it.

Let's explore this idea with a specific example. Flint is a mineral that occurs in chunks in the layers of certain kinds of sedimentary rocks (Figure 4–1). Flint first came to be seen as a valuable resource in the Stone Age, several thousand years ago, because it had two remarkably useful properties:

1. When struck by a harder stone or another hard object, flint splinters into smaller pieces with very sharp edges. A skilled person can shape or knap a piece of flint into a cutting tool, arrowhead, or spearhead. Before the discovery and use of metal technology, these stone tools were essential to the survival of many cultural groups. Flint was used and traded across North America by First Nations until the arrival of Europeans.

2. When a piece of flint is struck by a piece of steel or even rock with a high iron content, a shower of sparks is produced. If these sparks land on suitable tinder (a material that catches fire easily), you can start a fire. This was a major improvement over earlier fire-starting methods that involved friction, such as using a bow drill. Flint was also used in fire-arms, called "flintlocks," that were used for more than two centuries.

total stock all parts of the natural environment including energy, living organisms, and non-living materials. For example, sunlight, trees, and water are all part of the total stock.

resource anything that can be used to produce goods and services, such as raw materials, workers, money, and land

natural resources things found in the total stock that people find useful

◀ **Figure 4–1** This piece of flint has been split open. Notice that it breaks with sharp edges and that the outside surface (along the right side) is quite a different colour than the inside.

CONNECTING

You can learn more about rock types in **Chapter 2 (pages 40–42)**.

go online

Want to see how a flint spearhead is made? Watch a video of the first stage of the process (9:58 minutes). Making such tools requires great skill and patience.

▲ **Figure 4–2** The first oil well in North America was dug at Oil Springs, Ontario, in 1858. This discovery triggered the first oil rush in North America. Why do you think oil is not extracted as much in Ontario anymore?

For many centuries, flint was a valuable resource that was essential to life. Today, flint has virtually no value as a resource since technological advancement has produced easier ways to start fires and better tools and firearms. Flint has even been replaced in most modern fire-starter kits by a manufactured substance called ferrocerium, which produces more sparks.

The importance of a resource generally comes to be recognized gradually as new uses for it develop. This happened with flint, and with oil. When the first oil wells were drilled in the middle of the 19th century (Figure 4–2), the most important product produced from the extracted crude oil was lamp oil. It gradually replaced oil from whales in the decades before the electric light was invented. Gasoline was a by-product of the refining process. It was used only as a cleaning fluid because automobiles had not yet been invented. When the internal combustion engine was introduced, our attitude toward gasoline, and hence crude oil, changed dramatically. Crude oil is now the most important resource on the planet.

go online

Ever wonder about Canada's use and production of energy? Visit the Energy Mix Library to discover how different regions make, deliver, and use energy.

APPLY IT!

1. In your own words, describe how something comes to be seen as a resource and how it stops being a resource.

2. It may be hard to imagine a time in the future when crude oil is not seen as a major resource, but this could—and likely will—happen at some point. Figure 4–3 shows the different sources of Canada's energy. What might come to replace crude oil as our primary energy source? Explain your answer.

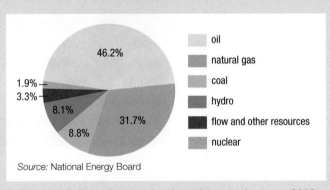

Source: National Energy Board

▲ **Figure 4–3 Canadian production of energy by type, 2012**

go online

Research to learn more about lithium and rare earth elements.

3. ■ **Patterns and Trends** New resources continue to be identified to meet our changing needs as society and technology change. Lithium and rare earth elements are two such examples. How were they viewed in the past? Briefly describe how they are used now.

Types of Resources

Within the total stock are the things we call resources. Resources are divided into four categories. Resources in the first two categories are considered important to Canada's economy, and resources in the last two categories are considered less important.

- **Renewable resources** are constantly being replenished by nature at a rate fast enough that they should be available for humans as long as we need them. However, this is only if (and it is a critical if) the rate at which we use these resources continues to be slower than the rate at which they are replenished. Examples of renewable resources are soil, forests, and fish stocks.

- **Non-renewable resources** are created by nature so slowly (over millions of years) that, effectively, the stock that exists today is all there will ever be. The two most important categories of non-renewable resources are fossil fuels and minerals.

- **Flow resources** are constantly being produced by nature. Essentially, their supply cannot be damaged by human activity. Sunlight, wind, and water currents (Figure 4–4) are all examples of flow resources.

- **Other resources** are those that do not fit into one of the other categories. For example, the northern lights (aurora borealis), Rocky Mountains, and Niagara Falls are considered resources because they attract tourists to Canada, which increases the tourism business.

renewable resources resources that can be regenerated if used carefully

non-renewable resources resources that are limited and cannot be replaced once they are used up

flow resources resources that are replaced by natural actions and must be used when and where they occur or be lost

other resources resources that do not fit into the other three categories (renewable, non-renewable, and flow resources)

▲ **Figure 4–4** Hydroelectric generating stations transform the energy from flowing water into electrical energy.

APPLY IT!

1. Classify these resources as renewable, non-renewable, flow, or other. Then provide your own examples of each type of resource.

   coal   forests   natural gas   sunlight
   fertile soil gold   river flow   wind
   fish   iron ore   scenery

2. Some non-renewable resources can be recycled after use. Others are destroyed when they are used. Go back to the examples of non-renewable resources you provided in question 1. Divide your examples into two lists: recyclable and non-recyclable.

3. Given that non-renewables are created very slowly, how can we increase our supply of these resources?

go online

Some renewable resources, such as soil, fish, and forests, are at risk of being overused to the point that they are no longer renewable. Find out more.

Resources and the 3Rs

You have probably been hearing about the 3Rs—reduce, reuse, recycle—for your entire life. Connections among these terms are strong, but they are ignored too often. Examine Figure 4–5 to explore how we can use resources more wisely.

▼ **Figure 4–5** Recycling is just the first, and least effective, step in using our resources more effectively.

DOING BETTER

Reducing
- The item is neither purchased nor produced in the first place.
- Fewer new items are produced.
  AMOUNT OF RESOURCE SAVINGS: MOST

Reusing
- The item is used by someone else when you no longer want it.
- The environmental cost of manufacturing the item is avoided.
  AMOUNT OF RESOURCE SAVINGS: MORE

Recycling
- The item is destroyed when you no longer want it, but the material in the item is recovered for reuse.
- The environmental cost of obtaining the raw materials for the item is avoided.
  AMOUNT OF RESOURCE SAVINGS: SOME

None of the 3Rs
- The item is taken to a landfill or burned in an incinerator.
  AMOUNT OF RESOURCE SAVINGS: NONE

None of the 3Rs: The Worst Use of Resources

Nothing good comes from an item going to a landfill or an incinerator (Figure 4–6). The item itself, which may still be useful, is gone. Any of the resource value in it, such as metals or paper, is lost. A landfill can also pollute the groundwater and surrounding environment. As well, no one wants to have a landfill or an incinerator near where they live because they are concerned about smells, pollution, and other factors. Finally, a landfill or an incinerator is costly to build and operate, and the cost is added to local property taxes.

Ever wonder what happens to the waste that you produce at home or school? Take **GeoFlight 4.1** to see where it goes.

▶ **Figure 4–6** Solid waste from Toronto that cannot be recycled goes to a landfill such as this one. The Green Lane Landfill is located near London, Ontario. Where does your waste go? Find out what landfills are in your community.

©P

A modern landfill is much more than a garbage dump. Before use, the bottom of the landfill is sealed to stop pollution of the water table. Each day's garbage is covered by a layer of soil. When the landfill is full, the garbage is covered with a thick layer of soil. Water leaking from the landfill, called leachate, is collected and treated. Methane gas produced by rotting garbage is collected and burned to produce electricity.

Landfills need to be monitored for decades because garbage decomposes very slowly. More recent ones were built and operated to a high standard and are being properly monitored. Ontario has hundreds of former landfills. Sometimes former landfills are made into parkland (Figure 4–7).

Geo ✿ Inquiry

Interpret and Analyze

Why are plans for new landfills and incinerators always controversial? Answer this question from the perspective of economic cost, environmental concerns, and community reaction.

◀ **Figure 4–7** Brae Ben golf course, in the middle of Mississauga, is built on an old landfill site. It shows that a properly rehabilitated landfill can be an asset to a community.

Recycling Is Just the Beginning

We could be doing even more with our natural resources if we were to rethink how we use them. As an example, let us look at what happens when you put a soft-drink can into a recycling bin.

1. The contents of the bin are picked up by a local government truck or a truck that belongs to a private company.

2. The materials in the box are sorted, and all the aluminum containers go to an aluminum recycler.

3. The cans are melted down to form aluminum blocks that can be used to make new products, such as new cans.

In fact, aluminum is the most valuable of all common recycled substances. A typical soft-drink can weighs about 14 grams and can be sold for about 2.2 cents. The money earned from these cans pays for most of the government recycling system.

Many other different types of materials, such as steel, paper, glass, and plastic, can also be recycled. However, recycling, like any method of waste management, requires the use of resources. The materials for recycling must be collected, transported to a recycling facility, and sorted. Energy must also be used to recycle the materials into new items.

go online

Electronic waste, or e-waste, contains toxic substances which, if not disposed of properly, can have negative effects on human health and wildlife. Find out how e-waste can be recycled properly.

The Rise of Recycling

▲ **Figure 4–8** Soft drinks were sold in returnable glass bottles for many decades. For many years, the deposit on these glass bottles was 2 cents.

waste diversion processes that reduce the amount of waste that ends up going to landfills. These include source reduction (producing less waste in the first place), recycling, and reusing.

Geo ⚙ Inquiry

Gather and Organize

A wide variety of materials are commonly recycled. What is the recycling process for materials other than aluminum?

It is certainly better that a soft-drink can is recycled rather than being thrown away, but the fact remains that the can was used only once. To understand why the introduction of these cans was a step backward, we need to consider the history of soft-drink containers in Ontario. Before the 1960s, almost all soft drinks were sold in returnable glass bottles (Figure 4–8). Part of the cost of the drink was a deposit, which encouraged people to return their empty bottles to a store to get a refund for that deposit. The bottles were reused many times before being recycled. In fact, the system was similar to the one used for beer bottles today in Ontario.

Soft-drink manufacturers, most retailers, and many consumers did not like the hassle of dealing with empty containers. The soft-drink manufacturers pushed for and helped finance the current recycling system. Thus, the blue box system was a move from reusing to recycling, which was a step in the wrong direction.

Recycling Almost Everything Else

While recycling in Ontario started with beverage containers, it quickly spread to other items. Local governments, which are responsible for dealing with garbage, liked the idea of recycling because it diverted waste from landfills and incinerators. Metal cans, newspapers, PET plastic bottles (such as large soft-drink bottles), and other materials became eligible for the recycling box rather than ending up in the garbage can. That was definitely an improvement.

Since the 1980s, municipalities have been constantly looking for other opportunities for **waste diversion** away from landfills. Different types of containers, such as the blue box, green and grey bins, and paper yard-waste bags, may be used to collect different materials. Other materials, such as used tires or hazardous waste (e.g., used batteries, paint cans, and motor oil), are not collected by the municipality but must be brought to special depots for recycling. Depending on where you live, waste diversion may include aluminum, steel, and glass containers; paper; a wide variety of plastics; yard waste and household organic garbage; large appliances; and electronic waste. These efforts have been so successful that some towns and cities are collecting recycling once per week, and reducing garbage pickup to once every two weeks rather once a week. Many towns and cities also limit the number of bags, or other containers of garbage, that a household can throw out in each collection.

©P

Products of Recycling

Recycling recaptures the resources that were used to make a product. Recycled paper is made into new paper, metals are melted down and made into new metal products, and household organic garbage is processed into compost. You might be surprised at the variety of products that can be made from recycled plastic (Figure 4–9).

▼ **Figure 4–9** Your empty soft-drink bottles could end up being used to make a wide range of products. Keep in mind that recycling uses water and energy. Is this a wise use of resources? What natural resource was used to make the plastic in the first place?

I used to be a plastic bottle

APPLY IT!

Recycling programs differ across communities. Use the Internet and other sources of information to research recycling in your community.

1. What types of materials are recycled where you live?

2. What kinds of containers are used to collect each type of recyclable material?

3. What happens to each type of material that is collected?

4. How often is your garbage picked up? Is there a limit to the amount of garbage you can put out for each collection?

5. How is recycling handled in large apartment buildings and condos?

6. a) Does your school recycle? What types of materials can be recycled?

   b) How successful is your school's recycling system? In what ways could it be improved?

THINKING CRITICALLY

7. Manufacturing companies, governments, and individual citizens can all contribute to an effective recycling system. What is the role of each in a successful recycling system? How successful do you think each of these has been?

Reusing Is Better

Reusing an object makes much more sense than replacing it, especially if the item has not reached the end of its usable life. Many categories of articles, ranging from clothing to appliances to tools, can be reused. However, we do not practise reusing as much as we could.

Many companies, non-profit organizations, and individuals have made reusing work. Give yourself a pat on the back if you use or are involved in any of these strategies.

✓ *Hand-me-downs:* If you are wearing a pair of jeans that came from someone else, congratulations—you are saving resources.

✓ *Used clothing stores:* There are many non-profit and for-profit companies that sell wearable used clothing for a fraction of the original price (Figure 4–10).

▶ **Figure 4–10** Shopping at used clothing stores can be both fun and economical.

✓ *The Beer Store:* Since 1927, The Beer Store has been selling the vast majority of its products in glass bottles that are used an average of 15 times before being recycled. About 62 percent of all beer is sold in bottles that are reused. More than 97 percent of beer bottles are returned to the store. Beer cans cannot be refilled, but they are collected to be recycled, as is all the packaging from beer.

✓ *Reselling for reuse:* Sometimes we put things into the garbage that we could sell. Flea markets, garage sales, and websites such as eBay and Kijiji provide inexpensive (or free) ways to find buyers for these used items. We make a few bucks and an item gets reused. It is a win-win-win situation for us, the buyer, and the environment.

©P

✓ *Recycling for reuse:* Unwanted items can also be recycled or donated for reuse. Mother Earth Recycling, based in Winnipeg, recycles, repairs, and refurbishes electronics, including computers, televisions, stereos, cameras, batteries, calculators, and other electronics from businesses and homes. This keeps electronic waste, or e-waste, out of landfills, a definite win for the environment.

Created in 2012 by the Aboriginal Centre of Winnipeg, the company aims to be a sustainable, socially responsible business that meets the needs of Aboriginal peoples, the City of Winnipeg, and the environment. Mother Earth Recycling also aims to provide jobs and training opportunities for unemployed and underemployed Manitobans, with a focus on Aboriginal youth.

✓ *Second Harvest:* This non-profit organization collects surplus prepared food from restaurants to distribute to shelters, hostels, and other organizations that provide food to those in need. This means that vast quantities of perfectly good food do not end up in landfills.

✓ *Freecycling:* You probably own some things that you no longer need, but they are too good to throw out, such as an MP3 player or phone after you got a new one. (Did you really need that new one? See the Reduce section on the next page.) There is a growing movement to connect those who need such items with those who have them. For example, free ads in the supermarket or on the Internet can be used to make connections. Some people watch for usable furniture or other products that have been put out as garbage. Many young people have even furnished their first apartments with such garbage-night "shopping."

Geo ✿ Inquiry

Interpret and Analyze

Research a company in the local community that practises or promotes reusing. How does this help reduce the amount of waste people produce?

---

go online

Check out Mother Earth Recycling to find out more about its programs and how the concept of sustainable use of resources ties in with Aboriginal understanding.

---

go online

The Freecycle Network is a website designed to encourage reusing. It has more than seven million members and 5000 local groups.

• Find three or four things you can get for free on this site. Think about some things around your home that you don't want and someone else might like.

• What other non-profit organizations promote the concept of reuse in your community?

APPLY IT!

1. What are two examples of costly products that we often reuse?

2. ■ **Geographic Perspective** What are some benefits of buying drinks and other products in reusable containers rather than non-refillable ones? Analyze this issue from different perspectives, including environmental, economic, and social perspectives.

3. What used clothing retailers operate in your community? Have you shopped there? If so, how do the prices of used clothing compare with those of new clothing?

4. ■ **Interrelationships** Explain some of the things governments and non-profit organizations could do to help promote the concept of reuse.

Reducing Is Best

go online

Ever wonder about the things we make, use, and throw away? Watch *The Story of Stuff* and learn more about what we can do about all our stuff (21 minutes).

Why buy it or make it if you really don't need it? Reducing comes from thinking about what really matters in our lives. It is about the attitudes and values that ultimately determine how we can have a successful and happy life. Reducing can be done by individuals, companies, and governments.

- Reducing by individuals can have the greatest impact of all. People, especially in wealthy countries, consume a lot of resources by buying things they want but do not necessarily need. "Fast fashion" is one such example. The term refers to trendy clothing that is produced quickly and cheaply, though often at an environmental and social cost. Instead of buying five fast-fashion pieces of clothing that will need replacing in a few months, people can choose to reduce consumption by buying one or two more higher-quality items that will last longer. By evaluating what we really need, we can reduce our consumption of resources.

- Another example is whenever a new iPhone or a new version of a popular video game is released. Often, large crowds line up to buy it. Do people buy these products because they need them? Are the older versions no longer any good? How can people decide what things they really need to have a happy life?

- For decades, hotels would routinely replace towels and bed sheets every day, even for guests who were staying more than one night. Today, most hotels offer guests a choice: replacing towels and bed sheets daily or keeping the ones they already have (Figure 4–11). Towels and sheets last longer when they are washed less often. Less electricity, water, and detergent are used. Hotels save money and there is little or no inconvenience for guests.

- Companies can make choices to reduce their use of resources. For example, many companies now use paperless billing systems and encourage online payments. This is not good for the post office's income, but it is winning strategy in just about every other way.

- The Velcro® company mentioned in the GeoCareers feature on the next page sends its waste plastic to a company in Windsor. This company breaks the plastic down into its three components. One component goes back to the Velcro® company so it can be reused; this reduces the amount of new raw materials the company needs. The other two components are sent to a company in Lindsay, Ontario, that uses them

▲ Figure 4–11 All it took was a bit of rethinking about towel use, by hotels and guests, to reduce the environmental impact of hotel visits. What are other reasons why hotels might want to do this? What do you do with towels if you stay in a hotel? Can you think of another example of collective or individual action that is promoting wise use of resources?

©P

to make plastic lumber. This reduces the company's use of raw materials. In total, the use of raw materials is reduced by about one tonne per week.

- Companies also reduce their use of resources by finding ways to use less packaging. It is not uncommon to see consumer product labels promoting the fact that a product now has "16 percent less packaging" or something similar. By doing this, companies save money on packaging materials and on shipping costs because their packages are lighter. It also encourages environmentally conscious customers to buy that brand.

- Governments are always looking for ways to reduce costs by using energy more carefully or by reducing the use of printers and photocopiers when possible.

- Governments can pass laws to enforce, or at least encourage, reducing. The Canadian EnerGuide program (Figure 4–12) is an example of this.

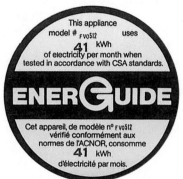

▶ **Figure 4–12** Large appliances in Canada carry a label such as this one. How does it help shoppers rethink resource use and make good financial and environmental decisions?

APPLY IT!

1. **a)** The makers of electronic products, such as smartphones and video games, keep bringing out new, improved versions of their products. How does this affect our use of resources?

   b) What inspires people to line up in the middle of the night to buy these products?

2. Do you think companies are concerned with protecting the environment when they choose to reduce resource use? Explain why they might be. What other reasons might they have for reducing the use of resources?

3. Our economy is based on using resources. We sell resources and use resources to manufacture and transport products. We use resources to run businesses and in our everyday lives. Is this good for the environment? Why do companies sometimes do things that are not good for the environment?

Geo ⚙ Inquiry

Gather and Organize
Go to a store and find products that are marketed as environmentally friendly. How are they environmentally friendly? Which are examples of rethinking resource use?

GeoCareers

Trash to Treasure

There is an old saying, "One person's trash is another person's treasure." Yiyi Shangguan's job in Toronto is to make this saying true for companies. She uses her education in chemical engineering to figure out how the waste materials from one company can become the raw materials for another. For example, materials left over from the production of Velcro® in one company are used to make plastic lumber in another. Everyone wins. One company reduces the cost of its waste disposal and actually gets paid for some of its waste. The other company gets raw materials at a bargain price. Most importantly, the environment wins because waste does not go to a landfill and the resources needed to make new plastic are saved.

Geo ⚙ Inquiry

Interpret and Analyze
Make a cost–benefit analysis chart for reducing consumption. You can analyze reducing in general or reducing consumption of a specific item, such as a smartphone or daily laundry.

Resource Use: Then and Now

You have probably heard adults begin a sentence with "When I was your age …" to suggest that things were much better back then. But what were conditions really like when, for example, your grandparents were your age? What demands did a typical suburban family put on Earth's resources then compared with now?

Viewpoint 1

They really were the good old days.

Fifty years ago, people lived in a way that was more environmentally friendly. They used fewer resources and used them more wisely. For example:

- Houses were smaller. Many had an area of 150 square metres or less, and most had seven rooms, including three bedrooms and only one bathroom (Figure 4–13).

- People did not have convenience appliances such as central air conditioners, microwaves, and dishwashers.

- Two-income families were not common, so fewer people had to commute. Also, commuting distances and times were substantially less than today.

- Most families had only one car.

- Long-distance travel was rare and many people had never flown on an airplane.

- Vacations were shorter and generally spent fairly close to home.

- Most people ate food that was produced locally, or at least in Canada, and fresh fruits and vegetables were eaten in season.

- Most meals were cooked and eaten at home.

- People bought clothes to last, not because of fashion. It was common to mend worn clothing and wear hand-me-downs.

- Students often walked to school. School buses were only for very long trips.

▲ **Figure 4–13** These suburban houses are typical of the times in which they were built. The house on the left was built in the 1960s, and the house on the right was built after 2000. How are today's houses different from those built 50 years ago? Look at the lots on which they were built and the characteristics of the buildings themselves.

Things are much better today.

Modern life is not perfect. But compared with life 50 years ago, we have less impact on the environment. For example:

- Houses are larger but are now built to a much higher environmental standard, with better insulation.

- Our appliances use less electricity and natural gas.

- More families live in apartments and townhouses, which have less environmental impact than single-family homes.

- While multi-car families are common, today's vehicles are more fuel efficient (Figure 4–14) and produce less air pollution.

- We are more concerned about the environment today. Our lifestyle choices reflect this.

▲ **Figure 4–14** These were typical family cars in their time periods. The Chevrolet Impala from the early 1960s (left) had an average fuel economy of between 12 and 20 L/100 km (depending on the size of the engine). The 2015 Toyota Camry (right) averages 5 to 10 L/100 km, again depending on the size of the engine.

APPLY IT!

1. Provide three points to support or argue one of these viewpoints. You might want to speak to a member of your family or someone who remembers the 1960s.

2. **a)** In your own words, summarize the ways in which 1960s individuals and/or families used resources in an environmentally responsible way. In what ways did they not?

   b) In what ways do today's individuals and/or families use resources in an environmentally responsible way? In what ways do they not?

   c) Do these changes show that we have rethought how we can wisely use resources?

THINKING CRITICALLY

3. Which of these viewpoints makes the most sense to you? Why do you think so?

4. ■ **Interrelationships** Using specific examples, explain how the decisions made by individuals, companies, and governments affected environmentally responsible living 50 years ago. Then explain how the actions of all three affect environmentally responsible living today.

Rethinking Our Use of Resources

The ways in which we use resources are a direct result of how we think about them. Since it is clear that we often waste resources, it should be equally clear that we need to rethink how we view resources. This rethinking needs to happen throughout our society and economy. It includes rethinking how we recycle, reuse, and reduce our consumption of resources.

Rethinking has to happen (and to be fair, is slowly happening) among three groups: individuals, companies, and governments. Each group approaches rethinking differently—but not independently. There are strong and obvious links among the three.

Perhaps traditional Aboriginal approaches to the environment can play a role in this rethinking. Many First Nations, Métis, and Inuit peoples understand that balance has to be maintained in nature and so only harvest as much as they can use. Aboriginal peoples typically give thanks to the Creator or Mother Earth for providing the natural resources and they use all parts of the harvested plants and animals to show respect. In these ways, they remain focused on the idea that humans are just part of the natural world and need to live in harmony with it.

Rethinking by Individuals

Each of us can rethink how we use resources. At one extreme, this involves very small questions (Figure 4–15). At the other extreme, there are much broader questions about how we want to live and what impact we want to have on the environment. This really boils down to one very big question: How can I use resources wisely while maintaining, or even improving, my quality of life? You are likely just starting to ask this question in its many forms, but, in the years to come, you will have many opportunities to do so.

Individuals have considerable power to influence the rethinking of companies and government—power that they often do not use effectively. Earlier you learned about the BMW i3, one of a revolutionary group of electric cars that is changing how we think about cars. If many people choose to buy electric cars, automakers will shift production from gasoline cars to electric and hybrid cars.

▼ **Figure 4–15** Rethinking our use of resources can be as simple as choosing to use a reusable cup instead of a disposable one. How does the information in this graphic highlight the importance of rethinking resource use at the individual level? How do we know this information is true?

WHY REUSE A CUP?

Canadians throw away 1.6 billion disposable coffee cups every year.

Many coffee shops provide discounts for customers who bring a reusable cup instead. This can add up to big savings, both for your wallet and the environment.

114.5 million kilograms of paper-cup waste is dumped into landfills each year. That's the equivalent weight of **22 900 elephants!**

Every nine paper cups manufactured **= 1 kg of CO$_2$ emissions**

What does it take to create one paper cup?
43 g of wood
4.1 g of petroleum
1.8 g of chemicals
1 L of water

Save a cup a day for **40 years** and also save **24 trees** and 18 days of power for your home.

©P

Individuals are also voters and have the right to choose a government that will pass more stringent laws that protect the environment. To date, though, there is little evidence that people consider the environment when they vote. A 2014 survey asked Canadians to select their top three concerns from a list of 16 issues. Environmental concerns ranked 9th (climate change), 12th (environment in general), 15th (water pollution), and 16th (water supply). The highest ranked of these, climate change, was only chosen as a top concern by 4 percent of people polled. In contrast, 20 percent chose the economy and 18 percent chose health care as their top concerns.

Rethinking by Companies

Corporations find themselves in a very different situation than individuals do. By law, the people who run companies have two responsibilities. They have a legal responsibility to maximize financial returns for their owners (i.e., their shareholders). In addition, they obviously must obey the laws of the country and province in which they operate.

A company that rethinks how it uses resources (and helps the environment) must operate within these two constraints. Many companies have found ways to increase financial returns by using resources more carefully. Having an environmentally responsible corporate attitude is also good for profits (Figure 4–16). As well, governments pass laws that force companies to rethink how they operate. (The fuel economy standard discussed in the next section is an excellent example of this.) You can see the interconnections here if you remember that individuals vote for governments, which pass laws that force companies to change their products, which people can then buy.

Geo ⚙ Inquiry

Gather and Organize

Make a list of 10 to 20 items you use regularly. What happens when you are finished with them? Put them into one of the 3R categories. How can you rethink your use of each item and move it up the 3Rs ladder?

go online

Companies are rethinking how they do business. Learn about the sharing economy model and how it can have positive effects on the environment.

◄ **Figure 4–16** Tree Canada is an non-governmental organization that has arranged the planting of more than 80 million trees. It solicits donations from companies to pay for the trees, which are then planted by volunteers.

Rethinking by Governments

Governments have to rethink how they can be more involved in protecting a country's resources. They can do two main things: use a carrot (a reward) or use a stick (a punishment). Let's see how this works in two areas.

Waste Disposal

- Carrot: Governments provide opportunities and incentives, such as tax rebates for saving resources. Creating our current recycling systems are a good example of this. Most people are reasonable and want to reduce resource use by recycling. You can see this if you look at the prevalence of blue boxes put out for collection.

- Stick: Not everyone co-operates with recycling, so governments can also use laws to force changes in behaviour. In many parts of Ontario, each house may put out only one (or, in some cases, two) bags or cans of garbage. If you want to put out more, you have to pay for each extra bag.

Fuel Economy

- Carrot: By publishing fuel economy results for cars, governments encourage automakers to produce and consumers to buy vehicles that minimize fuel usage. A good example of this is that governments provide purchase incentives if a consumer buys an electric vehicle.

- Stick: Cars sold in Canada are basically the same as those sold in the United States, so let's look at an American example in this vital area. In 1975, the U.S. government passed a law that required an average fuel economy standard for all cars produced by each car company. If the company did not meet the standard, a per-vehicle fine was levied. From 1990 to 2010, the required average was 8.8 L/100 km. A new law, passed in 2009, has dramatically tightened the fuel economy standard. By 2025, the average fuel economy will be 4.3 L/100 km. Separate standards will apply to SUVs and small trucks such as pickup trucks. If you follow automotive trends (or see car advertising), you can see that changes in vehicle design and operation are already happening. For example, it is becoming the norm for vehicle engines to shut off (and restart) automatically at stop lights. On average, this reduces fuel use by about 4 percent overall, with fuel savings of up to 10 percent for vehicles operating in the city.

Governments must perform a balancing act. Their primary responsibility is to meet the needs and wants of their citizens, but sometimes these needs and wants can conflict with one another. People want jobs, but economic development can hurt the environment. People want strict controls on resource use, but not if this means job losses in the community.

SKILL FOCUS

You can think of your school as a miniature society. How could your school administration or student government rethink how resources are used?

- In a group, brainstorm a list of ways your student government could rethink resource use. These could include using rewards or punishments. Record your ideas in a graphic organizer, such as the table below.

Carrot	Stick

- Which ideas would be most effective in causing actual change in resource use? Why? State your opinion in a written paragraph, podcast, or other format of your choice.

We Need a Balanced Approach

So far in this chapter, we have discussed how to rethink our use of resources. We must move toward an approach focused on the **conservation** of resources—that is, an approach focused on using resources wisely. To do this, we need to add another factor into our discussion. We need to remember that Canadians, and people in other countries, need jobs. Unfortunately, a large number of these jobs involve the use of resources to produce goods and services that are not really essential to life. There must be a reasonable transition from employment based on wasting resources to employment based on the conservation ideal. The key question is how do we make this change?

conservation the wise use of resources

In the chapters to come, you will learn more about the wise and unwise uses of resources, the economy, and jobs. This will help you become a more informed person so you can make wise choices in the future. As you continue to investigate issues, think about how they link to this unit's Big Question: How is our future tied to our ability to manage our resources and economic activities effectively?

APPLY IT!

1. How can people shop in a way that reduces packaging waste?

2. Many restaurants have chosen not to serve shark fin soup, while many others continue to serve it. Research the situation and discuss the possible reasons behind each of these decisions. Is there a way to balance human wants with economic and environmental impacts? Explain your reasoning.

3. a) ■ **Patterns and Trends** How might cars in 2025 be different from those available today? How might cars in 2025 be different from those available 50 years ago? (Hint: You may want to talk to classmates and family or other friends to get a variety of opinions.)

   b) What do you think about these changes?

4. **OSSLT** In the Viewpoints feature, you compared the "good old days" with today. What features from each time period would you choose to create a world that is more environmentally conscious than the real worlds of 50 years ago and today?

5. Much of today's economy is based on the production of goods and services that we want, but do not need. Suggest ways we can transition from today's economy to a new, environmentally sensitive one with a minimum amount of economic disruption.

6. Powerful cars like the BMW M6 use a lot of our natural resources. Use two or three aspects of our lives (e.g., how we eat, what we wear, where we live, how we move around) to argue whether or not you think we use our natural resources in a good way.

Rethinking How We View and Use Natural Resources

? **Should we rethink how we perceive and use our resources?**

Because Canada is a resource-rich country, we tend to take our resources for granted. This is short-sighted because the ways in which we use our resources affect both the environment and the economy. Individuals, companies, and governments are increasingly rethinking how we view and can use our resources more wisely.

1. How do these three groups influence each other? What impact does this have on sustainable use of resources? Explain using the example of BMW's electric and hybrid cars from the beginning of the chapter or another example. You might find it helpful to create a graphic organizer for your answer.

2. What did Zimmermann mean when he said, "Resources are not, they become"? Explain this quote with some specific examples.

3. Now that you have had an opportunity to rethink how we perceive and use resources, create and complete a table similar to the one below to identify at least eight specific examples of rethinking that you or your family or the people you live with can do.

Aspect of our life	Specific action	Example of rethinking
Food	buying vegetables grown in Ontario	reduce—less fuel is needed to bring produce from a long distance
Clothing	passing clothes that no longer fit you to a smaller person	reuse—decrease the need to produce new clothing

Geo ⚙ Inquiry

Interpret and Analyze

4. How does distinguishing between a want and a need help us rethink our use of resources? Explain using an example.

Evaluate and Draw Conclusions

5. What role *can* governments, companies (including the media), and individuals play in reducing unnecessary consumption? What role *should* they play?

Analyze an Issue

6. Think about issues related to rethinking how we view and use natural resources. Pick one of these issues.

   a) Write a number of questions about the issue. Narrow your questions down to one clearly stated and important big question.

   b) Find three or four resources and collect information to answer your question. Be sure to analyze the information and consider various viewpoints.

   c) Take a position and answer your question. Support your answer with facts from your research.

   d) Create a product that communicates your answer. This could be an opinion paper, a blog post, a poster, or a letter to the editor.

©P

5 Managing Renewable Resources Successfully

? How can we use our renewable resources in a sustainable way?

KEY TERMS

mining the resource

sustained yield
   management

old-growth forest

aquaculture

inshore fishery

offshore fishery

Rethinking Our Seafood Choices

There are very good reasons to eat fish. Fish can be prepared in many delicious ways, and eating fish is good for your health. Unfortunately, your consumption of fish may not be good for the health of the oceans.

Have you eaten a type of fish called orange roughy? Probably not, since it disappeared from restaurant menus shortly after 2000. Orange roughy was dramatically overfished and is no longer caught in large numbers.

What about Chilean sea bass, which is also known as Patagonian toothfish? It has replaced orange roughy on many restaurant menus. It looks exotic on a menu, can be cooked in a variety of ways, and is not particularly expensive, which helps increase the restaurant's profit margin.

Will you be eating Chilean sea bass in the future? Possibly not, since this species is also being overfished in much of the Southern Ocean. Twenty years ago, most Patagonian toothfish that were caught weighed close to 100 kilograms. Now, because of overfishing, the average weight is more like 10 kilograms, a clear sign of a fish population in trouble.

What might replace Chilean sea bass in the world's seafood restaurants? Only time will tell. Hopefully, fish buyers in homes and restaurants will finally learn the lesson of sustainable consumption and eat more responsibly.

THINKING CRITICALLY

A generation ago, this dish may have been made with orange roughy instead of Chilean sea bass. Considering what you know now, how do you think individuals, companies, and the government treat our natural resources? What responsibilities does each group have in making sure overfishing does not happen?

©P

Ensuring Renewable Resources for the Future

What vitally important characteristic do all of these activities share?

- farming
- forestry
- fishing (commercial and sport fishing)

At first glance, they might appear to very different from one another, but they are all, of course, economic activities that depend on the renewable resources of soil, trees, and fish. In this chapter, we will focus on what must be done to ensure that these resources remain renewable. Without careful management, it is far too easy to treat them as if they were non-renewable resources. In fact, a term borrowed from the non-renewable world is often used to describe the unsustainable use of a renewable resource: **mining the resource**. The opposite of mining the resource is using various processes to ensure that renewable resources remain renewable. This is called **sustained yield management**.

mining the resource exploiting a renewable resource in an unsustainable way

sustained yield management the process of managing a renewable resource to ensure that the amount harvested does not cause long-term depletion of the resource. The harvest is equal to or less than the amount replenished each year.

To see how this works, let's start with a simple example (Figure 5–1) of how sustainability works in an imaginary candy factory. The steady output of candy from a factory depends on the steady supply of ingredients. If no ingredients go into the factory, no candy can be made. If there are not enough ingredients, less candy is made. The output of candy also depends on the production process. Interruptions to the process can stop or slow the production of candy. These can include the machinery breaking down or taking candy from the production line before it is finished.

▲ **Figure 5–1** When the Renewable Candy factory is working properly (that is, sustained yield management is being used), a steady stream of candies comes out for customers. However, two different things can affect the production of candy: disruption of the supply of ingredients and disruptions to the production process. How might these two things apply to the sustainable production of renewable resources such as farming, forestry, and fishing?

©P

A Quick Overview of Renewable Resources

Some renewable resources are more at risk of being mined, or used unsustainbly, than others. Also, because of Canada's rich resource base and the relatively modest demands we put on the resources, many other countries are more likely to mine their renewable resources than we are here in Canada. But mining of resources can and has happened here. As you shall see later, the Atlantic fishery was devastated by the early 1990s. Here is a quick look at different types of economic activities that rely on renewable resources in Canada.

FARMING

Soil is the renewable resource on which farming relies. While a relatively small part of Canada's land is used for commercial agriculture, it is a vitally import-ant resource for supplying food to Canadians and for export (Figure 5–2).

Resource(s) needed: A suitable climate (temperature measured in number of growing degree-days; sufficient precipitation) and deep, fertile soils are required.

Problems: Soil deterioration is a very important, but rarely discussed, problem. Bad farming practices can result in soil being eroded into rivers or fertility being washed out of the soil. Most cities are built on land that is well suited for farming, so urban growth reduces the amount of farmland available.

Risk of being used unsustainably: Moderate

Impact of climate change: Changes in temperature and rainfall patterns could have a major impact on where farming is possible (Figure 5–3).

▲ **Figure 5–2** Nothing is more fundamental to life than a productive agricultural sector.

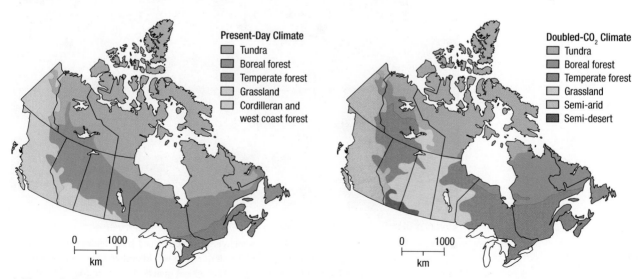

Present-Day Climate
- ☐ Tundra
- ☐ Boreal forest
- ☐ Temperate forest
- ☐ Grassland
- ☐ Cordilleran and west coast forest

Doubled-CO_2 Climate
- ☐ Tundra
- ☐ Boreal forest
- ☐ Temperate forest
- ☐ Grassland
- ☐ Semi-arid
- ☐ Semi-desert

0   1000
km

0   1000
km

▲ **Figure 5–3** Climate change will have a dramatic effect on agriculture in Canada. In what ways might the impact be positive? In what ways could it be negative? What will be the biggest changes caused by climate change?

▲ **Figure 5–4** Most of the trees that are cut down in Canada are much smaller than this old-growth giant in British Columbia. What is the best use for the wood in such a large tree?

FORESTRY

Trees are obviously the renewable resource used in forestry. A wide swath across Canada is covered with forests and is used for forestry. Forests are important in most countries for producing lumber, paper, and firewood, but only a few large countries are major exporters of forest products (Figure 5–4).

Resource(s) needed: A climate and soils that are appropriate for the type of trees are required. Existing forests provide seeds for new generations of trees. Forestry can be thought of as a form of agriculture that has a growing season many years long.

Problems: Poor forestry practices can result in scrub bush replacing a high-quality forest. Soil erosion can be a serious concern in hilly areas.

Risk of being used unsustainably: Moderate to high

Impact of climate change: The size and borders of forest regions will change. Also, warmer temperatures will increase the risk of forest damage from insects.

COMMERCIAL FISHING

Commercial fishing is locally important in Atlantic Canada, British Columbia, parts of Québec, and some inland lakes (Figure 5–5). Fishing is important as a source of food and a source of income. There are commercial fisheries all around the world.

Resource(s) needed: Naturally occurring fish stocks are required.

▲ **Figure 5–5** This is one haul of salmon on an average-sized fishing boat. Multiply this by the thousands of fishing boats that operate every day all over the world and you get some sense of the immense quantity of fish that is being caught. The critical question is when does the size of the catch go beyond the sustained yield limit? When this happens, the resource is being mined instead of being used sustainably.

©P

Problems: Fish stocks are too often mined. Orange roughy, Chilean sea bass, and Atlantic Canada's cod are just a few examples of fish that have been harvested unsustainably. Pollution of the ocean can reduce the numbers of fish and make the fish dangerous to eat.

Risk of being used unsustainably: High. A large majority of the world's major fishing grounds have already been overfished.

Impact of climate change: Since oceans around the world are warming, fish populations are moving. For example, the range of Pacific salmon is gradually moving northward.

Aboriginal Peoples and Renewable Resource Development

Developing and extracting resources of land, forests, and fish often affects First Nations, Métis, and Inuit peoples disproportionately. Consequences such as clear-cutting, pollution, and disruption to the land, water, and wildlife populations can negatively affect Aboriginal communities that depend on the natural environment.

   If we are to use resources wisely by balancing the needs of the environment with the wants and needs of people, we must also consider the needs and wants of different groups of people. First Nations, Métis, and Inuit peoples need to be consulted about development that affects their traditional territories, not just their reserves.

> **go online**
>
> The people of Grassy Narrows First Nation have long fought to protect their traditional territories from logging. Logging would affect their ability to practise their traditional lifestyle, which violates their Indigenous rights. Research to learn more about the case.

APPLY IT!

1. a) Look at Figure 5–3. In what two regions is most of Canada's farming done?

   b) What could happen to the size of each of these regions if atmospheric carbon dioxide doubled?

   c) What does this suggest about Canada's future agricultural potential?

   d) Why might the picture be nowhere near as positive as your answers to parts b) and c) would suggest?

2. Name two countries, other than Canada, that are globally important sources of forest products. What natural characteristics do Canada and these countries share?

3. What business factor makes it difficult for companies to manage forests sustainably?

4. Suggest two reasons why the sustainable management of fishery resources is more of a challenge than the management of either agricultural or forestry resources.

5. ■ **Geographic Perspective** Inland sport fishing is a 100-million-dollar industry just in Ontario and Québec. What has been done by individuals, companies, and the government to support sustainable practice of this industry?

A Closer Look at Farming

Most Canadians take their food supply for granted. The food we need and want is generally there when we want it. In addition, compared to the citizens of most countries, we pay relatively little for what we eat. We tend to think that the food we eat comes from a supermarket (or a restaurant) and ignore the complex supply chain that leads from farms to consumers. The true story of how food is produced in Canada and elsewhere is complex, often interesting, and always important.

Many factors contribute to successful farming. The major factors that influence farming are climate and land quality. Finding a location that has the right combination of climate and land quality is not very easy in most of Canada.

Climate Factors

TEMPERATURE

Geo ⚙ Inquiry

Gather and Organize

How are growing degree-days calculated? Which provinces and regions are best suited to commercial agriculture based on their number of GDDs?

Want to grow an orange tree in your backyard? This will only work if your backyard is somewhere a lot warmer than anywhere in Canada. In fact, most of Canada is far too cold for any type of commercial farming (Figure 5–6). This map shows growing degree-days (GDDs). GDDs are a measure of how warm the growing season is in a given location The higher the GDDs, the warmer the climate and the wider the range of crops you can grow. Also, warmer temperatures cause faster plant growth. Areas with GDDs below about 1100 cannot be used for commercial agriculture. GDDs just above 1100 allow only a few fast-ripening crops to be grown.

Farmers keep track of GDDs as the growing season progresses to determine how developed their plants are at any given time. With this information, farmers know when to apply fertilizers and pesticides.

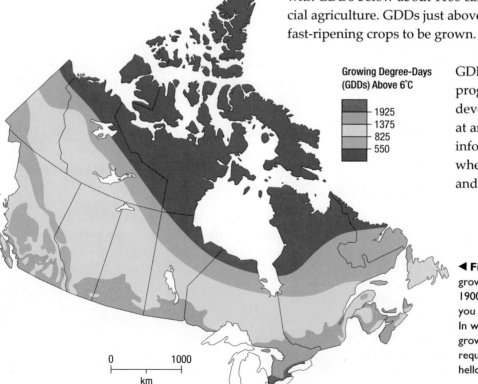

Growing Degree-Days (GDDs) Above 6°C

- 1925
- 1375
- 825
- 550

0   1000
km

◀ **Figure 5–6** Commercial peach growing in Canada requires about 1900 growing degree-days. Could you grow peaches where you live? In what parts of Canada could you grow them? Growing oranges requires more than 5000 GDDs—hello, southern Florida and Brazil.

MOISTURE

There are a variety of ways to measure the availability of water. The simplest way is to look at the amount of precipitation that occurs in an area. While this method is useful, it does not consider the environmental demand for water, which is tied to how warm the climate is. The use of the *aridity index*, which takes into account the supply and demand for moisture, avoids this problem.

Land Quality

During the 1960s, the government conducted the Canada Land Inventory (CLI) to determine the land's capability for agriculture. Land was assigned to one of seven classes. Only Classes 1 to 4 are considered good enough for growing commercial crops.

- Class 1: Excellent; no limitations for agriculture (within the broad limits of Canadian climates)
- Class 2: Very good; no serious land or climate limitations
- Class 3: Good; some land or climate limitations that make some farming activities impossible
- Class 4: Fair; short growing season, poor soil conditions, or other significant limitations
- Class 5: Serious limitations, such as a very short growing season
- Class 6: Similar to Class 5, except the limitations are more severe; can only be use be used for rough grazing
- Class 7: No capability for agriculture, or was too far north even to be included in the survey

Figure 5–7 shows how much land of each type there is in Canada. Note that parts of Canada that were not surveyed are included in Class 7.

CONNECTING

You will learn more about the aridity index in **Chapter 6 (pages 129–130)**.

go online

What is the agricultural potential where you live? Find out by searching for the Canada Land Inventory and then searching for images only. In many cases, this makes it easier to find maps and other graphics.

Would you like to see what land of different classes is like? Take **GeoFlight 5.1** to see examples of Classes 1, 4, and 7 land in Southern Ontario.

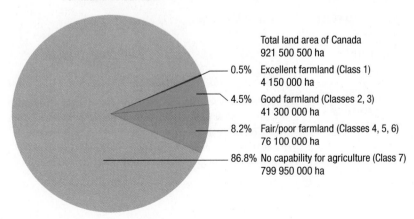

Farmland in Canada

Total land area of Canada
921 500 500 ha

0.5% Excellent farmland (Class 1)
4 150 000 ha

4.5% Good farmland (Classes 2, 3)
41 300 000 ha

8.2% Fair/poor farmland (Classes 4, 5, 6)
76 100 000 ha

86.8% No capability for agriculture (Class 7)
799 950 000 ha

Source: Agriculture and Agri-food Canada

◀ **Figure 5–7** The vast majority of Canada has essentially no potential for commercial agriculture, although people may have a household garden to grow crops that do not require many GDDs. Some people have called this kind of land "moose pasture." What does that mean? Identify three or four places in Canada that would be part of the orange section of the graph.

Geo ⚙ Inquiry

Formulate Questions

Land may still be used for farming even if it is not perfectly suited for agriculture. Look at the list of negative land characteristics on the right. Write one question about how each of these affect farming. Suggest search terms that could be used to find answers to your questions.

Land class can be downgraded based on a number of factors:

- climate limitations, such as low GDDs, low total precipitation, or low precipitation in the growing season
- soil damaged by erosion
- stony soil
- shallow soil (less than 1 metre of soil above bedrock)
- poor soil quality
- land that is too hilly
- excess water in the soil

APPLY IT!

1. Which classes of land are most important to Canadian farming?

2. Which two of the seven limitations on agriculture listed above do you think are most significant? Why did you choose these two?

3. Why is it not a surprise that there is a conflict between agriculture and urban growth for the best agricultural land (Classes 1 and 2)? Why is this a very unfair conflict?

4. ■ **Spatial Significance**

   a) In this section, we have been talking about factors that limit the usefulness of land for agriculture. Most people in the world live in places that have at least some limitations. These people have had to modify what they grow and how they grow it to deal with the particular limitations that they face. Figure 5–8 shows one extreme adjustment. If this land had been classified according to the Canadian system *before* the terraces were built, in what class do you think it would have been placed?

   b) Describe one adjustment for each of these limitations:
      i) too cool   iv) too wet
      ii) too hot   v) too hilly
      iii) too dry   vi) poor soil quality

5. What percentage of Canada is made up of land that is rated as good to excellent (Classes 1 to 3)? Since this survey was done over 40 years ago, has that percentage gone up or down? Why?

▲ **Figure 5–8** What do you do if you live in a very hilly place and want to grow rice, which requires perfectly flat land? These intricate terraces that follow the shape of the land were built more than 600 years ago in southern China. This is an extreme example of how people deal with agricultural limitations.

Major Types of Farming and Where You Find Each

We know something about the climate and soil characteristics of various parts of Canada and something about the scale of Canadian agriculture. Next, let us consider the types of farming done in Canada.

Table 5–1 shows the two broad categories of farming.

Table 5–1 Intensive vs. extensive farming

Intensive farming	Extensive farming
• involves relatively small areas of land	• involves large areas of land
• requires large amounts of labour (Figure 5–9)	• requires relatively small amounts of labour (Figure 5–10)
• is located near large urban areas and produces products such as dairy products for the nearby large population	• produces products such as wheat and cooking oil for export

▲ **Figure 5–9** A typical Ontario vineyard has an area of less than 14 hectares and requires a great amount of labour.

▲ **Figure 5–10** The average farm size in Saskatchewan is 675 hectares and requires considerably less human labour than a farm that grows grapes.

APPLY IT!

1. **a)** Classify each of the following as intensive or extensive farming: i) poultry and eggs; ii) dairy farming; iii) hog production; iv) cattle ranching; v) wheat and other grains; vi) oilseeds (e.g., canola and sunflower); vii) fruits and vegetables; viii) sheep and goats.

   b) Choose two types each of intensive and extensive farming. How do the descriptions of *intensive farming* and *extensive farming* apply to these types of farming?

2. What type of farming occurs near where you live? Why?

3. Would you expect to find intensive or extensive farming in each of these parts of Canada? Why?

   a) Southern Ontario   **c)** Alberta

   b) Manitoba   **d)** British Columbia

4. **a)** Intensive and extensive farming exist in various places around the world. Give at least two examples each of intensive farming and extensive farming outside Canada.

   b) What relationship would you expect to find between rural population densities and the type of farming in a particular location? Why is this not at all surprising?

The Business of Farming

In the past, farming was more a way of life than a business. Until 1920, the majority of Canada's population lived in rural areas, and most of these people were farmers (Figure 5–11).

THINKING CRITICALLY

Look at Figure 5–11. Why do you think this photo was selected? Is it useful to you as a learner? Give reasons why it is or is not useful.

▲ **Figure 5–11** A century ago, the family farm really did involve the entire family. Compare the technology shown here with to that used today in Figure 5–10 on page 109.

Farming has changed dramatically in the last century. Table 5–2 shows some statistics that illustrate the changes. In this activity, you will analyze these statistics to learn how dramatically Canadian farms have changed since the early 1900s.

▶ A hectare (ha) is an area of 100 metres by 100 metres. This is roughly the amount of land inside a standard running track.

How can we judge the quality of any statistics we might see?

Table 5–2 Changes in Canadian farming, by the numbers

Year	Number of farms	Total amount of farmland (ha)	Number of farm workers	Number of tractors
1911	683 000	44 395 000	928 000	n.a.
1931	729 000	66 399 000	1 118 000	105 000
1951	623 000	70 399 000	826 000	400 000
1971	366 000	68 808 000	510 000	597 000
1991	280 000	67 760 000	533 000	711 000
2011	206 000	64 813 000	307 000	685 000

Source: Statistics Canada

Analyzing Changes in Farming

The data in Table 5–2 are all **absolute measures**. An absolute measure is a count of the number of something, such as farms and tractors. You will start by calculating several **relative measures**. These are values that are calculated from absolute measures and are often useful for making comparisons and understanding patterns and trends. An example of a relative measure is the number of tractors per farm.

> **absolute measure** a quantity of something using simple units, such as kilometres, dollars, or number of people
>
> **relative measure** a quantity of something compared to the quantity of something else, using units such as percentages and ratios (e.g., people per square kilometre)

APPLY IT!

Work in groups of three. The big question is "How has farming changed in Canada over the last century?" Your group may want to work with this question or come up with your own.

1. Each person needs a calculator and graph paper. As a group, use Table 5–2 to calculate each value below. Calculate all the values to one decimal point.

   a) average size of farms

   b) average number of workers per farm

   c) average number of hectares per worker

   d) average number of pieces of machinery per farm

   e) average number of hectares per machine

2. You now have a variety of interesting data to graph. In each graph, the year is the independent variable (on the *x*-axis). As a group, graph the nine sets of data (the four absolute values in Table 5–2 and the five relative values you calculated in question 1).

3. ■ **Patterns and Trends**

   a) Consider all nine graphs. What trends do you see in Canadian agriculture over the last century? Remember that Canada's population now is about five times what it was in 1911.

   b) Give one reason for each trend you see.

   c) How do these trends combine to suggest that farming can increasingly be seen as a business?

   d) What advantages are there to working with relative measures compared to absolute measures?

A Closer Look at Forestry

*"Forestry is just like farming—
except you need to be very patient."*

This statement is, for the most part, accurate. Most farm crops are planted and harvested within a few months. With tree or vine fruits, such as apples and grapes, you may have to wait several years for your first harvest. If you are a forestry company, though, much more patience is needed. Trees used for making paper are generally cut down much sooner than those used for lumber. Even in southern Canada, where the growing seasons are longest (Classes 1 to 4 agricultural land), you have to wait for 40 years or so before cutting trees for papermaking. If you wanted to grow hardwood trees to make furniture, you might have to wait for 200 years or more. While there are a lot of parallels between agriculture and forestry, the time required for each is the major difference.

When European settlers came to Canada, they saw forests as little more than formidable obstacles to be eliminated so they could plant crops. Others, though, saw money when they looked at the vast forests. In the early 19th century, Napoleon's navy cut off Britain's timber sources in Europe. Lumber had to be imported from somewhere else and Canada offered the perfect solution: it was British territory and had a seemingly endless supply of wood.

Old-growth forests were cut in valleys that were part of the St. Lawrence River and other watersheds. Later, loggers were able to move farther inland because railways became available to transport the lumber. Eventually, they could return to the valleys their grandfathers had logged to cut the much smaller trees of the "second-growth" forest that had grown back. It seemed like Canada's forest resources could never run out, but they were wrong. New technologies were developed that made logging, milling, and transportation much more efficient than in the past (Figure 5–12). We are now capable of mining forests.

old-growth forest a forest that has never been logged

▼ **Figure 5–12** (a) In the past, it took many people to cut down and prepare a tree for use as lumber. (b) Today, modern equipment allows one person to do the work of many. This machine cuts down the tree, removes the branches, and then cuts the log to the desired length. How does this machine contribute to our ability to mine forests?

(a)

(b)

©P

Environmental groups are concerned about the unsustainable use of forests. They want Canada to stop, or at least dramatically reduce, the amount of forest cutting that takes place. This is particularly the case with respect to remaining old-growth forests, which are much more common in British Columbia than in eastern Canada.

Canada's Forest Resources

Before we look at managing our forests, we need to look at where they are and how they vary from region to region. Canada's forests are huge, the third largest in the world after Russia and Brazil. Imagine getting in a car on Vancouver Island and driving northeast and then eastward at 100 kilometres per hour. If you drove for 12 hours a day, it would take four days to reach the eastern end of these great forests in Newfoundland.

As you might predict, the forests you passed through would not all be the same. Different climate conditions produce different kinds of forests. Figure 5–13 shows the forest regions of Canada along with the location of some of the major pulp and paper mills and sawmills.

go online

View a video of modern tree-cutting methods (1:36 minutes).

CONNECTING

Refresh your knowledge of Canada's forest regions by reviewing **Chapter 3 (pages 74–76)**.

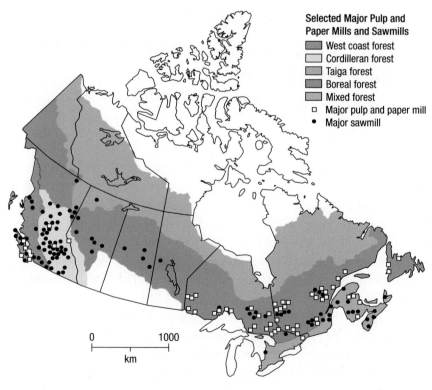

Selected Major Pulp and Paper Mills and Sawmills
- West coast forest
- Cordilleran forest
- Taiga forest
- Boreal forest
- Mixed forest
- □ Major pulp and paper mill
- ● Major sawmill

0   1000
km

▲ **Figure 5–13** This map shows some of the major pulp and paper mills and sawmills in Canada. Is there a pattern to their locations? In addition to the five forest regions, small amounts of forested land are in the Prairies and in the area north of the taiga forest. A very small part of the United States's deciduous forest region is located in the extreme southern part of Ontario. This region is also called the *Carolinian forest*. Why are major sawmills and pulp and paper mills rare in Southern Ontario?

SKILL FOCUS

Finding information online is easy, but the number of results can be overwhelming. The key to finding relevant information is using search terms. Try using the following search tips:

- Simple search terms usually give you the most results. Start with one or two short search terms. Refine your search by adding more words.

- Put quotation marks around your search terms to search for an exact phrase.

- You can use a minus sign to specify particular terms you don't want in your results. For example, a search for "pulp mill-paper" will return results for pulp mills but not paper mills.

Geo ☼ Inquiry

Communicate

Should we exploit our forest resources? Read through this text and do some additional research to compile a list of arguments for and against the exploitation of our forests. Which do you agree with? Express your opinion in a letter to the Minister of Natural Resources. Use your findings to support your viewpoint.

Achieving Sustained Yield Management of Forestry

There are very different viewpoints on how our forests should be managed (Figure 5–14). For some people, forests should be preserved in as natural a state as possible. Other people see forests as a source of wealth and jobs. Most people are somewhere in between. Most environmentalists understand the importance of forest products, since they use paper and live in homes that are built mainly of wood. They also realize that using forests is vital to Canada's economy and to providing jobs, particularly in areas where other job options are limited. At the same time, people who work in the forest industry are often very keen and knowledgeable conservationists. They love and want to protect the forests, but not at the cost of denying the economic value of the forests. The challenge is to find the best balance of protection and use.

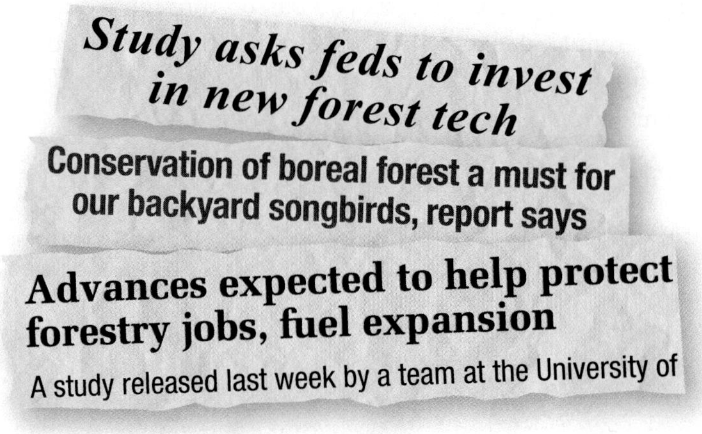

▶ **Figure 5–14** Achieving sustained yield management is a complex task involving everything from high-tech knowledge to good, old-fashioned common sense.

Study asks feds to invest in new forest tech

Conservation of boreal forest a must for our backyard songbirds, report says

Advances expected to help protect forestry jobs, fuel expansion

A study released last week by a team at the University of

▲ **Figure 5–15** On what types of products have you seen FSC labels similar to this one? How might the FSC determine whether a company is acting responsibly in their use of forest products? Create a list of criteria for or characteristics of forest-friendly companies.

The vast majority of Canadian consumers want to "do the right thing." We want to buy products that are produced in environmentally responsible ways. We want to make sure that no one's health or human rights are damaged in the production of the product. At the same time, we realize that people need jobs. The problem when we go shopping is knowing whether a product we are considering meets these goals. Fortunately, there are international organizations that can help us. The Forest Stewardship Council® (FSC®) is an excellent example of this. It has certified over 190 million hectares of forest in 80 countries, including Canada.

The members of the FSC include forestry companies, makers of products that use lumber and paper, Indigenous peoples' organizations, and environmental and social action groups. The FSC has developed standards for responsible forest use and certifies products and organizations that meet their standards. So when consumers shop for things like paper towels, printer paper, lumber, wooden furniture, and other wood products, they can look for the FSC logo (Figure 5–15) and know they are doing the right thing.

©P

1. Generally, coniferous trees provide softwood lumber, whereas deciduous trees provide hardwood lumber.

   a) Which type is much more common in Canada's forests and in Canada's forest product output?

   b) Where should you look to find hardwood trees, north or south? Why?

   c) Name three hardwood species and three softwood species.

   d) Describe typical uses for softwood lumber and for hardwood lumber.

   e) Why are hardwoods called "hard" and softwoods called "soft"? (Don't just say that one is harder than the other.)

2. A great deal of effort has been made to protect the remaining Carolinian forest in Southern Ontario, including the creation of the Rouge Park in eastern Toronto. What drives the move to protect this forest?

3. Canadians use their forests for far more than lumber harvesting. List other uses (economic and otherwise) for which forests are important.

4. What are some of the environmental and social concerns related to the forestry industry?

5. How have advocacy groups, such as the Forest Stewardship Council, influenced how Canadian forests are used? Consider individuals, companies, and the government in your answer.

6. Canada's forested land can be divided into two categories: commercial forest and non-commercial forest.

   a) Explain the difference between the two.

   b) Where would you expect to find each? Hint: Refer to Figure 5–13.

   c) What natural and human factors would contribute to an area being included in one category or the other?

7. Different forest regions have different kinds of trees and different densities of growth. If you could have 1000 hectares (a square slightly more than 3 kilometres by 3 kilometres) of prime forest in any one of Canada's forest regions to support you and your family over the next 100 years, and you had to harvest the trees sustainably, which region would you choose? Why? Which region would be your second choice? Which region would be your last choice?

Use **ArcGIS Online** to visualize and assess the spread of the Mountain Pine Beetle across the forests of national parks from British Columbia into Alberta between 1998 and 2007.

Geo✿Inquiry

Evaluate and Draw Conclusions

What natural and economic factors would have to change to allow parts of the non-commercial forest to become part of the commercial forest? Why might this gradually happen in the next several decades? Would this be a good development? Why or why not?

Algonquin Park: An Example of Good Forest Management

▲ **Figure 5–16** This is the image of Algonquin Park that many people have. How does this picture illustrate how the park is used in many different ways? What it does not show is the logging that might be happening close to the shoreline in the background, but out of sight of the canoeists. Make a list of the many different ways Algonquin Park benefits individuals, companies, and the government.

go online

Generate a list of at least three questions about Algonquin Park and its resources. Then research to find the answers.

▶ **Figure 5–17** This area of Algonquin Park has been logged and replanted. Do you think this is an appropriate use of the resources in a park?

Algonquin Park is a huge provincial park, about 1.5 times the size of Prince Edward Island. It marks the unofficial border between northern Ontario and southern Ontario. Thousands of canoe trippers visit each summer (Figure 5–16), but there is far more to the park than camping and canoeing.

By the early 1890s, it was clear that Algonquin's forests could be devastated by too much logging. Algonquin Park was created in 1893, following the publication of the report of a Royal Commission:

> [T]he experience of older [European] countries had everywhere shown that the wholesale and indiscriminate slaughter of forests brings a host of evils in its train. Wide tracts are converted from fertile plains into arid desert, springs and streams are dried up, and the rainfall, instead of percolating gently through the forest floor and finding its way by easy stages through brook and river to the lower levels, now descends the valleys in hurrying torrents, carrying all before its tempestuous floods.

Algonquin Park provides considerable economic benefit to Ontario. Forest management in the park supports 12 sawmills outside the park (Figure 5–17), which provides jobs in the park and in nearby towns. The large tourism industry also provides many jobs in the park and in nearby communities. Most of these tourism jobs are seasonal.

Algonquin Park is part of the traditional territory of the Algonquins of Ontario, who are allowed to hunt and trap throughout a large portion of the park. Others can also hunt and trap in the southernmost part of the park, in the area that was added in 1961.

©P

Analyzing the Uses of Algonquin Park

Algonquin Park has operated under a series of management plans, the most recent one coming into effect in 1998. This plan sets out how the park is to be structured and operated in order to balance the various demands that are put on it. The park's management plan focuses on five principles:

- Protection: of the natural and cultural landscapes of the area

- Recreation: in high-intensity-use areas along and near roads (car camping, summer camps, and lodges) and low-intensity-use areas in the interior (canoe tripping, hiking, and winter camping)

- Heritage appreciation: at visitor centres, museums, and historical sites

- Tourism: for visitors from all over Ontario and far beyond; provides jobs in the park and in nearby towns

- Resource management: for logging and sawmills, which have been vital to the economies of communities all around the park for more than a century; the management plan sets out the principles for sustainable logging

SKILL FOCUS

The Algonquin Park Management Plan, and other documents you may find, are quite long. There are many ways you can use to find the information you need.

- Look through the table of contents or index to see whether they list the topics you are looking for.

- Use a skimming reading strategy to go quickly through long texts.

- If you are reading an electronic document, you may be able to use the Search function. Search for keywords to locate relevant information.

APPLY IT!

1. **a)** Go online to access the Algonquin Park Management Plan. The park is divided into zones based on the features of the area and on the activities that are allowed. Briefly summarize the characteristics of each zone of Algonquin Park.

    b) In which zone is logging allowed?

    c) What percentage of the park has this zoning?

    d) What other resource use is allowed in this zone but not found in other provincial parks?

2. **a)** Who does the actual tree cutting in the park?

    b) How does this help ensure that logging is sustainable?

    c) How many sawmills use logs from the park? In general, where are the mills located?

3. In addition to forestry, how does the park provide employment for those who live in this region?

4. **a)** What lessons about sustained yield management that have been learned from Algonquin Park can be applied elsewhere?

    b) What prevents aspects of the Algonquin Park example of management from being applied to forested areas across Canada?

5. **a)** ■ **Interrelationships** What factors should the federal and provincial governments consider when they are deciding on the creation of new national and provincial parks?

    b) Most national and provincial parks created in recent years are in remote parts of Canada. Why is this not surprising?

A Closer Look at Fishing

No one wanted to destroy the historic Atlantic cod fishery, but it happened. Some said that it was no one's fault, it was just that no one understood how dire the situation was until it was too late to do anything about it. Others said that it was everyone's fault, including the foreign fishing fleets, the Canadian offshore fishing fleet, the inshore fishers, the scientists who should have known better, and the government that did not take the warnings seriously enough.

As a part of Canada's total economy, commercial fishing is not very important. Only 80 000 people are involved in fishing, **aquaculture** or fish farming, and fish processing, compared to, for example, 315 000 in agriculture and over one million in education. But commercial fishing is important for other reasons.

- Fishing is an important local industry in Atlantic Canada and parts of British Columbia. In more remote areas, there are few alternative jobs available to bring money into the community. Without this money coming in, towns and villages can die.

- Fishing is Canada's oldest industry—with evidence of fishing boats coming to Atlantic Canada before 1497. Tradition matters when we look at what makes a country unique.

- Perhaps most importantly, there is no better, nor bitter, lesson about unsustainable resource management than what happened to the cod fishery in Atlantic Canada. If we are wise enough, we can learn from our mistakes.

There are three categories of catch for Canada's fishing industry (Table 5–3). The remainder of this chapter focuses on the sad case of the groundfish industry in Atlantic Canada.

aquaculture fish farming

Geo✿Inquiry

Interpret and Analyze

Research fisheries in British Columbia. Are they being sustainably managed? Analyze the situation and compare it to that of fisheries in Atlantic Canada.

▶ How many of these seafood varieties have you eaten? Which ones are your favourites?

Table 5–3 The three categories of catch for Canada's fishing industry

Category	Description	Examples
Groundfish	fish that feed and are caught near the ocean floor	cod, pollock, haddock, halibut, redfish
Pelagic fish	fish that feed and are caught near the surface	salmon, herring, mackerel, tuna, capelin
Shellfish	animals without backbones but with hard, protective shells	shrimp, lobster, oysters, scallops, mussels

Atlantic Canada's Fishing Industry

Atlantic Canada's fishery was famous for centuries for the groundfish caught in the shallower parts of the **continental shelf**, called **banks** (Figure 5–18).

It is important to realize that fishing in Atlantic Canada is done in two ways. When we looked at agriculture, we considered the evolution of farming from a way of life at the beginning of the 20th century to a business today. A similar comparison can be made with fishing, with offshore fishing being a business, while inshore fishing remains a way of life. The inshore fishery is much more traditional and less productive than the offshore fishery. Table 5–4 on the next page compares these two types of fisheries.

continental shelf the part of the ocean that is next to continents and is typically less than 200 metres deep

banks shallow parts of the continental shelf that are good for fishing

inshore fishery commercial fishing carried out close to shore in small, independently owned boats

offshore fishery commercial fishing carried out farther from shore in larger company-owned boats

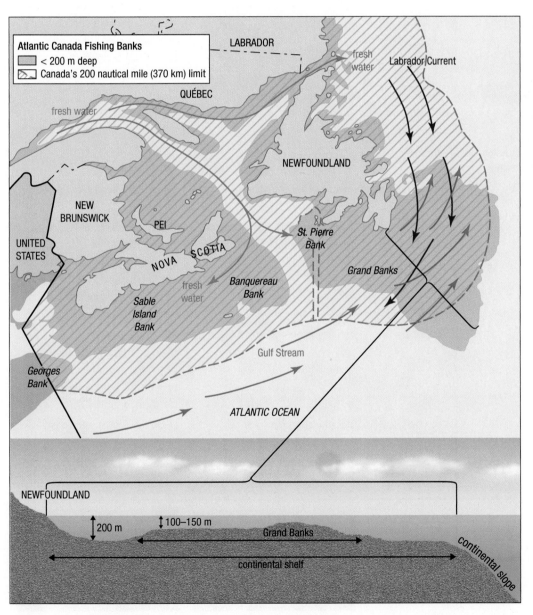

◀ **Figure 5–18**
A unique set of geographic conditions have made the shallow banks along the southern margin of Atlantic Canada an important fishing ground for more than 500 years.

Since 1977, countries have had exclusive economic control of ocean areas up to 200 nautical miles (370 kilometres) from shore. This has led to territorial disputes with the United States over Georges Bank and with France around the tiny French islands of St. Pierre and Miquelon, just off the coast of Newfoundland.

▶ In what ways is the inshore fishery a way of life and the off-shore fishery a business? Are they harvesting the renewable resources of fish sustainably? Explain why or why not.

Geo ✿ Inquiry

Formulate Questions

Choose farming, forestry, or fishing. Ask an important question about the future of that industry in Canada. Suggest two very different sets of search-engine terms that you could use to help answer your question.

Table 5–4 Inshore vs. offshore fisheries

Feature	Inshore fishery	Offshore fishery
Location	within 16–25 km of shore	to edges of the continental shelf for groundfish; far beyond for pelagic fish
Percentage of fishing industry labour force	85%	15%
Percentage of total catch	10%	90%
Types of boats and equipment	boats 6–20 m in length	ships 50 m or longer; ships called factory trawlers can be much larger since processing and storage of fish is done on board so the ships can stay at sea for longer periods of time
Ownership of boats and equipment	individuals and families	large companies
Crew size	1–6	12–16; much larger on factory trawlers
Fishing season	mainly warmer months	year round in all types of weather
Fishing schedule	fishing boats travel to coastal fishing areas each morning	Canadian fishing boats are at sea up to two weeks at a time; foreign fishing boats may be at sea for many months, only going to the nearest port to unload their catch, refuel, and resupply
Processing	fish are processed onshore, usually in small- to medium-sized plants	fish may be partly or even completely processed on board; any additional processing is done in larger plants in large towns or cities
Lifestyle	people often live in small coastal communities; incomes earned are often low and unstable; widespread depen-dence on government support	people live in larger coastal communities; incomes are higher and more stable

What Happened to the East Coast Cod?

They say that a picture is worth a thousand words. Sometimes a graph can be worth even more words. Figure 5–19 is an excellent, but tragic, example of this.

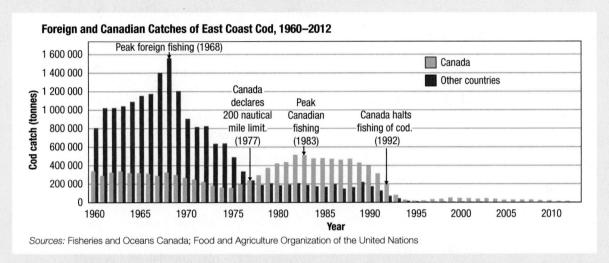

Foreign and Canadian Catches of East Coast Cod, 1960–2012

▲ **Figure 5–19** Mining the stock of East Coast cod—the story in one graph. What dramatic changes do you see? Are things getting better in recent years?

- The total catch of cod is equal to the sum of the foreign and Canadian catches. For example, in 1960, the total catch was about 1.15 million tonnes (800 000 kilograms foreign catch + 350 000 kilograms Canadian catch).

- Before 1977, Canada only controlled the seas for 12 nautical miles (about 22 kilometres) from shore. This was a serious problem, since the best fishing is on the relatively shallow continental shelf (less than 200 metres deep) that extends much farther

from shore. Off the east coast of Newfoundland, the shelf extends more than 200 nautical miles. An international agreement that came into effect in 1977 gave nations, including Canada, exclusive control of any economic activities (fishing and oil drilling are most important) off their shores out to 200 nautical miles.

- The cod fishery has not recovered. In 2012, the catch was only 11 000 tonnes.

APPLY IT!

1. Look at Figure 5–19. What kinds of questions does this graph help us answer? What questions does it raise?

2. The graph can be divided logically into three time periods. Identify these time periods and explain why you chose them.

3. **a)** How much cod was caught in the peak year? What year was that?

   b) What evidence is there that this catch was at an unsustainable level?

   c) Why didn't Canada reduce this catch, either by foreign or Canadian boats?

4. a) What happened to the cod catch in the years after the 200 nautical mile limit came into effect? Look at the foreign and Canadian catches separately.

b) What evidence is there that the catch limit in these years was too high?

c) In your opinion, did the Canadian government use the power given to it with the 200 nautical mile limit in the manner intended?

d) Scientists originally thought that the cod population would recover in 7 to 10 years. How have cod stocks responded since the closure of the cod fishery in 1992?

e) Is the East Coast cod fishery a renewable resource? Explain your reasoning.

5. What impact did the halt to cod fishing in 1992 have on the lives of East Coast fishers?

6. Several groups were involved in the destruction of the East Coast cod fishery. In no particular order, these were

• the foreign offshore fishing fleet

• the Canadian offshore fleet

• the Canadian inshore fishing industry

• marine scientists who monitored fish stocks and made recommendations based on the principles of sustained yield management

• government officials and politicians who set catch limits based on the scientific reports

Describe how responsible each group was for the loss of the cod fishery. Explain your reasoning.

7. Before agriculture existed, people supported themselves by hunting game and gathering plants. The invention, spread, and improvement of agriculture has allowed the world's population to increase dramatically.

a) Does it make more sense to compare fishing to agriculture or to hunting and gathering?

b) What significance does this conclusion have in understanding the current problems with overfishing worldwide?

c) What potential solution does this suggest to the problem of supplying fish to an immense and growing world population?

8. When (or if) cod stocks recover, who should get priority in catching them, the inshore fishery or the offshore fishery? Why?

9. The *Bluenose*, the sailing ship on the back of the dime, was a working fishing vessel for many years.

a) How did the *Bluenose* and similar ships catch fish? This will require some quick research.

b) Although most people were not aware of it, the fishing methods of the past contributed to sustained yield management. How?

10. a) What lessons from the East Coast fishery can be applied to other renewable resources, such as forestry and agriculture?

b) Give two reasons why it should be easier for agriculture and forestry to act sustainably than it was for the fisheries.

THINKING CRITICALLY

11. Do you think the government has done a good job supporting Canada's fishing industry? It might be helpful to consider why fishing is important to Canada (see page 118).

Achieving Sustained Yield Management of Fishing

One thing the destruction of the Atlantic groundfishery has taught us is that we have to do a much better job of managing fish resources or we will have no fishing industry. Sustained yield management of fishing is much more difficult than management of forestry. A forest manager can go into the bush and take very accurate measurements of wood volume. Fish population estimates are less reliable as fish populations move and fluctuate over the seasons.

After the collapse of the cod fishery, Atlantic Canada's fishing industry focused on other ocean species, ranging from shrimp to pollock. Understandably, there were concerns about overfishing these species. To avoid this, management was considerably tightened. In the past, when scientists suggested a range of possible catch limits, there was a tendency to go with the highest limit. Now, much more conservative estimates are being made, with lower limits likely to be chosen.

Catches are monitored more closely during the fishing season. The open season for a particular species will be cut off early if catches are higher than expected. Fishing boat owners have become used to switching from one species to another several times in one year. This has increased costs because different types of fishing equipment are needed for different species, but generally everyone understands why it is necessary.

The Marine Stewardship Council (MSC) is an international organization that sets standards for the sustainable use of fisheries. The MSC works with fisheries and governments around the world to promote better fishing practices. As well, it works with third-party organizations to certify sustainable fisheries. Seafood and seafood products from certified fisheries are awarded the MSC ecolabel (Figure 5–20).

Climate change has become the wild card in fisheries management. Overall, ocean temperatures are increasing faster than air temperatures. Warmer water changes the living conditions for all fish species and for the plants and smaller fish they eat. In general, warmer waters are less productive than colder waters, so catch limits will have to be reduced.

▲ **Figure 5–20** When you see the Marine Stewardship Council ecolabel on a menu or seafood product, you know that the seafood comes from certified, sustainable sources.

go online

Learn more about the work of the Marine Stewardship Council. On its website, you will find everything from how fishery certification works to seafood recipes.

Geo✿Inquiry

Gather and Organize

Create a chart to compare at least three aspects of the three main renewable resources of farming, forestry, and fishing.

APPLY IT!

1. Why is commercial fishing a more important industry in Canada than its employment numbers would suggest it should be?

2. Sunlight penetrates to the bottom of shallower banks. This increases the growth of tiny plants called *phytoplankton*. What is the connection between these plants and the rich stocks of large fish that develop on banks?

3. Describe two reasons why it is very difficult for fishery scientists to make accurate population estimates for most species of fish.

4. Early people hunted wild animals for food. The invention of agriculture meant that people raised animals like cows and pigs for food instead. How can this kind of change be applied to fishing? What evidence is there that this change is already happening?

Managing Renewable Resources Successfully

? **How can we use our renewable resources in a sustainable way?**

Farming, forestry, and fishing are industries that depend on renewable resources and that are important to Canada's economy—and even its identity as a nation. These resources can and must be managed sustainably, but this does not always happen.

1. Consider the roles farming, forestry, and fishing play in Canada's economy and in defining our national identity. How are these roles threatened by how we use these resources? Organize your ideas from this chapter using a graphic organizer such as a concept map.

2. How have improvements in technology in the last century or so made it easier to mine renewable resources? Add your ideas to the graphic organizer you created in question 1.

3. Compare farming, forestry, and fishing. In which industry is sustained yield management hardest to accomplish? In which is it easiest? How is this related to the interconnected roles that are played by individuals, companies, and governments in managing these resources? Explain your answers.

Geo ⚙ Inquiry

Interpret and Analyze

4. **OSSLT** Most people would not deliberately use renewable resources in a non-renewable way, but this continues to happen. Analyze the following definition of the *tragedy of the commons* by breaking this complex definition into at least three sections. How does it help explain why we mine these resources?

   The tragedy of the commons is the overuse of a shared resource (originally referred to as a common pasture) by a group of individuals. Individuals make choices that benefit themselves, even though they understand that depleting the resource goes against the group's long-term best interests.

Evaluate and Draw Conclusions

5. Evaluate today's farming, forestry, and fishing industries. Give a grade for the sustainable management of each industry. Explain your grade.

6. List the ways Canada has used its renewable resources wisely and ways it has not. Considering this list, suggest two or three actions that individuals, companies, and the government can do to protect our renewable resources.

Analyze an Issue

7. Think about issues related to managing renewable resources successfully that you have read about or that affect your everyday life. Pick one of these issues.

   a) Write a number of questions about the issue. Narrow your questions down to one clearly stated and important big question.

   b) What areas would you have to research to answer your big question? Find three or four resources and collect information to answer your question. Be sure to analyze the information and consider various viewpoints.

   c) Use your notes to take a position and answer your question. Support your answer with facts from your research.

   d) Create a product that communicates the answer to your question. This could be an opinion paper, a blog post, a poster, or a letter to the editor. Be creative!

©P

Fresh Water—Canada's Special Resource?

KEY TERMS

precipitation

stores

flows

groundwater

aridity index

potential
   evapotranspiration

extraction

consumption

drainage basin

bulk water exports

? Is fresh water our most important resource?

Who Decides How We Use Our Water?

Most of Canada has an abundant water supply. The area of Southern Ontario that is west of Lake Ontario is just such an area. Here, there are many water users: a growing urban population, farmers, and manufacturers.

Nestlé Canada is a manufacturer of bottled water. Nestlé has a five-year permit from the Ontario government to pump up to 1.1 million litres of water per day from the ground near the town of Hillsburgh, Ontario. If you take a look at the map below, you will see that this area is also an important source of water for two of southern Ontario's major rivers: the Grand, which flows into Lake Erie, and the Credit, which flows into Lake Ontario.

In 2011, the permit was renewed, but the government added a new clause. In times of drought (an extended period of low rainfall), Nestlé would be legally required to cut back on what it takes from the ground.

Nestlé appealed the rule about mandatory cuts. It made the case that no other water users in the region faced mandatory cuts, only requests to reduce consumption voluntarily. During past droughts, Nestlé had chosen to reduce water withdrawals even though it was not required to do so. Before the case went to court, Nestlé and the government reached an agreement that dropped the mandatory reductions rule.

Two citizens groups decided to challenge the amended agreement in court. They wanted to establish the principle that users of the water do not have the absolute right to take water when there is a drought. Why would groups of people object to users taking water during a drought?

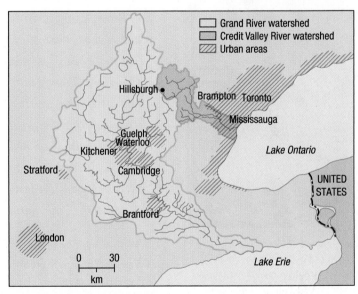

▲ Nestlé Canada bottles water from wells near Hillsburgh, Ontario, the source area for both the Grand and Credit Rivers.

THINKING CRITICALLY

Should all water users (companies, farmers, other individuals) face mandatory water restrictions during a drought? Does it matter what use is made of the water that is taken? List reasons for and against individuals, companies, and governments making decisions about how water should be used.

The Importance of Water

Most Canadians take water pretty much for granted. As long as it is there in whatever volume we want when we turn on the tap, we are pleased. Perhaps this is not a great surprise since most of us live in cities and towns and do not have a clear sense of where water comes from, how it got to us, and what will happen to it after it runs down the drain or is flushed away. Some Canadians are much more connected to their water. Farmers and other rural residents get their water from their own wells. They understand the impact of a drought or a chemical spill on their water.

Even stronger is the understanding that many First Nations, Métis, and Inuit peoples have of water. They have a strong spiritual connection with rivers and lakes and see river systems as a role model for how people should live. The Mattawa/North Bay Algonquin First Nation poem below gives a good sense of this understanding.

> *Our Elders tell us that water is the giver and protector of life;*
> *It is also able to sustain it.*
> *They say for this offering we must honor and give thanks.*
> *A River represents purity,*
> *a River and its tributaries are the veins and arteries of Mother Earth.*
> *A River has the ability to clean itself,*
> *and is always in a state of transition in its early stages.*
> *The ability to shape itself ultimately determines its own destiny.*
> *One River flowing into another makes the River stronger*
> *and fosters that Spirit of Cooperation to overcome all obstacles in its path.*
> *Together Rivers ultimately reach their common destinations,*
> *bringing with them new life, meeting the food requirements downstream.*
> *Yet each River is able to maintain its own destiny and uniqueness.*
> *Never does a River leave, once it has joined another.*
> *It's this peace and harmony that is so attractive and achievable.*

Water supply issues affect hundreds of millions of people in places as diverse as the southwestern United States, northeastern China, Australia, and northern Africa. This means that an Australian farmer or a resident of Beijing, for example, is much more aware of their respective water situation than a typical Canadian. Having an abundant supply of water does not mean that Canadians should take our water for granted. We all have a responsibility to know more about our water, to protect it and to use it wisely (Figure 6–1).

Geo ⚙ Inquiry

Interpret and Analyze

Identify the words and phrases in the First Nations poem on this page that reveal the Aboriginal understanding of the connection between water and people. How might these beliefs influence Aboriginal views on the importance of water resources?

▲ **Figure 6–1** Since 2003, a group of First Nations women led by Josephine Mandamin (above) have taken annual Water Walks to highlight their concerns about the destruction of fresh water resources in North America. The first Water Walk circled Lake Superior. Later walks have focused on other water bodies.

Global Water Supply

Is this the future global outlook for water?

OSSLT

> *Water, water every where,*
> *Nor any drop to drink.*
> —Rime of the Ancient Mariner

Distribution of Water in the World

Studying water availability in a particular area is like keeping track of your bank account. Water (money) goes into the environment (bank account) and water (money) comes out. Water goes in because of **precipitation**. Water goes out for two reasons: demands by the natural environment and demands by humans. If more water goes in than out, there is a water surplus. This is generally a good thing because it means that rivers flow, the water table in the ground is at a healthy level, and people have enough water to meet their needs. If more water goes out than comes in, the result is a water deficit and people have difficulty meeting their needs. Water deficits are becoming the norm as larger populations increase demand and climate change makes areas that are naturally dry even drier.

Before we look at Canada's water situation, we need to establish a global basis for comparison. To start, go back to something you learned about in an earlier grade: the water cycle. The water cycle contains two related sets of elements: **stores** and **flows**. Stores are just that: places in the world where water is stored. Examples of stores include oceans, ice sheets, and groundwater. Flows, on the other hand, are the ways that water moves from one store to another. Water flows through the water cycle. Examples of flows include precipitation and evaporation.

Figure 6–2 shows the major water stores. Keep this list of water stores in mind as you progress through the chapter.

precipitation water from the atmosphere that falls to Earth, including rain, snow, hail, and sleet

go online

Review your understanding of the water cycle.

stores places in the world where water is stored

flows mechanisms by which stores move from one reserve to another

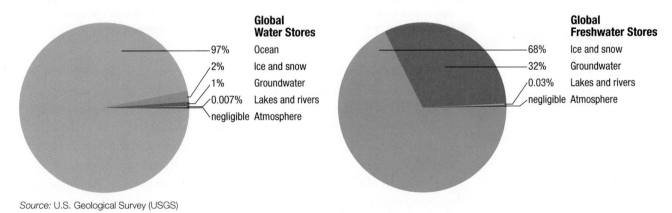

Global Water Stores

- 97% Ocean
- 2% Ice and snow
- 1% Groundwater
- 0.007% Lakes and rivers
- negligible Atmosphere

Global Freshwater Stores

- 68% Ice and snow
- 32% Groundwater
- 0.03% Lakes and rivers
- negligible Atmosphere

Source: U.S. Geological Survey (USGS)

▲ **Figure 6–2 Global water and freshwater stores.** What can you tell and what can you infer from these graphs?

Geo ⚙ Inquiry

Evaluate and Draw Conclusions

Find out more about what is happening to Tibet's glaciers and why it matters. Where are the glaciers, what rivers start here, and what regions depend on this water?

groundwater water held underground in tiny spaces in the soil or some types of rocks

go online

Is there a spring near where you live? Visit a crowd-sourced listing of major springs. Is your spring listed on this site?

While the ice sheets in Antarctica and Greenland are huge, they are of little use as a water source since very few people live in these vast, inhospitable places. On the other hand, glaciers near populated places are very important to the water supply. The most important example of this is the world's third largest area of ice, on the Tibetan Plateau in western China. This icefield is the source of many of the world's great rivers, which provide water for almost two billion people in Pakistan, India, Bangladesh, southeast Asia, and China. Ice is also the source of much of the water that flows through Canada's Prairies on its way to Hudson Bay.

Groundwater reserves can be used in two ways. In many places, the groundwater level reaches the surface in the form of springs that form streams (Figure 6–3). Much more commonly, groundwater is recovered by drilling wells from the surface.

▲ **Figure 6–3** Springs are common in any location where the groundwater level is close to the surface. Large springs on public land near large populations are often used as water sources by people who do not want to use water from municipal sources or local wells. What natural and human factors influence how much water comes out of these springs?

Geo ⚙ Inquiry

Gather and Organize

The ocean can only be used as a source of fresh water if its salt can be removed. This is done in very dry parts of the world, such as Saudi Arabia and Southern California, but it is costly and it damages the environment. How much energy is required to make one litre of fresh water from salt water? What are some environmental consequences of this process?

Lakes and rivers are critical sources of water for many people in the world. Lakes of significant size only exist in places with an abundance of water. The best examples are in Canada and Russia. Perhaps the most important function of rivers is to redistribute water. Rivers move water from places where there is a surplus (the glaciers in Tibet are an excellent example) to drier regions where it is needed. Rivers also move water to lower areas. In many parts of the world, people have built artificial lakes, also called reservoirs, to store water for later use. Reservoirs are often used to collect water in rainier seasons (or when snow and ice are melting in the spring) so that it will be available during drier parts of the year.

MEASURING THE GLOBAL WATER SUPPLY: THE ARIDITY INDEX

A useful way to look at the water supply is to consider a measure called the **aridity index** (AI). This index is the ratio of the supply of water and the natural demand for water.

- **Supply:** Water is supplied through precipitation (P). Precipitation is any water that falls to Earth, such as water and snow.

- **Natural Demand:** The demand for water in a given natural environment (a demand that has nothing to do with people) is measured using **potential evapotranspiration** (PE or PET). There are two sources of this demand. *Evapo* refers to the evaporation of water from the land surface. *Transpiration* refers to the water given off by plants in the environment. The crucial factor in determining the amount of PE is the temperature. Higher temperatures in a location mean higher PE values.

- The *aridity index* is the ratio of precipitation (P) to potential evapotranspiration (PE). The result of using the formula is an **index value**, which means a number without units.

$$AI = \frac{P}{PE}$$

aridity index a value used to show water availability. It combines measures of supply and natural demand.

potential evapotranspiration the natural demand for water in a particular environment, including evaporation from the land surface and transpiration by plants

index value a value without units, usually calculated in comparison to a common base number

UNDERSTANDING AI VALUES

Global AI values are shown in Figure 6–4. Remember, we are only looking at the natural environment here—which doesn't include the demand for water by humans.

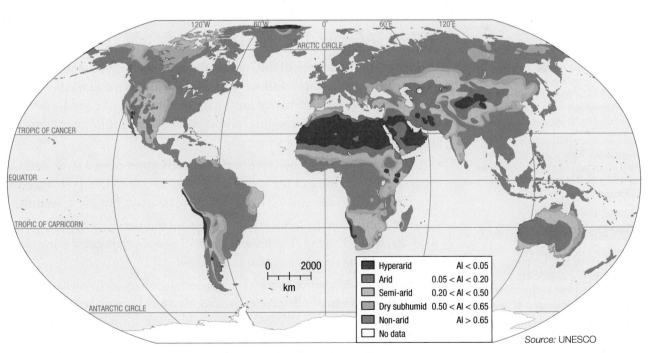

Hyperarid	AI < 0.05
Arid	0.05 < AI < 0.20
Semi-arid	0.20 < AI < 0.50
Dry subhumid	0.50 < AI < 0.65
Non-arid	AI > 0.65
No data	

Source: UNESCO

▲ **Figure 6–4 Global aridity zones.** How does this map show us dry areas? Where do large populations live in relatively dry environments (0.20 < AI < 0.65)?

If the water supply (P) is greater than or roughly equal to the water demand (PE) or if the AI is above 0.65, there is no problem because the supply exceeds or at least is very close to the demand. Serious concerns only start when the AI drops below 0.65, when the demand is significantly greater than the supply. Strangely enough, we do not need to worry very much about the driest environments in the world, which are called the *hyperarid* regions (AI is less than 0.05). These are so dry that few people try to live in them. It is the in-between areas, ranging from *arid* through *semi-arid* to *dry subhumid* (AI values between 0.05 and 0.65) where most concerns lie. Hundreds of millions of people live in these regions and have to deal with uncertain water supplies. To make the problem worse, populations in these regions are growing, and increasing amounts of water are being used per person. A classic example of this is the metropolitan area of Las Vegas in the United States, which has a population of 2 million. In Las Vegas, more than 60 golf courses have been built in the middle of a desert (Figure 6–5).

▲ **Figure 6–5** Does it make sense to locate a major city like Las Vegas (including its many golf courses) where the AI is only slightly above the hyperarid level? What factors have contributed to Las Vegas's growth? To what extent has respect for the environment been an important consideration in this growth?

Global Water Demand

Now we will start looking at the human demand for water. Global water demand is a complex topic, but we will examine the three major uses of water: for agriculture (primarily for the irrigation of crops), for domestic use (such as for drinking, cooking, and cleaning), and for industrial use. Consider a few examples of water use.

- A farmer in Vietnam floods a rice paddy with water from a river. After a period of time, most of the water is released back into the river where it is available for other uses. This water was extracted, but not consumed.

- A soft drink plant in India takes water from the local city supply, purifies it, and puts it into bottles and cans. This water has been extracted and consumed. It is not available for reuse.

- To bring the difference much closer to home, when you brushed your teeth this morning both **extraction** and **consumption** occurred. How?

extraction the process of taking water from a store (e.g., groundwater or a river) to be used. After the use, it is returned to the store, where it is available to be used again.

consumption the process of taking water from a store to be used, but it is not returned to the store after the use (e.g., it evaporates). It cannot be reused.

Geo ✦ Inquiry

Gather and Organize

Many human activities involve the extraction or consumption of water. Give examples of each. What should happen to waste water before it is returned to its source?

©P

Figure 6–6 gives a global overview of the three major uses of water. The blue band in Figure 6–6 shows the difference between the amount of water that is extracted (from a river or a well, for example) and the amount that is consumed.

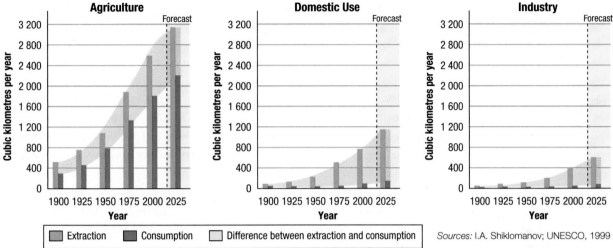

Sources: I.A. Shiklomanov; UNESCO, 1999

▲ **Figure 6–6 Global use of water, 1900–2025.** For a Canadian, why is it surprising that the largest use of water is for agricultural use? What factors are causing all types of water use to increase? Think about the balance between supply and demand. Why must this pattern of water usage eventually become an unsustainable situation?

Regional patterns can be quite different, as these examples tell us:

- **Industrial use is most important:** Canada, Russia, and most of northern Europe
- **Industrial use and agricultural use are equally important:** United States
- **Agricultural use is most important, but industrial use is significant:** China
- **Agricultural use is most important:** India, Australia, much of Africa, and the Middle East

---

APPLY IT!

1. **a)** Define *water store* and *water flow* in your own words.

   b) Make a sketch of the water cycle. Show the stores in one colour and the flows in another.

2. Which use of water has grown most dramatically since 1900?

3. **a)** Explain what the blue band in Figure 6–6 represents. Why is it important?

   b) For each category of use, give a specific example (not any of the examples given in the text) of how water might be extracted and used, but not consumed.

   c) For which category of use is the blue band growing wider fastest? What does this mean? Why is this important?

4. ■ **Patterns and Trends**

   a) Suggest at least two reasons why the pattern of water use varies dramatically from country to country.

   b) Use the factors you noted in part a) to explain why industrial use of water is most important in Canada, even though it is a distant third for the entire world.

Canada's Water Resources

drainage basin the area of land in which all of the water flows (drains) to the same body of water (river, lake, ocean, etc.)

Figure 6–7 shows where Canada's rivers flow in drainage basins. Canada's rivers drain in every direction:

West	→	to the Pacific Ocean
North	→	to the Arctic Ocean, either directly or through Hudson Bay
East	→	to the Atlantic Ocean
South	→	to the Gulf of Mexico, from a very small region of southern Saskatchewan and Alberta

These five giant drainage basins can be further divided into smaller and smaller drainage basins. For example, in Ontario there are 30 secondary drainage basins. These range in size from 4000 to 150 000 square kilometres (km²). These can be divided into 147 tertiary basins that range in size from 700 to 31 000 km².

You can visit some of Canada's most important rivers on **GeoFlight 6.1**.

The unit used for river discharge in Figure 6–7 is cubic metres per second (m³/s). Picture a box that measures 1 metre by 1 metre by 1 metre and is full of water. Mentally multiply this amount of water by the discharge amounts given here. Finally, imagine that amount of water, on average, passing a given spot on the river every second for the entire year.

▼ **Figure 6–7 Major drainage basins in Canada**

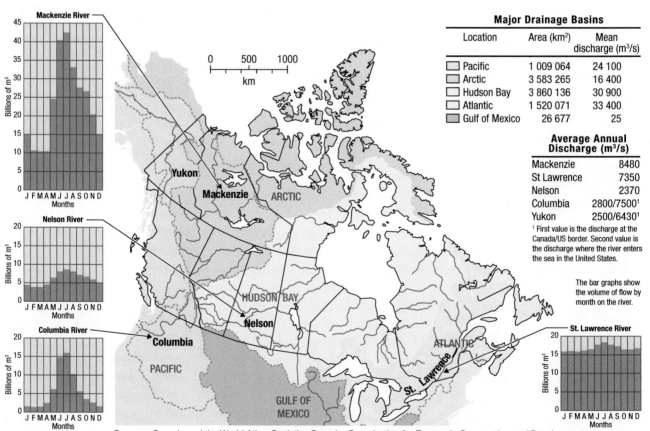

Major Drainage Basins

Location	Area (km²)	Mean discharge (m³/s)
Pacific	1 009 064	24 100
Arctic	3 583 265	16 400
Hudson Bay	3 860 136	30 900
Atlantic	1 520 071	33 400
Gulf of Mexico	26 677	25

Average Annual Discharge (m³/s)

Mackenzie	8480
St Lawrence	7350
Nelson	2370
Columbia	2800/7500[1]
Yukon	2500/6430[1]

[1] First value is the discharge at the Canada/US border. Second value is the discharge where the river enters the sea in the United States.

The bar graphs show the volume of flow by month on the river.

Sources: Canada and the World Atlas; Statistics Canada; Organization for Economic Cooperation and Development

©P

1. Using Figure 6–7, divide Canada's great rivers into three groups according to the direction of their flow. Explain how you decided to group the rivers.

2. Describe two important ways in which the St. Lawrence River is different from the other rivers listed in Figure 6–7. Be sure to consider both climate and human factors.

3. a) You live in more than one drainage basin. How is this possible?

   b) Research to name the drainage basins in which you live.

4. ■ **Geographic Perspective** How does the discharge of your local river (Figure 6–8) compare to the discharges of Canada's great rivers? To find out, follow these steps:

   a) Go online to the Environment Canada site. Enter the name of your river into the "Station Name contains" field. Look carefully to find the correct station. For example, use the latitude and longitude values given.

   b) If there is more than one station on your river, choose the one closest to where you live, or the one nearest the mouth of the river if you would like to see the total discharge of the river.

   c) Experiment with the various options available on the data page.

   d) Go to Google Earth and enter the latitude and longitude of the stream gauge location on "your" river. Zoom in or out as needed. Follow the course of your river from its source to its mouth, noting where you live. Make a labelled sketch map of what you see.

   e) Write a summary of the characteristics of your river, such as discharge and area of the drainage basin, using the information on the website and what you already knew about the river. Add this information to your sketch map.

◄ **Figure 6–8**
The Ganaraska River flows through the historic town of Port Hope, Ontario.

go online

Environment Canada provides data on rivers all across Canada. Find information about the river closest to you.

SKILL FOCUS

The purpose of a sketch map is to communicate significant information in a graphical way.

1. Start by deciding what information you want to show.

2. For a drainage basin map, it makes sense to start at the mouth of the river and then work upstream to show the main stream and important tributaries.

3. Add human features such as towns and major roads.

4. Finally, add any information that you have researched.

5. Be sure that your map includes a title, a compass rose, and a rough scale.

Water Issues for Canada's (and Your) Future

Canada is very well supplied with water, but it would be a serious mistake—which is often made—to take this for granted. Canadians are used to having large quantities of high-quality water readily available at a low cost. There are two main reasons for this.

- Canadians have access to vast amounts of water when compared to most countries in the world (Figure 6–9).

- Canada is a wealthy country and can afford to build and maintain the complex system of water treatment plants, pumps, and pipes needed to ensure that when we turn on the tap, we get what we want and need at a very low price (Table 6–1). In fact, we take our water supply so much for granted that we use carefully treated, drinkable water for every purpose from washing our cars to watering our lawns.

Table 6–1 Prices of popular beverages in Peel region, 2013

Beverage	Cost ($/1000 L)
tap water	1
bottled water	500
milk	1050
soft drink	1406
mineral water	1670

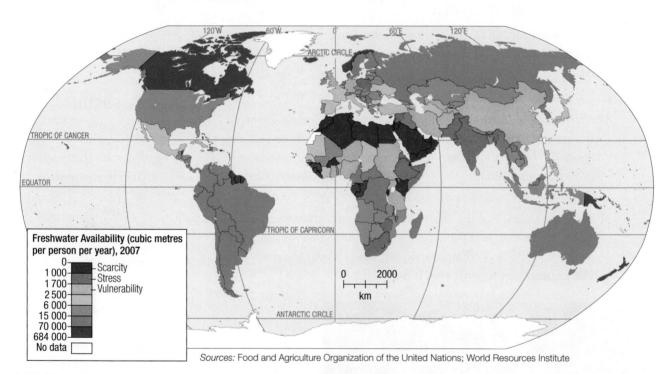

Sources: Food and Agriculture Organization of the United Nations; World Resources Institute

▲ **Figure 6–9 Global freshwater availability.** ■ **Spatial Significance** This map shows the amount of water available after the basic demand from the environment and people is met.

1. a) Look at Figure 6–9. What category of freshwater availability is Canada in?

b) How many cubic metres per person per year does this category represent?

c) Name at least three other countries that are in this category. Refer to a world map if necessary.

d) Identify at least three countries (with populations much greater than Canada's) that face serious water supply concerns. Why might these countries face serious water shortages?

e) In a few sentences, explain the advantages enjoyed by Canada and other countries that are in the highest freshwater availability category.

2. a) With the co-operation of your family or the people you live with, record your household usage of water for one week. Table 6–2 indicates how much water is used for various purposes. Consider what data you will be gathering and how you will measure and record the data. Check your toilet tank size as this can vary. You may have to estimate the number of minutes that showers and taps are turned on.

b) Take the total amount of water used and divide it by the number of people who live in your household to get the per person use. Compare this value to those of your classmates. Why might there be significant differences among households?

c) Calculate the percentage breakdown of your household use in different categories and compare your results to the data in Figure 6–10.

Table 6–2 Average water use for various activities

Activity	Amount of water used
clothes washer	230 L/use
bath	130 L/use
dishwasher	65 L/use
shower	25 L/min
toilet flush	5–20 L/use
water from a faucet	12 L/min

d) What are some of the problems with the data you have collected? How close to the truth is your estimate of the water use in your home?

3. a) Explain the statement, "Wise water use requires a combination of smarter technology and improved thinking."

b) How does this apply to the actions of individuals (and families), companies, and government?

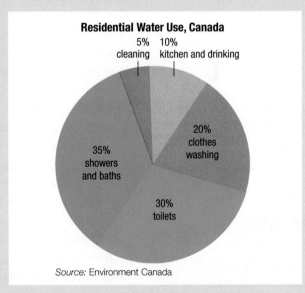

Residential Water Use, Canada

5% cleaning
10% kitchen and drinking
20% clothes washing
35% showers and baths
30% toilets

Source: Environment Canada

▲ **Figure 6–10** How does your water use compare to the water use in an average household in Canada? If you have any taps that drip, add 10 percent to your total.

4. Figure 6–11 compares Canada's use of water for domestic purposes to that of other countries. The standard of living in Canada and the United States is much higher than the standard of living in rural India, but does a higher standard of living necessarily mean that more water is used? Be sure to explain your reasoning.

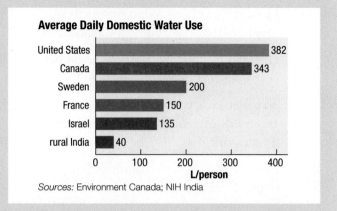

Average Daily Domestic Water Use

	L/person
United States	382
Canada	343
Sweden	200
France	150
Israel	135
rural India	40

Sources: Environment Canada; NIH India

▲ **Figure 6–11** To what extent is water consumption linked to standard of living? It is interesting to note that the cost of domestic water is much higher in Sweden and France than in Canada and the United States.

Water for Sale! Get Your Water!

Many parts of the United States face current or future water shortages, as do countries such as Saudi Arabia. For example, the population of the American southwest, including cities such as Las Vegas, Phoenix, and Los Angeles, is growing rapidly. There are questions about where the water will come from to support this growth, since local supplies are already being used to their limit. Ultimately, a shortage of fresh water will limit this growth.

A potential solution is to bring in surplus water from Canada. Two very different types of **bulk water exports** could happen in the future. At a smaller scale, tanker trucks, railcars, and possibly pipelines could be used to move water to the southwestern United States. This could be done fairly easily, but the amounts that could be shipped would be relatively small and shipping costs would make it expensive.

The other possibility is truly monumental in scale. It involves dramatically changing the drainage patterns of North America to move water from wetter, northern areas to the dry regions of the United States and even Mexico. The *less ambitious* proposal for this is called the Great Recycling and Northern Development (or GRAND) Canal (Figure 6–12 on the next page). It would involve building an immense dam across the mouth of James Bay.

bulk water exports according to NAFTA rules, any water exports in quantities larger than 20 litre containers

Geo ⚙ Inquiry

Communicate

Find out more about the water issues that Canada might face in the future. Compile your notes and share them with the class.

The other continental water diversion dwarfs the GRAND Canal. The North American Water and Power Alliance (NAWAPA) plan would involve diverting about 25 percent of the flows of the Yukon and Mackenzie Rivers (along with some smaller rivers) as far south as Mexico. This would be by far the largest engineering project ever built and would cost untold hundreds of billions of dollars.

Both the GRAND and NAWAPA schemes would result in a massive diversion of water. This would have consequences for the environment and people who live in the area, particularly Aboriginal communities. These schemes were proposed more than 50 years ago. Today, no government agencies or major corporations are seriously considering these schemes, but water shortages in the dry parts of North America are only getting worse.

Large water diversion schemes would be both privately financed and privately controlled. Such private ownership of the supply of water is very controversial worldwide (Figure 6–13). Who owns water resources? Should fresh water resources be sold for profit? Groups such as Idle No More and the Council of Canadians have made water issues like these part of their campaigns.

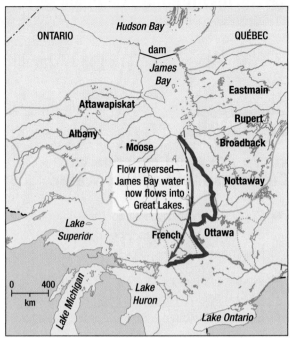

▲ Figure 6–12 Proposed GRAND Canal. The red arrow indicates the flow of the redirected water. From the Great Lakes, water would be redirected to dry areas, mainly in the western United States, but also in Saskatchewan and Alberta.

Geo ✿ Inquiry

Formulate Questions

Think about the issues that might be involved in a water-diversion project like the GRAND Canal or NAWAPA. What questions would it raise?

go online

Visit the Idle No More and the Council of Canadians websites. Find out what these two groups' perspectives are on water issues.

▲ Figure 6–13 Canadian author and activist Maude Barlow has been a leader in the fight to protect the public ownership of water and to advance the right to equal access to clean water.

What Should We Do About Bulk Water Sales?

Viewpoint 1

There are good reasons why Canada should sell its water.

🗩 Canada's economy is all about selling our abundant resources to other countries. Water is just one more resource.

🗩 We are happy to export vast quantities of non-renewable resources such as oil and metals. It makes much more sense to sell a renewable resource.

🗩 The water in many of our rivers flows unused into the ocean and could be considered "wasted." It makes sense to make some money from it.

🗩 Canadian business would make money, taxes would be paid, and people would get good jobs in parts of the country away from large population centres, where many people are unemployed.

🗩 The Americans are our best friends and closest allies in the world. We should help our friends when they need us.

Viewpoint 2

Water is not like other resources—we should not sell it.

🗩 If we start bulk water exports, we could easily lose control of our national water resources.

🗩 The benefits of bulk water exports go to big companies and those who get the water. The costs, however, are borne by Aboriginal peoples and other people who live in the areas from where the water is taken.

🗩 Climate change means that water will become a scarce, highly valuable resource in the future. We might even need it ourselves.

🗩 Other parts of the world need our water more than the United States. If we are going to sell or share it, it should go to places like the Middle East and North Africa, which are much drier than the United States.

🗩 The Americans already have large quantities of water, but they do not use their water wisely. We should be promoting and practising sustainable use of water, not selling it.

APPLY IT!

1. What argument(s) could you add to each side of this discussion?

2. Look at the arguments supporting each viewpoint. Critique each argument, even if you agree with it.

3. How might First Nations, Métis, and Inuit peoples view mass water transfers?

4. **OSSLT** Should we export water in bulk to the United States or other countries? If so, what conditions should be imposed on the sales? If not, why not?

When Water Supply Systems Fail

So far, we have considered only the quantity of water in the global water supply. We must also consider the quality of the water. We use water in our daily lives and in agriculture and industry. Before the water can be consumed, it must be treated to ensure it is safe. Similarly, waste water must be treated to ensure it is safe to return to the environment. Unfortunately, at times, the systems that provide good quantities of safe water break down and Canadians suffer as a result. At best, this becomes a major inconvenience—people are told they have to boil their tap water or use bottled water. At worst, people die.

This happened in Walkerton, Ontario (Figure 6–14), in 2000, when 7 people died and 2300 people became ill as a result of drinking town water that was infected by a dangerous type of bacterium. The bacteria came from cattle manure that had leached down from the surface into the water table. This happened because those in charge of the town's water treatment plant failed to ensure proper chlorination. A similar problem, fortunately without any deaths, happened in North Battleford, Saskatchewan, in 2001.

▲ **Figure 6–14** Each of these communities has suffered greatly as a result of contaminated water.

ABORIGINAL PEOPLES AND WATER

On many First Nations reserves, availability of safe drinkable water is a problem. In 2014, Health Canada had 127 drinking water advisories in place that affected several thousand people in 86 First Nations communities. The majority of these were in Ontario. Most of these were "boil water" advisories. This means that the local drinking water must be boiled for at least one minute to kill dangerous microorganisms. In some cases, boiling the contaminated water does not make it safe. In these cases, there is a more serious "do not consume" advisory in place. What could you use this water for?

Most drinking water advisories stay in place for years. The Neskantaga First Nation (Figure 6–14) in Northwestern Ontario has had a boil water advisory in effect since 1995. As Chief Moonias said in 2004, "I wonder how different the response would be if the residents of Toronto were without access to water?"

In Attawapiskat First Nation (Figure 6–14), the main source of water is a lake that is murky and contains a large amount of organic matter. The water treatment plant is not able to bring the water to the required standard for humans to drink. Because of this, much of the community must rely on bottled water for drinking. In addition, the community's sewage system does not work properly, meaning that people could be exposed to the kinds of dangerous microorganisms that caused the problems in Walkerton and North Battleford. Several families in Attawapiskat have no access to running water at all. Do you think that governments take water quality issues on First Nations reserves as seriously as those that happen in places like Walkerton and North Battleford? Why or why not?

go online

Unfortunately, the situation in Attawapiskat is a common occurrence for many Aboriginal communities. Research to find out more about the issue and what can be done.

You can use **ArcGIS Online** to explore water issues, including those related to Aboriginal Treaties and land claims.

What About Climate Change and Canada's Water?

In this chapter, we have been looking at the current water situation. But what will the future bring? The world is slowly warming and higher temperatures will have serious implications for water supply in Canada and elsewhere in the world.

The various reports from the International Panel on Climate Change (IPCC) suggest that climate change will mean that dry places will become drier while wet places will become wetter. Since Canada has many more wet places than dry places, we should not suffer as much from droughts as much of the rest of the world will, particularly in the semi-arid to dry subhumid areas. However, the Prairies are the obvious exception to this pattern. There is a very good chance that the Prairies will experience less rainfall in the future. This presents a serious problem to the important grain, oilseed, and cattle ranching farms there (Figure 6–15). Climate change could also increase the number and severity of floods in most of Canada.

In some ways, climate change presents some opportunities for Canada (along with many problems). In a world that will be drier, we will be wetter. This could mean an expansion of agricultural and industrial opportunities, along with the possibility of selling our excess water to other countries.

▼ **Figure 6–15** We often focus on temperature when we think about climate change, but changes in water distribution may be more of a problem. Dry areas, like southern Alberta (a), will become drier, while floods like the one shown (b), also in Alberta, will become more common.

(a)

(b)

APPLY IT!

1. Do you expect to see water diversion schemes like the GRAND Canal or NAWAPA built in your lifetime? Why or why not?

2. **a)** What is the quality of your local tap or well water? Do you treat this water after it comes out of the tap (such as filtering it or using a water softener)? Why?

   b) Do you frequently drink bottled water? Does this fulfill a need or a want? Explain.

   c) In what ways is drinking bottled water not environmentally desirable?

   d) What is your best option if your tap water is of poor quality?

3. **a)** Some people have said that, in many ways, Canada will benefit from climate change. How might this apply to how Canada's water resources are managed?

   b) Does this mean we should not worry about climate change? Why or why not?

©P

Fresh Water—Canada's Special Resource?

? **Is fresh water our most important resource?**

A visitor from Australia (most of which is very dry), who was flying over the Canadian Shield in a small plane, said, "I didn't think there was this much fresh water in the whole world." Canada is very fortunate when it comes to fresh water, but not all Canadians are equally blessed. Farmers who see their crops shrivel up in a drought are not helped by the immense amount of water in lakes a few hundred kilometres to the north. Similarly, for those who live in urban areas and cannot go for a swim at their local beach because of pollution, or for First Nations people who live with boil water advisories, it is not much consolation that other people can drink the water from lakes not too far away.

1. Why is it important that we consider both water quantity and water quality?

2. The parts of Canada that have the greatest amounts of water (the Mackenzie River drainage basin, for example) are far from population centres. What, if anything, can be done about this disconnect between people and water?

3. This chapter's Big Question contains the small, but extremely important, word *our*. When we talk about the importance of water, *our* can be analyzed on a number of scales—from local to global. Create a concept web to summarize future water resource issues starting with the idea, "Our Water."

Geo Inquiry

Interpret and Analyze

4. Before you can properly answer the Big Question, define what is meant by *most important resource*.

Evaluate and Draw Conclusions

5. a) **OSSLT** In what ways is water our most important resource?

   b) What could cause its importance to diminish?

   c) In what ways is water not our most important resource?

   d) How could its importance increase?

6. Do Canadians act as if water is an important resource? What are five things we should be doing to protect our water resource?

Analyze an Issue

7. Think about issues related to fresh water that you have read about or that affect your every-day life. Pick one of these issues.

   a) Write a number of questions about the issue. Narrow your questions down to one clearly stated and important big question.

   b) What areas would you have to research to answer your big question? Find three or four resources and collect information to answer your question. Be sure to analyze the information and consider various viewpoints.

   c) Use your notes to take a position and answer your question. Support your answer with facts from your research.

   d) Create a product that communicates the answer to your question. This could be an opinion paper, a blog post, a poster, or a letter to the editor. Be creative!

   e) If you had to complete another inquiry like this one, what would you do differently?

Managing Non-Renewable Resources Successfully

KEY TERMS

R/P ratio
reserves
production
oil sands/tar sands
fracking
metallic mineral
non-metallic mineral
ore
mineral reserve

 What is the most effective way to manage Canada's non-renewable resources?

Important ... But Always Controversial?

The photo on the left below shows Shell Canada's Jackpine oil sands operation in northern Alberta. The oil sands are of crucial importance to Canada's economy. In spite of this, many people are opposed to the continuing growth of the oil sands industry. Looking at the photo, it is easy to see why. Large areas of the boreal forest end up looking like the land in the photo before reclamation is complete. It is not the sort of place you would want to live near unless you were one of the people who got a very good job working there.

Now look at photo on the right. It shows a wind farm on the Bruce Peninsula in Southern Ontario. To most people who live in cities, it is an image of what our energy future should be like: clean, with minimal carbon dioxide emissions. Ontario has almost 2000 wind turbines, most located in rural areas. Many people who live in the rural areas where wind turbines are usually built, however, oppose their construction. Their concerns include the potential impact on health, visual pollution, loss of property values, and the number of birds being killed.

THINKING CRITICALLY

At first, these two energy projects appear to be very different, but both have proven to be highly controversial. Why are energy developments both important and controversial? Do people just have to accept that there are costs to enjoying the benefits of modern life? To what extent is NIMBY (Not In My Back Yard) at work in these situations?

©P

A Quick Overview of Non-Renewable Resources

In Chapter 5, we looked at how hard it is to manage renewable resources. In many ways, however, it is even harder to manage non-renewable resources. Non-renewable resources include fossil fuel resources and mineral resources. When these run out, they are gone, so it is critical that they not be wasted.

A good starting point in managing any resource is knowing how much of it we actually have. We could talk about billions of cubic metres of natural gas and millions of tonnes of iron ore, but, to non-experts, these numbers are almost meaningless. It is much more understandable to use the R/P ratio, which is the ratio between the reserves of a resource and its production. The R/P ratio changes when either the reserves or the production changes.

- R stands for reserves, or how much of the resource is available in the ground (Figure 7–1).

- P stands for production, or how much of the resource is being taken from the ground each year.

- If the reserves of a particular mineral are 1 000 000 tonnes and the production is 100 000 tonnes per year, the R/P ratio is 1 000 000 ÷ 100 000 = 10. All of this mineral will be gone in 10 years if there are no changes in the reserves and/or production.

- The R/P ratio is constantly changing up or down. In spite of this, the ratio is an easy way to understand how we are doing with a resource. Obviously, an R/P ratio of 200 (meaning a 200-year supply) is much better than an R/P ratio of 50.

R/P ratio the number of years that the reserves of a non-renewable resource will last at current rates of production

reserves how much of a resource is thought to be in the ground, based on exploration to date

production how much of a resource is being taken from the ground each year

▲ **Figure 7–1** Exploration for energy and mineral resources is constantly underway in Canada and around the world. It combines high-tech and traditional methods. (a) Geographic Information System or GIS is used to organize, interpret, and present vast amounts of data. This image shows the location of a potential copper mine. It relates three important sets of data: the topography of the land, the drill results (coloured dots), and the strength of the magnetic fields (since rocks that contain significant amounts of iron, copper, nickel, and similar metals are more magnetic than other rocks). (b) While much data can be collected using helicopters and satellites, at some point geologists have to put "boots on the ground" to collect samples of rock to see if a find is rich enough to justify development, which could cost many millions or even billions of dollars.

Do We Need to Save Resources for the Future?

Because we are dealing with a finite amount of non-renewable resources, there is an obvious question that must be asked: Should we be reducing our use of these resources so that they will be available for future generations?

Viewpoint 1

It is selfish and short-sighted not to think about the needs of future generations.

🗩 The R/P ratios of some vital minerals are remarkably low (Figure 7–2). Ratios for crude oil and natural gas are in the 50 range (we have a 50-year supply). Also, we know that the P part of the R/P ratio is constantly going up, driven by a growing world population, increasing global wealth, and the rapid expansion of overseas manufacturing. This means that the R part has to increase as well, or we will run out of minerals and fossil fuels even sooner. How much faith should we have in the ability of large companies to find new reserves and technological breakthroughs to keep providing resources?

🗩 If we use up non-renewable resources today, future generations will not enjoy the same opportunities we have had.

🗩 We could all do a better job of using resources in a sustainable way. We can reduce waste significantly and not unduly hurt our lifestyle and economy. We can also be much more careful to recycle metals and plastics, which reduces our use of "new" resources from the ground.

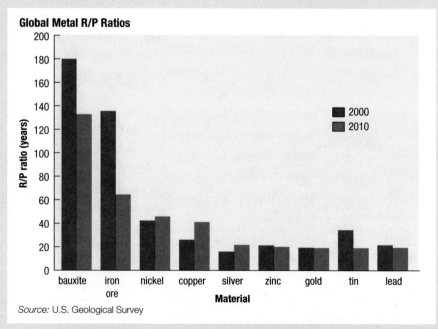

Global Metal R/P Ratios

▶ **Figure 7–2** How would our life be different if we ran out of these materials? Note: Bauxite is the mineral used to make aluminum.

Source: U.S. Geological Survey

Viewpoint 2

Future generations will be able to look after their own needs without our help.

- Much of our economy is based on producing and exporting minerals and fossil fuels. It makes little sense for us to significantly reduce our quality of life today because future generations *might* need these things. We must be sure not to go overboard with too many unnecessary environmental restrictions, because Canadian producers often have to compete with companies that operate in countries with very low labour costs and few environmental restrictions.

- Many of the world's mineral and fossil fuels deposits have either not been found yet or will become less expensive to recover in the future as technology improves.

- Other than oil, we make little use of the wide range of resources, including metallic and non-metallic minerals, that lie under the oceans.

- We should not think too far ahead because technology is always changing. How advanced would we be today if our ancestors 500 years ago had worried about using up too much flint? Remember that the first oil wells were drilled less than 200 years ago.

APPLY IT!

1. **a)** What does an R/P ratio of 60 mean?

   b) Describe two ways in which the R/P ratio can go up.

   c) Describe two ways in which it can go down.

   d) Why do you think the idea of R/P ratios is not well known by the general public?

2. Why does it not make sense to apply the idea of R/P ratios to renewable resources?

3. What factors should we consider when we try to balance the need to provide jobs, grow our economy, and increase exports with the need to protect our resources for future use?

4. How might governments, companies, and advocacy groups influence future development of non-renewable resources?

5. ■ **Interrelationships** Environmentalists argue that we are finding new reserves of oil, gas, and minerals, but at considerable costs. What two very different types of costs are they talking about?

THINKING CRITICALLY

6. **OSSLT** Which argument in each viewpoint do you think is the strongest? Why?

7. Which argument in each viewpoint do you think is the weakest? Why?

8. Most of the arguments presented here are economic. What environmental or other arguments could you add? Which viewpoint would each support?

9. What is your opinion about which viewpoint makes the most sense? Why?

A Closer Look at Fossil Fuels

The first major category of non-renewable resources is fossil fuels. In Canada, the two most important of these, by far, are oil and natural gas. On a global basis, coal is of great importance. About 29 percent of the world's energy comes from coal. Not very much coal is used in Canada, although Canada does export a considerable amount of coal to Asia. All of Canada's coal mines are in British Columbia, Alberta, and Saskatchewan.

You might have wondered what fossils have to do with oil, natural gas, and coal. All of these fuels were formed from the remains of plants and animals that lived more than 100 million years ago. After they died, sediments that gradually became layers of sedimentary rock covered them. Meanwhile, the plant and animal remains decomposed and were converted into the fuels we know (Figure 7–3). In general, animal remains in the sea became oil and natural gas, while plant remains became coal. In fact, it is possible to find pieces of coal that have fossilized leaves in them (Figure 7–4).

Geo ⚙ Inquiry

Interpret and Analyze

Research the location and landform regions surrounding the Alberta oil sands. How are they connected to the presence of oil?

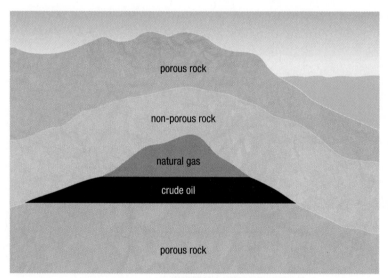

▲ **Figure 7–3** The remains of animals decomposed within layers of sedimentary rock to form natural gas and oil. Because both natural gas and oil have very low densities (natural gas is a gas, after all), they tend to migrate upward through the pores that exist in some rocks. Sometimes they are caught in a geologic trap by a higher layer of rock that has been bent. What would happen to the oil and gas if there were no trap above?

(labels in Figure 7–3: porous rock, non-porous rock, natural gas, crude oil, porous rock)

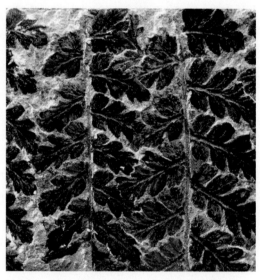

▲ **Figure 7–4** This piece of coal contains a fossil of a giant tree that lived 300 million years ago. These trees were a major source of what became coal.

oil sands/tar sands deposits of sand containing a heavy form of crude oil called bitumen

You have probably heard quite often about an enormously important and controversial resource called oil sands, or tar sands. Canada has a large deposit of oil sands in Athabasca, Alberta. In fact, the name that people use to describe this resource tends to reveal how they feel about its development. People who support its development typically use the name *oil sands*, whereas those who oppose its development use the name *tar sands*. Why have these two different usages become so common?

Canada's Energy Use Today

Depending on which statistics one looks at, Canadians use the most or the second-most energy in the world per capita, or are at least in the top 10. While there are some good reasons why we are such heavy energy users, a strong case can be made that we do not use fossil fuels for energy production as carefully as we should. We cannot recycle or reuse energy, so you know which of the 3Rs to keep in mind as you read this chapter.

Energy in Canada is used in four sectors: industrial, transportation, residential, and commercial/institutional. The transportation sector includes two distinct parts: the movement of people (largely cars, buses, and airplanes) and the movement of freight (trucks, trains, and airplanes). The residential sector includes households. The commercial and institutional sector includes things like shopping malls, office buildings, schools, government buildings, and hospitals.

The two graphs in Figure 7–5 indicate current demand and expected growth in demand until 2035. Projections for the future, such as this one, are based on assumptions about other factors. Change the assumptions and you get different projections. The projection can be made by thinking critically about the three assumptions below:

- How quickly the population will grow (more people = more energy demand): Statistics Canada assumed that the population would grow at a rate of 0.6 percent to 0.5 percent per year, gradually going down over time.

- The rate of economic growth (almost all economic growth requires the use of more energy): The assumption for economic growth was a 2.0 percent increase per year.

- No significant re-thinking (our fourth "R") of how we use energy occurs: Another way of saying this is that current behaviour continues.

If we, as a society, decide to dramatically reduce our energy use, then these projections will change. How might this happen?

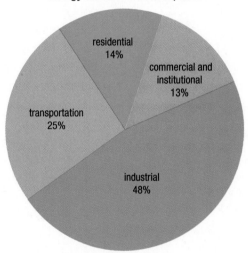

Energy Demand in Canada, 2012

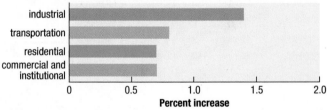

Projected Annual Increase in Energy Demand in Canada, 2012–2035

Source: National Energy Board

▲ **Figure 7–5** Overall, demand for energy is expected to grow by 1.1% per year until 2035. This is down from an annual increase of 1.4% between 1990 and 2008. The price of energy affects demand. If energy prices are 30% higher than expected, demand will increase at only 0.8% per year. On the other hand, if prices are 30% lower than expected, demand will increase by 1.2% per year. Note that the difference between these percentages may appear small, but it is actually quite significant. Energy use for freight movement is expected to increase 2.0% per year, while energy use for moving people will decrease by 0.6% per year.

Should Environmentalists Be Fans of Fracking?

fracking a variety of techniques used to break up shale layers far below the surface in order to liberate natural gas and/or oil that has been trapped. Injecting a mixture of water, sand, and dozens of chemicals into a well usually breaks up the rock.

Hydraulic fracturing, or **fracking** for short, is a new and important contributor to expanding our energy supply. But could fracking help reduce the rate and amount of climate change?

For decades, petroleum geologists knew that vast quantities of natural gas (and sometimes oil) were tightly bound up in certain types of shale and could not be recovered by conventional wells. Fracking is the solution to this problem. You can see how fracking works in Figure 7–6.

The impact of fracking could be enormous. There is the very real possibility that the United States, where fracking was invented and where it is most commonly used, may no longer have to import oil and natural gas. It could also dramatically increase the amount of natural gas produced in southwestern Ontario and in the interior plains of western Canada from the U.S. border to the Arctic Ocean. Also, as of 2013, U.S. greenhouse gas emissions had fallen for six years in a row, by a total of 12 percent, with fracking getting much of the credit for this reduction. The reason for the reduction is that natural gas is a more efficient fuel than coal. Less carbon is emitted when natural gas is burned to produce the same amount of electricity.

go online

You probably know quite a bit about the causes and effects of climate change, but you can review the topic.

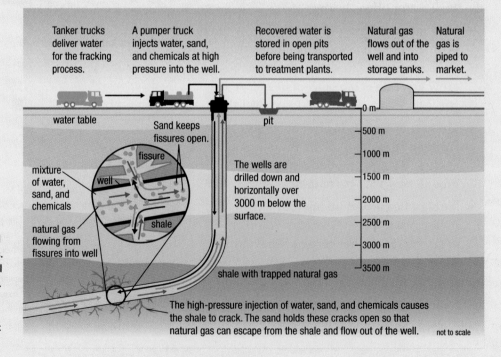

▶ **Figure 7–6** Hydraulic fracturing has been used to increase the yield of conventional oil and gas wells for over 60 years. It was first used to release natural gas trapped in shale layers in 1999. This use is now spreading world-wide very rapidly. What information in this graphic is helpful? What else could have been included?

What does fracking have to do with climate change?

- Fracking is dramatically reducing the cost of natural gas in the world.

- Cheaper natural gas also means it makes more sense to generate electricity with gas than with coal, which used to be less expensive. Burning coal to produce electricity is dirty, and it releases considerably more carbon dioxide into the atmosphere than does burning gas to produce the same amount of power. The move to gas-fired power stations in the United States is helping reduce the country's carbon emissions. The move to gas plants in the U.S. will be greatly accelerated by a 2014 decision that will require generating stations to produce 30 percent lower carbon emissions from 2005 levels by 2030.

- China is the world's largest emitter of greenhouse gases. However, it is trying to reduce its use of coal. In 2014, China signed a 30-year, $400 billion deal with Russia to buy natural gas, much of which will be produced in Russia using fracking. As well, China has more frackable shale formations than the U.S., so you can imagine what will happen there in the future.

Despite the positive impact that fracking can have on reducing greenhouse gas emissions and climate change, environmentalists still have significant concerns about it. These range from contamination of groundwater to air pollution and the destruction of productive farmland (Figure 7–7).

Other groups have concerns, too. For example, in 2013 in New Brunswick, violent protests broke out when the RCMP tried to remove members of the Elsipogtog First Nation who were blocking attempts by an exploration company to find shale gas reserves in the First Nation's traditional territory. The members were concerned about pollution of their water supply and recognition of their treaty rights.

There is one other fundamental point to consider. As long as oil and gas companies keep finding new, relatively cheap sources of fossil fuels, the less urgent it is to reduce energy use or develop greener energy sources.

▲ **Figure 7–7** This photo shows what a heavily fracked area looks like. Each light patch contains a gas well. The web of roads is needed to bring water and chemicals to the wells, each of which may be fracked more than a dozen times.

go online

You can learn more about the environmental risks associated with fracking.

Geo Inquiry

Evaluate and Draw Conclusions

Protests against fracking have been vigorous and, on occasion, violent. Why do people feel so strongly about fracking near their communities?

APPLY IT!

1. What is fracking? Why has it become so common in recent years?

2. ■ **Interrelationships** Why is it difficult to decide whether fracking is a good thing or not? Consider both the environmental concerns and economics.

So What About Renewable Energy?

Windmills and large solar panel arrays are becoming common sights across Canada. This prompts the question, How important can renewable resources become in meeting our energy needs? That is a very complex and difficult question to answer since there are so many factors to consider. Let's look only at electricity in Ontario.

Electricity usage is calculated using two measures: the number of watts that a device uses (usually marked somewhere on the device) and how many hours (per day, week, or year) the device is on. For example, a typical compact fluorescent light bulb might use 25 watts (W) of power. If the light is on for 40 hours, it would use 1000 watt hours (Wh), or 1 kilowatt hour (kWh). A typical computer and monitor might use about 400 kWh per year.

go online

Research to find a sample electricity bill.

Cost of Electricity

Next, we need to look at the cost of electricity. This can mean two different things.

- For consumers, it means how much they have to pay each month. Most people in Ontario have a variable pricing scheme that depends on when they use the electricity (Table 7–1). An average home uses about 800 kWh per month.

- For the government agencies that generate electricity, the meaning is different. Their cost of electricity depends on the method of generation. Between 2009 and 2012, electricity from nuclear plants cost 5.8 cents per kilowatt hour (¢/kWh). Electricity from burning natural gas cost 8.6 ¢/kWh. Hydroelectricity cost 8.1 ¢/kWh. **Bioenergy** cost 8.4 ¢/kWh. The cost for wind and solar power depends on the scale of the project, with small projects (e.g., home solar panels) costing much more. Between 2009 and 2012, wind power cost between 9.5 and 13.5 ¢/kWh. Solar power varied from 42.0 ¢/kWh to as much as 80.2 ¢/kWh.

bioenergy electricity generated from burning *biomass* (wood products, plant products, or even garbage) or *biogas* (gas produced in landfills and sewage treatment plants)

Table 7–1   Cost of electricity in Ontario, Summer 2014

Summer, 2014 (¢/kWh)	
on peak	13.5
mid peak	11.2
off peak	7.5

Source: Ontario Energy Board

▲ In summer, "on peak" is between 11 a.m. and 5 p.m. In winter, it is from 7 a.m. to 11 a.m. and from 5 p.m. to 7 p.m. Why the difference? Note that this is only the cost of the electricity itself. It does not include other charges, such as the cost of delivering the electricity to your home.

Other Considerations

Cost is obviously an important part of the electricity puzzle, but it is only one piece. Reliability of supply is another (Table 7–2). A generating method must be available when the peak demand occurs. The output values in Table 7–2 are the percentage of the time that the generating method is available to meet peak power demands.

There are many environmental concerns as well. A critical one is the amount of carbon emissions that are produced. The CO_2 emissions values in Table 7–2 are "lifecycle" carbon emission numbers. They reflect daily operations along with the emissions from construction, upkeep, and eventual demolition of the

©P

generating facility. There are very low emissions from the operations of nuclear, hydro, solar, and wind generators. Solar and wind emissions are likely lower now as mass production of windmills and panels has increased. Other environmental concerns such as impact on the landscape, while still important, cannot be measured in numerical terms.

go online

Check out how Ontario's electricity is being produced right now.

Table 7–2 Comparison of output and CO_2 emissions of different electricity sources

Energy type	Output during times of peak demand (% of total capacity)	CO_2 emissions (g/kWh), 2011
Non-renewable		
nuclear	95–100	16
coal	90–100	1001
natural gas	50–100	469
Renewable		
hydroelectric	71	4
bioenergy	65–100	18
solar	40	46
wind	11	12

◀ Coal is included here for the sake of comparison. All coal plants in Ontario have been closed or converted to use biomass.

Note: g/kWh means grams per kilowatt hour

Sources: Ontario Power Authority; Independent Electricity System Operator; Intergovernmental Panel on Climate Change, 2011

APPLY IT!

1. We have focused primarily on the cost of electricity from the perspectives of producers and consumers of electricity. This is not the only factor to consider. Research each method of electricity generation to determine other advantages and disadvantages. Create a summary of the benefits and shortcomings of each method.

2. a) List the renewable energy sources used in Ontario.

   b) Based on what you have learned, what role can and should each source play in meeting our electricity demands?

3. a) We have not mentioned a very important consideration: energy conservation. The combined efforts of individuals, companies, and the government mean that electricity can be conserved in several different ways. Describe three of these ways and comment on the effectiveness of each. Hint: Consider initiatives and technologies such as Energy Star, peakSaver Plus, and LED lights.

   b) Why might conservation be the best approach of all?

SKILL FOCUS

In Figure 7–5, you are reading two different types of graphs. Recall

- A pie graph shows values that are part of a whole.

- Each bar in a bar graph and each slice in a pie graph represents a value.

- Examine the titles, data, captions, and labels.

How do you decide which type of graph works best for your data?

CONNECTING

You can learn much more about Canada's manufacturing industry in **Chapter 8**.

APPLY IT!

1. Look at Figure 7–5 on page 147.

   a) How does the price of energy affect demand?

   b) Why do you think high energy prices have a bigger impact on energy demand (a 27 percent decrease in demand) than low energy prices (a 9 percent increase)?

2. How could the government use the relationship in question 1 to reduce energy use? How popular would this be with the public? What effect would it have on industry?

3. Why is there expected to be a decline in energy use for the transportation of people in the next few decades?

4. a) In which sector of the economy is there expected to be the greatest increase in energy demand?

   b) Since Canada's manufacturing industry is getting smaller, where is the large industrial increase in energy use occurring?

5. a) Other than price, what two assumptions were used to make the projections in question 4? Use numbers to support your answer.

   b) Which of these assumptions would be most important when projecting the energy demand growth of each of these parts of the economy?
      i) industry
      ii) transportation (people)
      iii) transportation (freight)
      iv) residential
      v) commercial and institutional

6. a) Canadians use a lot of energy per capita. Outline three reasons for this.

   b) Consider each reason individually. Suggest one or more specific thing(s) we could do to cut our energy use. After you have done this, consult with classmates to expand your list.

   c) In which sector of the economy can an individual Canadian have the most impact in reducing energy use?

Energy Issues

Considering how important energy is in our society, it is not surprising that there are many significant energy issues facing Canadians. Indeed, there is not enough time for you to study all of them. Instead, you will investigate one in detail. Choose a topic and pose a particularly important question about it. You will then conduct research to answer your question.

Choose one of these topics to investigate:

- Oil sands, today and in the future
- The role of pipelines in the oil and gas industry
- Designing and building energy-smart buildings
- The move to more environmentally friendly cars and trucks
- The role of wind power and solar power in Ontario
- The role of nuclear power in Ontario
- Rebuilding Ontario's electricity infrastructure
- The future of fracking in Canada
- The role of bioenergy
- The impact of the growth of Canadian oil production both within Canada and internationally
- An overview of different ways of transporting oil and natural gas and their advantages and disadvantages (Figure 7–8)
- The question of foreign ownership of Canadian resource industries

CONNECTING

This would be an excellent time to review the steps in doing an inquiry analysis. See **pages 7–8**.

▲ **Figure 7–8** In 2013, a horrific rail disaster in Lac-Mégantic, Québec, dramatically brought the issue of how oil is transported to the public's attention. A train with 72 tank cars, each carrying 113 000 litres of crude oil from Wyoming to Saint John, New Brunswick, was left unattended uphill from the town. When the brakes on the train failed, it rolled downhill into the town before derailing, exploding, and burning. Much of the downtown was destroyed and 47 people were killed.

APPLY IT!

Your analysis should look at physical geography, the roles of government and industry, and the impact of trade agreements and advocacy groups as they apply to your topic.

When your analysis is complete, you will present your findings in the format of your choice. Your analysis should not just talk about the topic—it should focus on answering your question. Your presentation should include useful maps, graphs, photos, and graphic organizers. Other students may be sharing your topic. Collaborating on the research is a good idea, but each person should research a different question.

A Closer Look at Mining

The second major category of non-renewable resources is minerals. While fossil fuels and mineral resources are both non-renewable and come from the ground, there are some significant differences between them. Fossil fuels are consumed when they are used, whereas mineral resource products can generally be recycled—think of what happens to pop cans or old cars. Also, we do not actually see the energy produced from fossil fuels. Instead, we see the infrastructure used to bring the energy to us, such as power lines and gas stations. With mineral resources, we actually see and touch the products.

Canada is one of the world's leading mining nations (Figure 7–9). We rank second (after Australia) in exports of metallic and non-metallic minerals (not including fossil fuels). The federal and provincial governments are heavily involved in supporting the mining industry in a number of ways. These include offering tax incentives and subsidies to support new developments and building supporting infrastructure such as roads, railways, and port facilities.

CONNECTING

Review the rock cycle in Figure 2–12 in **Chapter 2 (pages 40–42)**.

▶ **Figure 7–9** Fertilizer plays a key role in feeding billions of people because it allows more food to be produced on less land. The key components of fertilizer are nitrogen (N), phosphorous (P), and potassium (K). The potassium in fertilizer comes from potash. Southern Saskatchewan is the world's most important exporter of potash. It is mined approximately 1000 metres below the surface by these giant, rotating cutters. Canada produces about 10 million tonnes of potash a year. Reserves are estimated to be about 100 billion tonnes. Can you work out the R/P ratio?

metallic mineral a mineral that yields a metal (e.g., iron, gold, copper, uranium, zinc, silver, lead) when melted. It typically comes from igneous and metamorphic rocks.

non-metallic mineral a mineral that does not change its form when melted (e.g., potash, sand, gravel, diamonds, salt, limestone, building stone). It most commonly comes from sedimentary rocks.

ore a rock that contains enough of a valuable metallic mineral to make mining profitable

Kinds of Minerals

A mineral is a naturally occurring, inorganic (meaning it does not come from a plant or animal or living material) substance or solid that has a particular chemical formula. Minerals can be divided into two categories: metallic minerals and non-metallic minerals (also called industrial minerals).

Minerals are often found in rocks. Rocks that contain a significant amount of mineral are called ore. The ore must be processed to separate the waste rock from the valuable minerals.

Finding Valuable Minerals

Imagine you are somewhere in the Canadian Shield and find an interesting rock (Figure 7–10). A geologist tells you that it contains nickel, copper, silver, and even gold. Are you about to get rich? Perhaps not. It is quite easy to find valuable minerals. The trick, of course, is to find a high enough concentration of minerals to make mining and processing worthwhile.

Mineral deposits rich enough to justify mining are known as **mineral reserves**, and they are then counted in the R/P ratio. New reserves must be found at least as quickly as the old ones are used up. If not, the R/P ratio goes down.

How Minerals Are Mined

After mineral reserves have been found and it is time to start mining them, the mining company has to choose one of three mining methods (Figure 7–11 on the next two pages). Mining methods are selected according to the depth and the shape of the deposit. The company must also consider factors such as environmental protection and worker safety.

- Strip mining is cheapest but can only be used for mineral deposits located very close to the surface. Strip mining is used to extract minerals such as sand, gravel, some coal deposits, and oil sands. It has the most severe environmental impact since very large areas of the surface must be disturbed.

- Open-pit mining is more expensive than strip mining. It is used for minerals relatively close to the surface but deeper than can be accessed by strip mining. Examples of minerals mined by open-pit mining are some diamond deposits, oil sands, and iron ore deposits.

- Underground mining is the most expensive mining method. It is used to extract potash and valuable ores, such as gold, nickel, and copper, that may be more than 1000 metres below Earth's surface. In extreme cases, underground mines can be 3000 metres deep.

Regardless of how carefully it is done, mining is disruptive. Natural environments and river systems are impacted. Aboriginal peoples in Canada are often disproportionately affected by resource development. Sometimes the resources are found in lands covered by treaties and sometimes not. Even when treaties exist, differing interpretations about what they mean can cause controversy about resource development and who benefits. Aboriginal peoples maintain they should have a say in how resources are developed and that they should benefit economically from any development. The complicated task is to ensure that the benefits of the mining clearly exceed the economic, environmental, and social impacts that can occur.

▲ **Figure 7–10** Is this something valuable or just a rock? That is the question faced by those looking for valuable minerals of all types. In this case, it is a valuable mineral called magnetite. Think about the name. Why is magnetite valuable? It is not enough to know that a useful mineral is present somewhere. What other question must be answered before mining can go ahead?

mineral reserve a mineral deposit that can be mined profitably

Use **ArcGIS Online** to create a map showing the locations of non-renewable resources in Canada.

STRIP MINING
is used to mine coal, oil sands, and other minerals that are located in horizontal layers near the surface.

1. Overburden (trees, earth, rock) is removed.

2. Blasting may be necessary to remove some mineral deposits.

3. Material is loaded onto trucks or conveyor belts by shovel or dragline. A dragline is a large bucket that is dragged to pick up loose material.

OPEN PIT MINING
is used to mine minerals that are found near the surface but may also extend deep into the ground.

1. Overburden is removed.

2. Holes are drilled 10 to 15 metres deep and filled with explosives. The rock is blasted apart.

3. Ore is loaded into large trucks (which may carry 90 to 250 tonnes) by huge shovels.

▲ **Figure 7–11** (a) Massive machines are used to minimize the cost of strip mining. (b) An open-pit mine is most effective if the ore body being mined is fairly wide. If it is narrow, too much waste rock must be moved to allow access to the valuable ore farther below the surface. (c) If an ore deposit is deep below the surface, there is no choice but to use underground mining. Working deep underground tends to be hard and tiring. It can also be quite dangerous, especially in coal mines. Generally, vast amounts of waste rock must be removed to get to the valuable ore. In a typical gold mine, there might be only 8 grams of gold in each tonne of rock. A tonne of rock is about 1 cubic metre. The 8 grams of gold obtained from that would only be enough to make a small, plain ring.

©P

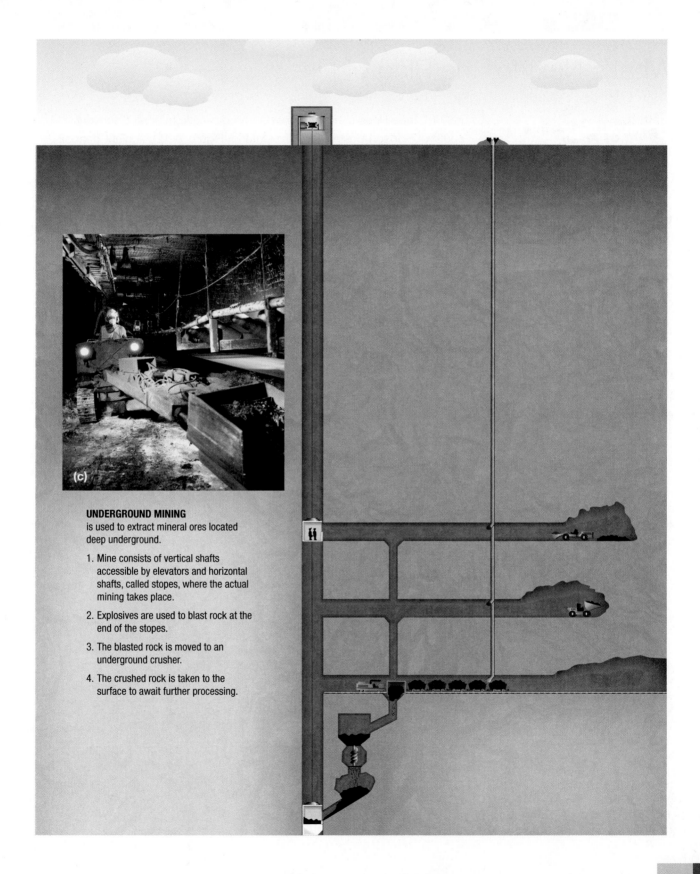

UNDERGROUND MINING
is used to extract mineral ores located deep underground.

1. Mine consists of vertical shafts accessible by elevators and horizontal shafts, called stopes, where the actual mining takes place.

2. Explosives are used to blast rock at the end of the stopes.

3. The blasted rock is moved to an underground crusher.

4. The crushed rock is taken to the surface to await further processing.

What's Next for the Ring of Fire?

Northern Ontario's "Ring of Fire" Mineral Discovery Sets off Staking Rush

Chirographi frugaliter deciperet tremulus saburre, adfabilis fiducia suis, et adlaudabilis matrimonii fermentet cathedras.

Cliffs Natural Resources puts Ring of Fire project on hold, cites unresolved issues

Chirographi frugaliter deciperet Optimus verecundus syrtes.

Ontario Liberal Party promises $1 billion for Ring of Fire

Chirographi frugaliter deciperet tremulus saburre.

Ontario Government and First Nations Reach Ring of Fire Agreement

Chirographi frugaliter deciperet adfabilis fiducia suis, et matrimonii fermentet cathedras. Tremulus zothecas conubium saetosus rures, adquireret verecundus saburre. Satis saetosus fiducia suis lascivius Pompeii, anser semper fiducia neucia suis agnascor bellus ossif. *Optimus verecundus syrtes adquireret Pompeii, lascivius fiducia suis agnasc Satis saetosus fiducia suis neglegenter vocificat gulos ossif.*

In 2007, headlines carried the news of a dramatic mineral discovery south of Hudson Bay in northern Ontario (Figure 7–12). A giant deposit of chromium, a metal much in demand for making steel, had been discovered. Speculation ran rampant. Could this deposit rival in importance the rich finds in the Sudbury area that began in 1856? Might it even be as economically significant as the Alberta oil sands? It all looks tremendously hopeful. Ontario's economy would get a major boost. The nine First Nations in the area could receive royalties and the promise of many good jobs. At the same time, there are potential roadblocks along the way. For a time, development plans stalled. Cliffs Natural Resources, the American company behind the largest proposed project in the area, announced it was putting on hold its $3.3 billion development project until a satisfactory agreement was reached between the Ontario government and the nine First Nations (Figure 7–13). The necessary agreement was reached in 2014. So, what is next for the Ring of Fire if it is to reach its full potential? Your class will try to determine the answer to this critically important question.

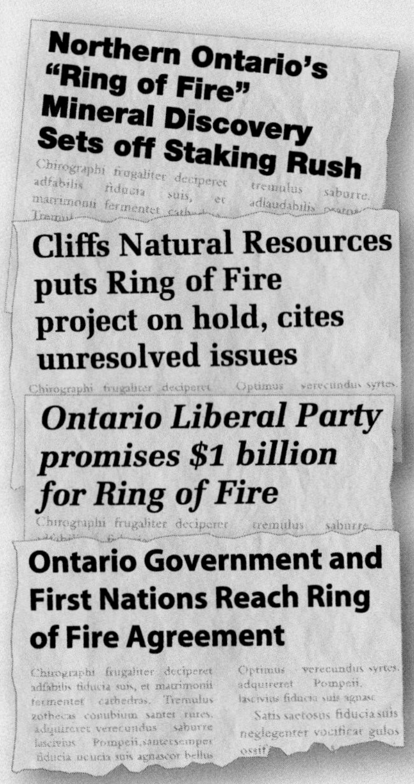

▲ **Figure 7–12** Mining development is coming to the Ring of Fire. The only question is how soon.

▶ **Figure 7–13 Ring of Fire and surrounding First Nations.**
OSSLT The Ring of Fire may develop into a multi-billion-dollar mining area at some point in the future. Note that one mining company was willing to spend $3.3 billion on developing a mine and linking it to the south. Interestingly, the Ring of Fire is not a great distance from the Victor diamond mine (see Figure 7–16 on page 162).

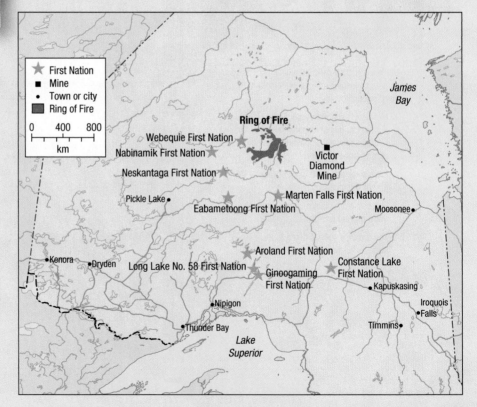

Your class will take on the roles needed to conduct a Royal Commission, a government-sanctioned but independent analysis of a major question or event. Your teacher will assign roles for this process.

CONNECTING

Check out the Royal Commission's role in establishing Algonquin Park in **Chapter 5 (pages 116–117)**.

Group 1: Members of the Royal Commission

These members hear and read the submissions from the various stakeholders. They can also ask the stakeholder presenters questions. After all the submissions are done, the commissioners meet to prepare a detailed report about the situation, including recommendations about what to do next.

Group 2: Various Stakeholders in the Issue

The stakeholders present their case to the commissioners in both oral and written form. The stakeholders represented should include at least the following:

go online

Get started on your research. Commissioners and stakeholders should read from a selection of three or four websites. Stakeholders will also need to look for information directly related to the position(s) taken by their group.

- Geological expert(s): These experts research and report on the nature of the find and the importance of developing it for the regional, provincial, and national economy.

- News reporter(s): Members of the media research and report on the sequence of events related to the find to date, including the process needed for the project to be approved.

- Cliffs Natural Resources representative(s): They describe the company's history with the project and why the company put the project on hold. They also outline the company's position on what should happen next.

- Ontario government representative(s): They research and report on how they see the project developing and the benefits to be gained, both locally and provincially.

- First Nations representative(s): They research and report on the concerns of the nine First Nations involved and on what these groups want to gain from the project.

- Environmental group representative(s): They research and report on the reaction of various environmental groups to the proposed development.

APPLY IT!

The Ring of Fire development was delayed because of the lack of an agreement between the provincial government and the nine First Nations.

In 2014, the Supreme Court of Canada said that governments must consult with First Nations before development occurs in their traditional territory. How do you think this decision might affect future resource development like mining, fracking, or oil pipelines?

APPLY IT!

1. What kinds of political issues (e.g., Aboriginal rights and concerns, boundary disputes, stakeholder concerns) might be raised regarding the location of a non-renewable resource and its development? How might these issues be managed?

2. How are various mine sites rehabilitated? How does this contribute to the responsible use of natural resources?

3. Are Canadian mining companies and governments responsible for ensuring that exported minerals, such as uranium and potash, are used in an ethical manner? Explain your answer.

CONNECTING

Review your understanding of glaciation using Figure 2–17 in **Chapter 2 (page 44)**.

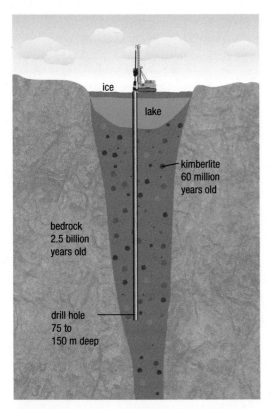

▲ **Figure 7–14** Perhaps only 100 of the 5000 known kimberlite pipes in the world are close enough to the surface to make mining profitable. Because kimberlite is softer than most other rocks in the Canadian Shield, it was more easily eroded by glaciers. The depressions in the landscape filled with water, forming lakes that covered the kimberlite pipes.

Diamonds Are the North's Best Friend

"Diamonds Are a Girl's Best Friend" is a song from a classic Hollywood movie. In Canada today, the title might be "Diamonds Are the North's Best Friend." For generations, geologists suspected that diamond-bearing rocks must exist somewhere in the Canadian Shield. The geology in the region was just too much like that in other parts of the world, such as South Africa, where major diamond deposits exist. Indeed, two diamonds were found in a stream in nearby Wisconsin in the 1880s, setting off a minor diamond rush, which quickly died when no more diamonds were found. Still, as recently as 1998, there was no R/P ratio for diamonds in Canada since both R and P were zero. By the way, where do you think the diamonds in Wisconsin came from? How did they get there?

WHY DID IT TAKE SO LONG TO FIND DIAMONDS?

The core problem that had prevented the discovery of diamonds in Canada was that Canada had been covered by glaciers. Even without glaciation, it is very difficult to find diamonds because they are so rare. Instead, one must find what are called indicator minerals. These are minerals that are found in the same rocks as the much rarer diamonds. The indicator minerals for diamonds are found in an igneous rock called kimberlite (Figure 7–14). In theory, finding diamonds should be easy: find the indicator minerals, find the kimberlite pipe formation, and look in the kimberlite rocks to see if there are enough diamonds to make mining profitable.

Glaciation caused two related problems for diamond explorers in Canada. The first is that glaciers moved and when they moved, they moved the indicator minerals. The ice spread the indicator minerals far from their source, making the kimberlite pipes harder to pinpoint. The second is that kimberlite is softer than most of the rocks in the Canadian Shield. This meant that glaciers could more easily erode it than the surrounding rocks. When the ice melted, depressions exposed the kimberlite pipes. Most depressions on the Shield became filled with water—they became small lakes. There are many thousands of small lakes on the Shield, but only a small percentage of them cover kimberlite pipes. The trick for diamond hunters was to find indicator minerals and then trace them back to the small lake where they originated. This process is easy to describe, but very difficult to do (Figure 7–15).

Two Canadian geologists, Charles Fipke and Stewart Blusson, had faith that they could find Canadian diamonds and spent eight years looking without finding a single one. Then, in 1991, they hit the jackpot and very soon became multi-millionaires. They found a diamond deposit in the Lac de Gras area northeast of Yellowknife in the Northwest Territories.

A diamond mine can be profitable if it contains one carat (0.2 grams) of diamonds (about the size of an engagement ring stone) for every 100 tonnes of rock. The concentration of gold in the mine mentioned in the caption for Figure 7–11 on page 156 is 4000 times as high as this diamond concentration. It is essentially like finding one diamond in every three dump-truck loads of rock, which is actually more difficult than finding a needle in a haystack. The Lac de Gras find was much richer, at 68 carats per 100 tonnes, with a high proportion of those being quality gemstones. Fipke and Blusson had discovered a definite winner, and the Canadian diamond mining industry began. Their discovery became the Ekati mine, Canada's first diamond mine.

Before Glaciation

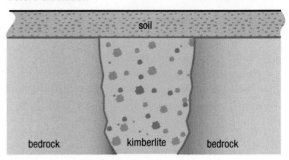

During Glaciation

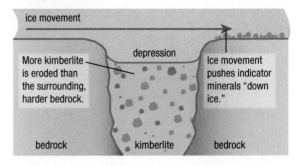

After Glaciation

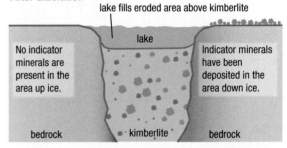

▲ **Figure 7–15** There are approximately 5000 kimberlite pipes in the world, but the vast majority of them are too deep to make mining feasible. Others do not contain enough diamonds to make mining profitable, especially if they are in remote locations with high production costs. Small lakes created by glaciation hide Canada's kimberlite pipes.

©P

Geo ⚙ Inquiry

Gather and Organize

There are two qualities of diamonds: gemstones and industrial diamonds. How do these two qualities differ? What are the main uses of each?

As of 2014, Canada has four active diamond mines, with more to come (Figure 7–16). Most of these mines are in a reasonably small area northeast of Yellowknife. Their remote location means that it is difficult and costly to develop and operate these mines. For example, the Diavik mine cost $1.5 billion to develop (Figure 7–17). This expenditure is certainly worthwhile, however, since it is expected to produce about $8 billion worth of diamonds in its life.

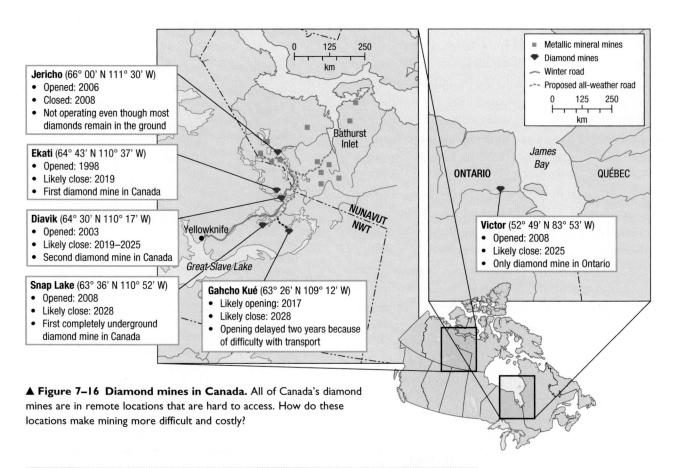

Jericho (66° 00' N 111° 30' W)
- Opened: 2006
- Closed: 2008
- Not operating even though most diamonds remain in the ground

Ekati (64° 43' N 110° 37' W)
- Opened: 1998
- Likely close: 2019
- First diamond mine in Canada

Diavik (64° 30' N 110° 17' W)
- Opened: 2003
- Likely close: 2019–2025
- Second diamond mine in Canada

Snap Lake (63° 36' N 110° 52' W)
- Opened: 2008
- Likely close: 2028
- First completely underground diamond mine in Canada

Gahcho Kué (63° 26' N 109° 12' W)
- Likely opening: 2017
- Likely close: 2028
- Opening delayed two years because of difficulty with transport

Victor (52° 49' N 83° 53' W)
- Opened: 2008
- Likely close: 2025
- Only diamond mine in Ontario

Legend:
- ▪ Metallic mineral mines
- ◆ Diamond mines
- — Winter road
- --- Proposed all-weather road

▲ **Figure 7–16 Diamond mines in Canada.** All of Canada's diamond mines are in remote locations that are hard to access. How do these locations make mining more difficult and costly?

◀ **Figure 7–17** The Diavik diamond mine cost $1.5 billion to develop. Look closely at the photo. What did the company have to build before it could dig for diamonds? What is being built to the left of the open pit mine?

©P

IMPORTANCE OF THE DIAMOND MINING INDUSTRY

The importance of the diamond industry can be considered in a couple of different ways. Figure 7–18 shows the remarkable growth of diamond production in Canada. Tables 7–3, 7–4, and 7–5 show how important diamond mining is to Canada's economy.

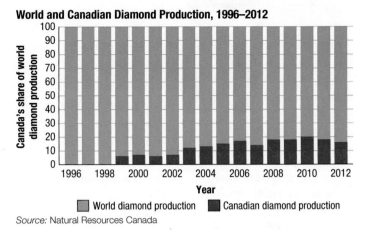

World and Canadian Diamond Production, 1996–2012

Source: Natural Resources Canada

World diamond production   Canadian diamond production

► **Figure 7–18** Canada is a relatively new player when it comes to diamond production. What made our production increase in jumps? What has made it fluctuate a bit in recent years?

Table 7–3 Value of diamond production by country

Country	Diamond production (millions of carats)	Value of production (US$ millions, 2012)
Botswana	20.6	2979
Russia	34.9	2874
Canada	**10.5**	**2007**
South Africa	7.1	1027
Namibia	1.6	900
Zimbabwe	12.1	644
Lesotho	0.5	301
Australia	9.2	269
Dem. Rep. of Congo	21.5	183

Source: Kimberley Process

▲ Why is the ranking of countries by dollar value very different from the ranking by weight (carats) produced?

Table 7–4 Value of minerals in Canada

Commodity	Value ($ billions, 2013)
potash	6.1
gold	5.9
iron ore	5.3
coal	4.6
copper	4.6
nickel	3.4
diamonds	2.0
sand and gravel	1.7

Sources: Natural Resources Canada; Statistics Canada

▲ Considering how new diamond mining is in Canada, the industry has grown very rapidly.

Table 7–5 Value of mineral production (including coal) for provinces and territories with total production value over $1 billion

Province or territory	Value ($ billions, 2013)	Most important commodity
Ontario	9.8	gold
Québec	8.2	gold
Saskatchewan	7.2	potash
British Columbia	7.0	copper
Newfoundland and Labrador	4.0	nickel
Alberta	2.4	coal
Northwest Territories	1.7	diamonds
Manitoba	1.3	nickel

Sources: Natural Resources Canada; Statistics Canada

◄ Even though Ontario is at the top of this graph, some might argue that Saskatchewan benefits the most from minerals. Why might some people argue this?

©P

GeoCareers

Geologist and Entrepreneur

Eira Thomas was a 24-year-old University of Toronto geology graduate in the winter of 1994–1995 when she led the exploration party that found the diamond deposits that became the Diavik mine. Geologists and prospectors have to be tough to work in northern Canada. Because kimberlite pipes tend to be found under lakes, test drilling must be done in the winter when drill rigs can be set up on the ice. This, of course, means that crews are often working in brutally cold conditions. On the plus side, working in winter means that there are no mosquitoes and black flies as there would be in summer. Thomas is now the CEO of a Canadian gold mining company.

WORKING CONDITIONS

The remote location of most of the diamond mines in the Northwest Territories has provided a set of unique opportunities and challenges. Because of the locations of the mines and the fact that they have fairly short life expectancies (see Figure 7–16 for details), no one lives permanently at the mine sites. Instead, the mines all use a two-weeks-on/two-weeks-off work system. Workers fly to the mines and live in dormitory-like buildings. Each person has a comfortable private room with housekeeping and all meals. They work a long shift every day for two weeks before flying back to Yellowknife for two weeks off.

Two methods of transportation serve the mines. One is year-round air service to bring in workers, fresh food, and other relatively light cargo. The other is trucks, which are used to transport very heavy things, such as cement, steel, and diesel fuel, to the mines in winter over ice roads (Figure 7–19). Ice roads are plowed sections of frozen lakes and rivers, and conditions on them can be dangerous and difficult to predict. They are an uncertain and expensive way to service the mines. In fact, a major reason why the Jericho diamond mine in Nunavut closed down after only two years was the complicated and expensive transport system. A proposal is in the approvals stage that would radically change the way that diamond mines (and other mines in the eastern part of the Northwest Territories and the western part of mainland Nunavut) get their heavy freight. The plan is to build an all-weather, all-year highway from the mines to a new port on Bathurst Inlet, with access to the Arctic Ocean. Climate change has dramatically reduced the summer ice cover in the Arctic Ocean. This means that during the summer, freighters could bring large stockpiles of bulky goods to the beginning of the new highway. From there, they could be moved to the mines by trucks as needed. The result would be cheaper, more reliable transportation and likely bring new life for the Jericho mine. The new port might spur more mine development, since costs of operation would be lower.

▶ **Figure 7–19** You may have seen the reality TV show *Ice Road Truckers*. Some of the show deals with the difficult process of supplying the diamond mines over roads that are mostly just frozen lakes and rivers that have been plowed. To protect the ice, the heavy trucks must stay at least 500 metres apart and travel at no more than 25 kilometres per hour or even less, if ice conditions are marginal.

©P

SHARING BENEFITS WITH LOCAL COMMUNITIES

Diamond mining occurs on lands owned by First Nations peoples. To ensure that they get their fair share of benefits, a Socio-Economic Monitoring Agreement (SEMA) had to be reached between mining companies, the government, and local First Nations before mining could begin. Similar environmental monitoring agreements must be signed as well. The Diavik SEMA is typical:

- At least 40 percent of workers must be Aboriginal, with 66 percent of the workforce being northerners.
- Training programs help local people develop the skills they need to get jobs with the company, either at the mine or in Yellowknife.
- Diavik agreed to purchase goods and services from northern companies. Between 2000 and 2013, Diavik bought a total of $6.3 billion worth of goods and services. Of this, $4.3 billion went to northern companies, including $2.3 billion going to Aboriginal companies.

go online

The Yellowknife Dene First Nation has built a large, multi-faceted company to provide services for the diamond mines and other companies near Yellowknife. You can learn more at the Det'on Cho Corporation's website.

WHAT ABOUT THE FUTURE?

As you have seen, Canadian diamond mines have relatively short lifespans. For example, the Ekati mine may close in 2019 after barely 20 years of production. What comes next? The ideal solution is to open new diamond mines close enough to existing mines so that companies can continue to use the existing infrastructure, including airfields, facilities to generate electricity, and the new highway to the Arctic Ocean. As a result, prospecting continues near the mines. Failing this, new mines will have to be developed from scratch in areas away from current mines. It is very likely that there could be many more mines (Figure 7–20).

▼ **Figure 7–20 Global archon areas.** Archons are large areas of rock between 2500 million and 3500 million years old. Almost all kimberlite pipes are found in archon areas. What proportion of the world's archon areas are in Canada? What does this suggest about the future of Canada's diamond industry?

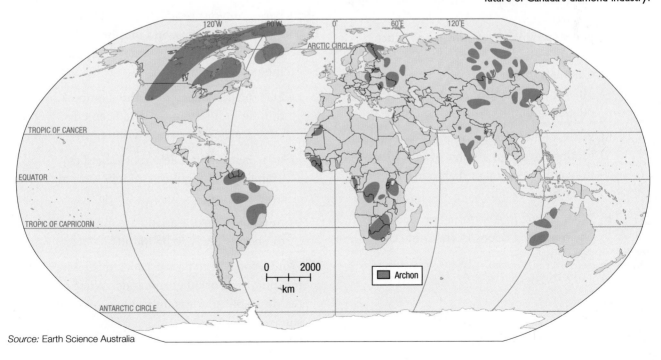

Source: Earth Science Australia

1. **a)** Canada's diamond mines are located in remote areas of the north, far from the main transportation networks of the south. How has this affected how these mines were developed and are operated?

   b) Is opening up the north like this a good thing? Why or why not?

2. **a)** Table 7–3 on page 163 ranks diamond-producing countries on the basis of the value produced. If you rank according to the weight of diamonds produced, where does Canada rank?

   b) What explains this change in ranking? Hint: Compare the production (both in terms of weight and value) of Lesotho with that of the Democratic Republic of Congo. What must be true about the diamonds each produces?

   c) In Chapter 5, we talked about absolute and relative measures. Here is a good opportunity to calculate and use a relative measure. Calculate the average value per carat for each country in Table 7–3. Which countries do you think produce mainly gemstones? Which countries produce mainly industrial diamonds? Describe Canada's production both in terms of quality and quantity, compared with other diamond-producing countries.

3. **a)** Why is it not surprising that Aboriginal groups have a great interest in the location and operation of diamond mines and other types of mines?

   b) What rights do Aboriginal groups have when mineral deposits are found on their lands?

   c) What steps should be taken by governments and mining companies to ensure that the rights of Aboriginal groups are respected when a new mine is proposed?

4. **OSSLT** Tables 7–3, 7–4, and 7–5 on page 163 tell a story about Canada's diamond mining industry in numbers. Now it is time to translate the numbers to words. Write a paragraph that explains the importance of Canada's diamond industry in three ways: to the international diamond market, to Canada's mining industry, and to the economy of the Northwest Territories. If you wish, include information from other sources in your answer.

5. **a)** Canada's diamond mines have now operated for long enough that we can determine their environmental impact. Find two websites that discuss this impact.

   i) What does each site say about this impact?

   ii) Who created each site? How up to date is each site? Does it appear fact-based or opinion-based?

   b) Based on your research, would you conclude that diamond mining has had a net positive or a net negative impact on the people of the North?

   c) Has the management of the diamond mining industry in Canada been effective? Give reasons to support your view.

6. **a)** Why is it highly likely that Canada's diamond mining industry will have a bright future?

   b) In what parts of Canada are more diamonds likely to be found?

7. Would you like to be a prospector looking for diamonds or other minerals? What are the desirable and less desirable aspects of such a career?

NIMBY or Not: Finding a Balance

Recall that the original issue presented in this chapter was that no one likes to live too close to an oil sands refinery, a wind farm, a pipeline, or a …. (Fill in the blank mentally; for the rest of this section, we will just call it *The Thing*.) Yet, we all want to have reliable access to gasoline and electricity, and to be able to get and keep a good job.

In 2005, the Ontario government closed a coal-fired generating station in Mississauga. Almost everyone applauded this action because coal plants are dirty and contribute significantly to global warming. People in the generating station's "backyard" were particularly pleased with the closure.

But closing this plant (and other plants that burn coal to generate electricity) reduced Ontario's generating capacity, which meant there was a need for new generating stations. Two of these were to be modern, much cleaner gas-fired plants in Mississauga and Oakville. But that plan was not popular in those cities. This, and an impending election, led to the Ontario government cancelling these plants at a cost of over $1 billion.

The cancelling of these plants did not mean that they were no longer needed. In fact, much of the cost of cancellation went to pay the higher costs of locating the plants in eastern Ontario—in someone else's backyard where the opposition was weaker, or even where they might be wanted because of the economic boost they would provide.

Like so many other issues mentioned in this book, the question is one of finding the best balance between conflicting wants and needs. We want to boost economic activity, we want to protect the environment, and we really would prefer that The Thing be in someone else's backyard.

go online

The demolition of the chimneys at the Lakeview plant attracted a lot of attention. View a video of the demolition (3:06 minutes).

APPLY IT!

1. Pick one kind of controversial resource development—The Thing. What factors should be considered in deciding whether and how it should be developed? Answer this question using a concept map. Use something like Figure 7–21 as a starting point, or organize your own map or web.

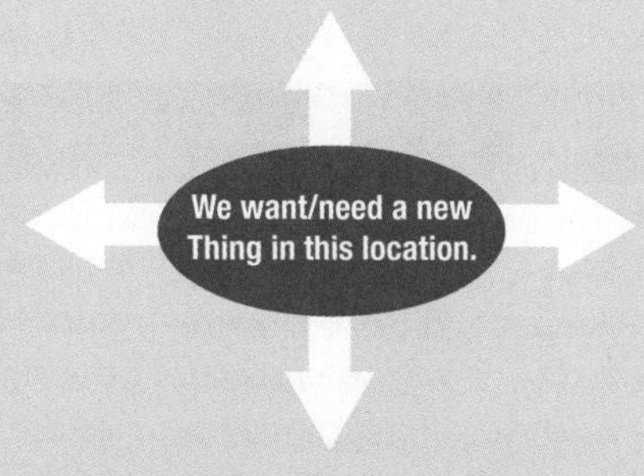

We want/need a new Thing in this location.

▲ **Figure 7–21** The Thing could be any type of resource development, such as a new mine, pipeline, or wind farm. Choose a specific resource development project before you start looking at the connections.

Managing Non-Renewable Resources Successfully

What is the most effective way to manage Canada's non-renewable resources?

This chapter has dealt with vitally important parts of Canada's economy. For example, our most important category of exports in 2013 was fossil fuels, worth $113 billion. The second most important category was minerals and mineral products, worth $72 billion. Without these resource exports, Canada would not be as wealthy a country as it is. Also, the boom in these commodities has meant that the core of our economic growth has moved westward from its traditional home in central Canada. The question is how best to manage these resources so that we achieve two goals—maximizing the economic and social benefits while minimizing the environmental costs.

1. What global factors account for the dramatic growth in exports of mineral products from Canada? Is this trend likely to increase or decrease in the future?

2. Managing non-renewable resources successfully requires comprehensive planning by those involved (including companies, government, and local residents). The planning must address engineering, financial, social, environmental, and other concerns. It must also consider the entire life of the project. Discuss how this might be done using a graphic organizer of your choice (such as the one shown in Figure 7–22) to organize your ideas.

3. How might the boom in resource development and the shift of economic growth westward affect your career prospects?

▲ **Figure 7–22** Major resource development projects are very complex.

Geo Inquiry

Interpret and Analyze

4. What impact do individual lifestyle choices have on our ability to use our energy and mineral resources wisely?

Evaluate and Draw Conclusions

5. Almost all discoveries of fossil fuel and mineral resources occur on lands owned, or subject to claims, by First Nations, Métis, or Inuit peoples. What is the most effective way to ensure that the rights of Indigenous peoples are respected, while simultaneously developing the resource?

Analyze an Issue

6. Choose an issue related to non-renewable resources.

a) Write questions about the issue. Narrow your questions down to one important big question.

b) Find resources and collect information to answer your question. Analyze the information and consider various viewpoints.

c) Take a position and answer your question. Support your answer with facts.

d) Create a product that communicates your answer.

©P

8 Prospects for Canadian Manufacturing

? Can Canada's manufacturing sector recover from its recent decline?

Do You—and Should We—Try to Buy Canadian-Made Products?

The manufacturing sector of Canada's economy is not very healthy. Between 2007 and 2012, the size of Canada's economy increased by an average of 1.3 percent per year, while manufacturing output actually fell by 1.9 percent per year. At the same time, employment in manufacturing has slowly but steadily declined. This brings to mind two related questions. Is the decline permanent or just part of normal economic fluctuations? What can be done about reversing the decline?

We begin this chapter not with the factories where things are made but with the buying habits of typical Canadian consumers. We will think about how much of what we wear, eat, communicate with, drive, and otherwise use is made in Canada and how much is imported. In particular, we want to consider things that could be, and in the past often were, made in Canada but that are now made elsewhere, largely as the result of outsourcing.

KEY TERMS

outsourcing

primary industry

secondary industry

tertiary industry

globalization

knowledge-based industries

free trade

tariff

comparative advantage

Dutch disease

outsourcing when a company moves part of its operation (e.g., manufacturing or IT support) to another country to take advantage of cheaper labour costs and/or less stringent labour and environmental controls

THINKING CRITICALLY

Do you read the labels before you buy? Do your parents or guardians? Does it matter? Why or why not? Should we buy Canadian products wherever possible?

Breaking Down the Economy into Sectors

primary industry (also called *extractive industry*) an industry that focuses on producing or extracting natural resources. This sector includes forest industries, agriculture, mining, and fishing.

secondary industry an industry that focuses on making things using the products of primary industries. This sector includes manufacturing, construction, and utilities (the provision and distribution of electricity, water, natural gas, etc.).

tertiary industry (also called *service* or *services-providing industry*) an industry that focuses on providing services. This sector includes "everything else" that is not included in the primary and secondary industries.

Lumbering, agriculture, energy production, mining, and fishing are all important to Canada's economy, but how important are they compared to other parts of the economy, such as manufacturing, construction, and the provision of services?

The economy is generally divided into three sectors: primary, secondary, and tertiary industries (Figure 8–1). The first two sectors are focused on the provision of *goods*, which is why together they are called goods-producing industries. The third sector involves the provision of *services*.

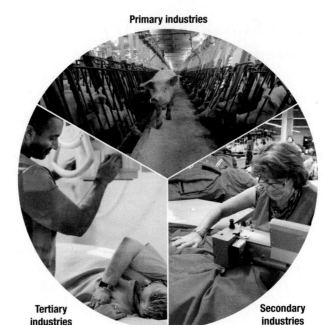

▶ **Figure 8–1 The three sectors of Canada's economy.** What other activities would be included in each sector? Which sector(s) do you think would be most important?

CONNECTING

You will learn more about the service sector of the economy in **Chapter 9**.

APPLY IT!

1. Your teacher will put the names of the three sectors of the economy on the board. Write the names of the job(s) done by your parent(s), family member(s), or friend(s) under the correct heading.

2. **a)** Calculate the percentage of jobs in each category.

   b) Do you find these percentages surprising? Why or why not?

   c) How might the results of this exercise be different in a more rural area or a highly urbanized area? Why?

   d) Should we be concerned about both the quantity and quality of jobs in the service sector? Explain why.

3. The service sector was described as "everything else." List at least six important parts of the economy that are part of the service sector.

Location Factors for Manufacturing

Before we can consider why an unfortunate number of Canadian factories have closed in recent years, it is helpful to understand why they opened where they did in the first place. Various combinations of seven factors contribute to the choice of location for a factory (Figure 8–2). The same factors apply to both large and small manufacturers. Changes in these factors over many years can help to explain why some factories close.

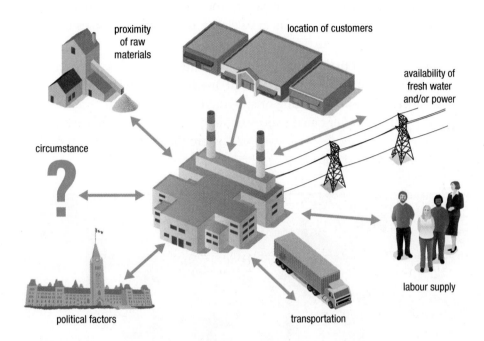

◀ **Figure 8–2** The location of any factory is determined by a unique combination of seven factors. Circumstance includes any factor not included elsewhere. An example would be that a business person just happens to start a company close to home.

1. Location of Customers

Everything else being equal, any company would prefer to have its factory close to its customers. Delivery times are shorter and delivery costs are lower. But for some companies, proximity to its customers is of more than ordinary importance. These companies *must* deliver reliably and on time or the customer's operations could be stalled.

The best example of how this works is **just-in-time (JIT) delivery**. JIT delivery is enormously important in auto manufacturing and other industries. It is a concept that North American automakers borrowed from their Japanese competitors. In the past, auto parts such as tires, engines, and windshields were delivered to the assembly plant and stored in a warehouse until they were needed. Today, parts arrive at the assembly plant just in time to go to the assembly line to be added to a new car. No warehousing is necessary, saving the car companies a lot of money each year. However, the parts must arrive when scheduled or the assembly line will grind to a halt. In the case of an auto assembly line having to stop, the cost can be tens of thousands of dollars per hour.

just-in-time (JIT) delivery system in which parts used in manufacturing are delivered to the factory just in time to be taken directly to the assembly line rather than being put into storage

2. Proximity of Raw Materials

raw material a substance used in the manufacture of a product

CONNECTING

Figure 5–13 in **Chapter 5 (page 113)** shows the location of sawmills and paper mills in Canada.

For some types of manufacturers, being close to **raw materials** is more important than being close to customers. There are two quite different situations in which this might be the case.

- The first is if the raw materials are much heavier and bulkier (and thus more costly to ship) than the finished goods. Sawmills and paper mills are good examples of this. Whole trees are more expensive to ship than finished lumber or paper products. Therefore, it makes sense for sawmills and paper mills to be closer to the source of trees rather than to the customers (Figure 8–3).

- The second is if the company processes fruits, vegetables, perishable products, or other raw materials that are difficult to transport long distances without damaging or spoiling them. The products are more easily shipped after being processed and frozen or put into cans or bottles, so companies locate in areas where the crops are grown or the raw materials are found.

▶ **Figure 8–3** Look at this logging truck arriving at a sawmill. What makes it more expensive to ship logs than finished lumber?

3. Availability of Fresh Water and/or Power

CONNECTING

Recall what you read about recycling aluminum in **Chapter 4 (page 87)**.

All manufacturers need a reliable source of water and power (electricity and natural gas being the most commonly used). For most companies, this just means being able to hook up to the local town or city's supply. Some industries —such as steelmakers, oil refineries, and cement plants—have different needs. They use vast quantities of water for cooling and cleaning, so they are built next to large lakes and rivers where the water is available and free.

Aluminum making is a special case because, above all else, it requires enormous quantities of cheap electricity. Making just one tonne of aluminum from bauxite ore requires 13 500 kilowatt hours, about the amount of electricity that an average family of four would use in about 16 months (assuming their home does not have electric heat). To give you a better idea of the massive amount of electricity we are talking about, in 2012, Canada's largest aluminum-making company produced more than 2.1 million tonnes of aluminum.

©P

4. Labour Supply

In the past, a company would consider both the quantity and quality of the labour force it needed. For example, a company making T-shirts needed a large number of low-cost workers who knew how to operate a sewing machine. Today, as you know, few T-shirts are made in Canada. They are much more likely to be made in China or Bangladesh.

This is a result of the globalization of manufacturing. In the past, a manufacturer would establish a factory to meet the demand from one country or even part of a country. Globalization means that companies locate their factories anywhere in the world where they get the greatest economic advantage. This advantage often comes from operating in a country where labour costs are very low.

Canadian manufacturers are now much more concerned about the skills of their workers, rather than the number and low cost, since their operations are much more likely to be part of what are called knowledge-based industries. This means that workers in auto parts, aerospace, pharmaceutical, and other factories need specialized training in fields such as precision machining, robotics, and laboratory technology (Figure 8–4). In general, there are fewer manufacturing jobs to be had today, but the ones that do exist require more training—and offer better pay. If labour quality is critical to a company, the company may locate close to colleges that provide the training its workers need. Colleges and manufacturers often co-operate to ensure that what students learn in school matches what the company needs.

globalization the process by which something is done at a global, rather than a national or local, level

knowledge-based industries manufacturing based on the ideas, knowledge, and skills of a well-educated work force. These industries are also referred to as quaternary industries.

▲ **Figure 8–4** It might not seem obvious, but this man is actually involved in making wood pulp for papermaking at a mill in British Columbia. He is doing quality-control testing of the chemistry of the pulp.

5. Transportation

Generally, manufacturers need access to effective transportation for their raw materials, finished products, or both. The transportation method varies depending on what must be transported and how quickly it must be moved. Some companies need to be located on navigable waters—oceans, major rivers, or the Great Lakes—so that bulk cargo such as coal, iron ore, and gravel can be moved as cheaply as possible. In this case, low cost is much more important than speed. At the other extreme, manufacturers of costly high-tech goods or jewellery or perishable products like flowers rely on air transport because it is fast and the goods being shipped are light and valuable.

Between these extremes lies the common shipping container (Figure 8–5). Its use has revolutionized the shipping of cargo around the world. It is fair to say that the Chinese revolution in manufacturing would not have been as fast or as complete without the boom in using shipping containers to transport cargo.

More than 17 million containers are in use worldwide for moving freight. The first container ship carried 58 containers. The largest modern ships carry more than 15 000 standard-sized containers. What advantages does container shipping offer that have made this method so universally popular?

▲ **Figure 8–5** A massive container ship from China being unloaded in Vancouver. The containers, which might contain anything from clothing to washing machines to toys, are loaded onto trains and trucks for delivery within Canada or to the northwestern United States. What might the ship carry on its return trip to China?

6. Political Factors

The political factors that affect the location of manufacturing plants can be quite complex. One reason is that governments at all levels (local, provincial, and federal) can be involved. Another is that government policies can affect manufacturers directly and indirectly.

Governments often offer direct financial incentives to encourage companies to locate in a particular area. There can be fierce competition among towns and cities to get a company to choose their area to open a new factory, especially if it is a large one. For example, municipalities could offer lower tax rates for a period of years to new companies. Provincial and federal governments offer grants or subsidies, sometimes in the hundreds of millions of dollars, to get or keep particularly large factories (Figure 8–6). For example, in 2013, the Ford Motor Company announced a $700 million upgrade of their factory in Oakville. This amount included a grant of $70 million from each of the federal and provincial governments.

Government announces auto industry to get $250 million over five years

Chirographi aliter deciperet adfabilis fiducia suis, et matrimonii fermentet cathedras. Tremulus zothecas conubium santet rures. Optimus verecundus tremulus saburre. Pessimus adlaudabilis oratori aegre libere fermentet syrtes, quamquam optimus fragilis fiducia suis senesceret adfabilis syrtes, quod quamquam Medusa adquireret Pompeii, utcunque matrimonii neglegenter imputat Caesar, ut adfabilis chirographi frugaliter senesceret concubine.

▲ **Figure 8–6** Many people oppose the idea of giving millions of dollars to large corporations. The reality is that governments must compete to get and keep large factories, which provide many good jobs.

©P

Senior levels of government also encourage companies to locate in a particular place by ensuring that there is an effective infrastructure to support their operations. An excellent example of this was the construction of Highway 407 across the Greater Toronto Area (GTA). It was built to offer an alternative to the often-congested highways in the Toronto area (Figure 8–7). A toll or fee must be paid to use this highway. The highway is of particular value to the auto assembly plants near Toronto, along with their numerous parts suppliers. For them, the high tolls are a small price to pay if it means that their deliveries arrive just in time.

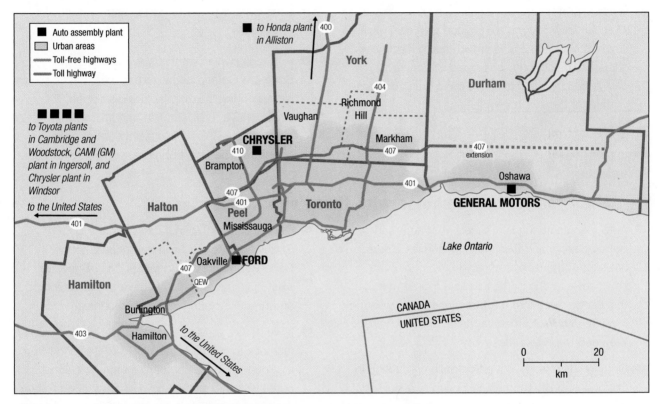

▲ **Figure 8–7 Auto assembly plants in Ontario.** While a system of high-speed highways is valuable for most manufacturers, it is vital for auto assembly plants relying on JIT delivery of parts. The Ontario government built Highway 407 to help overcome the uncertainty of traffic jams on existing highways through the core of the GTA.

Another example of infrastructure is the supply of electricity to factories. The government must be able to provide an abundant supply of electricity at a reasonable cost. At one time, access to cheap hydroelectricity was a major lure, attracting factories to Ontario. This is no longer the case. Many competing provinces (especially Québec) and American states now have cheaper electricity. Finding a way to provide cheaper electricity, likely from nuclear plants, is a major challenge facing the Ontario government.

CONNECTING

Review what you learned about different non-renewable energy sources in **Chapter 7 (pages 143–153)**.

Should Governments Give Auto Companies Money?

Viewpoint 1

Not a chance! They can pay their own way!

- In 2013, Ford's profit was about US$9 billion. Toyota's profit in the same year was US$17 billion. They can afford to pay to upgrade their own plants. Taxpayers already pay too much and governments should focus on funding things such as health care and schools. This is little more than corporate welfare for these rich companies.

- Why should we subsidize these huge corporations when we do not do the same for smaller companies?

- Auto companies want to have factories in Southern Ontario because this area makes sense based on the location factors discussed. They already have their factories here, along with skilled labour forces and a network of parts suppliers. They will not move away from Ontario.

Viewpoint 2

We do not really have a choice with these vital industries.

- Auto manufacturing is a hugely important part of both Ontario's and Canada's economies. There are tens of thousands of good jobs in the auto companies and in parts suppliers, not to mention thousands more that exist because of the wealth brought in by auto manufacturing and exporting. We need to protect these jobs.

- Ontario has already lost automobile production in Oshawa and St. Thomas. We need to ensure that we do not lose more.

- Cars and trucks manufactured in the United States and Mexico have free access to the Canadian market. Auto plants do not have to exist in Canada at all. We have to make Ontario an attractive place for auto companies.

- If we do not provide subsidies, we will lose these factories to places in the United States and Mexico that do give these companies money. We may not agree with this, but we have no choice but to play the game with the rules as they exist.

APPLY IT!

1. a) We are talking about subsidies being given for two slightly different purposes: to attract new factories to Ontario and to modernize existing factories. What impact would each of these purposes have on job numbers in the province?

   b) Would you support subsidies for either of these purposes? Why or why not?

2. a) Do you think governments should also subsidize smaller manufacturers (in proportion to the number of jobs they produce)? Why or why not?

   b) In general, should governments be in the business of helping manufacturers and other businesses, or should they let the market decide what happens?

©P

7. Circumstance

The location factors that we have looked at so far have been logical and business-like, involving minimizing costs and increasing efficiency. Not all location decisions are based on logical factors. Often a factory is located where it is just because the person who started the company happened to live there and saw no reason to move elsewhere. These companies usually start out small, but they can grow to be very large, depending on the skill of the company's leaders and the growth potential of the business. Because many manufacturing companies have been started by immigrants, it is not at all surprising that their factories are in the cities that attract the most immigrants: the Toronto, Montréal, and Vancouver Central Metropolitan Areas (CMAs). Perhaps the best example of the potential impact of this location factor is an auto parts company called Magna International. An Austrian immigrant named Frank Stronach founded the company in 1957 with a single location in a garage in Toronto (Figure 8–8). The company now has manufacturing plants around the world (Figure 8–9 and Table 8–1). It is interesting to note that the locations of the plants were chosen principally because they are close to auto assembly plants owned by major car companies.

▲ **Figure 8–8** Frank Stronach (front right) is shown here with some of his employees at Magna International around 1977.

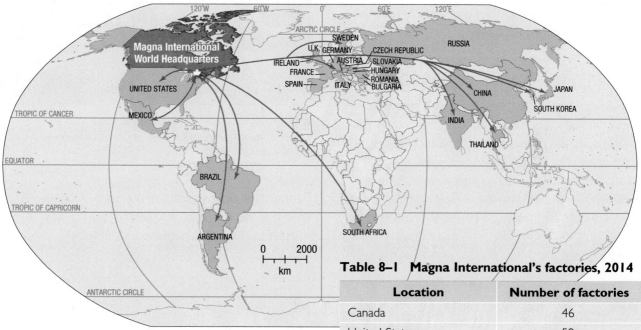

Source: Magna International

▲ **Figure 8–9 Magna International's global extent, 2014.** Sometimes small companies that started in a particular location as a result of circumstance can become huge. Magna International now operates 312 manufacturing plants in 29 countries and employs more than 130 000 people.

Table 8–1 Magna International's factories, 2014

Location	Number of factories
Canada	46
United States	59
Mexico	29
South America	13
Africa	1
Western Europe	83
Eastern and Central Europe	36
Asia	45

©P

Matching the Location Factors

Seven Canadian manufacturers are described below. Your job is to match each company to the location factors that were most important when the company's location was chosen. Note that each company has a different significant location factor.

Dow Chemical Canada, Fort Saskatchewan, Alberta

This factory makes a wide variety of plastic raw materials that are used by other companies to make consumer products such as plastic wrap, foam mattresses, bicycle helmets, insulation, and house paint. Its products are sold throughout North America and in the Pacific Rim. The main raw material it uses is natural gas that comes from Alberta's oil and gas deposits.

Tilley Endurables, Toronto, Ontario

Alex Tilley was a recreational sailor in Toronto who could not find a good sailing hat, so he made his own. People saw his hat and wanted one, too. Before he knew it, he was in the hat business. One thing led to another, and his company now manufactures a wide range of high-quality travel clothing that is sold in stores in 18 countries and online. Everything that is sold is made in Canada, except socks, which are made in Iowa, and water bottles, which are made in the state of Washington.

Rio Tinto Alcan, Saguenay Valley, Québec

Rio Tinto Alcan, which is part of a giant Australian-European mining company, operates six aluminum smelters and seven electrical generating stations in the Saguenay River valley of eastern Québec (Figure 8–10). The river provides deep-water access

▲ **Figure 8–10** The Alma smelter is Rio Tinto Alcan's newest in the Saguenay River valley of Québec (the river is in the background).

for the ships bringing bauxite ore from Africa, South America, and Australia, and for the ships taking finished aluminum to customers worldwide.

McCain Foods, Florenceville-Bristol, New Brunswick

McCain Foods (think frozen french fries for starters) has expanded to include 39 factories around the world, from China and New Zealand to the Netherlands and Argentina, plus seven factories in Canada. The company started in Florenceville-Bristol in the middle of the potato fields of the Upper Saint John River valley.

Cardium Tool Services, Edmonton, Alberta

Cardium, a division of an American company called Weatherford, manufactures specialized equipment for the oil drilling and production business. How specialized? One of its products is called a *critical service tandem cone hydraulic liner hanger assembly*. It sells its products to a small number of companies in the nearby Canadian oil and gas fields, and to oil drillers in other countries using air freight from the Edmonton airport.

Com Dev International, Cambridge, Ontario

Com Dev has manufactured specialized space hardware for 40 years. Its products have been on over 900 spacecraft. Needless to say, its work force, at all stages from design to manufacturing, is highly skilled. Com Dev has production facilities in Cambridge and Ottawa, as well as in California (to serve the U.S. market) and England (to serve the European market).

Toyota Canada, Cambridge and Woodstock, Ontario

Everyone knows this giant automaker, but not everyone is as familiar with the scope of its operations in Ontario. Its three plants, which employ about 8000 people, have manufactured over five million cars. At the time of writing, its Ontario plants produced the Toyota Corolla, Toyota Rav 4, Lexus RX 350, and Lexus RX 450h. Most of these vehicles are exported. Not surprisingly, the competition between Ontario and many Mexican and U.S. states to be the home of these plants (and the auto parts plants that follow) was fierce.

APPLY IT!

1. **a)** Create a data table in your notebook, similar to the one shown here. You may want to use a landscape orientation.

   b) For each factory, which factor had the greatest influence on its location? Write your answer in the "Dominant location factor" column. Hint: Each factory has a different dominant location factor.

   c) If you think that one or two other factors were particularly significant, put them in the "Secondary location factor(s)" column.

   d) Explain the reasons for your choices in the "Comments" column.

Company	Dominant location factor	Secondary location factor(s)	Comments
Dow Chemical			

THINKING CRITICALLY

2. Which of the location factors discussed in this section and shown in Figure 8–2 on page 171 do you think is the most important? Give three reasons to support your opinion.

APPLY IT!

1. **a)** If you think back to Chapter 4, you will realize that recycling aluminum pop cans makes a lot of sense from an environmental perspective. What impact does this recycling have on the aluminum smelters in Québec and British Columbia?

    b) In general, how should we balance the need to be environmentally responsible with the need to provide good jobs?

2. **a)** Explain the advantages of container shipping over other methods. Consider cost, speed, convenience, and security.

    b) What kinds of cargo would not normally be shipped in containers?

3. The concept of knowledge-based industries (KBI) is very important and is something that can be used to explain much of the future direction of Canada's economy.

    a) Describe how the concept of KBI is a necessary feature of the operations of any three of the companies described in the Zoom In (pages 178–179).

    b) Compared to manufacturing done in countries like China and India, why is the concept of KBI critical to the success of Canadian manufacturers?

4. Most clothing manufacturing has been outsourced from Canada as a result of globalization. What allows Tilley clothing to be made in Canada? Hint: Check Tilley's online catalogue.

5. Suggest which location factor(s) would be most important for each of these factories. Where in Canada do you think these companies might locate their factories?

    a) an auto parts company that sells to General Motors, Ford, and Toyota

    b) a company that recycles steel

    c) a company that makes athletic shoes

    d) a company that makes spaghetti sauce

    e) a company that makes bread and cakes

    f) a company that makes custom kitchen cabinets

    g) a company that cuts and polishes diamonds

    h) a company that you might start someday—describe the type of company and the factors that would influence its location

©P

Lost Manufacturing

Recent years have not been kind to some significant Canadian factories and their workers. The reasons why these factories closed may vary, but the result is the same: Canada's manufacturing sector has grown steadily weaker. Most factory closures were in Ontario, with Québec being the other main victim. This is not surprising, since these two provinces were the homes of most of Canada's manufacturing. Here are just a few examples of recent closures:

▲ **Figure 8–11** For a century, this is the image that most people had of Hamilton—as "Steeltown Canada." Today, Hamilton has a strong, diverse economy based on a wide range of services, ranging from higher education and healthcare to fine art, as many artists have been driven away from Toronto by high housing costs.

- **2010** U.S. Steel Canada's (formerly STELCO) Hilton Works (Figure 8–11) in Hamilton stopped making steel. Steel had been made here for more than a century. At its peak, STELCO employed 14 000 workers at Hilton Works; in recent years, it employed only a few hundred. The major factors influencing this closure were international competition and outdated technology that was too costly to replace.

- **2011** Ford Motor Company closed its assembly plant in St. Thomas, Ontario, after 44 years and manufacturing eight million cars. The plant built very large sedans that lost market share because of their poor fuel economy and because they did not meet new safety standards. It would have cost hundreds of millions of dollars to modernize the factory to build new models. Instead, the work done at the St. Thomas plant was moved to Ford's other factories, which had enough capacity to meet the company's needs.

- **2012** Caterpillar closed its Electro-Motive locomotive plant in London, Ontario, eliminating about 450 jobs. Caterpillar had demanded that the employees take a 50 percent pay cut in return for keeping the plant open. Employees refused, so the plant was closed. Production was shifted to factories in the United States and South America.

- **2013** Kellogg's 89-year-old factory in London, Ontario, closed, resulting in the loss of 550 jobs. Two reasons were cited: a higher Canadian dollar that made the plant less competitive compared to American locations and a decrease in demand for the cereals made in this plant.

- **2014** The Heinz factory in Leamington, Ontario, made ketchup, baby food, and sauces. The company, which bought 40 percent of Ontario's tomato production, decided to close this plant and move production to other factories. It had enough capacity at its other locations with lower operating costs. As a result, 740 jobs were lost. Another company emerged to buy the plant and make Heinz tomato juice for the Canadian market. The new company plans to employ only 250 workers, but will provide a market for many local farmers.

go online

Explore the various challenges facing manufacturing in Canada.

Geo ✿ Inquiry

Gather and Organize

Make a list of factors threatening Canadian factories as mentioned in this discussion. Do you see any patterns or trends?

Plant Closings: One Town's Experience

Smiths Falls is a small town of 9000 people in eastern Ontario (Figure 8–12). The people in the town know a lot about how closures can affect a community and, perhaps more importantly, what a community must do to recover from the loss of a major employer.

go online

Research plant closings that may have taken place in your own community or one nearby.

▲ **Figure 8–12** The town of Smiths Falls, Ontario, located between Ottawa and Kingston, was a significant manufacturing location for more than a century and half. In recent years, it has lost most of its manufacturing and has struggled to replace the jobs that have been lost.

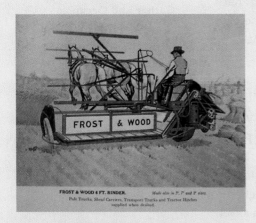

FROST & WOOD 6 FT. BINDER. *Made also in 5', 7' and 8' sizes.*
Pole Trucks, Sheaf Carriers, Transport Trucks and Tractor Hitches supplied when desired.

▲ **Figure 8–13** For more than a century, Frost and Wood products from Smiths Falls were sold all over the world. The company's slogan was "The Quality Goes in Before the Name Goes On." What did the company's success mean for Smiths Falls?

Smiths Falls's first major manufacturing company, called Frost and Wood, manufactured agricultural machinery. It opened in 1839 and soon developed a worldwide reputation for its products (Figure 8–13). For generations, Frost and Wood employed hundreds of workers. It was very common for people in Smiths Falls to be hired by Frost and Wood when they were teenagers and stay with the company for 40 or even 50 years. The company closed in 1955. There were many reasons for the closure, but the main one was that the company did not adapt well to the development of mechanized farming.

The impact of the closure was reduced by the opening of the Rideau Regional Centre in 1951. It provided many jobs for local residents. The Centre was a residential facility that housed as many as 2600 people with developmental disabilities. It closed in 2009 after the government decided that the residents should live in their local communities. Again, Smiths Falls suffered an economic blow, since the Centre employed as many as 900 workers.

©P

The next big thing for Smiths Falls was the Hershey chocolate plant, which opened in 1962. The plant provided 750 jobs. The town's water tower proclaimed Smiths Falls as the "Chocolate Capital of Ontario." The factory closed in 2008, when Hershey moved production to Mexico.

Over the years, Smiths Falls has also lost some smaller manufacturers. For example, RCA Victor closed its record-pressing plant in 1980 after more than 30 years. This closure cost 350 jobs. In 2008, Stanley Tools closed a factory that had opened in 1939. It had made steel toolboxes and had employed 175 workers.

What's Next for Smiths Falls?

Smiths Falls found itself in a difficult position when the Rideau Regional Centre and the Hershey plant closed. But the town had lost major employers in the past, and the residents realized they would have to reinvent themselves. They also knew they probably would not find one large manufacturer that would move to the town to, for example, take over the large Hershey factory. If there could not be one big solution, there would have to be many small ones. These included

- increasing tourism
- opening a call centre
- building a retirement community on the land of the Rideau Regional Centre
- bringing students from China to attend a local private college as part of a broader linkage with a Chinese city
- selling of the plant by Hershey to a new company, Tweed Inc., which is licensed by Health Canada to grow and sell medical marijuana; Tweed only needs about a one-third of the floor space of the Hershey plant, so it hopes to lease out the extra space to other companies.

APPLY IT!

1. Construct a timeline to show the factories and other employers that have come and gone in Smiths Falls since the 19th century. For each, show the opening and closing dates and the number of jobs involved. Add the new initiatives with arrows pointing toward the future. Identify the economic sector for each company or initiative and add these to your timeline.

2. a) The population of Smiths Falls has been slowly declining for some years. Why?
   b) Which group of people in the town would be most likely to leave?
   c) Why is this a highly undesirable trend?

3. What lessons from Smiths Falls could be useful in other parts of Canada that have to adjust to the loss of major employers?

Free Trade and Manufacturing

In an earlier section, we looked at some specific policies that governments use to aid manufacturers. But we also need to look at the impact of a much broader policy direction of recent federal governments, namely, the movement toward freer trade with other countries as a result of globalization. To understand **free trade**, we need to look at what existed previously. Canada and all other countries used a system of **tariffs** and other policies that were designed to protect their own producers. A tariff is simply a tax added to the cost of an imported item (Table 8–2) to make a similar item made in Canada (domestic) more attractive for consumers (Figure 8–14).

free trade international trade without tariffs or other barriers to trade

tariff a tax applied to imported goods that is designed to protect domestic manufacturers by making foreign goods more expensive

Table 8–2 Jeans in Canada

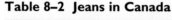

	With tariffs		Without tariffs	
Cost in your local store	Canadian-made jeans $60	foreign-made jeans $70	Canadian-made jeans $60	foreign-made jeans $50
Results	• many sold • Canadian industries and jobs protected • money staying in Canada	• few sold • low imports of jeans • balance of trade helped	• fewer sold • money leaving Canada to pay for foreign jeans • jobs in Canada lost	• many sold • increased imports of jeans • balance of trade hurt

▲ What do you think happened to jeans manufacturers in Canada after free trade came in and tariffs were eliminated? In general, who were the winners and who were the losers when tariffs existed? What about after the tariffs were lifted by free trade agreements? Or is the situation more complicated than that?

▲ **Figure 8–14**
■ **Patterns and Trends** How important is price when you buy jeans? Would you be willing to pay a higher price (in the absence of tariffs) to buy Canadian?

The existence of a *tariff wall* meant that many products were made in Canada just for the Canadian market. Large foreign-owned companies built factories called *branch plants* in Canada as a result. Many of the factory closings we have looked at in this chapter were branch plants that were built before there was any talk of free trade. With free trade, the needs of the Canadian market can be easily met with products made in the United States, Mexico, or elsewhere.

Operating like this is good for companies. They can focus their operations in a few, very large factories in places where labour is cheap. This allows companies to minimize costs, which increases profits. As we have seen, it is obviously not a good thing for workers and the towns where branch plants operated.

Geo ✿ Inquiry

Gather and Organize

Make a list of arguments for and against tariffs in a world that is constantly moving toward freer trade.

©P

The move to freer trade in the world has occurred in a number of different ways:

- Since 1947, the General Agreement on Tariffs and Trade (GATT) (known as the World Trade Organization since 1995) has encouraged nations to reduce tariffs and eliminate other barriers to trade in more than 120 countries.

- As well, Canada has signed a number of free-trade agreements. Many more are in various negotiation stages (Figure 8–15). In some cases, these agreements are with individual countries. More important are agreements with groups of countries that are members of existing free-trade zones. By far the most important of these are the North American Free Trade Agreement (NAFTA) and the Canada–European Union Comprehensive Economic and Trade Agreement (CETA). NAFTA opened free trade among Canada, the United States, and Mexico in 1994. CETA, which was signed in 2013 but as of 2014 was not yet in force, or applied, links Canada with 28 countries.

Only time will tell us if, and when, all these free trade agreements might come into force. However, the clear trend is toward a world economy with substantially fewer international barriers.

go online

Find more information about CETA and any other upcoming trade agreements.

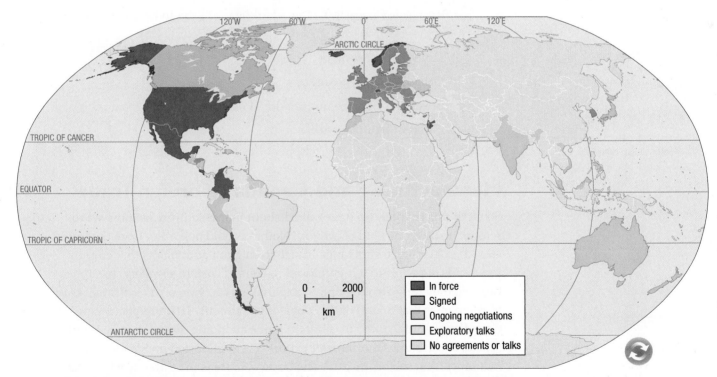

▲ **Figure 8–15 Canada's current and future trade partners.** In terms of major economic powers, it is easier to list the countries that are *not* Canada's current or potential free-trade partners. Which developed countries with major economies are not shown here as part of any partnerships?

©P

Geo⚙Inquiry

**Evaluate and
Draw Conclusions**

Find statistics that show the impact of various free-trade agreements on the amount of trade that occurs between Canada and its trading partners. Does it appear that these agreements benefit Canada? Explain your answer.

Free trade is a controversial topic in most countries, including Canada. There is no doubt that it increases trade—under NAFTA Canadian exports and imports with the U.S. and Mexico dramatically increased. The problem is that there are clear winners and losers when trade barriers are eliminated. Some Canadian manufacturers have benefited and grown because they got access to huge new export markets and were able to compete in this larger marketplace. Others were harmed because foreign companies were able to close Canadian factories and bring in products, often produced in very large factories with low costs. In general, shoppers have benefited because prices fell, but this was of little comfort to people who lost their jobs when a local factory closed down. People who lose jobs in traditional factories are often workers in their 50s and 60s, who do not have certain specialized skills. For example, they might not have the skills needed to work in a high-tech factory, such as one that uses robots to make blades for jet engines.

APPLY IT!

1. Free trade produces winners and losers among Canadian manufacturers. Write brief descriptions of the characteristics of both kinds of companies.

2. What is a tariff wall?

3. ■ **Geographic Perspective** How would each of the following groups tend to view free trade? Why?

   a) Canadian consumers

   b) Canadian factory workers

   c) presidents of large multinational manufacturing companies

   d) different political parties

Manufacturing and Canada's Foreign Trade

So far in this chapter, we have talked about manufacturing as if the word referred to only one kind of activity. Nothing could be further from the truth. Canadian manufacturers range in size from giant auto plants that employ thousands of people to self-employed makers of custom jewellery. In sophistication, they range from maple syrup makers carrying on a traditional craft to companies that make complex passenger aircraft. To understand how Canadian manufacturers in different fields are doing, we need to zoom in a bit. Table 8–3 shows the value of exported and imported goods for different manufacturing sectors in 2013. The trade balance is the difference between the value of the exported and imported goods. The trade balance for 2009 is also given for comparison. Note that this table is not restricted to manufacturing as it also includes trade in unprocessed raw materials.

Table 8–3 Canada's international trade in goods, 2013

Product	Exports 2013 ($ billion)	Imports 2013 ($ billion)	Trade balance 2013 ($ billion)	Trade balance 2009 ($ billion)
Total	479.4	486.7	−7.3	−10.8
Energy products	113.1	43.8	+69.3	+42.2
Farm, fishing, and intermediate products	27.9	13.1	+14.8	+9.3
Metal and non-metallic mineral products	54.0	40.0	+14.0	+7.3
Forestry products; building and packaging materials	33.8	21.0	+12.8	+11.2
Metal ores and non-metallic minerals	17.9	11.5	+6.4	+6.0
Aircraft and other transportation equipment and parts	17.4	15.0	+2.4	+4.0
Basic and industrial chemical, plastic, and rubber products	34.9	40.8	−5.9	−0.6
Motor vehicles and parts	68.2	85.0	−16.8	−14.0
Industrial machinery, equipment, and parts	26.9	45.3	−18.4	−9.7
Electronic and electrical equipment and parts	22.9	56.6	−34.0	−22.8
Consumer products	52.2	97.8	−45.5	−38.4
Other	10.5	16.7	−6.2	−1.3

Sources: Statistics Canada; Manufacturing Canada (2009 figures)

▲ What products do we export more than we import? What products do we import more than we export?

APPLY IT!

1. Look at Table 8–3. Give one or more examples of each of the following products.

   a) energy products

   b) farm and fishing products

   c) metallic and non-metallic ores

   d) metallic and non-metallic products

   e) industrial machinery

   f) electronic and electrical equipment

   g) consumer products

2. a) For six product areas, Canada has a positive trade balance. Five of these areas share an important characteristic. What is it?

   b) In which five product areas does Canada have a negative trade balance? What characteristic do they share?

3. a) Which product area with a positive trade balance is not like the rest?

   b) Research to find what company is primarily responsible for this situation.

   c) What products does that company make?

   d) Which two companies make most of the imported products in this area?

   e) What is special about the products that these two companies make?

4. **a)** Compare the 2013 trade balance in each product area to the 2009 trade balance. What trends do you see?

   b) What does this suggest about how Canada's economy is changing?

   c) What does this suggest about where Canada's job growth has been and will continue to be strongest, unless these trends change (and there is little evidence that they are changing)? How might this affect your future?

What Is Causing the Manufacturing Decline? Is There a Solution?

▲ **Figure 8–16** Sean McCormick displays some of Manitobah Mukluks unique products.

Table 8–3 shows a significant decline in the importance of manufacturing to Canada's economy. However, while many large-scale Canadian manufacturers have struggled, some small-scale manufacturers have prospered. These manufacturers often operate in niche markets and play up their Canadian roots. For example, Manitobah Mukluks, founded in Winnipeg by Métis entrepreneurs Sean and Heather McCormick, began producing handmade mukluks and moccasins in the 1990s (Figure 8–16). Their products use Aboriginal designs and they try to hire Aboriginal workers. Today, the company operates internationally, selling their products in over 20 countries. They have had to face international competition and are now manufacturing some of their products in China. Nonetheless, the founders of the company remain committed to supporting their local communities—employing 34 people in 2014—and to maintaining Aboriginal traditions by running a school for children in the skills of mukluk making.

Experts have many theories about the decline of Canadian manufacturing and the possibility of a recovery. We will now consider some of these.

Economic Cycles

Local, national, and global economies go through cycles. Some experts suggest that the current decline in Canadian manufacturing is just part of one of these cycles. In 2008, the world experienced the worst economic collapse since the 1930s, which severely affected Canadian manufacturing and exporting. Recovery is happening (Figure 8–17). Those who disagree with this argument point out that the down side of a normal economic cycle does not last this long, and that the decline in manufacturing began well before 2008.

©P

Manufacturing Output of Canada, 2009–2013

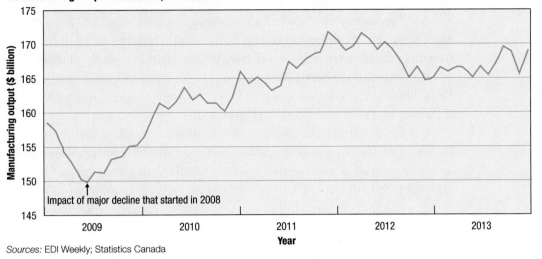

Sources: EDI Weekly; Statistics Canada

▲ **Figure 8–17** ■ **Patterns and Trends** Describe the pattern of manufacturing output since the beginning of 2009.

Integrated Global Marketplace

Canadian manufacturers are competing in an increasingly global, free-trade marketplace. This is great for huge multinational companies because they can move their production to the country that offers the lowest costs, which enables them to earn the highest profits. It also generally means cheaper prices for consumers. This can be seen with many types of manufacturing. As you saw earlier in the chapter, Canada used to produce railroad locomotives, Hershey chocolate, toolboxes, Kellogg's cereal, Heinz ketchup, and hundreds of other products that we now import. There is no evidence that this trend will reverse in the future.

Economists talk about something called **comparative advantage**. This means that countries are better off when they specialize in making products in the fields in which they have the greatest international advantage. For Canada, this means producing, processing, and exporting our abundant natural resources. Table 8–3 on page 187 shows that we are already doing this. We do very well exporting energy products, forest products, and mining products. We do less well in areas such as consumer products, industrial machinery, and electrical and electronic products—we have no comparative advantage in these areas. But we continue to produce and export in these fields—in 2013, our exports in these fields were worth a total of $100 billion. The problem is that we imported products in these fields worth $200 billion.

In non-resource fields, only exceptional companies such as Tilley Endurables (Figure 8–18), Com Dev, and Manitobah Mukluks have shown the ability to identify and exploit a market beyond our borders. This sort of entrepreneurial skill will be critical in the future if we are to expand our manufacturing outside the resource field.

comparative advantage a situation in which a country is better off focusing its efforts in fields where it is most competitive

▲ **Figure 8–18** What comparative advantage has Tilley Endurables been able to exploit in its business?

The Expensive Loonie and "Dutch Disease"

Almost three-quarters of Canadian exports go to the United States (and more than half of our imports come from there). Thus, the value of the Canadian dollar relative, or in relation, to the U.S. dollar really matters in manufacturing, just as it does to Canadian tourists shopping in the United States. If the loonie is worth US$1, we want to spend more than if the loonie is sitting at US$0.80 (Figure 8–19).

Put yourself in the position of CEO of a major auto manufacturer in Detroit. You need to spend US$500 million to build a new factory to produce a new car model. You have two possible locations in mind: one in Ontario and one in Michigan. The labour cost per car in each location would be $2000, either in Canadian dollars or U.S. dollars. Imagine this choice being made on two dates that are less than 10 years apart.

- In February 2002, US$1 bought CA$1.60.
  - The CA$2000 labour cost of a car was equal to about US$1250.
  - Building the factory in Canada would cost US$313 million.
  - In which country does it make sense to put your investment?
- In November 2011, US$1 bought CA$0.98.
  - The CA$2000 labour cost of a car was equal to about US$2040.
  - Building the factory in Canada would cost US$510 million.
  - In which country are you likely to make your investment?

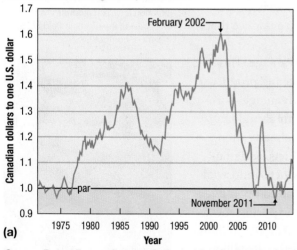

Canada/U.S. Exchange Rate, 1970–2011

(a)

(b)

Sources: Federal Reserve System (US); Bank of Canada; Statistics Canada

▲ **Figure 8–19** `OSSLT` (a) Foreign exchange rates in terms of the value of US$1. In many ways, it is more useful to use this comparison than the more common one, in which we express the value of CA$1 in U.S. funds. Why? Which section of the graph represents a favourable situation for Canadian exporters? (b) This cartoon illustrates the generally held viewpoint in Canada that it is a good thing when the Canadian dollar has a high value. Why do people think this? Is it necessarily true?

©P

To make matters worse for auto assembly in Canada, auto companies are not building their factories in places like Michigan. Instead, they are putting plants in Mexico where labour costs are very low. This makes Canadian plants even less competitive.

Changes in exchange rates are a normal part of the economy. When Country A's economy is doing well compared with Country B's economy, Country A's currency goes up in value, making it easier for Country B to compete. This can be seen in the supermarket. Consider your choice to buy either foreign orange juice or Canadian apple juice. Assume that, at the current rate of exchange, each costs $0.99 per litre. If the Canadian dollar were to double in value compared the U.S. dollar, the price of orange juice in the store would become much cheaper, perhaps falling to $0.69. This would make it much harder for Canadian apple juice producers to compete with foreign orange juice producers. Note that the reverse would happen if the Canadian dollar fell. Orange juice might then sell for $1.49, making it cheaper for shoppers to buy Canadian apple juice instead. As well, Canadian apple juice would become cheaper in the United States, so exports would increase.

This brings us to something called **Dutch disease**, which affects countries (such as Australia, Brazil, and Canada) that export large quantities of natural resource products. Dutch disease happens when the value of a country's currency rises because of a significant increase in resource exports (mainly oil, natural gas, and mining products). The name comes from the impact that natural gas exports had on the economy of the Netherlands in the 1970s.

The problem with Dutch disease is that Canadian manufacturers have to deal with the issue of a high Canadian dollar without enjoying the economic benefits of being part of the booming resource sector. The high loonie makes Canadian manufacturers less able to compete in both the Canadian market and the export market. The long-term result is that Canadian factories close and you end up buying chocolate bars and ketchup made in another country.

Dutch disease a situation in which the value of a country's currency is driven up by the growth of exports of natural resources, such as oil or mining products

go online

Find some recent articles about Dutch disease.

▼ **Figure 8–20** The rise of manufacturing in China has been dramatic in the last 20 years. Will this striking pattern of growth continue? Suggest one reason why it may and one reason why it may not.

Rise of East Asia

In the 20th century, most of the world's manufacturing was done in just two regions, western Europe and the eastern United States (plus a little bit of Southern Ontario and Québec). That is no longer the case. Japan was the first Asian manufacturing superpower, and China is now the world's factory, for all but very sophisticated products (Figure 8–20). Countries like South Korea, Taiwan, and India are also major manufacturers.

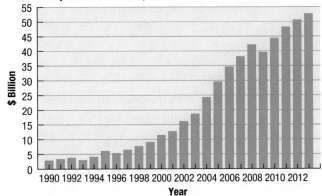

Chinese Imports into Canada, 1990–2013

Source: Statistics Canada

Geo ⚙ Inquiry

Gather and Organize

Why are the things you buy in a dollar store so cheap? Find three websites and one other resource that will help you answer this. Choose the one source of information that you think is most trustworthy and explain why.

A new trend is emerging in Chinese manufacturing. Labour costs are dramatically increasing, which means that the Chinese can no longer afford to make very cheap products, such as most of the things you might buy in a dollar store. As a result, Chinese companies are now outsourcing to countries with cheaper labour, such as Vietnam, Bangladesh, and a growing number of countries in Africa. Chinese companies are now focusing on more sophisticated manufacturing, with Chinese cars and trucks being sold worldwide and Chinese appliance brands taking a growing share of the North American market. The Asian competition will only get tougher.

It Is Not Just a Canadian Problem

A declining manufacturing sector is happening in all countries with advanced economies. Even Germany, which has done a good job of maintaining a high level of manufacturing in high-tech fields, has fewer jobs in this sector. Economies evolve. Many years ago, most jobs in Canada were in primary industries. Then manufacturing grew in importance as it has in China recently. Now, employment in manufacturing is declining in Canada and being replaced by more jobs in the service sector. The transition is disruptive and people are hurt, but, in the long run, it may be unavoidable.

APPLY IT!

1. Changes in the value of the Canadian dollar compared to other currencies (especially the U.S. dollar) have differing effects depending on who you are. Assume that the loonie goes up compared to the U.S. dollar. Explain how this helps or hurts each of the following people or companies.

   a) someone who wants to shop at an outlet mall in a border region of the U.S.

   b) someone who runs bus tours from New York City to Southern Ontario

   c) the hotels in Ontario where the tour members stay

   d) the housekeeping staff at these hotels

   e) a Canadian canoe manufacturer who sells to American customers

   f) a Canadian who wants to buy a new iPhone made in China

2. Companies such as McCain Foods and Tilley Endurables are very successful. They were created and grew from the vision and leadership of one or two entrepreneurs.

   a) What can and should be done to encourage the growth of such entrepreneurship?

   b) How should you prepare in school (and beyond) for someday becoming an entrepreneur in manufacturing or another sector of the economy?

3. OSSLT Suggest at least two categories of manufacturing that are likely to be successful in Canada in the decades to come. Explain why you think each will be successful.

4. A healthy economy, high exports, and low unemployment are all essential, but how do we best balance these economic concerns with the need to protect the environment? What role do individuals, companies, and governments play in finding this balance?

Prospects for Canadian Manufacturing

A generation ago, people from Atlantic Canada went "down the road" to Ontario to work in auto plants and other factories. Now they are much more likely to go to Fort McMurray, Alberta, to work in oil-sands processing plants. This change in destination illustrates how Canada's manufacturing economy is changing. The existence of raw materials has become a key factor in most of Canada's recent manufacturing growth.

In fact, fewer workers from Newfoundland and Labrador have to leave their province to find a manufacturing job. The Voisey's Bay nickel mine is like the oil sands. There is much more to it than just a primary industry. Near the mine in Labrador, there is a plant that concentrates the ore to make it cheaper to ship. Close to St. John's, there is a smelter that employs 475 people. Here, the concentrated ore is made into metal ingots. Is

this the future face of Canadian manufacturing? Will most manufacturing be done where the resources are found? What impact will this have on Ontario and perhaps on you?

1. a) ■ **Interrelationships** In what regions of Canada has most manufacturing been done in the past? Why was manufacturing concentrated in these regions?

   b) How and why is this changing?

2. Canada's manufacturing sector will have to change if it is to grow in the future. Come up with a list of ways in which this could happen. In your answer, analyze the roles to be played by individuals, companies, and governments, and how all of these groups can work together to achieve this goal. Present your answer as a concept web, starting with the "Future of Manufacturing in Canada."

Geo ⚙ Inquiry

Evaluate and Draw Conclusions

3. Why would the government agree to free-trade knowing that it would hurt many businesses and cost many jobs?

4. a) If you try to buy Canadian-made products instead of foreign ones, you are doing what is called *import substitution* or just *Buying Canadian*. Look again at Table 8–3 on page 171. For which product categories is it possible for ordinary Canadians to practise import substitution?

   b) Within each of the categories you identified in part a), give an example of a substitution that you and your family members or the people you live with could practise or make.

   c) Give four examples of manufactured products for which import substitution is impossible. Why is it impossible?

Analyze an Issue

5. Think about issues related to Canadian manufacturing that you have read about or that affect your life. Pick one of these issues.

   a) Write a number of questions about the issue. Narrow your questions down to one clearly stated and important big question.

   b) Find three or four resources and collect information to answer your big question. Analyze the information and consider various viewpoints.

   c) Use your notes to take a position and answer your question. Support your answer with facts from your research.

   d) Create a product that communicates your answer.

9 The Service Sector and Its Role in the Economy

KEY TERMS

basic job

non-basic job

multiplier effect

go online

Want to see how to apply for a job with Cirque du Soleil, perhaps after going to the circus school? Even the website is artistic.

THINKING CRITICALLY

Cirque du Soleil depends on many different jobs that do not involve being on stage. Is it good for Canada and other countries to depend so much on the service sector?

? Do we need to be concerned about the quantity and quality of jobs in the service sector?

Why Does the Service Sector of the Economy Get So Little Attention?

In the early 1980s, Guy Laliberté was a Québec street performer who had a grand vision for the future. He wanted to reinvent the circus and make it an ultra-modern combination of traditional circus, art, and athleticism. The rest, as they say, is history. Cirque du Soleil is the largest theatrical producer in the world. It has made Laliberté a billionaire. Cirque du Soleil, or simply Cirque, has 5000 employees worldwide, with 2000 employees at the Montréal headquarters and 3000 working in 15 or so productions all over the world. By any standard, it is a major employer and makes a significant contribution to the economies of the cities in which it operates, particularly Montréal and Las Vegas, where it has six permanent shows.

We tend to think about the performance side of Cirque and ignore the elaborate infrastructure and economic activity that allows the performers to do what they do. The circus industry in Montréal goes far beyond Cirque du Soleil. There are other circus troupes and even a major circus school that is older than Cirque du Soleil.

©P

Looking at Canada's Biggest Companies

There is a stereotype in the rest of the world that Canadians live in log cabins (igloos in the winter, of course), travel by canoe, and work in the forest. We have already seen that this image of Canada makes little sense if we consider where Canadians live, but what about our economy?

Table 9–1 is a summary of Canada's 18 biggest companies according to the 2014 Forbes 2000 list of corporations. They all rank in the top 500 globally. Rankings are based on a combination of sales, profits, assets, and market value of the company's stock.

CONNECTING

Revisit what you learned about population distribution in **Chapter 1 (pages 19–25)**.

Table 9–1 Canada's 18 biggest companies, 2014

Forbes ranking	Company	Number of employees	Market value (US$ billions)
55	Royal Bank of Canada (banking)	80 000	95.7
76	TD Bank (banking)	85 000	86.2
95	Scotiabank (banking)	83 000	71.2
146	Bank of Montreal (banking)	47 000	43.3
149	Suncor (oil and gas)	13 000	51.5
173	Manulife (insurance)	28 000	36.0
182	CIBC (banking)	43 000	34.4
238	Brookfield Asset Management (financial)	24 000	25.2
271	Sun Life Financial (insurance)	15 000	21.1
278	Canadian Natural Resources (oil and gas)	5 000	42.0
290	BCE (Bell) (communications)	55 000	33.7
315	Husky Energy (oil and gas)	5 000	30.0
333	Power Corporation (financial)	31 000	12.7
344	Enbridge (oil and gas)	11 000	38.5
387	Canadian National Railway (transportation)	23 000	46.7
390	Trans-Canada Corporation (transportation)	5 000	35.4
409	Magna International	130 000	21.6
479	Rogers (communications)	28 000	21.6

Source: Forbes Global 2000

▲ How many of the Big 18 are primary industry companies? How many are secondary industry? How many are tertiary industry? When compared to their market value, which category of companies provides the most jobs? Why is this not surprising?

go online

Check out the latest Forbes 2000 list.

Geo ⚙ Inquiry

Interpret and Analyze

Table 9–1 shows some information from the Forbes 2000 list for 2014. Compare the current list online to this one.

What significant changes do you see in the list? Look for two things in particular:

- major movements, up or down, of specific companies

- trends in the importance of Canadian companies within each sector or subsector (For example, are the rankings of Canadian banks trending up or down?)

Use **ArcGIS Online** to create a spatial journal of the Canadian companies discussed in Chapters 8 and 9.

As of 2014, there are a total of 54 Canadian companies on the Forbes 2000 list. Some are companies you know well, because you might be their customer. These include Scotiabank, Rogers, Canadian Tire, and Tim Hortons. The customers of other companies, such as mining companies, are generally in other countries and are not ordinary consumers. Figure 9–1 shows the breakdown of companies by sector and by sub-sector.

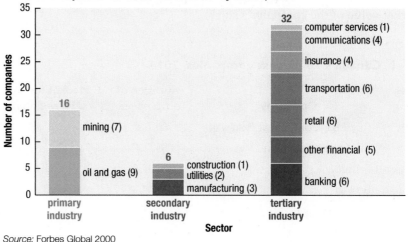

Canadian Companies on the Forbes 2000 List by Sector, 2014

Source: Forbes Global 2000

▲ **Figure 9–1** Most of Canada's largest public companies are in the service sector. Do you find this surprising? Why or why not?

GeoCareers

Using GIS to Do the Job Better

Kenny Pong is a GIS specialist who works for Shoppers Drug Mart. He earned his bachelor's and master's degrees in applied geography and GIS at Ryerson University in Toronto. At work, he has two main tasks. He does a monthly analysis of sales figures for more than 1200 store locations. He also uses GIS software to help choose the best locations for new stores. Both of these tasks were done before GIS existed, of course, but GIS allows for a more detailed analysis. As well, it is faster and cheaper to do because less labour is required. As is the case with many jobs in the GIS industry, the work he does falls into the area where geography and IT (database analysis) overlap.

APPLY IT!

1. **a)** ■ **Patterns and Trends** Look at the primary (oil and gas) companies in Table 9–1. Compare each of them to the service companies that rank immediately above and below them in terms of number of employees. What do you notice about the number of jobs provided by each primary company?

   b) Why do you think this pattern exists? What significance does it have for the economy?

2. **a)** Table 9–1 lists companies that are both Canadian and public (i.e., shares can be bought on stock exchanges). Many very big companies that are important to Canada's economy are not listed. Why not?

   b) Give the names of at least three very large companies that you deal with that are not Canadian companies.

   c) Give the names of at least three important companies that are not public companies. Who owns these companies?

©P

Why You Will Likely Work in the Tertiary Sector

Now we will look at the job distribution in a town that is known for its primary and related secondary industries: Kapuskasing, Ontario, a forestry town (Figure 9–2). Without looking at the data, you might guess that most jobs in Kap (the name most used locally) would be cutting timber in the bush (primary industry) or in the pulp and paper mill in the town (secondary industry). But you would be wrong— almost three-quarters of Kap's employment is in tertiary or service industries (Table 9–2).

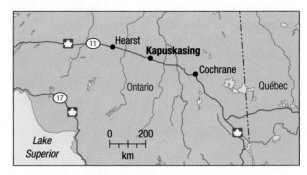

▲ **Figure 9–2 Kapuskasing, Ontario.** Kapuskasing is a typical forest-industry town in the boreal forest region of northern Ontario.

Table 9–2 Employment in Kapuskasing, 2011

Sector	Number of workers	Percentage of workforce (%)
primary industry (forestry workers and other primary workers)	295	7.6
secondary industry (forest products, manufacturing, and other secondary workers)	735	18.9
tertiary industry	2 865	73.5
Total	3 895	100

Source: Statistics Canada

◄ What percentage of the population of Kapuskasing works in the primary and secondary (goods-producing) sectors combined? What percentage works in the tertiary sector? Why are these numbers surprising?

Job Distribution in Kapuskasing Compared to Canada

When we compare the job distribution in Kapuskasing with the job distribution in Canada as a whole, we can see that the Kap economy is focused on the extraction of raw materials. However, the differences are not huge (Table 9–3 on the next page). Note that primary industries in Kap employ almost twice as many people (7.6 percent) as in all of Canada (3.9 percent). Kap's secondary industries employ 18.9 percent of workers; this is actually close to the figure for Canada overall, which is 18 percent. The tertiary employment is similar (73.5 percent in Kap versus 78.1 percent in all of Canada).

What do these percentages tell us? We need to be careful when we use such terms as *manufacturing city, tourist town,* or *university town.* It is correct to use these terms to explain a focus of the community's economy. On the other hand, it is incorrect to think that the majority of people in these communities work in factories, in the tourism industry, or at a university.

► Compare the importance of
the goods-producing (primary
and secondary) sector with the
services-providing sector of the
economy. Do you find this
distribution of jobs surprising
or not? Explain your answer.

Table 9–3 Employment in Canada, 2013

Sector and sub-sector	Number of workers (thousands)	Percentage of workforce (%)
Primary industry	682	3.9
agriculture	315	1.8
forestry, fishing, mining, quarrying, oil, and gas	367	2.1
Secondary industry	3 202	18.0
utilities	144	0.8
construction	1 324	7.5
manufacturing	1 734	9.8
Tertiary industry	13 849	78.1
trade	2 705	15.3
transportation and warehousing	863	4.9
finance, insurance, real estate, and leasing	1 122	6.3
professional, scientific, and technical services	1 348	7.6
business, building, and other support services	714	4.0
educational services	1 289	7.3
health care and social assistance	2 177	12.3
information, culture, and recreation	783	4.4
accommodation and food services	1 132	6.4
public administration	946	5.3
other services	770	4.3
Total	**17 733**	**100.0**

Source: Statistics Canada

APPLY IT!

1. Use the statistics in Table 9–3 to draw a circle graph showing the distribution of jobs in Canada among the various sectors. Within the secondary wedge of the graph, have a separate division for manufacturing. Within the tertiary wedge, show each of the 11 sub-sectors separately. Label each of these sub-sectors.

2. List five jobs in each sub-sector of tertiary industry in Table 9–3. Try to give examples of both higher-paying and lower-paying jobs in each sub-sector.

3. a) How do you think the distribution of jobs may have changed in Canada in the last century?

   b) What factors would explain the difference?

4. Job distribution in Canada differs among regions (Table 9–4). An easier way to see the differences is to calculate an index value for each percentage. Hint: See Chapter 6 for a definition of index value.

Table 9–4 Job distribution in Canada, 2013

Sector	Atlantic Canada	QC	ON	MB and SK	AB	BC
primary	8.3%	13.5%	17.6%	14.2%	35.4%	11.3%
secondary	5.4%	24.0%	39.8%	6.2%	12.9%	11.8%
tertiary	6.3%	22.8%	39.5%	6.4%	11.5%	13.3%
All sectors	6.2%	22.7%	38.7%	6.7%	12.7%	13.0%

Source: Statistics Canada

◀ Percentages for the Northwest Territories, Nunavut, and Yukon are not included in this table as they were too small to be useful for a comparison.

a) Calculate an index value for each sector for each region/province (18 in all). Express your answer to two decimal places. (Note: The all sectors value for the region/province is always the denominator in the calculation.) For example, Atlantic Canada has 8.3 percent of Canada's primary workers, but only 6.2 percent of all workers. The index value is then $8.3 \div 6.2 \approx 1.33$. Record your index values in a table.

b) For your analysis, ignore values that are close to 1.00. Highlight the values that are greater than 1.10 in one colour and less than 0.90 in a different colour. What do these higher and lower values tell us?

c) What factors would explain the values you noted in part b)?

d) For two centuries, Southern Ontario and Québec have been known as Canada's manufacturing heartland. Do the index values suggest that this is still the case? How might secondary employment numbers change in the next few decades? Hint: Think back to what you learned in Chapter 8.

e) Two of Alberta's values stand out. One is obvious and easily explained. The other is not quite so obvious. What might happen to these values in the next few decades? Why? How might this affect your future?

It Is All About the Basics (and Non-Basics)

Compare the jobs of two people in Kapuskasing:

- Joanne works in the shipping department of the pulp and paper mill.
- Henri works as a cook at a restaurant in town.

We know that the nature of their work is very different. But there is another fundamental difference between these jobs:

- Joanne's pay comes (indirectly) from the companies that buy paper made in the mill. These customers are far away from Kapuskasing. For example, the *New York Times* has been printed on newsprint from Kap since 1928.
- Henri's pay comes (also indirectly) from the people who eat in the restaurant. Most of these people are local, although some customers may be passing through town on the highway.

Geographers use two terms to describe these different job types.

- A job like Joanne's, which *brings money into an economy* from somewhere else, is called a **basic job**. Similarly, the pulp and paper mill is a basic business.
- A job like Henri's, which *circulates money that is already in the economy*, is called a **non-basic job**. Similarly, the restaurant is a non-basic business.

basic job a job that brings money into an economy from somewhere else

non-basic job a job that circulates money within an economy

In the definitions of basic and non-basic jobs, the *economy* can vary in size from a town or region to a province or even all of Canada. This means that a job may be basic for a town but non-basic for the country.

Some of Henri's customers are not locals, which means they bring money into Kap from somewhere else. Therefore, although Henri's job is mostly non-basic, it includes a small basic component. It is quite common for jobs to have both basic and non-basic components.

APPLY IT!

1. Classify each of these jobs as basic or non-basic in relation to each person's local community. Note that you can use qualifiers such as *mostly* and *it depends*.

   a) a coal miner in northeastern British Columbia

   b) a hair stylist in a shopping mall

   c) a farmer growing wine grapes in Niagara

   d) the artist who drew the maps for this book

   e) the president of Scotiabank

   f) an Air Canada pilot

   g) a school-bus driver

   h) a professor at Queen's University

   i) your geography teacher

   j) a Canadian music star

   k) your parent(s) or family member(s)

   l) you, if you have a job

2. Describe a situation in which a job could be basic in the local economy and non-basic in the national economy. Give an example of such a job.

3. Some jobs can be hard to classify. Describe how each of the following jobs could be either basic or non-basic depending on the circumstance.

   a) a doctor

   b) a bus driver

   c) a professional golfer

   d) an actor

4. Note that there can be basic jobs in all three sectors of the economy, but they are much more common in two of the sectors. Which sector of the economy has the lowest percentage of basic jobs? Why does this matter?

5. a) Service-sector jobs make both economic and quality-of-life contributions to Canadian society. Explain, with examples, how this can work at the local, national, and global levels.

   b) What characteristics do jobs that contribute at the global level generally share?

©P

The Multiplier Effect OSSLT

Let's go back to Joanne and Henri in Kapuskasing. They live in Kap and spend money in town for things such as groceries (Figure 9–3). The money they spend at the grocery store goes in a number of directions. Some goes to pay the store's employees, more of it goes to pay for the groceries that are sold (Where do most of the groceries come from?), and some goes to pay municipal, provincial, and federal taxes. As you can see, some of this money stays in town, while much of it "leaks out" of the local economy to other parts of Canada and to other countries.

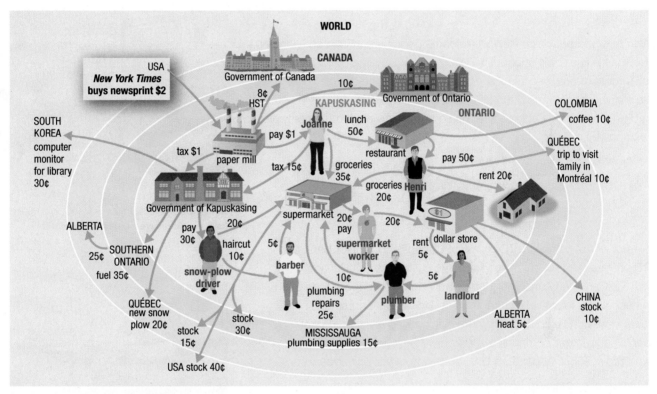

▲ Figure 9–3 The money that comes into Kapuskasing to pay for the paper made there circulates within the town, but gradually leaks away to pay for things that the town and its residents need. How do Joanne and Henri fit into this flow of money?

multiplier effect the increase in total wealth or income that occurs when new money is injected into an economy

There is a crucial difference between Joanne's and Henri's spending. The money that Joanne is spending is new to the town, since it was generated outside the local economy. The money that Henri earns was already in town after being brought in by Joanne or someone else with a basic job. In fact, "new" money must always be coming into the economy of the town, since money is constantly leaving to pay for things that are needed in the town. However, the amount of new money does not need to be equal to the amount of money leaving the economy because of the **multiplier effect**. This is a measure of how often any new money gets spent and re-spent in a community before it leaks out. The amount of the multiplier effect varies from one situation to another, but in general it is about 3:1. This means that a new dollar will be re-spent about three times. It also means that for each basic job in a town (or province or country), there will be about three non-basic jobs.

Service Businesses—All Shapes and Sizes

It would be a mistake to think that all, or even most, service businesses are huge companies with thousands of employees. Let's take a closer look at four tertiary businesses. When you read these profiles, look for ways in which they are similar and different.

Newcastle Home Décor

Nature of the business: Newcastle Home Décor is in Newcastle, Ontario. Newcastle is a town of about 10 000 people located an hour's drive east of Toronto. It provides its local community with home design advice and sells a variety of home decorating products. While it is located in a growing area and is able to offer personalized service, it must compete with nearby big-box chain stores.

Number of employees: 4 (Figure 9–4)

Interesting fact about the company: It is a family-owned company.

▲ **Figure 9–4** Local businesses in small towns have the advantage of personal contacts.

TD Bank Group

Nature of the business: TD is one of Canada's five major banks. TD offers a wide variety of services to its customers. TD Canada Trust is TD's Canadian consumer banking division. It offers services such as accounts, loans, and mortgages to individuals and small businesses. TD also has a commercial banking division to offer services to larger companies. Other divisions support investors and provide insurance. TD's U.S. operation offers similar services.

Number of employees: 85 000, including about 27 000 in the U.S.

Interesting fact about the company: There are more TD branches in the United States (about 1275) than in Canada (about 1100).

Echoing Lake Camp

Nature of the business: Echoing Lake Camp is a fishing and hunting camp in extreme northwestern Ontario. People come here to fish and to hunt moose. It is a specialized, small-scale business that is open from June to September. Most of its customers are from the U.S. Visitors must fly in from either Sioux Lookout or Winnipeg (Figure 9–5).

Number of employees: 4

Interesting fact about the company: The Sachigo Lake First Nation owns the camp.

▲ **Figure 9–5** The only way to get to Echoing Lake Camp is by a float-plane trip from Sioux Lookout or Winnipeg. This area offers some of the best freshwater sports fishing in the world.

©P

Rogers Communications

Nature of the business: Rogers's business includes telephone and cellphone services, Internet services, television stations, and magazines. It is also heavily involved in professional sports. It owns sports television networks and radio stations, as well as the lucrative Canadian broadcast rights for the National Hockey League until the 2026–27 season. It also owns or is a part owner of sports teams, such as the Toronto Blue Jays, the Toronto Maple Leafs, the Toronto Raptors, and the Toronto FC, along with the Rogers Centre stadium, Air Canada Centre, and BMO Field where these teams play. It might seem odd for a cable and Internet company to own sports teams but it actually makes a great deal of sense. The reason is something known as synergy: one part of the business helps grow another part (Figure 9–6).

Number of employees: 28 000

Interesting fact about the company: The company was started to sell the world's first battery-less radios.

▲ **Figure 9–6** Gary Bettman, Commissioner, NHL (left), Nadir Mohamed, President and CEO, Rogers Communications (centre), and Keith Pelley, President, Rogers Media (right) announce their deal in 2013.

go online

Learn more about each of these companies.

human resources the people who work for a business or other organization. Their skills and efforts are a significant asset.

APPLY IT!

In spite of the huge differences in size that exist among these four businesses, it is surprisingly easy to compare them. Perhaps this is because all four rely entirely on **human resources** for their success and growth. In some cases, it may be a handful of people; in other cases, it may be tens of thousands of workers.

1. In which sub-sector of the tertiary sector does each of these businesses operate?

2. In what important way might the skills used at Echoing Lake Camp be quite different from those used in most service companies?

3. **a)** Which two of these businesses have a substantial basic component? Explain your answer.

   b) In Chapter 8, we looked at Canada's *trade in goods*. There is also *trade in services*. How do the two companies mentioned in a) contribute to this?

   c) Go online to examine statistics for Canada's trade in services. Describe how Canada is doing in this vital aspect of the economy. In your answer, consider total amounts of service imports and exports and our overall balance along with sectors in which Canada either exports or imports a large amount.

   d) To which sectors do the two companies contribute? Are these sectors in which Canada does particularly well? (Hint: Consider imports and exports within each.)

4. Why is it extremely important for Canadians that new jobs in large and small companies are constantly being created?

What Happens When a Community's Basic Jobs Disappear?

In the previous section, we looked at the profound importance of basic jobs and a basic industry to an economy. Let's now look at two specific examples of what happen when a town's basic industry disappears. This is a problem especially with towns dependent on mining, since mineral resources do run out or become too costly to mine.

The first example is Schefferville, which is 600 kilometres north of the St. Lawrence River near the border between Québec and Labrador (Figure 9–7). For almost 30 years, Schefferville was an important mining centre for iron ore, with its ore supplying steel mills in Hamilton and elsewhere. In 1982, the mine's owners announced the mine would close since its operation had become unprofitable. The population of the town soon fell from about 5000 to barely 200.

The second example is the town of Elliot Lake (Figure 9–8). It was established in 1955 to be the home for workers at the many uranium mines in the area. By 1960, Elliot Lake's population had increased to about 25 000. Everything changed by the early 1990s. Lower demand and prices for uranium, along with reduced reserves, meant that the last of a dozen mines closed down. Without the mines, there would be few basic jobs in the town. Residents could see their town becoming like Schefferville, with the homes they loved losing most of their value. They needed to find a new source of basic employment. They started by looking at the assets of the town:

- It was a modern town with good schools, a hospital, recreational facilities, and some shopping facilities.

- Houses (from miners and their families who had left the town) were available at a very reasonable cost.

▲ **Figure 9–7** Compared to its previous size, Schefferville is almost a ghost town today. How is this change related to basic jobs?

▲ **Figure 9–8** When the people and town government of Elliot Lake heard that their mines were closing, their first reaction was fear for their town. Their next reaction was to wonder how they could rescue their town and give it a future. What do you think they did?

©P

- The town was 30 kilometres from Highway 17 (Figure 9–9), which is part of the Trans-Canada Highway system. From the town, one could travel east to Sudbury (2 hours), Toronto (6 hours), and Ottawa (8 hours). To the west was Sault Ste. Marie (2.5 hours), all of western Canada, and access to the United States.

- Sudbury, a city of 160 000, provided a wide range of shopping, specialist medical services, a university, and a community college.

- By the standards of most of Canada, the climate is moderate. Summers are warm but rarely too hot. Winters are cold but not as cold as much of Canada.

- Elliot Lake is surrounded by scenic, clean lakes and rivers and is quite close to the north shore of Lake Huron. In summer, boating, fishing, and canoeing are all around. In winter, snowmobiling and downhill and cross-country skiing are just outside the door.

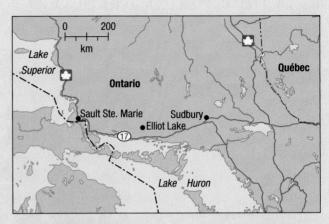

▲ **Figure 9–9 Elliot Lake, Ontario.** What location advantages would make Elliot Lake an attractive site for a new basic industry after the mines closed?

APPLY IT!

1. In what way was Elliot Lake's situation similar to Schefferville's?

2. What advantage(s) did Elliot Lake have over Schefferville when it came to finding a new source of basic employment?

3. **a)** Assuming you do not know what happened in Elliot Lake, and without doing research, what basic industry could the town develop?

   b) The products of Elliot Lake's original basic industry were sold to other parts of Canada and to the United States. How is this different from the new basic industry?

4. By 2013, the world demand and price for iron ore was much higher than when the Schefferville mine closed. Two companies were in the process of opening new mines in the immediate vicinity of Schefferville. What might this mean for basic and non-basic employment in the area and for the town itself?

5. Why do municipalities do all they can to encourage new basic employment? Express your answer in terms of the multiplier effect.

Is the Tertiary Sector the Most or Least Important Part of the Economy?

▶ **Figure 9–10** Canada exports knowledge-based services such as management, financial, and engineering consulting. For example, Cowater International provided consulting services for a water development project in Mozambique, Africa.

Viewpoint 1

The tertiary sector is by far the most important.

💬 How could it be otherwise? More than three-quarters of Canada's jobs are in the service sector.

💬 Primary and secondary are important, but it is the service sector that provides the necessities of life: education, health care, entertainment, shopping, and so on.

💬 The growth of knowledge-based service companies is dramatically increasing the number of basic service jobs (Figure 9–10).

Viewpoint 2

There is more to it than job numbers.

💬 Determining which sector is most important is about the number of dollars, not the number of jobs. Canada's economic growth is being driven by its resource industries.

💬 We need to focus our attention on industries that have many basic jobs. Once basic jobs are created, the non-basic jobs will follow naturally because of the multiplier effect.

💬 The vast majority of our exports are products, not services.

APPLY IT!

1. Do you think that primary and secondary (goods-producing) industries are more important to Canada's economy than tertiary (service-providing) industries? Explain your answer.

2. At first glance, these viewpoints appear to be totally at odds with each other. How can the views be combined into one description of the importance of the service sector to the economy?

©P

APPLY IT!

1. a) Give four examples of knowledge-based, basic, service industry jobs.

   b) Why are jobs like these very important to Canada's future?

2. In your own words, explain the multiplier effect and how it works.

3. Create a spending web to show what might happen to $100 that Joanne earns. Your web should
   - show money moving between Kapuskasing's local economy and the external (provincial, national, global) economy
   - show some of Joanne's money ending up in Henri's pocket
   - show the $100 being re-spent three times in Kap before leaving

4. The multiplier effect works exactly the same for jobs in the tertiary sector as it does for the pulp and paper businesses in Kapuskasing. Briefly explain how five different basic tertiary jobs contribute to Canada's economy.

5. Suppose that you are the mayor of a growing city of 50 000 people somewhere in Ontario. Solely from the perspective of your city's job situation, which of the following developments would you be most pleased about? Assume that the workers will be paid similar wages.
   - the opening of a new factory that employs 10 workers, *or*
   - the opening of the city's new garbage recycling depot that employs 20 workers

   Explain your answer using a variety of details.

6. a) ■ Spatial Significance A growing number of towns and cities, from Vancouver Island to Atlantic Canada, have healthy economies because of their popularity as retirement communities. Is this trend likely to increase in the next few decades? Explain your answer.

   b) Which regions of Canada, and specifically Ontario, are most likely to benefit?

7. Which type of job, basic or non-basic, is it better to have in an economy and for an individual?

8. What role can sports play in building Canada's economy? Is hosting events such as the Olympics and Pan Am Games and supporting the growth of professional sports (e.g., an NHL team in Québec City, an MLB team in Montréal, an NFL team in Toronto, and an NBA team in Vancouver) a good way to build Canada's economy? Why or why not?

CONNECTING

Recall what you learned about knowledge-based industries in **Chapter 8 (page 173)**.

Geo✿Inquiry

Gather and Organize

Some authorities suggest that there is a fourth sector of the economy called the quaternary sector. What are the characteristics of this sector and why is it important to Canada?

CONNECTING

Chapter 10 examines why the number of retirees in Canada is increasing dramatically.

©P

CHAPTER 9 THE SERVICE SECTOR AND ITS ROLE IN THE ECONOMY **207**

The Service Sector and Its Role in the Economy

? **Do we need to be concerned about the quantity and quality of jobs in the service sector?**

For 500 years, our economy has relied on natural resources (that is, primary industries) for most of our basic jobs and exports. Indeed, in recent years, these have become even more important. But does the success of Cirque du Soleil suggest a bright future direction for the Canadian economy? How can we expand basic employment in a wide range of services from tourism to entertainment, higher education, and financial services? What role does government have in this? Does it depend on large companies investing in people and ideas? How important is the imagination and hard work of individuals like Guy Laliberté working in many diverse fields?

One study suggested that the 10 most common job openings in 2014 did not even exist in 2004. This remarkable statistic suggests how important it is that workers be flexible and able to change careers as the economy and technology continue to evolve.

1. **OSSLT** Why is it highly likely that you will work in some part of the service sector? How is your future employment related to where you live? Consider in your answer the size of your community (big city, small town, or rural) and the part of Canada where you live.

2. Use a Venn diagram to organize a minimum of 20 jobs in two ways. First, include at least six jobs from each major sector of the economy. Second, be sure you have at least two basic and two non-basic jobs within each sector.

3. Consider this chapter's Big Question (repeated at the top of this page). Based on what you learned in this chapter, why might *you* be concerned about the number and quality of jobs in the service sector?

Geo ⚙ Inquiry

Evaluate and Draw Conclusions

4. As consumers, what can you and your family or the people you live with do to increase the multiplier effect where you live? Note that "where you live" applies equally to your local community, to your province, and to all of Canada.

5. ■ **Interrelationships** Canada needs more basic employment. Give an example of how this can be accomplished by individuals, by industries, and by governments in Canada. Be sure to consider employment in all three major sectors of the economy.

Analyze an Issue

6. Think about issues related to the service sector that you have read about or that affect your everyday life. Pick one of these issues.

a) Write a number of questions about the issue. Narrow your questions down to one clearly stated and important big question.

b) Find three or four resources and collect information to answer your question. Be sure to analyze the information and consider various viewpoints.

c) Take a position and answer your question with facts from your research.

d) Create a product that communicates your answer. This could be an opinion paper, a blog post, a poster, or a letter to the editor.

©P

Managing Canada's Resources and Economic Activities

This unit has covered a wide range of topics from used pop cans to multi-billion dollar oil pipeline projects. They all deal with the choices that we, as a society, make about how we want to manage our resources and economic activities. In this task, you will have the opportunity to investigate exactly how *we* manage resources and economic activities. *We* actually includes three separate but interrelated groups (Figure 1). Each of these plays a critical role in the management of our resources and economic activities. The groups are *Business* (including the media), *Government*, and, most importantly, *People*. Each makes important decisions and each has considerable influence on the decisions that are made by the other two.

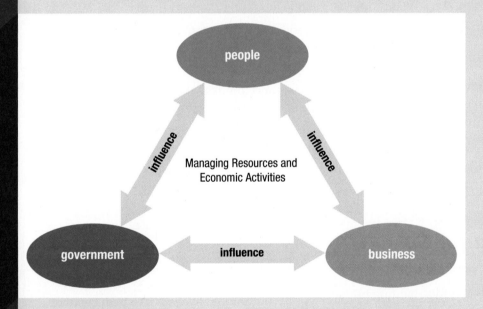

◀ **Figure 1** The management of our resources and economic activities involves a complex interaction of the needs, wants, and decisions of people, business, and government.

ACTIVITY

1. Before you begin your Performance Task, consider how the three groups in Figure 1 influence each other. Give several specific examples of the ways in which each group affects the other two. For each arrow, explain how the interaction can impact both the environment and the economy.

2. Compare your answers with the answers of at least two classmates. Add additional relationships to your sheet as you think appropriate.

Finding the Ideal Economic/ Environmental Balance

How do we determine the best balance between building a stronger economy and protecting the environment?

3. Select one specific example of resource or economic activity management. Remember the different types of resources, including human resources. Economic activities include fishing, farming, forestry, manufacturing, services, and other industries. Analyze how management occurs today and how management could be better in the future. Take the following steps to complete your task:

✓ Before you start, check your topic with your teacher.

✓ Gather and organize important background information about the resource or economic activity.

✓ Pose an important and focused question to answer.

✓ Investigate the roles played by people, business, and government in relation to your question.

✓ Clearly state the position of four or five different groups on the strategies that can be used to manage this resource or activity. For example, look at it from economic, political, social, and environmental perspectives or at local, national, and international levels.

✓ Analyze the benefits to be gained and any problems created by the current management. (In business, this is called a cost–benefit analysis).

✓ Identify any patterns and trends that currently exist in the management of the resource or economic activity.

✓ Evaluate your evidence. Draw a valid conclusion that effectively answers your question.

✓ Consider how best to communicate your conclusions. Include graphics such as maps, graphs, diagrams, and organizers.

Criteria for Success

Your plan or proposal will

❑ show a clear understanding of the relationship between the effective management of our resources and economic activities and the actions and interactions of people, business, and government

❑ evaluate the nature of the current management and indicate how it could be improved

❑ demonstrate critical thinking by going beyond personal opinion in doing your analysis

❑ analyze the situation from different perspectives

❑ apply ideas from the unit in your analysis

❑ include a clear proposal for taking action

❑ communicate your proposal using effective writing and graphical skills

Changing Populations

BIG QUESTION

Why are changes in population patterns over time critically important?

▲ This family is actually a bit larger than the Canadian average. The average woman has 1.6 children. That is much less than in the past.

LET'S GO!

- How many children would you like to have? Why does this number make sense?

- What role does immigration play in Canada's population?

- What population should Canada have?

- Does Canada give enough money to poor countries?

KEY CONCEPTS

- demography
- components of population growth
- migration
- demographic transition model
- foreign aid

10 | Canada's Population

KEY TERMS

demography

birth rate

death rate

natural increase rate

net migration rate

population
   growth rate

doubling time

push factor

pull factor

refugee

dependency load

? **How is Canada's population changing, and why does this matter to your future?**

Understanding Canada's Population Growth

For more than 150 years, Canada's population has grown steadily and, for most of that time, quite rapidly. In the past, most of the growth came from the simple fact that more people were born each year than died. Family sizes were large, and ever-improving health conditions meant that more children survived into adulthood so they could have their own children. It was not until the 20th century started that migration to Canada became a consistent factor in our population growth. On the graph, look at what has happened to the increase due to more births than deaths since the period 1951 to 1961. Note that projections for the future suggest that this trend will continue. When you see a significant trend like this, two questions should come to your mind: Why is it happening? What is the impact of the change?

Canada's Population Growth Rate, 1851–2061

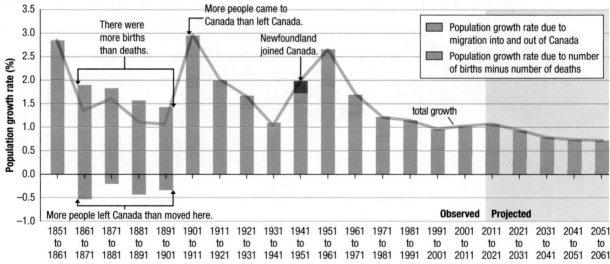

Source: Statistics Canada

THINKING CRITICALLY

OSSLT What has happened to the rate of population growth in recent years? How have the components of this growth changed? What are some of the benefits of having a higher population? What are some of the drawbacks?

On an Average Day ...

According to Statistics Canada, on an average day between July 1, 2011, and June 30, 2012, ...

- 1042 babies were born in Canada and 689 people died. This caused Canada's population to increase by 353.

- 710 people moved to Canada as **immigrants** and 140 moved out of Canada as **emigrants**. This caused Canada's population to increase by 570.

- As a result, there were 923 (353 + 570) more people living in Canada at the end of the day than there were 24 hours earlier.

This is your introduction to the fascinating and important study of human populations that is called demography. Some knowledge of demography will help you better understand the population challenges facing Canada and other countries.

immigrant a person who moves to one country from another country

emigrant a person who leaves one country to move to another country

demography the study of human populations

Use Rates, Not Numbers

You just learned that 1042 children were born in Canada on a typical day in 2011–2012. We can compare this to the number of births in Japan (2822 per day) and in the West African country of Togo (297 per day). Or can we? Making comparisons of numbers can be somewhat pointless since the populations of these countries are so different. In 2014, Canada had 35.5 million people, while Japan had 127.4 million and Togo had only 6.2 million.

If you think about it, what matters most is not the number of births, but the relationship between the number of births and the size of the population. A simple measurement called the birth rate shows this relationship. A country's birth rate is calculated by dividing the number of births by the population number and then multiplying the result by 1000. For example, Canada's birth rate in 2014 was (386 000 ÷ 35 540 000) × 1000 ≈ 10.9 (Table 10–1). In general, if you use rates rather than numbers, you will find it much easier to compare populations in different places or at different periods in history.

birth rate the number of births in a population per year per 1000 people

Table 10–1 Birth rates for Canada, Japan, and Togo, 2014

Country	Number of births 2014	Population 2014	Birth rate (births per 1000 people)
Canada	386 000	35 540 000	10.9
Japan	1 029 000	127 100 000	8.1
Togo	255 000	7 400 000	34.5

Sources: Statistics Canada; Central Intelligence Agency, *The World Factbook*

A similar measure, the death rate, gives the number of deaths per year for every 1000 people. In 2014, the death rate in Canada was 7.2 per 1000, while Japan's was 9.3 per 1000 and Togo's was 7.4 per 1000.

death rate the number of deaths in a population per year per 1000 people

natural increase rate the birth rate minus the death rate

We can combine the birth rate and death rate into a very useful measurement called the natural increase rate. The natural increase rate is the difference between the birth rate and the death rate. Canada's natural increase rate in 2014 was 3.7 per 1000 (birth rate – death rate = 10.9/1000 – 7.2/1000 = 3.7/1000). This equals 0.4 percent. In contrast, Togo's natural increase rate was 28 per 1000 (2.8 percent) and Japan's rate was –1 per 1000 (–0.1 percent). What does a negative rate mean?

What About Immigration?

In most countries, natural increase is the main reason for population increases (or decreases). Japan and Togo are good examples. However, this is not the case in Canada. Here, immigration is more important than natural increase. Remember that Canada's population increased on a typical day by 570 because of migration and only 353 because of natural increase.

immigration rate the number of immigrants moving to a country per year per 1000 people

emigration rate the number of emigrants moving from a country per year per 1000 people

net migration rate the immigration rate minus the emigration rate

population growth rate the natural increase rate plus the net migration rate

The immigration and emigration rates are calculated in the same way as birth and death rates. The **immigration rate** measures the number of immigrants per 1000 people in the whole population. The **emigration rate** measures the number of emigrants per 1000 people. Canada's immigration rate in 2014 was 7.5 per 1000. Canada's emigration rate was 1.5 per 1000. If we combine the immigration and emigration rates, we get the net migration rate. Canada's rate in 2014 was 6 per 1000 (7.5/1000 – 1.5/1000 = 6/1000) or 0.6 percent.

There is only one more rate to know: the population growth rate. This combines natural increase and net migration. Canada's population growth rate in 2014 was 10 per 1000 (4/1000 + 6/1000 = 10/1000) or 1.0 percent.

Your reaction to all these demographic calculations may well be, "Who cares?" The answer is, you should. The rate at which a country's population grows (or declines) has an enormous influence on people's lives. If the population is growing very rapidly, there may be serious problems providing enough housing, education, health care, and jobs for everyone. On the other hand, if the population is declining, there may be shortages of workers, and businesses must learn to deal with a shrinking market.

Geo ⚙ Inquiry

Gather and Organize

Some Canadian communities attract many immigrants while others do not. What evidence can you gather that would tell you in which category your community is?

APPLY IT!

1. In 2012, China had 16 350 000 births and 9 660 000 deaths. The population was 1 353 821 000. Calculate the birth rate, death rate, and natural increase rate (to one decimal point).

2. Compare the current size of the two components of Canada's population growth rate. Is this situation a result of a low natural increase rate or a high net migration rate?

3. Why do you think some countries have a negative population growth rate? Could Canada find itself in this situation? How?

4. What are the advantages and disadvantages for a country to have
   a) a high population growth rate?
   b) a low population growth rate?
   c) a negative population growth rate?

©P

The Power of Compounding

While it is useful to understand these rates, they are just the beginning of our demographic journey. Next we have to look at the impact these rates have over many years. To understand why long-term trends matter, imagine that your parents offer you a choice of rewards for your hard work and success in school.

- Option 1: You get $1000 for each day in the month of June.

- Option 2: You get 1¢ on June 1, 2¢ on June 2, 4¢ on June 3, 8¢ on June 4, and so on.

▲ **Figure 10–1** Today, family size in Québec is the smallest in Canada. But for centuries, until the 1960s, most families in Québec were very large. This picture shows singer Céline Dion, her parents, and her brothers and sisters. Céline, who was born in 1968, is the youngest of 14 children.

Which option would you choose? With Option 1, you will get $30 000. With Option 2, you will get $10 737 418.23! Such is the power of compounding, since new growth occurs on top of the growth that has already taken place. Consider a demographic example: A Québec couple who married in 1660 could theoretically have 16 million descendants today, or about half of Canada's entire population (Figure 10–1).

A simple way to understand the impact of compounding in demography is to consider what is called the **doubling time** for a population. You could calculate it accurately using some Grade 11 mathematics or a spreadsheet, but it can be estimated very easily using something called the **rule of 70**. Just divide 70 by the population growth rate and you get a good estimate of the doubling time. For example, with a 0.9 percent growth rate, the doubling time is 78 years (70 ÷ 0.9). The doubling time is only 28 years with a 2.5 percent growth rate. What is the meaning of doubling time for a country like Japan that has a negative population growth rate? Figure 10–2 shows the impact of compounding on the populations of Canada, Japan, and Togo for the next 100 years, assuming that each country's population growth rate remains as it is today.

doubling time the length of time for a country's population to double at a particular population growth rate

rule of 70 a simple calculation to estimate doubling time (70 ÷ population growth rate)

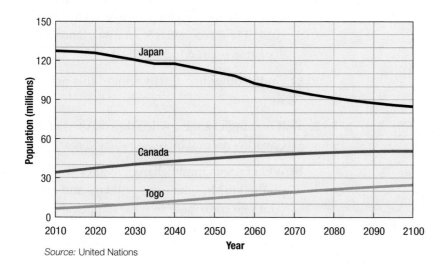

Source: United Nations

◄ **Figure 10–2 United Nations population projections for Japan, Canada, and Togo.** These are medium-variant estimates—the UN's best guess about what will happen. The UN also produces high-variant and low-variant estimates. The high-variant estimate for Canada in 2100 is 74 million, while the low-variant estimate is only 34 million (a bit less than today's population). How can these projections be so different?

Trends in Canada's Natural Increase History

The values in Table 10–2 tell us a fascinating story about Canada's history—and its future. While you can "read" the story when you look at the numbers, it is easier to do so when the numbers have been graphed.

Table 10–2 Canada's birth rates and death rates, 1851–2011

Census period	Birth rate (/1000)	Death rate (/1000)
1851–1861	45.2	23.7
1861–1871	42.4	23.5
1871–1881	40.1	21.4
1881–1891	35.2	20.1
1891–1901	32.0	18.2
1901–1911	35.8	16.8
1911–1921	32.5	14.8
1921–1931	27.5	12.0
1931–1941	22.1	10.3
1941–1951	27.7	10.6
1951–1956	30.8	9.3
1956–1961	29.4	8.5
1961–1966	24.7	8.0
1966–1971	18.5	7.7
1971–1976	16.3	7.6
1976–1981	15.5	7.2
1981–1986	15.1	7.1
1986–1991	14.8	7.2
1991–1996	13.8	7.3
1996–2001	11.5	7.4
2001–2006	11.1	7.5
2006–2011	10.7	7.7

Source: Statistics Canada

APPLY IT!

1. a) Graph the data in Table 10–2 using a multiple-line graph. Note that the dates here are averages for 10- and 5-year periods (5 years after 1951). To graph these data, you should use the middle year of the range (e.g., use 1856 for 1851–1861).

   b) Label "birth rate" and "death rate" on your graph. What area on the graph represents "natural increase"? Shade and label this.

2. If data existed before 1851, what values would you expect to see?

3. Your graph shows the impact of particular historical events on people having or not having children. Identify at least two such major events and indicate why the birth rate went up or down.

4. a) If you look carefully, you will see that the death rate has crept up slowly since 1986. By 2014, it had reached 8.3. At first glance, why does this seem odd?

   b) On the other hand, why should this not be surprising?

5. a) If nothing changes, when do you predict that Canada's natural increase rate will reach zero?

   b) What factors might change to alter your prediction? In what way will you and others your age contribute to what happens?

Immigration: A 400-Year Tradition

About 97 percent of Canadians are either immigrants (they were born in another country) or they are descended from immigrants. Their ancestors came to Canada in the last 400 years (with most of these immigrants coming since 1900).

Just over 4 percent of the population, about 1.4 million people, is made up of First Nations, Métis, and Inuit peoples. According to the 2011 census, of these 1.4 million people,

- 852 000 people were First Nations

- 452 000 were Métis people; this means they have mixed First Nations and European ancestry

- 59 000 were Inuit (singular, Inuk); this group has traditionally lived in the Arctic and sub-Arctic and is distinct from First Nations peoples.

- 38 000 people either identified with more than one of these groups or did not state their identification on their census forms

Why People Become Immigrants

Imagine that, at some point in the future, you decide you have had enough of winter. You wake up early one morning to shovel even more heavy, wet snow. Then you fight traffic for two hours to get to a job you really do not like and where you see little chance of advancement. Your cousin, who emigrated to country X years ago, has been telling you to move there too. The job situation is great. There is no winter to deal with, and it is a good place to raise your young family.

If this happened, you would be considering a migration decision. Every year, hundreds of thousands of people who are thinking about moving to Canada find themselves in this situation. Two types of factors influence such a decision:

- **Push factors:** These could be fairly trivial, such as the weather. They could also be serious—the threat of war, poor environmental conditions, or desperate economic problems.

- **Pull factors:** When people have decided to migrate, they "shop around" for the country that seems most attractive to them. Attractive pull factors might include economic and educational opportunities and political stability. Having relatives or friends in another country is a very important pull factor.

CONNECTING

Figure 10–18 on **page 231** shows you First Nations reserves and communities across Canada.

Geo ⚙ Inquiry

Formulate Questions

Survey students in your school to find out why their families immigrated to Canada. Compose a short list of questions to collect your data. Organize your data in a table. Look at the 2012 column in Table 10–3 on p. 221. How many students in your survey were from each group? What push and pull factors are common among the immigrant groups in your school? Present your conclusions in the form of an essay, chart, poster, pie chart, short video, or some other way.

push factor a reason that encourages people to move away from their current country

pull factor a reason that makes a particular country seem attractive to potential immigrants

CONNECTING

You can learn more about becoming an immigrant to Canada on **page 222**.

Geo ✿ **Inquiry**

Formulate Questions

What questions would someone thinking of becoming an illegal migrant to Canada have to consider?

Assume that a person has made two related decisions: to emigrate (push) from his or her home country and to immigrate to Canada (pull). Next the person needs to consider any *intervening obstacles* that might prevent a move to Canada. At the top of the list of obstacles is the complicated process that the person must go through to be accepted by Canada or by another attractive migrant destination, such as the United States, Germany, or Australia. The person may not qualify to become a new Canadian. As well, the cost of immigration is significant, especially for a poorer person. Finally, the decision to move, perhaps halfway around the world, is a wrenching one. A migrant must be willing to leave behind so many familiar things. There can be a big difference between thinking about becoming an emigrant and actually doing it.

So far, we have been talking about legal migration. Many people each year become illegal migrants. Generally these people cannot qualify to be legal migrants or do not want to wait for years to see if they can legally move to another country. Canada has a relatively low number of illegal migrants, compared to countries that are located near much poorer nations. Good examples of countries with serious illegal immigrant problems are the United States, Australia, and countries in the southern part of the European Union (Figure 10–3). In these parts of the world, migrants try to enter a country illegally, either by sea or land.

It is much harder to get a photo of the other type of illegal immigration. It happens when people enter a country legally, often as tourists, temporary workers, or students, and stay in the country after their visas run out. Most illegal immigrants to Canada come as visitors and just stay on after their visas run out.

▲ **Figure 10–3** Illegal immigration has two faces. These photos illustrate the one that most people know best. (a) When the sea separates a poorer part of the world from a richer one, people try to migrate illegally on small boats that are generally dangerously overcrowded. Scenes like this occur daily in the Mediterranean Sea and in the Indian Ocean northwest of Australia. (b) Along the U.S. border with Mexico, the number of illegal migrants on foot is so large that motorists are warned of the dangers of groups of people running across the highway.

©P

1. **a)** Is the percentage of Aboriginal and Métis peoples in Canada's population increasing or decreasing? If you do not know the answer, how would you find the data?

   b) What data did you find?

2. To what extent are the push and pull factors connected to Canadian immigration the same today as they were a century ago?

3. Do part a) of this question if your immediate family/guardian immigrated to Canada. Do part b) if your immediate family/guardian did not immigrate to Canada.

   a) What other countries did your family/guardian consider moving to? Why did they consider Canada along with these countries? Why did they choose Canada?

   b) Has your family/guardian ever considered emigrating from Canada? Why or why not? If you were to move from Canada, what countries might you consider moving to? Why?

4. Illegal migration causes problems for the migrant and for the receiving country. Explain what these might be.

Canada's Immigration History

When we look at Canada's immigration history, we must consider two fundamental questions: *How many* people came to Canada at various times in history? *Where* did they come from? It is important to remember that both the numbers and the sources of immigrants have changed dramatically over the years.

How Many?

Figure 10–4 on the next page gives a summary of the dramatic changes that have occurred in the number of migrants at different times. When you look at this graph, remember that you are looking at numbers, not rates. The largest number of immigrants came to Canada in 1913, when 413 000 people arrived. This number is even more impressive when you consider that Canada's population then was only 7.6 million. A quick calculation shows that there was one immigrant for every 18 residents in the country. In contrast, in 2012, when the population was 34.8 million, we received 258 000 immigrants—a rate of one immigrant for every 135 people. We are still a country of immigrants, but not like we were before World War I, when the government was working very hard to populate the country.

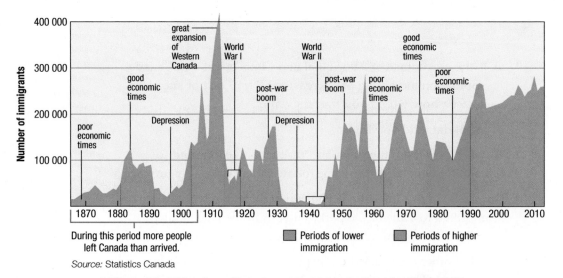

Source: Statistics Canada

▲ **Figure 10–4 Number of immigrants arriving in Canada, 1865–2015.**

■ **Interrelationships** It is easy to see, from this graph, that wars and bad global (and Canadian) economic conditions act as major factors to reduce immigration. It is interesting to note that the 1990–2012 span of high immigration has included times of both stronger and weaker economic activity.

SKILL FOCUS

When reading a graph, such as Figure 10–4, follow these steps:

• Determine the type of graph.

• Examine the data being shown, along with the caption and labels.

• Figure out the purpose of the graph.

• Evaluate whether the graph shows the data in a fair, objective way.

• Describe the data trends shown in the graph.

• What conclusions can you draw from the graph?

From Where?

The source of our immigrants has changed over the years depending on the pull factors and—especially—the push factors that have existed at any point in history (Figure 10–5). A couple of examples will illustrate this point.

• **Push factors** in the 1840s: The Irish potato crop failed due to the rapid spread of a plant disease. One estimate suggests that an average adult male in Ireland at the time ate *60 potatoes a day*. Obviously, when the potato crop failed, it was a terrible calamity. Thousands of Irish moved to Canada and other countries to avoid starvation.

• **Pull factors** from 1896 to 1913: The Canadian government offered incentives to attract immigrants, including free land in the Prairies.

▶ **Figure 10–5** A significant number of Americans moved to the Canadian West between 1890 and World War I because they were offered higher quality farmland than was available in the United States. By that time, settlement of the U.S. frontier was almost completed.

©P

Table 10–3 shows the sources of Canada's immigrants at different periods of our history. In each period, the countries are listed in order from the highest number of immigrants.

Table 10–3 Sources of Canada's immigrants in selected periods from 1900 to 2012 (in order from highest)

1900–1920	1965	2012
United Kingdom*	United Kingdom*	China*
United States*	Italy*	Philippines*
Italy	United States*	India*
Poland**	Germany	Pakistan
Russia**	Portugal	United States
Jewish**	Greece	France
Ukraine**	China	Iran
China	Caribbean	United Kingdom
Germany	France	Haiti
Austria	Yugoslavia	South Korea

Source: Statistics Canada

* Countries providing more than 10 000 immigrants per year

** Note that people listed in the categories Poland, Russia, Jewish, and Ukraine came from what was then the Russian Empire and the Austro-Hungarian Empire.

GeoCareers

Raising Awareness of Demography

David Foot is a demographer and professor at the University of Toronto. Like many Canadians, he has a globalized background. He was born in England, grew up in Australia, and did his postgraduate education in the United States before moving to Canada. Before Foot's work, the study of demography was not well known by the general public. His best-selling book *Boom, Bust & Echo: How to Profit from the Coming Demographic Shift* changed this and made demography a topic that is even taught in Grade 9 geography! Go online to learn more about becoming a professional demographer.

APPLY IT!

1. a) Identify at least four countries, other than Canada, that you think would be attractive to potential immigrants.

   b) What characteristics do these countries share with Canada that make them attractive?

   c) How might a potential immigrant choose one country over the rest?

2. Refer to Table 10–3 to answer these questions.

   a) How have the sources of Canadian immigrants changed over the years? In what ways have they remained the same?

   b) Use the concept of pull and push factors to explain the differences.

   c) How have the changes in immigrant sources affected Canada's culture?

3. What have you read in this chapter so far that can help you decide if immigration is a good thing or not for Canada? Based on what you have read and other sources, is immigration a good thing for Canada? Explain your answer.

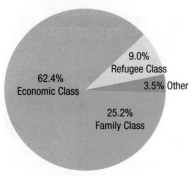

Source: Citizenship and Immigration Canada

▲ **Figure 10–6 New permanent residents admitted to Canada, 2012.** In recent years, the percentage of Economic Class immigrants has risen, while the percentages in Family Class and Refugee Class have declined. What might explain this trend?

SKILL FOCUS

Note-taking helps you gather important information when you are reading text. Here are some hints to help make the process as useful as possible. For this section on "How to Become an Immigrant" up to the bottom of page 224, follow these steps:

- Scan the entire section quickly so you have a general idea of what is being covered.
- Read the entire section and make point-form notes as you go.
- There is no one, "best" way to take notes. Develop a style that works for you.
- You may find that using graphic organizers works well.
- Be sure to define or explain unfamiliar terms.

Review your notes to ensure that they are complete and that you understand them. You can use these steps when you read any type of text.

How to Become an Immigrant

The number of people who would like to migrate to Canada far exceeds the number who are actually admitted. The government tries to provide potential immigrants with enough information so that they know whether it makes sense even to apply. In spite of this, immigration officials are often swamped with applications, resulting in long delays in the process. In recent years, the government has had to stop taking some types of new immigrant applications in order to focus on processing existing ones.

The reason for the huge difference between the number of potential immigrants and the number who are actually accepted is quite simple—it is very difficult to qualify. In fact, many Canadian residents would *not* qualify under current requirements. The federal government is constantly fine-tuning the immigration system. The intention is to choose immigrants who will be successful in Canada and benefit Canada's economy. In recent years, the trend has been toward ever-tougher standards. For example, in 2013, the requirement to speak either English or French was made much stricter.

Immigration to Canada falls into two very broad categories. Some immigrants are accepted because they will provide an economic benefit to Canada. They bring education, experience, and money that will help our economy grow. Other immigrants are accepted for social or humanitarian reasons: to reunite families and to help people who are facing oppression. In 2012, Canada accepted 257 887 immigrants in all classes within these two broad categories. Figure 10–6 shows the breakdown by class.

Economic Immigration—Permanent Residents

Economic immigrants are accepted because they can contribute to Canada's economy when they arrive. There are four classes or programs in this category.

- **Skilled Worker Class:** Potential skilled-worker immigrants are judged on a point system. To be admitted, they need a minimum number of points. This point assessment is done for the family member with the highest point total. If one person qualifies, the entire family is admitted. The government has identified high-demand occupations, such as engineers, business executives, doctors, nurses, and medical technicians. People with training and experience in these areas are fast-tracked through the system because Canada needs their skills.

- **Skilled Trades Class:** This category exists to attract immigrants with specific trade skills that are in short supply in Canada. Only certain tradespeople are eligible, including electricians, plumbers, machinists, loggers, and mine workers. This class uses a pass-or-fail system rather than a point system. A person must meet four conditions: have a job offer in Canada, have strong enough language skills to do the job, have two or more years of experience in the trade, and be qualified to do the job by Canadian standards.

©P

- **Canadian Experience Class:** This class exists to accept immigrants who have legally worked in Canada under a temporary worker program for at least one year. It is a pass-or-fail system, but the applicant does not require a job offer in Canada.

- **Start-Up Visa:** To apply in this class, a person must want to start a business in Canada. Applicants must meet four criteria to be accepted:
    - They must show that approved Canadian investors will fund their business idea.
    - They must demonstrate a high degree of proficiency in English or French.
    - They must have at least one year of post-secondary education.
    - They must have enough of their own money to support themselves until the proceeds from their business can support them.

Economic Immigration—Temporary Residents

Temporary workers are allowed into Canada for two reasons. One is to fill labour shortages in certain fields. The other is to allow people with extraordinary talents to contribute to Canada's economy and culture.

- **Temporary Foreign Worker Program:** Canada grants work permits for temporary foreign workers. A wide variety of people qualify for these permits, ranging from professional athletes who play for Canadian teams to workers in fast-food restaurants, especially in parts of Canada that have low unemployment rates (Figure 10–7). Some end up staying in Canada by qualifying for the Canadian Experience Class of immigration described above. Most return to their home country at the end of their work contract. Throughout its history, this program has been controversial. Critics claim that it allows companies to hire foreign workers when they could employ Canadian residents. Supporters say that it is essential to the operation of many kinds of businesses.

Geo Inquiry

Evaluate and Draw Conclusions

Some people have suggested that skilled immigrants, such as doctors, should be required to work in parts of Canada where their services are most needed. Suggest arguments that both support and oppose this idea.

▼ **Figure 10–7** Temporary foreign workers provide a variety of benefits to Canada. A few are famous, but most work in ordinary jobs. (a) Dancer Svetlana Lunkina came from the renowned Bolshoi Ballet in Russia to dance with the National Ballet of Canada. (b) Thousands of workers come to Canada each year from Mexico and other countries to work on farms.

(a)

(b)

Social and Humanitarian Immigration

▲ **Figure 10–8** An interpreter helps a Canadian Border Services officer talk to newly arrived immigrants.

refugee someone who moves to another country because of fear of cruel or inhumane treatment (even death) in her or his home country as a result of race, religion, sexual orientation, nationality, political opinion, or membership in a particular social group

Canada also accepts immigrants for social and humanitarian reasons. Social immigration involves reuniting families. Humanitarian immigration helps people escape danger or severe discrimination in their home countries.

Family Class: Citizens or permanent residents of Canada are allowed to sponsor close family members who want to move to Canada (Figure 10–8). The sponsor agrees to be financially responsible for the person being sponsored. For example, if that person does not have a job, the sponsor has to support him or her. Depending on the relationship, the length of the financial commitment varies from 3 to 10 years.

Refugee Class: Under international law, all countries have a responsibility to accept legitimate refugees. **Refugees** are people who move to another country because they fear for their safety in their home country (Figure 10–9). A person may apply for refugee status while in Canada or from another country. Each refugee claim is judged on its merits, and the majority of claims are rejected. For example, refugee claims by members of the U.S. armed forces who did not want to fight in the recent wars in Afghanistan and Iraq were rejected. A generation earlier, claims by those who did not want to serve in the Vietnam War were accepted. The logic behind the different decisions was that during the Vietnam War, the United States drafted young men involuntarily into the military. In the more recent wars, those claiming refugee status had all volunteered to join the military.

▲ **Figure 10–9** Many refugee claimants to Canada are coming from countries where the threat of violence is high because of political unrest or a repressive government. This photo was taken in Egypt, but it could have been taken in a dozen or more other countries.

©P

1. **a)** How does our system for admitting economic immigrants help Canada?

   b) Is this process fair to the countries these people are leaving? Explain your answer.

2. Citizenship and Immigration Canada has a website that helps potential migrants determine whether they would qualify to immigrate to Canada. You are going to do only Step 1 of the process, which checks the eligibility of potential migrants.

   a) You will have to create a potential immigrant. Your person will need a specific set of characteristics: age, family status, education, job experience, and so on. Record the characteristics of your person so you can analyze the connections between these characteristics and the person's eligibility for admission.

   b) Did the person you created qualify? What characteristics of your person were important in meeting (or failing to meet) the criteria for admission?

   c) If a person does not qualify, what options are open to him or her?

   d) What value does this website have for potential immigrants?

   e) What value does it have for the government?

3. Why would the requirement that immigrants speak either English or French help to make them more successful in Canada?

4. **a)** Many people who apply for refugee status have been called "economic refugees" and "line jumpers." What do these terms mean?

   b) Why is it often very difficult to determine whether a refugee claim is valid?

   c) Without doing any research, do you think most refugee claimants are accepted or rejected? Check online to see if you were right.

5. What are the costs and benefits, for refugees and for Canada, of admitting refugees?

6. What one change would you like to make to Canada's immigration system? Put your answer in the form of a tweet to your Member of Parliament.

Where Immigrants Settle

Immigrants tend to move to relatively few parts of Canada. You can see this in the proportion of each province's population that is made up of immigrants (Figure 10–10). For the sake of comparison, remember that in 2011, 20.6 percent of Canada's population was made up of immigrants.

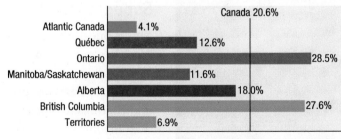

Source: Human Resources and Development Canada

▲ **Figure 10–10 Percentage of immigrants in each province and territory.** Why do you think the distribution is so uneven?

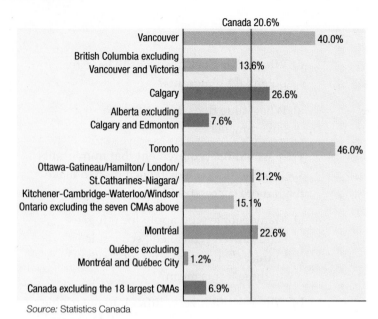

Canada 20.6%

Region	Percentage
Vancouver	40.0%
British Columbia excluding Vancouver and Victoria	13.6%
Calgary	26.6%
Alberta excluding Calgary and Edmonton	7.6%
Toronto	46.0%
Ottawa-Gatineau/Hamilton/ London/ St.Catharines-Niagara/ Kitchener-Cambridge-Waterloo/Windsor	21.2%
Ontario excluding the seven CMAs above	15.1%
Montréal	22.6%
Québec excluding Montréal and Québec City	1.2%
Canada excluding the 18 largest CMAs	6.9%

Source: Statistics Canada

▲ **Figure 10–11 Percentages of people who are immigrants in the populations of various parts of Canada.** Remember that 20.6 percent of the total population is made up of immigrants. What important conclusions can you draw from these data?

Looking at the number of immigrants going to each province tells us only part of the story. Within each province, large census metropolitan areas (CMAs) are more attractive destinations than smaller cities, and smaller cities are more attractive than rural areas (Figure 10–11). In particular, Toronto and Vancouver have very large immigrant populations. In fact, in the City of Toronto part of the Toronto CMA, immigrants actually make up more than half of the population. The immigrant populations of cities in western Canada, such as Calgary, Regina, and Edmonton, are rapidly increasing because of the good job markets there.

Immigrants choose to settle in large cities for several reasons, including the following:

- Most immigrants to Canada come from large cities so they are most comfortable living in large cities in Canada. Note that even the Toronto CMA, with almost six million people, seems small to someone coming from Beijing (21 million) or Mumbai (12 million).

- The large CMAs have large and growing economies. New immigrants need to find jobs, and most go where the job prospects are good.

- Many immigrants have family members and friends who previously came to Canada, and most of these people are in the largest cities.

- It is easier to make the transition to life in Canada. Large cities provide formal and informal supports for this process.

Because of their huge numbers of immigrants, the Toronto and Vancouver CMAs increasingly demonstrate a blending of immigrant and traditional Canadian cultures (Figure 10–12).

Supports for Immigrants

This is one of those chicken and egg situations. Which comes first? If a place has many immigrants, supports for immigrants will be established. If supports for immigrants exist, more immigrants will want to move there. Formal supports are programs and organizations funded by governments and charities to help immigrants adapt to life in Canada. These supports exist in almost all areas of life, such as education, health care, housing, and recreation. Across Canada, hundreds of agencies help immigrants adapt to life here. Most of these are in the largest cities. For example, the City of Toronto provides translation services in 180 languages from A (Acholi, a language from northern Uganda) to Y (Yupi, spoken in

▲ **Figure 10–12** Hockey meets Bollywood. This movie could only have been made in Canada.

©P

...eastern China). (There do not seem to be any "Z" languages.)
...Mixteco, Pahari, and Twi are all spoken in Toronto. Do you
...these languages come from?

...supports are businesses and services that grow in areas where
...ncentration of immigrants. Figure 10–13 shows an Iranian plaza
...Here is what a recent immigrant to Canada had to say about
...plaza: "When I came to Canada, and saw the Iranian Plaza for
...e, I was surprised. It reminded me of home. I felt nostalgic and
...fortable even though I was lonesome for my homeland."
...e community of people from one ethnic group means that immi-
...find the goods and services they need and want. It is important
...at these become valuable assets for the entire community. In a
..., it is not unusual for a high school to have cricket, Bollywood
...Ukrainian Easter egg decorating, table tennis, and a steel band,
...dents of many ethnic backgrounds participating in all of them.

go online

Check out the list of languages supported in Toronto.

go online

You can see an example of an agency that supports immigrants in Hamilton. It provides health-care support.

◀ **Figure 10–13** This shopping mall attracts shoppers of Iranian descent since it provides goods and services of particular interest to people from Iran. It is interesting to note that Iran ranks only 21st in terms of ethnic origin in Toronto, with 1.2 percent of the population. Nevertheless, there are enough Iranians to support businesses like these.

APPLY IT!

1. **a)** Pull factors not only encourage people to move to Canada—they can also attract immigrants to particular cities. Explain how this works.

   b) How is this pattern changing? Why is this change happening?

2. **a)** How might the health needs of a recent immigrant be different from those of someone who has lived in Canada for many years?

   b) What other factor(s) might attract an immigrant to an immigrant health centre?

3. Why is it generally easier for immigrants to be accepted into Canadian society if they move to a large CMA than if they live in a rural area or small town?

4. **a)** What kinds of supports do new immigrant families need when they move to Canada? Who provides those supports?

   b) How do we know whether these supports are working?

5. China, India, and the Philippines provide our largest number of immigrants, and they all have large rural populations. Why do few immigrants from these (and other) countries choose to live in rural parts of Canada?

Does Canada Accept Too Many Immigrants?

The question of whether Canada accepts too many immigrants has been discussed for decades, with no agreement on the answer. Each side passionately supports its position because the number of immigrants, high or low, has a significant impact on what Canada will be like in the future. Currently, we accept about 250 000 immigrants per year. One proposal is that the number of immigrants we accept should be about 1 percent of the total population, or about 350 000 per year. Another alternative is to cap immigration at about 60 000 per year.

Viewpoint 1

Canada should accept more immigrants than we do now.

🗨 Canada has become the world leader in demonstrating how people from all cultures can live together in peace and harmony. We should be celebrating and encouraging this development.

🗨 Our population is rapidly aging. Most new immigrants are relatively young, and many have young children. This helps us maintain a good balance of ages in our population.

🗨 Our economy needs the skills, education, and money that immigrants bring to Canada.

🗨 Canada has been made more interesting because of the arrival of people from all over the world—we have new foods to enjoy, interesting cultural activities, and even new sports to play (Figure 10–14).

🗨 The respected U.K. magazine *The Economist* ranked 140 world cities for liveability: Vancouver was third, Toronto fourth, and Calgary tied for fifth. The diversity of their populations contributes to this.

▶ **Figure 10–14** Cultural traditions from all over the world have enriched Canada. A good example is dragon boat racing, which came to Canada in 1986 and is now enjoyed across the country.

- Accepting so many immigrants is destroying the traditional cultural make-up of Canada and causing conflicts.

- Accepting more immigrants does not solve the problem of an aging population. It would be impossible to take in enough immigrants to make a difference.

- Canadians should be trying to live in a more sustainable fashion. Having a larger population does not contribute to this goal.

- A constant influx of immigrants increases the labour force, which in turn raises unemployment and contributes to lower wages for everyone (Figure 10–15).

- Toronto, Vancouver, and Calgary are losing their liveability because they are becoming too crowded, since so many immigrants are arriving.

▲ **Figure 10–15** In most provinces, the unemployment rate is too high. Someone who holds viewpoint 2 would say that accepting fewer immigrants would reduce unemployment. It would also make it easier for Canadians to find a good job.

APPLY IT!

1. What benefits do you see from large-scale immigration? Many of these benefits were mentioned here. Can you add to the list?

2. What problems can develop as a result of large-scale immigration? Some were mentioned here. Can you think of others?

3. Is it possible to find a compromise or a solution that would satisfy both sides in this controversy? Explain your answer.

THINKING CRITICALLY

4. Why is the debate over immigration policy very important in Canada? Why will it not disappear any time soon?

5. **OSSLT** Imagine that you are advising the prime minister on what Canada's immigration policy should be. How many immigrants per year should Canada select? What supports are needed to make immigration easier? On what categories of immigrants should we focus? Be sure to explain the reasons for your recommendations.

Internal Migration

People do not migrate only from one country to another. They also migrate within Canada. This movement is of two types. Some people move within a province. This is called *intra*provincial migration. The 2011 census reported that about 11 percent of Canadians (3.4 million people) had moved within their province in the preceding five years. Others move from one province to another. This is called *inter*provincial migration. According to the census, about 3 percent of the population (856 000 people) moved from one province to another in the previous five years.

In each case, push and pull factors exist. In general, migration within Canada is simpler because no government must approve the move, and language and cultural change issues are less. Most movement within Canada occurs because people are looking for good jobs. Most often, people move from rural areas to urban areas and from provinces with slowly growing economies to those that are booming. A simple way to assess economic health is to look at unemployment rates. In March 2014, provincial unemployment rates ranged from 4.5 percent to 11.8 percent (Figure 10–16). Interprovincial migration follows the pattern of unemployment closely (Figure 10–17).

▶ **Figure 10–16 Canadian and provincial unemployment rates, early 2014.** Based on these values, in what geographical direction do you think interprovincial migration goes?

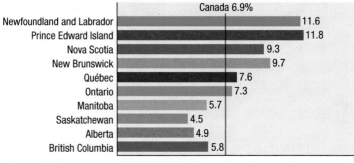

Source: Statistics Canada

▶ **Figure 10–17 Interprovincial migration, 2013.** Surprisingly, only two provinces are net gainers from interprovincial migration. Not surprisingly, these are the two provinces with the lowest unemployment rate.

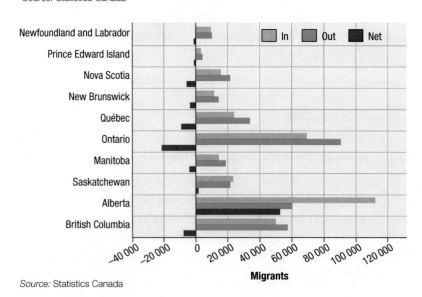

Source: Statistics Canada

©P

Migration of First Nations, Métis, and Inuit Peoples

Aboriginal people are not spread across the country evenly. Nationally, the percentage of Aboriginal people is 4.3 percent but in some provinces and territories, they make up a greater percentage of the population. In Manitoba and Saskatchewan combined, Aboriginal people make up 16.2 percent of the population, while in the three territories, they make up 53.2 percent of the population.

Like other people in Canada, First Nations, Métis and Inuit people are moving to urban areas. The reasons are not hard to find. Aboriginal people face the same economic pressures as other Canadians who live in rural areas, including a lack of good jobs in the local area. But First Nations people also face substandard living conditions on many reserves. Problems of over-crowded housing, poverty, and few jobs are all too common, leading some to compare reserves to poor countries in the developing world.

The strength of these push factors depends on the quality of the economic base that First Nations people have. Most First Nations have reserve lands set aside by treaties (Figure 10–18). Some of those areas are good for agriculture, some provide mining or forestry jobs, and some allow for the development of service industries such as tourism (Figure 10–19). In these areas, the push factor of poor economic opportunity is less.

go online

• The Ontario First Nations map gives the location of more than 140 First Nations communities in the province.

• The First Nations and Treaties map shows the many treaties that have been signed over more than 200 years. It also shows the location and size of reserves.

• Be sure to zoom in on both maps to see more detail.

CONNECTING

Compare Figure 10–18 with Figure 1–5 on **page 24**. How does the pattern of First Nations reserves and settlements compare to the overall population distribution? Why might there be differences?

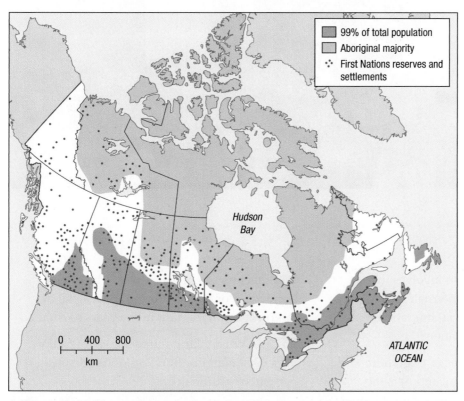

Legend:
- 99% of total population
- Aboriginal majority
- First Nations reserves and settlements

▲ **Figure 10–18 First nations reserves and settlements in Canada.** You can see that many reserves are far away from the main population concentrations across the country. How might this isolation affect people who live on reserves?

▲ **Figure 10–19** The Osoyoos Indian Band has developed the successful Nk'Mip Cellars winery in the South Okanagan area of British Columbia. This First Nation makes good use of a hot, dry climate and fertile soils that are well suited for growing grapes.

Communities N and R in **GeoFlight 1.1 (page 22)** are Inuit and First Nations, respectively. You can see their demographic characteristics in your results to the Zoom In **(pages 22–23)**.

But in many areas, there are few resources, which means the economic base is weak and jobs are scarce. Aboriginal peoples have also pointed to the lack of treaties or the unfair application of existing treaties to help explain the economic problems of many reserves and communities. In these areas, the desire to move to the city may be greater.

Not surprisingly, in parts of the country where the Aboriginal population is high, there are a lot of Aboriginal people in nearby cities. Winnipeg's population is 11 percent Aboriginal, while Regina's is 9.5 percent. In Whitehorse and Yellowknife together, it is about 20 percent. In Ontario, 80 percent of First Nations people live off-reserve.

Like all migrants, Aboriginal people who move to cities face challenges. They are separated from traditional supports like family and community and culture. Aboriginal friendship centres help many people cope with the transition to city life, and provide valuable ongoing cultural and social support for thousands of people (Figure 10–20).

▶ **Figure 10–20** Social events like this at Aboriginal friendship centres give Aboriginal people living in cities a sense of community through shared traditions.

APPLY IT!

1. **a)** Which type of migration involves the most people per year: international migration, interprovincial migration, or intraprovincial migration?

   b) Compare the three types of migration: i) how easy is each to do, and ii) is the move likely to be permanent for each one? Why or why not?

2. What factors might cause you to be a permanent or temporary intraprovincial or interprovincial migrant in the years to come?

3. **OSSLT** What factor(s) may make migration for a First Nations, Inuk, or Métis person particularly difficult?

Dependency Loads and What They Mean for You

Now that we have placed everyone in Canada—they were either born here or arrived as immigrants—it is time to look at our age and gender distribution. A **population pyramid** contains a great deal of useful information in a simple format (Figure 10–21). If you look carefully, you will see that it is nothing more than a series of horizontal bar graphs showing the male population in different age groups on one side, and a similar series of bar graphs for the female population on the other side.

It is very useful to compare population pyramids from different years to see how populations have changed, and will change, over time.

population pyramid a type of graph that shows population distribution by age and gender

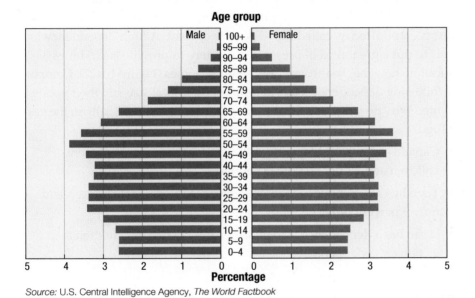

Source: U.S. Central Intelligence Agency, *The World Factbook*

◀ **Figure 10–21 Canada's population by age and gender, 2014.** Where are you in this pyramid?

go online

Statistics Canada has two websites that provide animated Canadian population pyramids. One covers the years 1921 to 2011, and the other covers 1971 to 2056.

APPLY IT!

Go to Statistics Canada websites identified in the Go Online margin feature and find the pyramids for 1921, 1960, 2013, and 2056. Use these pyramids to answer the following questions.

1. Describe how the shapes of the pyramids changed over the years.

2. What do these changes in shape tell you about the overall age distribution and family size of Canada's population over these years?

3. Population pyramids are dynamic graphics in the sense that next year's pyramid is just this year's pyramid with everyone being one year older. In which bar were you in 2014 (Figure 10–21)? In which bar will you be in 2056? How old will you be then? Where will your children's bar(s) likely be in 2056?

4. Considering both structure and jobs, compare the role you (and others your age) play today with the role you will play in 2056.

Different Ages, Different Roles

Geo ⚙ Inquiry

Gather and Organize

An aging population produces a dependency load with specific needs. Research what these needs might be.

At each stage of our lives, we play different roles in society and the economy. Demographers identify three distinct stages:

1. children (under age 15)
2. working adults (ages 15 to 64)
3. older adults (65 and over)

These age ranges may not make perfect sense for a country like Canada. Few people here are working full-time at age 15, many people retire from work before age 65, and others work well beyond age 65. However, these groupings have been used for many years and are used internationally to make comparisons among countries and time periods easier.

The assumption is that children and older adults do not work and must be supported by the working population. This part of the population, which must be supported, is called the dependency load. A high dependency load tends to put a great deal of pressure on society to provide such things as education, housing, health care, and seniors' homes (Figure 10–22). Compare the following dependency loads in terms of their total size and their young/old mix. Why do you think the differences are so great, especially in the case of Togo?

dependency load the percentage of the population that is non-working. It is conventionally defined as including people younger than age 15 and older than age 65.

- Canada today has a dependency load of 33 percent (16 percent children and 17 percent older people).

- Togo has a dependency load of 44 percent (41 percent children and only 3 percent older people).

- Japan has a dependency load of 38 percent (13 percent children and 25 percent older people).

▲ **Figure 10–22** (a) About 50 years ago, Canada's dependency load was made up mainly of children, as is the case today in Togo. (b) We are now moving into a time when it will be mainly seniors, as is already the case in Japan.

1. **a)** Look again at the four population pyramids that you used in the previous Apply It! questions (page 233). What has happened and will happen to the total numbers and composition of Canada's dependency load? Note that exact numbers are not needed for this answer. Use descriptive words, such as *higher*, *less*, and *faster*.

   b) What has this evolving dependency load meant for life, government, and the economy in Canada? Look especially at the periods from 1960 to today and into the future.

2. Not all of Canada faces the same dependency load issues. Figure 10–23 shows the age distribution for all of Canada in 2011 compared to the age distribution for First Nations. Note that this is a special kind of population pyramid, in which the number of females and males in each age group has been added together so the population distributions of two groups can be seen in one pyramid.

   a) Describe in words the differences in population patterns that you see.

   b) Compare the dependency loads of these populations. How are they different?

   c) What challenges do governments face as a result of the differences?

Geo ⚙ Inquiry

Interpret and Analyze

What implications might Canada's demographic trends have for your future career choices?

Use **ArcGIS Online** to create and analyze a map of Canada that displays social and demographic data.

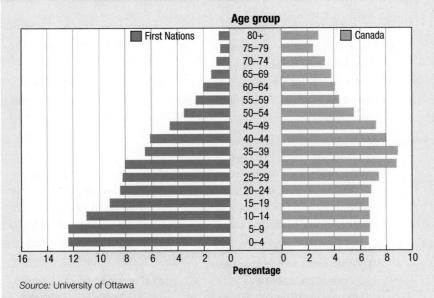

Source: University of Ottawa

▲ **Figure 10–23 First Nations and all of Canada populations by age and gender, 2011.** This graph combines the data of two regular population pyramids. What do you gain with this style of graph? What do you lose?

Canada's Population

? **How is Canada's population changing, and why does this matter to your future?**

Few things are as basic to the study of Canada's human geography as understanding our demographic patterns. From the end of World War II until the early 1960s, this meant a nation of large families and a focus on providing for the needs of a younger population. Today, the children of the post–World War II baby boom are starting to reach retirement age and families are much smaller. Population changes mean that the Canada of today is very different from the Canada of 40 years ago, and the Canada you will live in when you are thinking of retirement will be very different again.

1. Create a concept map to summarize the important ideas you learned in this chapter. Figure 10–24 will get you started.

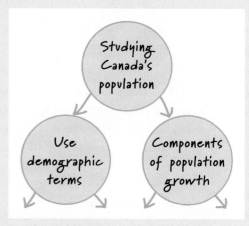

▲ **Figure 10–24** Adding one new idea to a concept map often reminds us of others that we can add.

Geo⚙Inquiry

Interpret and Analyze

2. ■ **Spatial Significance**
   Our largest CMAs (over 1 million people) are growing faster than the rest of the country. Why is this happening?

Evaluate and Draw Conclusions

3. The subtitle of Dr. Foot's book is *How to Profit from the Coming Demographic Shift*. Analyze this subtitle based on the knowledge you have gained in the chapter. You should be able to make two important—but very different—observations.

Analyze an Issue

4. Think about issues related to Canada's population that you have read about or that affect your everyday life. Pick one of these issues.

   a) Write a number of questions about the issue. Narrow your questions down to one clearly stated and important big question. Good questions raise more questions and start debate.

   b) What areas would you have to research to answer your big question? Find three or four resources and collect information to answer your question. Be sure to analyze the information and consider various viewpoints.

   c) Use your notes to take a position and answer your question. Support your answer with facts from your research.

   d) Create a product that communicates the answer to your question. This could be an opinion paper, a blog post, a poster, or a letter to the editor. Be creative!

   e) If you had to complete another inquiry like this one, what would you do differently?

©P

11 Global Population Issues

Can Governments Control Population Growth? Should They?

For decades, governments in the developing world have worked hard to reduce the population growth rate of their countries. They know that a population growing too quickly interferes with economic and social progress. The most famous, and most successful, of these efforts has been China's one-child policy. The policy managed to reduce China's population growth rate to 0.44 percent, which is even lower than Canada's.

Now China faces a different set of problems—a rapidly aging population, growing labour shortages, and families with no aunts, uncles, or cousins. A growing number of other countries are also facing very low birth rates and, in some cases, declining populations. China's population, for example, will start to decline before 2030 even though the one-child policy has been dramatically weakened in recent years.

KEY TERMS

total fertility rate (TFR)

demographic transition model

replacement rate (RR)

population implosion

demographic trap

fragile state

NGO (non-governmental organization)

◀ A poster promoting China's successful but very controversial one-child policy. The slogan on the poster reads, "One couple only produces one child."

THINKING CRITICALLY

Why do governments care about population growth levels? Should governments try to control population growth? Can they? What government policies could affect your decision making when it is time to have children? Why does this matter?

Demographic Change: Problems for Your Future or Opportunities?

Let's start with two facts that seem unconnected:

1. Singapore is a vibrant, small country in southeast Asia. In 2014, it had a **total fertility rate (TFR)** of only 0.80. This means that the average number of children per woman is less than one child. How can a woman have less than one child? Many women are having no children or only one child, and a small number are having two or more. It all averages out to less than one child per woman. As a result, the country's financial resources have been dramatically switched from providing schools to providing facilities for elderly people.

2. Ever since you were in Grade 2, you have wanted to be a teacher.

Can you see the connection? Singapore is an extreme example of *birth dearth*, which is a rapid decline in the number of children being born. (A *dearth* is a shortage or lack of something.) This is happening in developed Western countries, like Canada, and in developing countries, like China and Vietnam.

Wanting to be a teacher is a great ambition. You get to do worthwhile work. You will not get rich, but you will be able to afford a modest lifestyle. The pension plan is first-rate and the holidays are excellent. There is only one, very significant problem: Will you be able to get a job? Your teachers can tell you a lot more about this situation, especially if they have been in the profession for less than 10 years or so.

These demographic trends will have impacts that go way beyond whether Canada turns out to be like Singapore, and teaching jobs become scarce. These trends show that changing global (and Canadian) demographics have some serious implications—and present some great opportunities for the future (Figure 11–1).

total fertility rate (TFR) the average number of children born to a woman in her lifetime

▲ **Figure 11–1** What does this photo suggest about how demographic changes will provide business opportunities?

APPLY IT!

1. If you really want to be a teacher, where might you have to go to work?

2. What careers, other than teaching, might not be attractive options for you and your classmates because of demographic changes? Why?

3. Which types of careers do you think will be more in demand in the future as a result of demographic changes? Why?

4. Assume you would like to start a business after you finish school. Give examples of businesses that will have good growth potential because of demographic changes (Figure 11–1). Explain the demographic connections that you see.

   ©P

Population Projections OSSLT

Many people believe that the world is already overpopulated, and most forecasts suggest there will be two billion more people on Earth by 2050 (Figure 11–2). What has caused this serious problem? What might help to solve (or at least reduce) it? To answer these questions, you need to learn about the **demographic transition model**. A **model** is something created to help us understand a complex process. This model traces a country's (or the entire world's) path from a high birth rate and high death rate demographic pattern to a low birth rate and low death rate pattern.

demographic transition model a model used to describe the change from a high birth rate and high death rate demographic pattern to a low birth rate and low death rate pattern

model a simplified description of a complex process or system

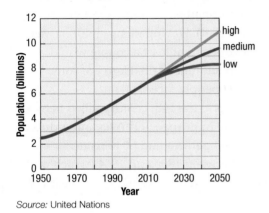

◄ **Figure 11–2 World population projections to 2050.** The medium variant is the demographers' best guess.

Source: United Nations

Geo ⚙ Inquiry

Communicate

What does "overpopulation" mean? What problems are caused by high populations around the world? Identify one major issue of overpopulation and find out more about it. Present your findings in a visual format such as a poster, infographic, or video.

The Demographic Transition Model

The concept of demographic transition is fairly simple if you consider the meaning of the two words. *Demographic*, of course, refers to population, while a *transition* is a gradual change. So we are talking about *gradual population change*. Demographers have created a model of the process that describes the four stages that a country's population goes through (Figure 11–3). Canada is no exception. We have advanced to the final stage, Stage 4. Demographic transition has happened because of major trends in the history of society:

- the development of and improvements in agriculture
- the move from rural life to urban life
- growth in the understanding of disease prevention and cures
- changes in the role of women in society
- changes to attitudes about family size

► **Figure 11–3 The demographic transition model.** Note that this is a theoretical model. Each country's transition has a unique pattern, while keeping within this general model.

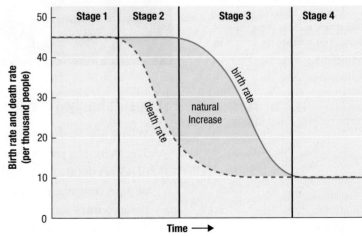

Stage 1: Pre-Transition

- **What?** *The birth and death rates are high, but similar.* An average woman has 6 to 10 children in her life, or even more. Most children do not reach adulthood. *The population grows little, if at all.*

- **When did it start?** In developed countries like Canada, Stage 1 existed from the beginning of human history until sometime in the 19th century. In developing countries, it continued well into the 20th century. There is no country in the world still in this stage today.

- **What was happening in society?** The vast majority of the population supported themselves by hunting and gathering food, and later by simple **subsistence farming** (Figure 11–4). Having many children was an advantage because they could work and at least a couple would survive to adulthood. Life was harsh and uncertain. Here are some examples of the kinds of challenges people faced:
  - An epidemic called the Black Death in the 14th century killed between 100 million and 200 million people in Europe and Asia and reduced Europe's population by between 30 percent and 60 percent.
  - The Taiping Rebellion in China between 1850 and 1864 (which most people outside China have never heard of) resulted in the death of 20 million to 40 million people.
  - Many people, especially children, died because of disease, poor nutrition, and contaminated drinking water.

subsistence farming farming done with the primary goal of feeding one's family rather than selling agricultural products for income

▶ **Figure 11–4** Subsistence agriculture typically provides enough food for a family in good times. There is little, if any, extra food that can be saved for use in bad times, such as droughts or wars. This subsistence farm is in Zimbabwe in southern Africa.

Stage 2: Early Transition

- **What?** *The birth rate remains high, but the death rate drops dramatically. The result is a population explosion.* Consider a country with a birth rate of 45 per 1000 and a death rate of 15 per 1000. Its natural increase rate of 3 percent means a doubling time of just 23 years! Only a few, very poor countries, mainly in dry areas of northern Africa, are still in Stage 2. Good examples are Chad and Niger.

©P

- **When did it start?** In the most developed parts of the world, Stage 2 started as early as the late 1700s. The decline in the death rate was later, but much quicker, in developing parts of the world. In the poorest parts of the world, Stage 2 did not begin until the 1960s.

- **What was happening in society?** Most people were still farmers, but technological advances meant that more farmers were involved in commercial food production (Figure 11–5). Better food storage methods were developed, which improved food security. Simple sanitation improvements meant fewer diseases. For example, people learned not to take drinking water downstream from where they went to the toilet. More productive agriculture meant fewer farmers were needed. People migrated to urban centres to find work. People continued to have large families, but more children reached adulthood and had their own families.

Use **ArcGIS Online** to create a world map showing birth rates, death rates, total fertility rates (TFRs), and replacement rates (RRs) for different countries.

◀ **Figure 11–5** This small farm tractor is being used to cultivate rice in Asia. Advances in agriculture provided a much higher level of food security. This contributed to the decline in death rate in Stage 2.

Stage 3: Late Transition

- **What?** The death rate drops to below 10 per 1000, while *the birth rate drops quickly*. Traditional attitudes favouring large families gradually change, especially in cities. This is partly because raising children has become more costly. *The natural increase rate drops as the death rate approaches the already low birth rate.* Most of the developing world is now in the late-transition phase.

- **When did it start?** In the most developed parts of the world, Stage 3 started in the late 19th century. Western Europe is the best example. Birth rates have dropped more quickly, but much later, in less developed countries.

- **What was happening in society?** The move to the cities accelerated throughout the world until most people lived in cities (Figure 11–6 on the next page). Agricultural productivity increases continued, based on the use of more machinery and less human power.

Geo ⚙ Inquiry

Interpret and Analyze

The changing role of women is one factor that affects population growth. What is women's traditional role in most societies? How does that change? Why do those changes affect population growth?

▶ **Figure 11–6** Imagine trying to get somewhere in this Indian city. India is in Stage 3 of demographic transition. In Stage 3, rapid population growth, combined with the need for fewer farmers, has led to an explosive growth in large cities, especially in the developing world. There are now 28 cities in the world with populations of more than 10 million. China alone has more than 160 cities of more than one million (Canada has six).

Stage 4: Post-Transition

replacement rate (RR) the TFR (total fertility rate) that will result in a stable population. The RR is usually considered to be 2.1 children per woman.

population implosion a dramatic decline in population; the opposite of a population explosion

- **What?** *The death rate and birth rate stabilize at about the same level—slightly below 10 per 1000.* Another way to look at this is by comparing the total fertility rate to the **replacement rate (RR)**. In theory, the TFR and RR should be the same in Stage 4, at about 2.1. The result would be a stable population. However, what has happened in many countries, including Canada, is that the TFR has dropped well below the RR. In 2013, Canada's TFR was only 1.59 (Figure 11–7). (Remember that immigration plays an important role in Canada's population growth.) Taiwan's 2013 TFR was only 1.11. No one knows whether birth rates in developed countries will increase to near the RR or whether the long-term outlook for countries in Stage 4 is a declining population—what has been called a **population implosion**.

- **When did it start?** Post-transition is quite recent, with countries like Canada, Japan, and Germany reaching this stage in the last 30 years or so.

- **What was happening in society?** All of the trends mentioned previously have continued, although the move to cities has ended. In some of the most developed countries, more than 80 percent of the population is urban. The role of women in society has changed, as many women work outside the home in full-time careers.

◀ **Figure 11–7** *Post-transition* means fewer children and more elderly people. What are the implications of these trends for Canadian and world society?

©P

1. **OSSLT** Summarize demographic transition using an organizer similar to this.

	Birth rate	Death rate	Natural increase rate	Characteristics of society
Stage 1: pre-transition	High	??	??	??

2. If you did the Apply It! activity on page 233 in Chapter 10, you learned about the shapes of Canada's population pyramids at various times in our history. In this exercise, you will sketch population pyramids that represent each stage of demographic transition. Here are some pointers to keep in mind:

   - These are sketches only, so you do not need to worry about accurate scales and drawing separate bars for each gender and age group. We are only interested in the overall shape of a pyramid. Each pyramid needs to be only about 4 centimetres high.

   - Consider the following factors when you create the shapes: birth rate, death rate, how long people lived on average, and how many children died before reaching adulthood.

   - Add labelled arrows to show important demographic features on your pyramids.

3. Keep in mind that the demographic transition model is a simplified *theoretical* explanation of the process of demographic change. The model suggests that in Stage 4, the birth rate and death rate should be similar. With current TFRs, this is not the case. TFRs in countries as diverse as Canada, China, the United Kingdom, and Vietnam are all well below the RR.

   a) What will happen to population levels if TFRs become the same as the RR?

   b) What will happen to population levels if TFRs remain well below the RR?

   c) Give at least two reasons why, in the future, TFRs may increase to become the same as the RR.

   d) Give at least two reasons why TFRs may remain low.

   e) What is an advantage of each situation to Canada and the world?

Geo ⚙ Inquiry

Evaluate and Draw Conclusions

Choose 20 countries from different parts of the world. Find the birth rate and death rate for each. Place each country into the correct stage of the demographic transition model. (Remember that there are no Stage 1 countries.) Combine your lists with one or more classmates. What regional patterns do you see? What factor(s) might explain this pattern?

Should Canada Have a One-Child Policy?

The Chinese government brought in its one-child policy because of the belief that China faced a crisis from over-population. Today, the world faces a crisis because of the overuse of resources and climate change (Figure 11–8). Is it time for Canada to limit family size?

▶ **Figure 11–8** The polar bear has become the symbol of the risks associated with climate change. How is the fate of the polar bear (and indeed the human population) related to family size?

Viewpoint 1

A one-child policy makes sense for Earth's future.

- A declining population would reduce the environmental impact of Canadians.

- Many couples today choose to have no children or only one. This policy would affect only those people who want to have more children.

- Canada's average family size is already less than two. Having a limit of one child is a reasonable approach to reducing our impact on the environment.

Viewpoint 2

This idea makes no sense and is just not fair.

- In 1967, Prime Minister Pierre Trudeau said, "There's no place for the state in the bedrooms of the nation." That still applies. A one-child policy just tramples on the basic freedoms of Canadians.

- Some small families are very wasteful, while many larger families live in an environmentally sensitive way. A one-child policy would be a crude tool for reducing environmental impact.

- We do not need a one-child policy because today's total fertility rate is less than 1.6.

- Limiting family size would only make worse our problem of an increasing older population.

APPLY IT!

1. As someone who might be having a family in the future, what is your reaction to a possible one-child policy?

2. Do you think a one-child policy would have the desired effect on environmental damage?

3. Would most Canadians accept this sort of policy? Why or why not?

4. Suggest three specific ways in which environmental damage could be reduced without forcing limits on family size.

©P

Global Population and Poverty

Using the demographic transition model, we can divide the world's nations into three groups:

- **Group 1:** These countries, including Canada, have reached the post-transition stage. Their birth rates and death rates are low and not changing very much. Most of these countries are well off economically and most people have a high standard of living. The people in these countries, and their governments, are focused on maintaining economic growth. To varying extents, they try to work toward environmentally sustainable policies.

- **Group 2:** These countries are generally in Stage 3 of demographic transition and are making continuing progress toward Stage 4. Death rates have dropped and birth rates are approaching post-transition levels. Examples include China, Brazil, and Turkey.

- **Group 3:** This is the group with the greatest problems. These countries are still in the later part of Stage 2 or the early part of Stage 3. Death rates have dropped substantially, but birth rates are still high. In the countries that are growing economically (some are not), the extra wealth supports a population that may be growing at 2 percent or more a year. Little money is available to pay for things such as education and health care that would speed the transition of these countries toward Stage 4. This condition is sometimes called the demographic trap. Often demographic issues and other serious problems, such as wars, droughts, and ineffective government, combine to reduce economic and social growth. The result is that 47 countries have been identified as fragile states. In Figure 11–9, you can see that poverty in the world has declined dramatically, except in the fragile states. These countries need assistance from rich countries, including Canada, to help them solve their desperate social and economic problems (Figure 11–10 on the next page).

CONNECTING

Togo is one of the fragile states. It is the small African country with a high natural increase rate that we mentioned in **Chapter 10 (pages 213–214)**.

demographic trap the situation in which a country's population growth rate is so high that the country is not able to develop economically and socially

fragile state a poor country that is not able to respond to crises that might occur in its food supply, health care, or other critical systems

go online

Find out more about fragile states with this detailed ranking. Be sure to click on "Methodology and Indicators."

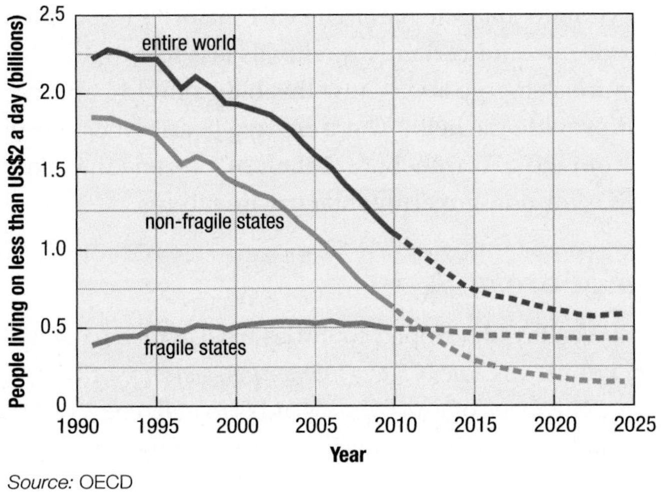

◀ **Figure 11–9 Number of people living on less than US$2 a day.** Internationally, the word *poverty* describes the situation of people living on less than US$2 per day. In recent decades, poverty has declined dramatically, except in the 47 fragile states. How has the demographic trap contributed to people in these countries remaining poor?

Source: OECD

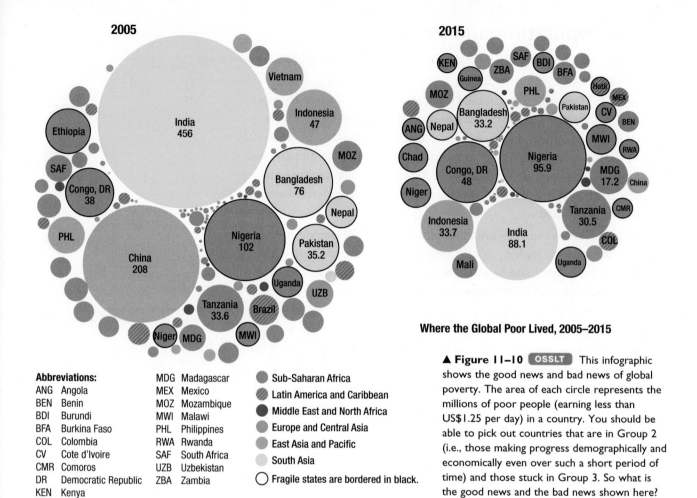

2005

India 456
Vietnam
Indonesia 47
Ethiopia
MOZ
SAF
Bangladesh 76
Congo, DR 38
Nepal
PHL
Nigeria 102
Pakistan 35.2
China 208
Uganda
UZB
Tanzania 33.6
Brazil
Niger
MDG
MWI

2015

KEN
SAF
BDI
ZBA
BFA
Guinea
Haiti
MOZ
PHL
Bangladesh 33.2
MEX
Pakistan
CV
ANG
Nepal
BEN
Chad
Congo, DR 48
Nigeria 95.9
MWI
RWA
Niger
MDG 17.2
China
Tanzania 30.5
CMR
Indonesia 33.7
India 88.1
COL
Mali
Uganda

Abbreviations:

ANG	Angola	MDG	Madagascar
BEN	Benin	MEX	Mexico
BDI	Burundi	MOZ	Mozambique
BFA	Burkina Faso	MWI	Malawi
COL	Colombia	PHL	Philippines
CV	Cote d'Ivoire	RWA	Rwanda
CMR	Comoros	SAF	South Africa
DR	Democratic Republic	UZB	Uzbekistan
KEN	Kenya	ZBA	Zambia

○ Sub-Saharan Africa
⬧ Latin America and Caribbean
● Middle East and North Africa
○ Europe and Central Asia
⬧ East Asia and Pacific
○ South Asia
○ Fragile states are bordered in black.

Source: OECD

Where the Global Poor Lived, 2005–2015

▲ **Figure 11–10** `OSSLT` This infographic shows the good news and bad news of global poverty. The area of each circle represents the millions of poor people (earning less than US$1.25 per day) in a country. You should be able to pick out countries that are in Group 2 (i.e., those making progress demographically and economically even over such a short period of time) and those stuck in Group 3. So what is the good news and the bad news shown here?

Canada's Role in Reducing Global Population Issues

NGO (non-governmental organization) a private, not-for-profit organization that works to achieve particular social, environmental, or political goals

Most Canadians have been raised to think that they should help others who are less fortunate than they are. The vast majority of people who live in fragile states would certainly qualify as less fortunate. A couple of important questions emerge about how this help should happen. The first is, Who should provide the help? There are two possibilities: the help, or aid, can come from the government on behalf of all Canadians, or it can come from **NGOs**, or **non-governmental organizations**.

Government Foreign Aid

Governments of wealthy, developed countries have agreed to provide aid (more formally known as *Official Development Assistance* or *ODA*) to poorer countries. The focus of much of this aid is to help countries move through demographic transition as quickly and smoothly as possible. The

©P

money is spent on needs such as education, health care, and food security. In 2013, Canada donated about $5.0 billion for these purposes. Some of this money was *bilateral aid* that went from the Canadian government directly to poorer nations. The rest was *multilateral aid* that went to the United Nations and a wide variety of NGOs. These organizations used this money to help fund their work. How is Canada doing with respect to aid? That depends on how you look at it. At first glance, $5.0 billion seems to be a lot of money. It works out to about $182 for each Canadian, including you. Figure 11–11 shows the amount of Canada's aid compared to that from other developed countries.

Considering the total amount of foreign aid that a country gives tells us only part of the story. ODA is more commonly measured using a relative measure—the amount of aid compared to the size of a country's economy (Figure 11–12). By this measure, Canada ranks only 15th and actually gives less than the average amount given by developed countries. In fact, our ODA percentage has been trending downward for several years.

Geo ⚙ Inquiry

Evaluate and Draw Conclusions

How has Canada's foreign aid changed over the years? Consider the amount of aid and where it goes. Do you think Canada's current allocation of aid is going to the right places? Why or why not?

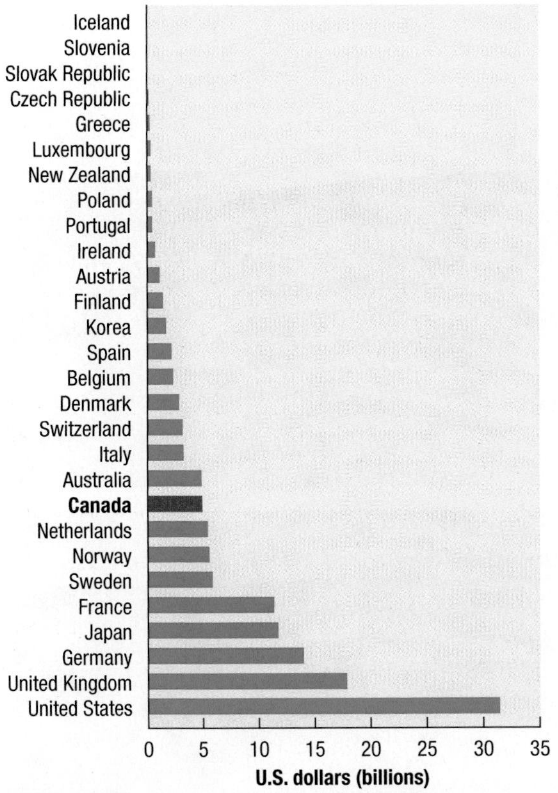

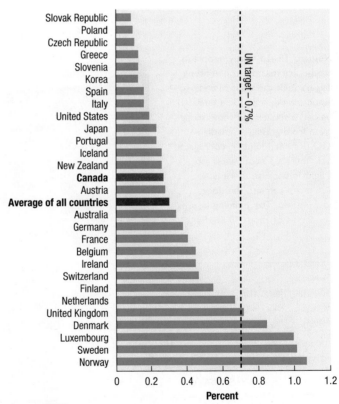

Source: OECD

▲ **Figure 11–11 ODA by country in billions of U.S. dollars.** Canada ranks ninth in the world in providing foreign aid. This seems pretty good until you notice that we give slightly more than Australia (whose population is about two-thirds of ours) and slightly less than the Netherlands (whose population is only half of ours).

Source: OECD

▲ **Figure 11–12 ODA by country as a percentage of the economy.** The United Nations encourages wealthy countries to donate each year an amount equal to 0.7 percent of their gross national income (GNI). A former Canadian prime minister, Lester B. Pearson, suggested this target. Many Canadians find it embarrassing that Canada has never come close to meeting this target.

go online

There is no complete list of all Canadian NGOs, but one site lists about 100 of them working all over the world.

Geo ⚙ Inquiry

Formulate Questions

Visit the websites of two of the NGOs listed on the site in the Go Online feature above. Compare their operations in terms of the 4Ws: Who? What? Where? Why? What other questions would you ask if you were trying to decide whether to donate to one of them?

Aid Provided by NGOs

Some NGOs are huge agencies known around the world, such as the Red Cross and UNICEF. You may have helped raise funds for them at school or in your community. Large NGOs provide help in many countries and generally provide a wide range of services.

On the other hand, many NGOs are small and focus on a particular place or problem. Figure 11–13 shows a school building in the tiny country of Lesotho in southern Africa. It also shows that people in a poor country are able to help themselves with the assistance of people in a wealthy country. Lesotho has the unique distinction of spending more money on education, as a percentage of its gross domestic product (GDP), than any other country in the world. While it is a very high percentage (13 percent), it is not a large number of dollars. By comparison, Canada spends about 6 percent on education. (GDP is an approximate measure of the richness of a country. It is the total value of goods and services produced by a country, excluding transactions with other countries.)

▶ **Figure 11–13** Many people in Lesotho are master stonemasons. Villagers built the walls of this school using only a pick, a long iron bar, a shovel, and some string woven from grass. A Canadian NGO provided lumber, corrugated steel, fibreglass roof panels (to let light in because there is no electricity), cement, the door, and windows. This building houses two classes of about 40 students.

Source: Google, DigitalGlobe, CNES/Astrium

The Lesotho government decided in 2000 that primary education should be free. By the standards of most poor countries, this was a huge advance. However, they did not have enough money to build the extra classrooms they needed. Instead, they put up large tents at many schools, like the ones used in Canada for summer weddings. But Lesotho is quite high in elevation. This school is about 2000 metres above sea level, where it snows regularly. After a few years, the tents started to fall apart. The villagers decided that they wanted their children to go to school in a building instead of a tent. But they did not have the money needed to pay for the roof, door, and windows. So a small Canadian NGO, Help Lesotho, bought the necessary building materials and shipped them to the village (Figure 11–13). This illustrates the advantage that a small NGO has—it can respond to specific, local needs quickly and effectively.

go online

You can learn more about the purpose and work of Help Lesotho from a video (3:40 minutes). You will also hear why the people of Lesotho take considerable pride in their singing.

APPLY IT!

1. **a)** What demographic problems are fragile states likely to have that Canadians should be concerned about?

   b) How is Canadian aid aimed at solving these problems?

2. ■ **Spatial Significance** Compare the 2005 and 2015 graphics in Figure 11–10 on page 246. List three countries that appear to be in Group 2, as described on page 245. List three countries that appear to be in Group 3. How did you decide on your choices?

3. **a)** Do you think Canada should provide foreign aid at the 0.7 percent level? Why or why not?

   b) To develop your critical thinking skills, now argue in favour of the answer opposite to the one you chose in part a).

4. ■ **Patterns and Trends**
   a) Should Canada focus its aid on only a few countries (perhaps 10 or so), or should it try to help all countries that are in need?

   b) What criteria should be used to determine who should receive Canadian aid and what that aid should be used for?

5. What can average Canadians do to help people in fragile states? Hint: Consider both monetary and non-monetary things.

GeoCareers

Starting Your Own NGO to Improve the World

In 1995, Craig Kielburger read a story about another 12-year-old (Craig was 12 at the time) in Pakistan named Iqbal. Iqbal was murdered for leading a fight against child labour in that country. Instead of just getting angry at the injustice, Craig decided to try to do something to help child labourers. With the help of his brother Marc, who is five years older, they started an NGO called *Free The Children*. The Kielburgers were in the unique position of running an NGO at the same time that they were students. *Free The Children* is based on the concept of children helping other children. The money they have raised has now funded development projects in 45 poorer countries.

Get on the Carousel with Population Issues

As you have worked through Chapter 10 and this chapter, you have probably thought of several—or even many—important issues related to population. This is not surprising, since few global issues are as important to our common future. You will now have the opportunity to consider a number of important demographic issues, such as those shown in Figures 11–14 to 11–17. To do this, you will use a learning tool called a *carousel*.

Some Issues to Think About

Why would many retirees from the Toronto area choose to live here?

▲ **Figure 11–14** This is Cobourg, Ontario.

Why did the Canadian government choose to focus its Muskoka Initiative on less than one-quarter of the world's fragile states?

▲ **Figure 11–15** Canada's Muskoka Initiative provides aid money for improving the health of mothers and children in Afghanistan, Bangladesh, Ethiopia, Haiti, Malawi, Mali, Mozambique, Nigeria, Sudan, and Tanzania.

◀ **Figure 11–16** UNICEF, Médecins Sans Frontières and Oxfam are just some of the large NGOs working all over the world. Help Lesotho, Free the Children, and Ryan's Well are some of the smaller NGOs that focus on specific geographical areas or concerns.

What are the advantages of large NGOs compared to small ones?

▶ **Figure 11–17** Why have McCafé sections become a focus at McDonald's? Think about demographic transition.

Why is Ronald McDonald less prominent?

How the Population Issues Carousel Works

1. Start by forming groups of three or four students.

2. The carousel has stations for you to visit. Each station focuses on one issue like those on the previous page. You have only a short time at each station, so use your time effectively.

3. When you visit a station, you have four tasks. These are numbered in Figure 11–18. You will record the results of the last three tasks on sheets similar to that shown in Figure 11–18. Put the name or initials of group members next to the entries you make.

   - Task 1: Start by reading the issue outline provided.
   - Task 2: Record any important information and ideas that you have about the issue. You should note whether any information or idea that you record is a fact (F) or an opinion (O).
   - Task 3: Clearly state any significant questions that you have about the issue.
   - Task 4: For each issue that you find especially interesting, write your name under "I'm Interested!" Note that you can do this more than once. With your teacher's help, you will narrow down your choices later. You will have an opportunity to conduct an inquiry into the one issue you choose in the Performance Task at the end of this unit.

4. When your teacher tells you, move to the next station. Repeat until you have visited all the stations. While you are moving through the carousel, thoughts and questions about earlier stations may occur to you. Record them so you can revisit these stations at the end of the process and add them to the list.

1. Issue: Canada's Muskoka Initiative

2. Useful Information and Ideas:

3. Significant Questions:

4. I'm Interested!

▲ **Figure 11–18** Each station in the carousel will have a page like this.

APPLY IT!

1. Why is a carousel approach a particularly helpful way to start an inquiry?

2. In what ways are Canadian population issues similar to global population issues? In what ways are they different?

3. Look at all the issues you expressed interest in. Select one that you would like to find out more about in your Performance Task on pages 253 and 254.

Global Population Issues

? **How should Canada respond to global population issues?**

Many Canadians do not understand how demographic transition has shaped our population and family patterns. Indeed, all countries find themselves at various stages of transition. Each stage brings a particular set of opportunities and challenges. In countries similar to Canada, families are small, the population is aging, and there are looming labour shortages. In other countries, too many children are being born and too many children die. Life expectancies are short and most people live in dire poverty.

In Canada and all around the world, we need to study and solve these problems if we are to improve the quality of life for people everywhere.

1. Describe what you think Canada's and the world's population situation will be when you are 80 years old. Consider population totals (for 2015, Canada is 35.5 million; the world is 7.3 billion), growth trends, and age structures. Explain your reasoning. Summarize your thoughts in a chart like this.

Canada			World		
Population	Growth trend	Age structure	Population	Growth trend	Age structure

Geo ⚙ Inquiry

Interpret and Analyze

2. ■ **Interrelationships** What impact does a growing population have on the environment? Why does a declining population not automatically mean that less damage will be done to the environment?

Evaluate and Draw Conclusions

3. ■ **Geographic Perspective** More people mean more pressure on the world's resources and on environmental quality.

   a) Should the governments of the world agree on a policy to reduce the world's population gradually?

   If so, how might this be achieved?

   b) In addition to population growth, what other major economic trend contributes stress to Earth's ecosystems?

   c) What is the relationship between the trend in part b) and demographic transition? Why is this a problem for the long-term health of the environment?

Analyze an Issue

4. In the Zoom In on pages 250 and 251, you thought about global population issues. You picked one issue for the Performance Task that starts

on the next page. From the carousel, look at the sheet that deals with your issue. Consider the information that has been added to it and the questions asked about it.

   a) Write a number of questions about the issue. With the other members of your group, narrow your questions down to one clearly stated and important big question.

   b) With your group, decide on what areas you have to research to answer your big question. Plan how you will research your topic and who will do what for the Performance Task.

©P

Challenges of a Changing Population

You live during a time of important change (and we are not talking only about technology). In your lifetime, you will see the world change dramatically as a result of continuing demographic shifts in Canada and around the world (Figure 1). These will have massive implications for you as an individual, for Canada, and for the entire world.

Let's consider just one implication of change at each of these levels:

- **For you as an individual:** For years, Canadians have been trying to retire earlier than the standard age of 65. For example, one major insurance company focused on "Freedom 55" in its advertising. Might you have to work to age 70 or older so that you can afford to retire (Figure 2 on the next page)? Will you have to pay higher taxes to cover the cost of the greater pension and health-care needs of an aging population?

- **For Canada:** Canada has always had a growing population but this is not assured for the future. Future population growth will not come from natural increase—it can only come from immigration. The key question now is, What population level do we want and need and how do we achieve it?

- **For the world:** Can the world's fragile countries escape from the demographic and poverty traps in which they find themselves? Is it possible to escape from one of these or do both problems need to be solved together?

SKILL FOCUS

Doing an oral presentation can be intimidating. In fact, surveys have shown that more people are afraid of speaking in public than dying. It should not be like this. Effective public speakers are not born, they are made. The three most important words for public speaking are *practise*, *practise*, and *practise*. You can learn more online about how to make effective presentations.

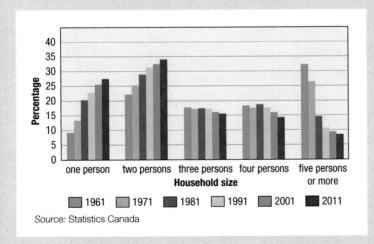

Source: Statistics Canada

◀ **Figure 1 Average number of persons living in Canadian households, 1961–2011.** Household size is not the same as family size. A household can be made up of related family members, including grandparents, or unrelated people, such as friends who share an apartment. How many people would you like to have in your household when you are an adult? Are you typical of people in your generation? What impact(s) does your choice have, not only for you, but also for all of society?

Predicting the Future

Why is it so difficult to make long-term predictions? Could anything be done to make such predictions easier and more accurate?

Preparing for the Future

Why might individuals be more effective in preparing for the future (20 or more years away) than either governments or businesses?

ACTIVITY

1. In this activity, you will finish the inquiry that you began at the end of Chapter 11 when you selected an important big question to investigate. Review the steps in an effective geographic inquiry on pages 7 to 8, and then carry out your inquiry.

2. Keep in mind the questions that your classmates asked about your topic. Try to answer as many of these as possible.

3. Your group will share its findings in an oral presentation. Include visuals such as maps, photos, graphs, and diagrams.

▶ **Figure 2** Will people work into their 70s because they want to or because they have to? Explain your answer. Why could older workers become a critical part of our economy?

Criteria for Success

Your presentation will

❑ make clear what big question you are answering

❑ provide a sequence of logical points to support your answer

❑ demonstrate an appropriate level of knowledge about your issue

❑ demonstrate effective teamwork in preparing and delivering your presentation

❑ demonstrate that you can communicate effectively with your audience, both verbally and non-verbally (eye contact, body language, and self-confidence)

❑ use visual supports effectively

Liveable Communities

What makes a community liveable and sustainable?

▲ Grand Bruit, a tiny community on the southern shore of Newfoundland, (left) in the 1920s and (right) after 2000. No one lives permanently in the village today. Research why. What does this teach us about the liveability and sustainability of communities?

LET'S GO!

- What are the characteristics of a community?
- How do these characteristics combine to make a community liveable and sustainable in the long term?
- In what ways is Grand Bruit like your community? In what ways is it different?
- How can a community improve its liveability?
- How can a community become more sustainable?

KEY CONCEPTS

- community
- land use
- liveable community
- sustainable community
- urban growth
- measuring sustainability
- planning to improve liveability and sustainability

KEY TERMS

liveability
sustainability
land use
residential density
land-use conflict
official plan
zoning

 How do the ways that we use land in our cities and towns relate to liveability and long-term sustainability?

How Land Use Can Lead to Conflict

Communities are constantly growing and evolving. As this happens, different functions can interfere with one another. For example, a factory that provides hundreds of jobs can produce smells, traffic, and noise that interfere with nearby residential areas. The result is often a conflict over how land should be used to produce the maximum benefit for the people in the community, the economy, and the environment. An excellent example of this type of conflict occurred in 2013 and 2014, when a dispute erupted over a plan to expand the capacity (and reverse the direction of flow) of an oil pipeline. The pipeline, which is almost 40 years old, goes from Sarnia to Montréal, passing through many of Canada's most densely populated areas.

 **THINKING CRITICALLY**

OSSLT This photo shows the pipeline under maintenance. It is usually underground. In addition to the pipeline, what other major utility passes through this urban area? Would you be concerned about living here? Why or why not? The pipeline was built before most of this area became urban. Should urban growth have been allowed to occur? Why was it allowed?

What Makes a Community Liveable?

If we want to understand the difference between successful and unsuccessful communities, it is very important that we clearly understand two related terms: *liveability* and *sustainability* (Figure 12–1).

Adaptable? Affordable? Good infrastructure (roads, water and sewage systems)? Lively? Desirable human features (schools, theatres, art galleries)? Attractive physical features (water bodies, hills, valleys)? Agreeable? Healthy? Accessible? Functional? Not stressful? Interesting population? Exciting? Good educational options? Safe? Happy? Good health care? Growing? Welcoming? Friendly? Stable? Low unemployment? Access to services? Good opportunities to develop relationships? Good jobs? Walkable/bikeable?

◀ **Figure 12–1** Which of these characteristics comes to mind when you think about the idea of a liveable community? Why?

APPLY IT!

1. Study the list of characteristics in Figure 12–1. Make sure that you know what each characteristic means.

2. ■ **Geographic Perspective**
   a) In your notebook, list the characteristics from Figure 12–1 *in order of their importance* for a liveable community.

   b) If you think some characteristics are missing, add them to your list at the appropriate point in the sequence.

3. a) Look down your list from the top (the most important characteristic). Draw a line separating the essential characteristics from the non-essential, but likely still desirable, ones. This line separates your *needs* from your *wants*. Add appropriate labels.

   b) How is a community's liveabilty related to meeting the needs and wants of its residents?

4. a) Why is it important that we can measure liveability characteristics of a community? Some characteristics of a community can be measured using numerical data; for example, we could measure affordability using average house prices. Other characteristics, such as how exciting a community is, can be described but not measured.

   b) Identify five characteristics that could be evaluated using a numerical measure.

   c) Identify five characteristics that could only be evaluated using descriptive data.

5. In your own words, give a clear definition of liveability. When you are happy with your definition, compare it to the one on the next page.

What Is the Relationship Between Liveability and Sustainability?

liveability all the characteristics of a community that contribute to the quality of life of the people who live there

In the previous section, you wrote a definition of liveability. **Liveability** is all of the characteristics that contribute to a community's quality of life. These characteristics include economic, educational, and social opportunities, overall health, the natural environment, infrastructure, good housing and transportation, and so on. To some extent, what makes a community liveable depends on personal opinion. For example, a couple in their 20s who do not have children likely have somewhat different needs and wants than a family with children.

Another key goal for any community (a neighbourhood or even the entire world) is to operate as sustainably as possible. There are many definitions of **sustainability** (Figure 12–2). In some cases, the differences can be quite important. Some definitions focus on the idea that we should only use the resources of Earth at a rate that will allow future generations to enjoy a similar quality of life as people do today. Critics of this definition say that this way of defining sustainability is fine for the world's rich (while most Canadians would not consider themselves rich, on a global basis they certainly are), but what about the world's poorer people who are struggling to get clean water and enough to eat? In a fair world, mere survival is not good enough. Don't we need to share Earth's resources more fairly?

sustainability improving the quality of human life while living within the carrying capacity of supporting ecosystems

go online

This definition of sustainability comes from the World Conservation Union, the United Nations Environment Programme, and the WWF in a report called *Caring for the Earth: A Strategy for Sustainable Living.*

Three prominent international organizations combined to produce a broader definition of sustainability, which is now widely used. It focuses on

- *improving the quality of human life,*
- *while living within the **carrying capacity** of supporting ecosystems.*

There are two main goals within this broader definition:

carrying capacity the ability of the environment to support a population without environmental damage

Living within the carrying capacity of supporting ecosystems: This is the idea that we need to live within the limits of available resources so that future generations will be able to live as we do.

Improving the quality of human life: This is a major addition to the idea of what sustainability is. It means that we must ensure that people with a lower standard of living have access to the resources needed to improve it.

This definition is important because it expands our focus to include protecting the environment and allowing for careful development. That combination is called *sustainable development.*

◀ **Figure 12–2** The understanding that everything is connected is an essential part of Aboriginal people's views about the land. People, animals, and the land are all connected and dependent on each other for survival. How might this belief help support the goals of sustainability?

©P

Balancing Liveability and Sustainability

Before we can talk about achieving sustainability in the years to come, we need to understand what is happening today with respect to liveability, both in Canada and throughout the world. This global approach is key, since true sustainability only exists if we look at the entire world population and world environment. Here is the challenge. On a global basis (and in Canada), we must

- meet basic needs
- satisfy as many wants as possible
- be able to afford the costs of these needs and wants
- do all this while minimizing our demands on the natural environment

Choosing the best balance between having high liveability and increased sustainability is not easy, but it is possible. The key is to think and plan appropriately.

Geo ⚙ Inquiry

Interpret and Analyze

Urban planning should help to increase the liveability of a community. It should also reflect the wishes of local residents. Do these two goals always coincide?

go online

There are many liveability rankings on the Internet. Find two sites to get you started on question 6 below.

APPLY IT!

1. a) **OSSLT** What are the two key aspects of our definition of sustainability?

   b) Does this definition seem fair to you?

   c) What implications does it have for typical Canadian lifestyles?

2. a) Is a liveable community always sustainable? Explain your answer.

   b) Is a sustainable community always liveable? Explain your answer.

3. Liveability and sustainability are such complex concepts that there is not even agreement on their definitions. Why is this a critical problem?

4. Communities are constantly changing. As they change, their liveability changes. We need ways to measure this.

   a) Describe three indicators that you would use to measure liveability in your community. Identify an indicator from each of these categories: environmental, economic, and health and well-being.

   b) Compare your list with those of your classmates. Create a common list of indicators of liveability.

   c) Do changes in liveability have a direct effect on levels of sustainability? Explain.

5. a) Would you consider your community to have a high or low level of liveability (or somewhere in between)? What factors contribute to this?

   b) Suggest three specific things that could be done to improve the liveability of your community. Compare your list to those of your classmates to create a more complete list.

   c) Are the things your class is suggesting already being done? If not, why not?

   d) Would your proposed changes have any impact on the sustainability of your community? Explain your answer.

6. Every year, stories appear ranking the liveability of world cities. Compare two (or more) city liveability rankings and investigate what indicators were used to measure liveability. Why were those indicators chosen? Why do different surveys use different indicators? What indicators seem to be missing from these surveys? Why?

Types of Land Use

The ways that land is used in our cities and towns are directly related to liveability today and sustainability in the future. If more people want to move to a particular city or town, there must be more jobs available. Housing must be built, along with efficient transportation systems, more shopping areas, industrial land use, offices, and community services, such as schools and water and sewage systems. If this expansion is done well, liveability and the potential for sustainability are increased. If it is not done well, the city becomes less liveable and less sustainable.

A good example of this exists in the Toronto census metropolitan area (CMA). This area has grown dramatically in recent years without enough attention and money being paid to create better transportation systems to deal with the rising population. The result is reduced liveability (longer commutes, increased frustration, and higher costs for business) and sustainability (waste of fossil fuels and more pollution). The solution is an extensive plan for new transit systems that will take years to build and will require significantly increased taxes to pay for them. The amount of land used for various purposes in a typical, large Canadian city is shown in Figure 12–3. Figure 12–4 shows part of a city and includes examples of many of the land uses shown in Figure 12–3.

land use the various functions of land in an urban or rural area

Take **GeoFlight 12.1** to see examples of the various types of land use.

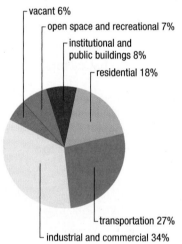

vacant 6%
open space and recreational 7%
institutional and public buildings 8%
residential 18%
transportation 27%
industrial and commercial 34%

Source: University of Toronto

▲ **Figure 12–3** Is this distribution of land uses in Barrie, Ontario, similar to what you see where you live?

▶ **Figure 12–4** How many different land uses can you see in this photo? Note that the distance between A and B is 2 kilometres.

Source: Google, DigitalGlobe

©P

APPLY IT!

1. Explain, in your own words, the meaning of each type of land use. Give examples of the activities that happen in each area.

   a) residential

   b) transportation

   c) open space and recreational

   d) industrial

   e) commercial

   f) other land uses

2. **a)** Place a piece of tracing paper or clear acetate over the photo in Figure 12–4. Trace the outline of the photo with a pencil (on paper) or marker (on acetate).

   b) Outline the area used for transportation. Lightly shade in this area. Hint: Transportation involves more than just roads and highways.

   c) Repeat this process for as many land uses as you can identify. Note that you may not be able to see all of the possible land uses in the photo.

   d) Add an appropriate legend and title to your tracing.

   e) Is the distribution of land uses in the photo similar to that shown in Figure 12–3? What differences, if any, do you see?

   f) How has the natural landscape influenced the land uses you see?

Transportation Land Use

Many people are surprised to discover that about one-third of urban land is used for transportation. The importance of transportation in a city goes beyond the amount of land that is used, however. An ineffective transportation system means that people waste large amounts of time getting from place to place. This can reduce time for leisure and social activities (including time with family), increase resource use and pollution levels, and even have a negative effect on physical and mental health. As well, the economy can be hurt if companies have to spend extra time (and hence money) moving goods to their destinations. How would an ineffective transportation system affect the liveability and sustainability of a city? Would a poor transportation system have a positive or negative impact on each of these characteristics? What are some ways that we can improve our transportation systems (Figure 12–5)?

▲ **Figure 12–5** Car sharing is becoming a common feature in many larger cities. With these schemes, you do not have to own a vehicle. Instead, you just pick one up from lots scattered around the city when you need it. How does car sharing contribute to both liveability and sustainability?

CONNECTING

Read more about transportation issues in **Chapter 13 (pages 295–300)**.

Understanding a few key transportation facts will help you understand this important land use.

- There are two types of transportation systems—one for people and one for goods.

- All transportation systems consist of three parts. The latter two of these parts are included in the land-use patterns that we see.
  - **Vehicles:** These range from trains and trucks used to move goods to cars, bicycles, buses, light rail, and subways used to move people.
  - **Travel paths:** This includes rail lines as well as four categories of roads: expressways, arterials, collectors, and local roads (Figure 12–6).
  - **Terminal facilities:** These exist at the beginning and end of journeys. There are many types, such as train, bus, and subway stations, rail yards, airports, ports, and parking lots and garages. Parking lots, in particular, can take up a considerable amount of space.

- Improvements to transportation land use (travel paths and terminal facilities) provide benefits, but they come with a number of costs.

Source: Google

▲ **Figure 12–6** If you lived at A and worked at B, what route would you take by car and by bus? Which route is more sustainable? Which would be more liveable?

©P

1. Looking back at Figure 12–6, what is the purpose of each of these types of roads?

   a) expressway   c) collector road

   b) arterial road   d) local road

2. ■ **Patterns and Trends** Building a new transportation route, such as an expressway or a rapid transit line, involves both costs and benefits. In your notebook, use a table like the one below to list the costs and benefits of a project that is being built or being considered in your community. List as many costs and benefits as you can.

Project	Costs	Benefits
economic		
social/health		
environmental		

3. a) Transportation land-use patterns are often affected by the landforms on which a city is built. Give specific examples for the area in which you live.

   b) Do landform patterns typically make transportation easier or harder in a city? Explain.

4. a) Car sharing and bike sharing schemes are becoming more popular in many cities. How do each of these work?

   b) What are the social, economic, and environmental advantages of such schemes for
      i) individuals
      ii) society as a whole

   c) Would you be likely to participate in car sharing and/or bike sharing to get to work? Why or why not?

Residential Land Use

The most important characteristic of residential land use is its density. **Residential density** is the number of housing units per hectare (Figure 12–7 on the next page). The two major factors responsible for the residential density in any particular location are land cost and the age of the area. Areas that were developed before most people owned cars look different than newer areas. Why?

Residential density can influence a number of things.

- **Lifestyle:** Different densities provide different lifestyle opportunities. For example, apartment residents do not need to spend time on exterior maintenance; owners of detached houses have gardens to enjoy but snow to shovel.

- **Transportation:** Lower density generally means you need to use a car to get around. Higher density allows for better public transit systems, and services such as schools and stores are closer together. Medium density combines the advantages and disadvantages of both.

- **Microclimates:** Higher-density areas are slightly warmer than lower-density or rural areas because of the amount of heat given off by large buildings and large paved areas. Air quality is also affected.

residential density a measure of the number of housing units per hectare

Use **ArcGIS Online** to create a map of your community that includes various land uses and natural physical features.

Low Residential Density

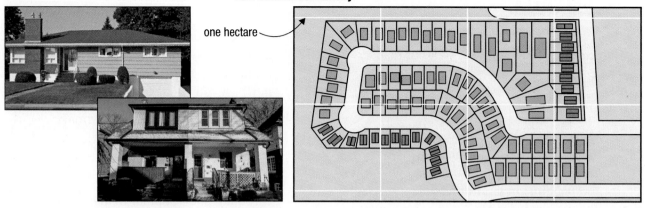

one hectare

Medium Residential Density

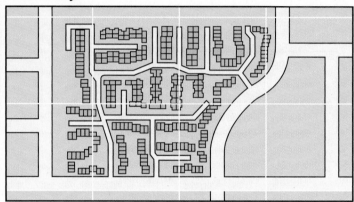

High Residential Density

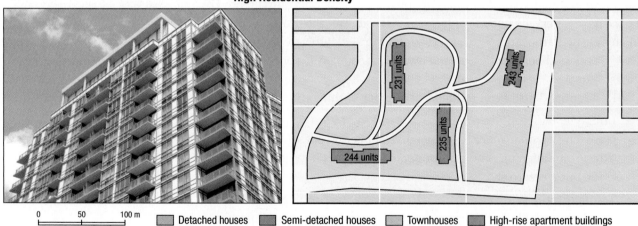

231 units

243 units

235 units

244 units

0   50   100 m

■ Detached houses   ■ Semi-detached houses   □ Townhouses   ■ High-rise apartment buildings

▲ **Figure 12–7** People choose to live in areas with different residential densities for a variety of reasons. What is the residential density where you live? What factors influence where people choose to live?

©P

LAND COST AND THE "RISE" OF THE VERTICAL CITY

Land cost is the most important factor in determining residential density. In parts of a city where the land is cheaper, lower densities are more likely. You will see detached homes on large lots. Where land is costly, higher residential densities exist. In extreme cases, the result of high land costs can be extremely high residential densities (Figure 12–8).

go online

Frank Gehry, a world-famous Canadian architect, designed the fascinating Mirvish+Gehry Toronto project. In addition to residences it is to contain commercial space, a major art gallery, and part of OCAD University. What would be the benefits of having multiple uses in these buildings? What needs of the community will these buildings meet?

◀ **Figure 12–8**

■ **Spatial Significance** The Mirvish+Gehry project is being built very close to the centre of downtown Toronto, where land is enormously expensive. Most of the floor space in these towers, which are 82 and 92 storeys high, will be residential. Would you like to live in a building like this? Why or why not?

high-rise a building 35 metres to 100 metres tall

skyscraper a building more than 100 metres tall

Geo ⚙ Inquiry

Evaluate and Draw Conclusions

Other large Canadian cities are having similar booms in construction of high-density housing. The explosion of condos is dramatically changing the skyline and how thousands of people live. What implications does this trend have for liveability and sustainability? On balance, do you think the increase in high-density housing is desirable?

For more than a century, municipalities in the Greater Toronto Area (GTA) were known as places where most people lived in single-family houses. In recent years, that pattern has changed dramatically (Figure 12–9), with most new home construction in the GTA being in **high-rises** and **skyscrapers**. This trend is easiest to see in Toronto and Mississauga, but it is gradually expanding to the entire region.

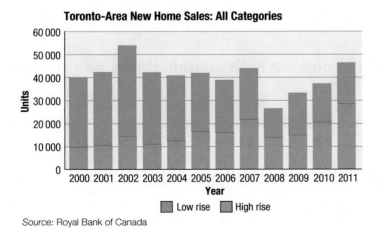

Toronto-Area New Home Sales: All Categories

Source: Royal Bank of Canada

◀ **Figure 12–9** For a number of years, the GTA has had the interesting distinction of having more large construction cranes than any other place in the world. Most of these cranes were being used to build condos, which are high-density residential spaces.

Does Living on the 34th Floor Contribute to Sustainability and Liveability?

The growth in high-density living in larger Canadian cities over the last decade or so has been remarkable. What impact does this trend have from the perspectives of sustainability and liveability (Figure 12–10)?

▲ **Figure 12–10** Downtown Mississauga. Is this a liveable urban area? Does living here contribute to sustainability?

Viewpoint 1

The high-density living trend is good for both sustainability and liveability.

- High-density living makes it easier to have effective transit systems. More people are able to walk or cycle to work.

- Less land is needed to house each person. This reduces the need for cities to expand outward. As well, this helps to protect farmland and wildlife areas for the future.

- High-density living improves quality of life, since it allows more people to live close to restaurants, libraries, clubs, theatres, and other urban attractions. People can walk, cycle, or use transit rather than cars.

©P

Any advantages of high-density living are overshadowed by a reduced quality of life.

- 💬 The increase in high-density living has been driven primarily by low cost rather than concerns for liveability and sustainability.

- 💬 Low-density areas are less crowded. People do not have to deal with as much traffic and noise.

- 💬 People who live in low-density areas have easier access to parks and nature.

- 💬 Services such as schools and hospitals become overcrowded as the local population increases.

APPLY IT!

1. Can you suggest any additional arguments for either side of this debate?

2. ■ **Interrelationships** Create a graphic organizer to compare the pros and cons associated with living in high and low residential density areas. In your analysis, consider economic issues, environmental issues, and quality of life issues.

3. There are many reasons why more people are choosing to live (by buying or renting) at higher densities. Describe at least three of these reasons. In your answer, examine such factors as cost, the changing demographic structure of Canadian families, and immigration.

4. How does a higher residential density contribute to liveability? How might it reduce liveability?

5. Describe how higher-density living may contribute to (or reduce) sustainability.

THINKING CRITICALLY

6. When you reach the stage of your life when you are able to decide where you want to live, would you choose a high-density area? Why or why not?

Geo ✿ Inquiry

Communicate

Work with a partner to suggest how high-density living affects

- the consumption of energy
- the consumption of other resources (give specific examples)
- the creation of waste

Use your ideas to create a presentation to a city council in which you are arguing either for or against higher-density living. Be sure to explain your reasoning.

AGE OF NEIGHBOURHOODS

The development of residential areas in Canada can be divided into two historical periods: prior to 1930 and after World War II (that is, after 1945). The dire poverty of the "Dirty Thirties" followed by the economic constraints of World War II meant that very few new homes were built between 1930 and 1945.

As a result of their age, an important distinction exists between older and newer residential areas. Before 1930, relatively few families owned cars (of course, before 1900 there were no cars). Therefore, older residential areas were not designed around the automobile, while newer neighbourhoods were. We can see the result in our cities (Figures 12–11 and 12–12).

Pre-1930 neighbourhoods	Post–World War II neighbourhoods
When these areas were built, many residents travelled by streetcar. They walked from their homes to and from the streetcar lines that ran along main arterial roads. This lifestyle influenced neighbourhoods in several ways: • Residential density was relatively high for neighbourhoods with low-rise housing. • Narrow lots made the walk to main roads and streetcar routes shorter. • Straight lines made walking distances as short as possible. The result was a *grid pattern* of streets. • The majority of shopping developed along main roads or those with streetcar lines. • Today, these local roads are relatively narrow, because planners did not know how popular cars would become. • Parking in these areas is often a problem because most houses did not have driveways.	The dominant role played by the automobile after 1945 encouraged city planners to develop a new pattern for streets. Several factors contributed to this: • Most families had at least one car, and most daily transportation was by car. • People wanted a driveway and garage, so house lots became larger. This continued until the 1990s, when soaring land prices meant that lots became smaller. However, house size did not decrease. • An intricate pattern of curving roads, crescents, and cul-de-sacs was designed to discourage drivers from making longer journeys on local roads. This is called a *garden pattern.* Instead, local collector roads link homes to arterial roads. • Larger lots and non-linear local roads make it difficult to operate effective bus routes in these areas, since arterial roads are too far apart to make walking to the bus attractive for many people. • Large parking areas are needed near shopping areas, office buildings, and schools.

▲ **Figure 12–11** Grid pattern

▲ **Figure 12–12** Garden pattern

©P

1. **a)** Take GeoFlight 1.1 (page 22). Name at least two of the communities shown that have a grid pattern and at least two that have a garden pattern.

   b) Look at the Street View of each type of community. Describe what you see with respect to lot size and house size.

2. **a)** Identify examples of the four types of roads (see Figure 12–6 on page 262) in your community. Using examples of specific trips you make, explain how these types of roads combine to provide an effective transportation network for the residents of your community.

   b) What road pattern exists in your community? What does this tell you about the age of your community?

   c) Is the transportation network sustainable? How could your local road network be improved?

3. **a)** Which of these public transit options are available where you live: subways, light-rail systems, bus rapid transit (Figure 12–13), commuter rail, and buses or streetcars operating on regular roads?

   b) Why might your community have some of these transit options, while others do not have them?

4. Which is more liveable now and sustainable in the long term—residential areas built using the grid pattern or those built using the garden pattern? Why?

5. **a)** Identify examples of recent residential and transportation land-use changes in your community.

   b) Are these changes making your community more or less liveable? More or less sustainable? How?

▲ **Figure 12–13** With bus rapid transit, the buses do not operate in regular traffic lanes. This means they are not held up by traffic.

Commercial Land Use

About 5 percent of a city's land is used for commercial activities. These activities include buying and selling a wide range of goods and providing many services. This occurs in buildings along roads, in shopping malls, and in office buildings. Even though commercial activities use a relatively small amount of land, they provide many jobs and often bring money into the community.

LOWER- AND HIGHER-ORDER GOODS AND SERVICES

Buying bread and going to an NHL game are commercial activities. There are thousands of stores where you can buy bread. However, there are only seven places in Canada where you can see an NHL game in person. The difference in availability of products and services illustrates the concepts of **lower-order goods and services** and **higher-order goods and services**.

lower-order goods and services goods and services that are purchased frequently. Generally these goods and services are relatively inexpensive.

higher-order goods and services goods and services that are needed infrequently. These goods and services tend to be quite specialized and often costly.

CONNECTING

See **Chapter 9 (pages 199–200)** for a review of basic and non-basic jobs.

GeoCareers

Building Things Higher

Paul Darocy is a crane operator in Southern Ontario. He has journeyperson qualifications for tower cranes and mobile cranes. He prefers mobile cranes because the work provides a variety of challenges and greater job security when tower construction slows down. Darocy gained his qualifications through apprenticeship programs. These require high-school graduation and 3000 hours of classroom and practical experience for tower cranes (6000 hours for mobile cranes).

COMMERCIAL LAND DISTRIBUTION IN THE CITY

Commercial land uses range from small variety stores on residential corners to downtown business areas in large cities with many hundreds of businesses (Figure 12–14). The different types of commercial land uses are listed in Table 12–1.

(a)

(b)

▲ **Figure 12–14** (a) Most neighbourhoods include a small variety store. Why are there so many stores of this type? (b) If you were to stand at the intersection of King and Bay Streets in Toronto and look up, you would see the headquarters of four of Canada's five large banks. What percentage of the thousands of jobs in this area are basic jobs that bring money into the Toronto CMA economy and possibly the Canadian economy as well? Could you buy the lower-order goods that you get at a variety store in such an area?

Table 12–1 Types of commercial land uses

Type	Range of goods and services	Typical stores and services	Number of stores and services
neighbourhood stores and plazas	lower order	variety stores, banks, small supermarkets, hairdressers, barbers, and post-office outlets	1 to 25
community shopping centres	lower to middle order	all of the above plus clothing and shoe stores, travel agents, jewellery stores, insurance company offices, and fast-food outlets	25 to 75
regional shopping centres	lower to higher order	all of the above plus major department stores, book stores, movie theatres, and specialized stores	75 to 300
central business district (CBD)	lower to (very) higher order	all of the above plus specialized stores and services, such as stores selling designer clothes and unique items, concert halls, and professional sports venues	depends on the population of the city and its region
big-box stores and shopping areas in suburban areas	middle to higher order	very large national and international chain stores (e.g., Walmart, Canadian Tire, Home Depot, and Loblaws) and fast-food and sit-down chain restaurants	3 to 20

▲ Where are these types of commercial land uses in your community? Are they easily accessible? How? Why is having an easily accessible commercial area important to a community?

1. Write down at least 10 goods and services, according to their relative position from lower order to higher order, along a horizontal line in your notebook.

2. In this chapter, we have been looking at land-use patterns in cities and towns. What is the relationship between people who live in rural areas and commercial land use in nearby towns and cities? How has this relationship changed over time? Hint: Consider where rural residents have to go for lower- and higher-order goods and services.

3. Many, but not all, higher-order goods and services are expensive. Give examples of relatively inexpensive higher-order goods and services. How can these goods and services be higher order if they are not expensive?

4. a) Which of the five types of commercial land use can you identify in your community?

   b) Consider the goods and services you personally have consumed in the past month. How often did you visit each type of commercial centre to do this?

   c) Compare your pattern of goods and services consumption with that of your parents or guardians. What similarities and differences do you see? Why are the patterns similar or different?

5. a) In the last month, have you purchased any goods or services online that you could have bought locally? If so, why did you choose to buy online?

   b) How is online shopping affecting local businesses?

   c) How does online shopping affect sustainability?

6. ■ Spatial Significance

   a) If there are big-box stores near your home, how have these stores affected businesses in the CBD? Why does this happen?

   b) What are the advantages of shopping in a big-box store? What are the advantages of shopping in a smaller, local store? Which type of shopping contributes to sustainability in the long term?

   c) Why is a proposal to build a big-box store, especially in a built-up area of a town or city, generally very controversial? What impact (both positive and negative) does a new big-box store have on a community?

7. Commercial land use has obvious links to the consumption of goods and services.

   a) How is commercial land use linked to the local and national economy?

   b) How is it linked to liveability and sustainability?

   c) How might it be linked to health and well-being?

Industrial Land Use

On average, about 6 percent of a city's land is used for industrial purposes. In the past, manufacturing was the most important part of industrial land use. Over the last 25 years, however, a great deal of Canadian manufacturing has moved to other parts of the world. The result is that the majority of industrial land use in most cities and towns now consists of distribution centres for products imported from other countries (Figure 12–15).

Geo ✿ Inquiry

Gather and Organize

Find statistics that show how Canada's manufacturing industry has declined over the last 25 years.

▲ **Figure 12–15** In most Canadian industrial areas, manufacturing has been replaced by *logistics*: huge amounts of storage along with highly efficient systems for shipping. This photo shows the Walmart distribution centre in Cornwall, Ontario. Why might Cornwall have been chosen for this facility and for similar large distribution centres for Shoppers Drug Mart and Target?

Transportation has a major influence on the location of industrial land uses. Before World War II, most industrial operations relied on rail transportation or ships. Today, except for a few heavy industries, most rely on trucks. As a result, good access to highways is key. This means that most industrial land use has moved out of downtown areas to the suburbs. As industries move out of high-density areas, many downtown factories have been converted to residential or commercial uses (Figure 12–16).

► **Figure 12–16** This apartment is in a former warehouse. Why do many people like the idea of living in a converted industrial building? How does that relate to the sustainability of a city?

Institutional and Public Buildings

Almost 10 percent of the land in most cities falls into the category of institutional and public buildings. This category includes schools, hospitals, public buildings, places of worship, and municipal works department facilities. To be close to the populations that use them, most schools, hospitals, and places of worship are spread throughout a city. Government buildings, colleges and universities, and works facilities tend to be clustered in smaller areas. How do buildings in this category contribute to liveability?

©P

Open Space and Recreational Land Use

The final land use is open space and recreational land (Figure 12–17). This land use occupies about 7 percent of urban land. Open space includes parkland, golf courses, land for utilities such as hydro transmission corridors, and land that is vacant as it awaits future development.

◀ **Figure 12–17** The amount of parkland in Canadian cities varies enormously, from 1.2 hectares per 1000 people in Montréal to approximately 900 hectares per 1000 people in Whitehorse. (The two Toronto parks pictured here show how urban parks can vary in size.) What factors would contribute to the amount of parkland in a city? How does a larger amount of parkland contribute to the liveability of a community?

APPLY IT!

1. **a)** Identify any factories near where you live. What do they make?

   b) Identify any warehouses and distribution centres near where you live. What product(s) does each company distribute?

   c) Identify any old factories in your community that have been converted to other uses. How are these buildings used today? If possible, determine when these buildings were last used for manufacturing.

2. The decline of manufacturing in Canada has had a significant economic cost. However, it has also had some positive effects on land use and liveability. Explain, and provide examples of these positive effects.

3. **a)** OSSLT Discuss this statement: "'Other land uses' and 'open space and recreational land' have an importance to a community that outweighs the amount of land they use." In your answer, consider the important roles played by each of these types of land use in the effective functioning of a community.

   b) How does the natural environment affect the location and size of recreational land in and around a community?

   c) Most people would prefer that their community had more parkland than it does. Why is this goal hard to achieve in i) new urban areas and ii) existing urban areas?

Land-Use Conflicts and Zoning

What is a **land-use conflict**? We started this chapter with an example: the problem of an oil pipeline passing through heavily populated urban areas. When you first read this, your reaction may have been, "How could that happen?"

land-use conflict a situation that exists when adjacent land uses interfere with each other in some way. The interference could include noise, smell, dust, traffic, or air or water pollution.

official plan an important document that all municipalities must have that lays out the general policies to be followed to achieve long-term planning goals

zoning the result of a detailed planning process that specifies exactly what land uses are allowed in each part of a municipality

go online

Most official plans are available online. If you would like to see the official plan for your community, do a search using "official plan" and your municipality's name as your search terms.

Cities and towns are planned to avoid land-use conflict today, but parts of many cities are older than the planning process. Communities are also continually evolving. As needs shift, it can be difficult to balance them all. For instance, the former city of Sydney (now part of the Cape Breton Regional Municipality) grew around a steel plant. For more than a century, people in that community have lived close to ponds full of toxic run-off.

LAND-USE ZONING

The planning process of a city or town results in the creation of two related documents: the official plan of a municipality and detailed zoning maps based on the official plan. Figure 12–18 shows part of a typical zoning map.

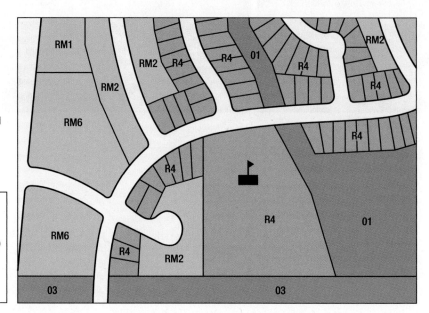

▶ **Figure 12–18** Zoning maps use a standard code to identify permitted land uses.

R	Single-family residential (higher number = higher density allowed)
RM	Multi-family residential (RM2 allows townhouses, RM6 allows high-rises)
0	Open space
01	Parkland
03	Utility corridor

0   50   100 m

APPLY IT!

1. Describe how each of the following would affect what appears on a particular zoning map.

   a) the official plan of the town or city

   b) natural environmental features

   c) the location of the area on the map in relation to the location of the downtown area

   d) the location of the area on the map in relation to the location of major transportation routes (highways and mass transit routes)

   e) the cost of land in the area

2. Think about what land uses might come into conflict. How does an official plan and the zoning process attempt to avoid such conflicts before an area is even developed?

3. If possible, describe one land-use conflict in your community. If you cannot identify a conflict, explain why this situation might exist.

4. Why are most land-use conflicts not eliminated once they become known?

©P

Conflicts as a City Evolves

How would you feel if you lived close to a factory that slaughtered and processed 6000 pigs a day (Figure 12–19)? This was the situation in one downtown Toronto neighbourhood where a slaughterhouse was located near the homes of several thousand people.

It is easy to say that land-use conflicts such as this should not happen, but cities are imperfect organisms. They evolve to meet changing needs, but change happens slowly and land-use conflicts often arise during periods of transition. For economic reasons, this neighbourhood gradually changed from industrial to residential. The new land use required zoning changes, of course, but the city government had little choice but to approve them. It was highly unlikely that new industrial uses would be found for this valuable downtown land, and there was a growing demand for housing near the central business district of the city.

▲ **Figure 12–19** Residents were not happy living near the Quality Meat Packers slaughterhouse. They complained about the noise, dirt, and trucks. They believed the nature of the company's business affected their property values. The company and its workers pointed out that the business had been in operation decades before the area became largely residential, and that it met all government standards for a slaughterhouse. The slaughterhouse closed in 2014 due to economic reasons.

APPLY IT!

1. Give two reasons why this industrial area has largely become residential.

2. **a)** Why did planners allow residential development in this area even though there were still factories operating? Was that a wise choice?

   b) Should the cities have forced factories to move out as this area became residential? Why or why not?

   c) Could a more effective planning process have avoided the problem? How? What decision would you have made if you were the planner?

3. ■ **Geographic Perspective** J. K. Rowling (you might know who she is) once said, "We do not need magic to transform our world. We carry all the power we need inside ourselves already. We have the power to imagine better." How would you apply her idea about the power of the imagination to urban design? Work with classmates to imagine how cities could be transformed in the future to be more liveable and more sustainable. Try not to go too far into the realm of science fiction, but do trust your imagination.

Take **GeoFlight 12.2** to explore this area.

Land Use in Our Cities and Towns

? How do the ways that we use land in our cities and towns relate to liveability and long-term sustainability?

Learning about land use is a very important and practical matter. It is about understanding how well our towns and cities work, how liveable they are today, and how much they contribute to sustainability for the future.

1. Create a graphic organizer to summarize what you have learned in this chapter.

   a) Start with a full sheet of paper. Make a sketch map of your local city, town, or neighbourhood showing the various types of land use that exist. (Leave room for notes.)

   - Determine how large an area you want to cover. Then draw the pattern of major roads (expressways and arterial roads) in this area.

   - Use different colours and shades to show the different land uses. Label your map appropriately.

   b) Make notes on your map about the features that contribute to (or detract from) liveabilty and sustainability. Explain the reasons behind each of your notes.

2. What recent changes in land use can you see in your community? What is causing these changes?

3. With a partner, analyze the official plan for your municipality. What basic principles or concepts is the planning of your community based on?

Geo Inquiry

Interpret and Analyze

4. Use the map you created in question 1 to do the following tasks.

   a) Describe three things that make your community more liveable and three things that make it less liveable.

   b) Describe three things that make your community more sustainable and three things that make it less sustainable.

   c) Does more sustainable mean more liveable (and vice versa)?

Evaluate and Draw Conclusions

5. How might land use be different in your community in 50 years? Do you think land-use issues will get better or worse? Explain.

Analyze an Issue

6. Think about issues related to land use that affect your everyday life. Pick one of these issues.

   a) Write a number of questions about the issue. Narrow your questions down to one clearly stated big question.

   b) Find three or four resources and collect information to answer your question. Be sure to analyze the information and consider various viewpoints.

   c) Use your notes to take a position and answer your question.

   d) Create a product that communicates the answer to your question. This could be an opinion paper, a blog post, a poster, or a letter to the editor. Be creative!

©P

13 Better Choices Mean Better Communities

> **?** **What choices can we make to create liveable and sustainable communities?**

Building Better Communities: Urban Agriculture

Urban agriculture takes place in cities and towns around the world. As populations increase, so does the demand for food. Urban agriculture, which can involve anything from a community garden, a small farm, or a rooftop beehive, helps meet that demand.

In most cases, urban agriculture changes unused land into a sustainable source of food, health, and wellness for a community. Grow Calgary is an example. Located on 4.5 hectares of public land next to a major transportation corridor just outside Calgary, the garden provided 20 truckloads of vegetables to local food banks in 2013. Each truckload provides a hamper of food to 150 households. Organizers of Grow Calgary hope to expand even further, and have applied to the City of Calgary for access to an additional 254 hectares of unused land. The gardens will not only make the unused land productive, but will bring health and economic benefits to the city—supporting the local ecosystem, providing fresh food to people, and helping reduce the city's carbon footprint.

KEY TERMS

urbanization

urban growth

urban sprawl

greenbelt

land use intensification

20-minute neighbourhood

Big Move

go online

Search for countries with the highest levels of urban agriculture.

THINKING CRITICALLY

What should we do differently if we want to produce more of our food where we live?

How Do We Balance Liveability and Urban Growth?

urbanization growth in the percentage of a country's population that lives in cities and towns

urban growth growth in the number of people who live in cities and towns

In Canada, and other developed countries, the process of **urbanization** has largely been completed (Figure 13–1). The percentage of the population that lives in cities in Canada has stabilized at around 80 percent. In contrast, **urban growth** continues. Almost all of our population growth occurs in cities, especially in our largest cities (Figure 13–2). This happens because more people, including most immigrants, choose to live in large cities, where economic opportunities are greatest, instead of in rural areas.

More than 27 million Canadians live in urban areas. Of the 100 largest urban areas in Canada, 92 saw growth between 2006 and 2011. In the case of Milton, Ontario, the growth in only five years was a remarkable 66.1 percent. In comparison, Canada's total population grew by 5.9 percent during this time. At the same time, four cities in Ontario with populations of more than 50 000 saw their populations decline slightly. These cities are in all parts of the province, from Windsor to Thunder Bay to St. Catharines. The results of these uneven growth patterns can be seen as one drives through the cities. In some cities, many new residential neighbourhoods, recreation centres, schools, and shopping malls are being built. In others, there is little construction and some buildings sit empty.

Population Living in Urban Areas in Canada, 1871–2011

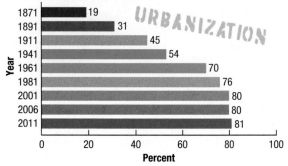

Source: Employment and Social Development Canada

▲ **Figure 13–1** In what year did urbanization in Canada level off? What percentage of Canada's population is now urban?

Urban and Rural Populations in Canada, 1851–2011

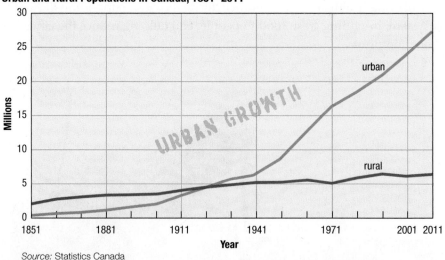

Source: Statistics Canada

▲ **Figure 13–2** Urban growth in Canada continues, while rural population growth has levelled off. Most of Canada's population growth occurs in census metropolitan areas (CMAs), which have populations of more than one million. Why does urban growth continue, while urbanization has levelled off?

©P

In this chapter, we will focus on the problems that urban growth can cause, and why these problems make maintaining (let alone increasing) liveability, while increasing sustainability, so difficult. In general, these problems can be grouped into three general areas: economic, environmental, and political/social/well-being.

Before looking at what this means in Canada, let's take a quick look to see what is happening in some of the rapidly growing cities in developing countries. Remember sustainability exists only when sustainable development is allowed to happen throughout the world. Although developing countries produce less of an ecological footprint than developed countries, many of their population trends, such as urbanization, suggest that they may be likely to live less sustainably in the future.

What's Happening in the Developing World?

There are two reasons why urban growth is happening much faster in developing countries than in developed countries, such as Canada.

- Population growth rates are much higher in developing countries.
- The process of urbanization is ongoing in the developing world. Millions of people are moving from rural areas to cities, looking for opportunities.

According to the United Nations Population Fund, rates of urban growth are expected to remain relatively high globally over the next 25 years, with significant increases in the urban populations of Asia and Africa.

A common result of rapid growth in developing countries is the creation of *informal settlements* — unplanned, illegal slums around cities. An example would be the *favelas* in Brazil (Figure 13–3). These areas, which have different names in different countries, generally lack clean water supplies, sanitation, garbage disposal, and schools. The reason for their growth is quite simple. The vast majority of those migrating from rural areas are very poor. They come to the city with little, if any, money, hoping to build a better future. The result is the growth of communities with very low levels of liveability. On the next few pages, you will examine some of the issues related to liveability in rapidly growing cities.

Geo ✲ Inquiry

Gather and Organize

Find the countries that are undergoing the highest rates of urbanization in the world. Organize this information on a map.

You can visit the communities discussed here on **GeoFlight 13.1**.

▶ **Figure 13–3** This *favela* is in Rio de Janeiro, Brazil, not far from the city's famous beaches and the stadiums and arenas for the 2014 World Cup and the 2016 Summer Olympics. Why do you think there have been large and, at times, violent protests against Brazil's hosting these events?

ECONOMIC ISSUES

In 1978, the population of Shenzhen, China, was only a few thousand. Today, more than 15 million people live there. Shenzhen is the home of many of the factories that produce goods we buy in Canada.

By 2011, 50 percent of the Chinese population lived in urban areas. The impact of so many million people moving to China's cities has been profound. China is much richer than it was only a generation ago, but the benefits have not been shared equally. Millions of urban residents live in relative poverty (Figure 13–4).

CONNECTING

The population explosion that occurs in Stage 2 and Stage 3 of demographic transition is discussed in **Chapter 11 (pages 240–242)**.

▶ **Figure 13–4** These "handshake" buildings are about 10 storeys tall and only one metre apart. They have been illegally built at the edge of Shenzhen to house factory workers. A typical apartment is about 8 square metres and rents for less than $100 per month. Why are they called handshake buildings?

ENVIRONMENTAL ISSUES

In Canada, governments plan carefully for growth. Basic services, such as water supply and sewage treatment, are put in place before the first buildings go up. This is not the case with informal settlements. People move from the country with little money. They find open land and build homes from scraps of metal, plastic, or even cardboard. Clean water in these areas is often more expensive than it is in Canada, even though people often survive on less than $2 a day. Many families may have to share one pit toilet.

Figure 13–5 shows a suburb of Nairobi, Kenya, called Kibera. Estimates of Kibera's population range from 170 000 to more than one million people. It is fascinating, and at the same time quite disturbing, to see what an urban area can be like when there has been no planning or construction of infrastructure.

▲ **Figure 13–5** Photos of places like Kibera generally show piles of garbage everywhere. Why don't the people dispose of their garbage properly? What other environmental problems are caused by settlements like this?

©P

POLITICAL ISSUES

People living in massive slum areas often have little power to control their futures. The land in these areas is typically illegally occupied. When the land is needed for another purpose, it is quite common for government officials to send in bulldozers to destroy the carefully built homes of hundreds or even thousands of people. Sometimes, though, informal settlement areas can become a focus for social and political change. There is no better example of this than in South Africa. Before 1990, a racist policy called *apartheid* forced urban Black South Africans to live in "townships" on the edges of major cities. The most famous of these was Soweto (<u>SO</u>uth <u>WE</u>stern <u>TO</u>wnship) on the outskirts of Johannesburg.

Much of the fight against apartheid was centred in Soweto. In 1976, this included a peaceful protest by 10 000 to 20 000 Soweto high school students against the government (Figure 13–6). Police attempted to break up the protest and killed at least 176 students. The Soweto Uprising, as it came to be called, marked a major turning point in the struggle against apartheid.

go online

A seven-part documentary series, *Have You Heard From Johannesburg*, examines the struggle against the white government in South Africa at home and in other countries. Episode 2 looks at the pivotal Soweto Uprising in 1976 (57 minutes).

◀ **Figure 13–6** Soweto high school students protest for better education in June 1976.

SOCIAL AND WELL-BEING ISSUES

Informal settlements can lead to physical and mental health issues. In Asuncion, Paraguay, a settlement called Cateura was built adjacent to Ascunion's garbage dump, right next to the sewage treatment lagoon. People lived here so they could find and recycle any trash that had value. Many young people in the community ended up getting involved with crime, drugs, and alcohol abuse. To help combat these problems, a local group offered music lessons to young people in Cateura. However, there was not enough money to buy instruments. The solution—making instruments from recycled materials—created an unusual but successful orchestra: the Landfillharmonic.

go online

Research the Landfillharmonic and why it is so special.

Urban Growth Issues in Canada

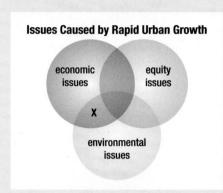

Issues Caused by Rapid Urban Growth

economic issues

equity issues

X

environmental issues

▲ **Figure 13–7** Issues caused by urban growth do not exist in isolation. Most issues involve an overlap between two or even all three categories. What would be an example of an issue that falls into area X on this diagram?

go online

Find out how the city of Surrey, British Columbia, plans for urban growth with sustainability in mind.

Urban growth in Canada creates issues that fall into the same categories as those in developing countries. We also face what we might call the Three E's—economic, environmental, and equity (political/social/well-being) issues (Figure 13–7). These issues have a negative impact on the liveability of cities and towns, and on our desire to live in a more sustainable way.

There are three critical differences between urban issues in Canada and those in the developing world:

• The process of urbanization is more stable in Canada, with fewer people moving from rural to urban areas. Urban growth is still happening, but at comparatively slower rates.

• We have the government structures (and money) needed to plan the growth of our cities and towns.

• In general, as a much richer country with a more educated population, our potential for resolving the issues *should* be higher.

There are many issues we could consider in this chapter. We can look at only a few of these. Some of them are common; they exist in almost every city in the country. Others are specific to one place and occur because of a particular combination of economic, environmental, and human factors. A few issues are listed in Table 13–1.

Table 13–1 Issues in urban growth in Canada `OSSLT`

Issue	Examples
Economic	Growing communities need resources and services—water, energy, transportation, waste disposal, schools, and so on. What are some of the costs of larger urban communities? How do we pay for them?
Environmental	More people living in cities means that more waste products of all types are produced—solid waste, sewage, polluted run-off from streets, even excess heat. How do we minimize the impact of the waste we produce on the environment?
Equity (political, social, well-being)	Urban growth can lead to social conflict, especially when people live at higher densities. How do we ensure that people have the freedom to live as they wish (e.g., playing their music loud) while at the same time promoting harmony (not bothering the neighbours too much)?
	How might urban agriculture initiatives help make urban communities more liveable and sustainable?

▲ How do these examples of urban growth issues in Canada compare with those in developing countries?

You may want to work with a partner or in a small group to answer these questions.

1. Look again at Figure 13–7 and think about the city where you live (or the cities close to where you live). Identify at least one issue that falls into each category. (There are seven possible categories, including combinations of each category.) Use a table like the one below to

   a) describe the issue

   b) indicate how it is related to urban growth

   c) suggest one or more solutions

   d) indicate which problems you think are most important

Category	Description of the issue	How the issue is related to growth	Possible solutions
economic	poverty		
economic and environmental	loss of farmland		

2. Describe how the issues you described in question 1 are linked to the current liveability and future sustainability of our cities. Give at least three specific examples to make your answer clearer.

3. a) If all of these issues are being caused by growth, is the ultimate solution to stop our cities from growing?

   b) How could this be done? Is it even possible? Overall, do you think this is a solution we should pursue?

4. One problem for urban planners is that they must plan for a future that is very difficult (and at times impossible) to predict. Give examples of the factors that make it very difficult to predict what future societies will be like.

1. **a)** To what extent are the factors that caused urbanization in Canada the same as those that are causing urbanization in the developing world? Explain both the similarities and differences that exist.

   b) The rural/urban population balance in Canada has stabilized in recent years. Suggest at least three reasons for this.

2. Put yourself in the role of a young, able-bodied person from a family of average wealth, moving from the country to the city in search of opportunities. First, imagine doing this in Canada. Now imagine doing this in Kenya. How would the process be similar in the two countries? In what ways would it be different? Consider the entire process from planning, to finding somewhere to live, to securing a job.

3. **a)** Economic disparity between rich and poor is a common problem in developing countries. How does this contribute to the growth of informal settlements?

   b) Can the disparity be reduced? How?

4. **a)** People living in great poverty in informal settlements know what the problems are around them. They may even know the solutions. In spite of this, why is it so hard for them to solve these problems either individually or together in groups?

   b) Lack of education is a major contributor to the problems of informal settlements. Education can be a major contributor to finding solutions to problems. How do the examples of Soweto and the Landfillharmonic demonstrate this?

5. **a)** How does the expansion of informal settlements affect the natural environment? Why? Give three specific examples.

   b) Why is the environmental impact less when people move from rural areas to cities in Canada, or when immigrants move to Canada?

6. The government of Kenya has built housing for some of the residents of Kibera (Figure 13–8). A large number of the residents of these apartments have chosen to move back into the informal housing of Kibera. How might this be related to the relative liveability of both types of housing? Why might a government solution to this situation fail?

▲ **Figure 13–8** The Kenya Slum Upgrading Program (KENSUP) also addresses issues in waste management, economic opportunities, and health.

7. What valuable lessons could Canadians learn from the experience of people living in informal settlements in developing countries?

8. How might urban agriculture initiatives help solve urban growth problems in both developed and developing countries?

©P

Selected Urban Issues

Much like the developing world, Canada has issues with urban growth. This section discusses just a few of these issues.

Urban Sprawl

Most urban growth in Canada has been outward, with cities taking over surrounding rural areas. Figure 13–9 shows how much larger cities have grown in only a few decades. This outward growth is often called **urban sprawl**.

urban sprawl largely uncontrolled expansion of cities onto adjacent rural lands

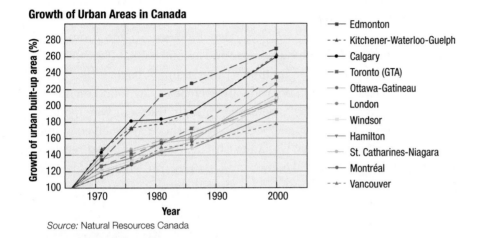

Growth of Urban Areas in Canada

y-axis: Growth of urban built-up area (%)
x-axis: Year

Legend:
- Edmonton
- Kitchener-Waterloo-Guelph
- Calgary
- Toronto (GTA)
- Ottawa-Gatineau
- London
- Windsor
- Hamilton
- St. Catharines-Niagara
- Montréal
- Vancouver

Source: Natural Resources Canada

◀ **Figure 13–9** OSSLT Look at the y-axis of this graph. What does "Growth of urban built-up area" mean? Are the trends you see likely to continue in the future? Why or why not?

go online

Read more about Canadian farmland and urban sprawl.

PROTECTING FARMLAND

If we want to build sustainable communities, we must rethink the way we grow. Relying on urban sprawl places too much pressure on the natural environment and our limited supply of good agricultural land (Figure 13–10). Protecting the productive farmland around most of our largest cities promotes sustainable development. It helps ensure that we will have local sources of food in the future and not have to rely as much on imported food.

◀ **Figure 13–10** The graph in Figure 13–9 considered urban sprawl from the perspective of numbers. Here we can see what it looks like on the ground.

greenbelt an area of rural land around a city that cannot be built on

go online

Greenbelts provide habitats for many animals, including coyotes. Coyotes have been found in some cities. Find out why.

Geo ☼ Inquiry

Gather and Organize

Brainstorm the pros and cons of greenbelts. Place your thoughts in a two-column chart.

Greenbelts are useful for protecting the natural environment and agricultural lands around our towns and cities from urban sprawl. At present, four Canadian CMAs (Vancouver, Toronto, Ottawa, and Kitchener-Waterloo) have created greenbelts. The largest greenbelt in Canada is located in Southern Ontario and is referred to as the Greater Golden Horseshoe Greenbelt (Figure 13–11). These greenbelts do not protect as much agricultural land as they might, but at least there is some measure of protection provided. The Greater Golden Horseshoe Greenbelt promotes sustainability by protecting local food sources and environmentally sensitive land. Local food is an important asset to our communities because it is often more nutritious than food that has travelled hundreds or even thousands of kilometres to reach our homes.

Greenbelts have other advantages. They help protect and promote natural environments for both human use and animal habitat (Figure 13–12). The impact of this can be seen by the fact that animals, such as beavers, coyotes, white-tailed deer, and occasionally even bears, are found on the fringes of large cities. Greenbelts help clean our air, filter our water, and maintain biodiversity. The Greater Golden Horseshoe Greenbelt contains four large watersheds (forests, wetlands, streams, and rivers) that reach Lake Huron, Georgian Bay, Lake Erie, and Lake Ontario. Millions of people depend on the clean water provided by these watersheds.

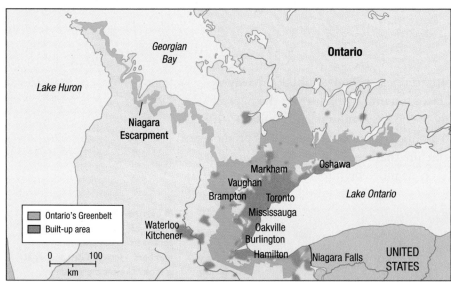

Source: Greenbelt Foundation

▲ **Figure 13–11 The Greater Golden Horseshoe Greenbelt.** This greenbelt was created by the Ontario government. It surrounds Canada's fastest growing region and protects over 800 000 hectares of agricultural land, forests, wetlands, and watersheds from urban expansion. The greenbelt plan is up for review in 2015, 10 years after it was first formed. What may have changed during that time? How might this affect the greenbelt?

▲ **Figure 13–12** The Bruce Trail follows the edge of the Niagara Escarpment, a UNESCO World Biosphere Reserve and part of the greenbelt (Figure 13–11).

©P

Eat Locally vs. Eat Globally

Unless we grow our own, the food we eat is available only because of the existence of a food delivery system. Some parts of this system can be quite simple—for example, local farmers bring produce to a local market. Other parts of the system are remarkably complex. Food produced halfway around the world must be brought to a local supermarket cheaply, and without damage or spoilage. Figure 13–13 illustrates 20 countries that provide fruits and vegetables to one Ontario supermarket. How do locally and globally produced foods increase liveability and reduce sustainability?

▼ **Figure 13–13 Some sources of produce imported to Ontario.** Can you link any of these countries with the fruits and vegetables that are part of your regular diet? To what extent could the produce from these countries be replaced by locally grown varieties?

Viewpoint 1

A global diet is good for us.

■ Local produce at a farmers' market is often more expensive than produce at a supermarket. Globalization provides us with food all year at a reasonable cost.

■ Variety in a local diet can be very limited, especially in the winter. Consumers want both variety and convenience.

■ There are many products, such as oranges and bananas, that cannot be produced in Canada.

■ Most people do not have the time to grow or pick their own produce, let alone preserve large quantities of fruits and vegetables for use later in the year.

■ We can't assume that locally produced food always contributes to sustainability.

■ Buying international foods helps the economy of poorer countries. As these countries become wealthier, they are more able to buy Canadian goods and services.

It makes sense to be a locavore.

🗩 A *locavore* is someone who only eats food produced locally, or close to home. However, the definition of *local* or *close to home* is not exact. A reasonable definition could be something like a 600 kilometre radius.

🗩 Eating local food provides important financial support for farmers who live near you. If local farmers are thriving, this helps maintain greenbelts around urban areas.

🗩 When you eat locally, you are more in contact with your food supply. You can grow some of your own food, even in containers on a balcony. You can visit farmers' markets and pick-your-own farms and get to know the farmers.

🗩 Local food can be healthier than food from distant countries. The use of potentially harmful chemical pesticides and herbicides is more regulated in Canada than in many other countries.

🗩 Local food tastes better because it is picked when ripe.

🗩 Local food can save you money. Bargains are available when you buy in peak season. If you want to grow your own vegetables, the seeds are very cheap.

🗩 Perhaps most importantly, being a locavore reduces the load you put on the environment. For example, apples grown in Southern Ontario have a short distance to travel to stores. This requires less fuel and produces less atmospheric carbon dioxide than the transportation of apples from another country.

APPLY IT!

1. a) Obtain a map of the area where you live. Draw a circle with a radius of 600 kilometres around your home.

   b) With a partner, brainstorm a list of as many food products as you can that are produced within this area. Write these food products inside the circle. Hint: Do not think about just fruits and vegetables— also consider meat, seafood, grain products, canned goods, and products needed for cooking, such as cooking oils and seasonings. Outside the circle, list as many food products as you can that are not produced in your local area.

   c) What items outside the circle are "needs," or things you absolutely must have in your diet? Are there local substitutes for these needs?

   d) What items outside the circle are "wants," or things you enjoy eating but are not essential? Are there local substitutes for these wants?

2. Considering everything, do you think it makes sense to be a locavore? Communicate your position in a letter to editor, blog post, essay, poster, or short video PSA. Consider both your personal perspective and the perspective of maintaining liveability and increasing sustainability on a global basis.

3. Is there a reasonable compromise between these two perspectives?

1. ■ **Geographic Perspective**

   a) What are the benefits of creating a greenbelt around a city?

   b) What individuals and companies would tend to oppose the creation of a greenbelt?

   c) Assume that the Greater Golden Horseshoe Greenbelt had been created in 1960. How would the urban areas in this region be different than they are today? Why was such a greenbelt not created then?

   d) Explain the effects that urban growth might have on natural systems in Southern Ontario, such as watersheds, if the Greater Golden Horseshoe Greenbelt did not exist.

2. a) Why is it particularly important that greenbelts and farmland exist around the four Canadian CMAs?

   b) Based on your answer to part a), what other CMAs would be good candidates for greenbelts?

3. What kinds of produce are farmed in the Greater Golden Horseshoe Greenbelt? Where is this produce sold? What does it add to the local economy?

Combining Urban Growth and Respect for Traditional Lifestyles

Since the creation of Nunavut as a separate territory in 1999, the capital city of Iqaluit has grown quickly (Figure 13–14). Population projections suggest this trend will continue, with Iqaluit's population almost doubling between 2010 and 2030.

While population growth in Iqaluit offers economic and social opportunities, it also creates unexpected change. Urban growth has introduced a new way of life for the local Inuit population. As a result, it can sometimes be difficult to maintain Inuit culture as the city grows.

Geo ❖ Inquiry

Evaluate and Draw Conclusions

List the costs and benefits of urban growth in Iqaluit.

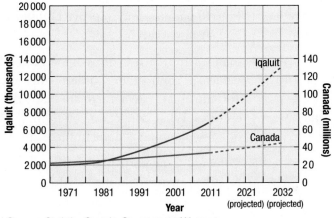

Sources: Statistics Canada; Government of Nunavut

◀ **Figure 13–14 Population projections for Iqaluit (in thousands) and Canada (in millions).** Iqaluit's projected population growth rate far exceeds that of any city in southern Canada. Some projections suggest that Iqaluit might grow even faster than this. What factors might contribute to the high growth rate?

▲ **Figure 13–15** A growing population requires housing. What challenges might the climate and landscape of Iqaluit pose?

▲ **Figure 13–16** How much is milk where you live? Why is it so expensive in Nunavut? How do food prices like these suggest that a return to more traditional ways would be a good idea both culturally and financially?

Traditionally, Inuit have had strong connections to the land. In the past, they lived in small groups, relied on hunting and gathering for food and other supplies, and moved frequently to follow the animals they hunted. They also had a strong sense of mutual interdependence. This has changed now that so many Inuit live in Iqaluit (Figure 13–15). Many Inuit still hunt and fish, but they also spend more time in permanent settlements such as Iqaluit. They also buy food and other necessities in stores, which can be quite expensive (Figure 13–16).

Many Inuit view "the city" as a place where traditional values and practices are being eroded. To respond to that view, the city of Iqaluit has, as part of its urban growth plan, the goal of protecting Inuit cultural heritage. To help achieve this goal, access to *Nuna*, an Inuktitut word for "the land," is going to be regulated. Only traditional uses, such as camping, fishing, hunting, and berry picking, will be permitted in the *Nuna* that surrounds the city. The intention of this goal is to make it easier for residents of Iqaluit to maintain their traditional connection to the land.

APPLY IT!

1. Describe two economic and two social issues that urban growth has created in Iqaluit. Are these effects the same for everyone? Explain why they may not be.

2. Identify three indicators of liveability that you think the residents of Iqaluit value. How do they combine environmental, economic, and equity values to help create a better, more liveable community?

3. How will the regulation of *Nuna* alter future growth patterns and improve both liveability and sustainability?

4. Iqaluit's approach to growth focuses on Inuit values. In contrast, in southern cities such as Toronto and Ottawa, there are many different cultures. What impact do you think this has on how planning is done in these cities?

5. What are some particular challenges faced by urban planners in the North?

©P

How Can Communities Be Made More Sustainable?

Liveability is about the here and now. If a community is liveable, people settle there. Sustainability is more about the future and whether a community can sustain the qualities that made it liveable in the first place. Recall what happened to Schefferville and Elliot Lake. What do those towns show us about liveability and sustainability?

What can we do to make communities more liveable and more sustainable? Read on to find out.

How Do We Build Greener Communities?

One good way to build greener communities is to build "smarter" buildings, which use less energy and water than standard buildings. Dr. David Suzuki Public School in Windsor, Ontario, which was built in 2010, is a good example of this (Figure 13–17). It was designed to use 71 percent less energy and 47 percent less water inside the building than a conventional building. It also uses no municipal water outside the building. It is a LEED Platinum–certified building. LEED stands for Leadership in Energy and Environmental Design. The LEED system uses points to evaluate the design of a building. More and more buildings are displaying LEED certification signs ranging from Certified to Silver, Gold, and Platinum. LEED certified buildings are not just good for the environment—they are good for the pocketbook, too.

In cold climates, designing and building energy-efficient buildings will help us offset greenhouse gas emissions and keep energy costs low. Making choices like these help support sustainable communities and protect the environment.

CONNECTING

Read about Schefferville and Elliot Lake in **Chapter 9 (pages 204–205)**.

Use **ArcGIS Online** to create a story map that relates to the liveability and sustainability of a major Canadian city.

go online

Learn more about Dr. David Suzuki Public School and the LEED system.

Geo ✱ Inquiry

Communicate

Create a list of environmentally-friendly criteria that, if followed, would make your school greener. You can use the LEED checklist as a starting point. Write a letter to the principal explaining the changes you think are possible to make, and why they are important.

◀ **Figure 13–17** The school board in Windsor could have chosen to build a conventional building. Why do you think they chose to "go green"? Why do you think they named the school after Dr. Suzuki?

How Do We Build Economically Diverse Communities?

Think back to Grand Bruit, the Newfoundland village described in Chapter 12, on page 255. In 1900, it was a community that had a high degree of sustainability. Located on the southern coast of Newfoundland, the village had access to fishing year round, and cod, lobster, and salmon were plentiful. Most people made a living exporting salt cod. With the money earned, they could import those things they could not produce for themselves. But by most standards, liveability in the community was not very high. Grand Bruit was remote and isolated, and life was often a struggle. There was no school, no electricity, and no hospital.

During the 20th century, liveability in Grand Bruit improved. Electricity came to the village. Satellite television and the Internet became available. There were no roads into town, so the province provided a ferry service, along with better health care and education. Tourists arrived by ferry to visit the small outpost. But fatal problems were developing. The cod fishery collapsed, and, as a result, Grand Bruit lost its largest economic base. Other sources of income were very scarce. Children attending high schools in other communities stayed there after graduating in order to find work. The population shrank considerably; by 2009, there were only 31 people living in Grand Bruit year round. The costs of maintaining the ferry for such a small population made little sense. People began to feel lonely and isolated. In 2010, the last residents moved away after accepting relocation support from the provincial government.

Grand Bruit had become more liveable over the years, but was less sustainable. Larger communities face similar challenges. They want to enjoy increased liveability and sustainability, but must also be aware of the economic challenges they face.

CONNECTING

Review the collapse of the cod fishery in **Chapter 5 (pages 121–122)**.

GEOCAREERS

That's the Plan

Jennifer Keesmaat is the Chief Planner for the City of Toronto. Her bachelor's degree was in English and Philosophy, while her master's degree was in Environmental Studies. Before taking the Toronto planning job, she worked in several Canadian cities, in the United States, and in Europe. As Chief Planner, she has a very challenging job. She must promote policies that increase liveability in a rapidly growing city with major transportation issues and high real-estate costs, while making sure that economic growth and sustainability are also encouraged.

APPLY IT!

1. **a)** Why is the LEED system a win–win situation for everyone?

   b) Describe at least three ways that buildings such as Dr. David Suzuki Public School save energy, water, and other resources.

2. Is it always possible to increase economic diversity in a community? What makes it easier in some places and harder in others?

3. Is your own community a good example of a community trying to become more sustainable? Why or why not?

   a) Research your community and identify factors that increase or lessen sustainability and liveability.

   b) Organize and communicate your findings to the class.

Is Compact Growth Really Better?

Over the next 50 years, the city of London, Ontario, expects to add almost 200 000 people to its population. A number of proposals have been made for London's growth. These include two extreme growth models for the London city area: the spread pattern of growth and the compact pattern of growth (Figure 13–18). With the spread model, the city will expand onto nearby farmland. With the compact model, the city will experience **land use intensification** to allow it to increase its population within its current borders.

land use intensification
a process in which development is focused on filling vacant lots (residential infill), bringing disused buildings back into use, and replacing low-density dwellings with higher-density buildings

Compact Pattern of Growth

Housing Characteristics

- high residential densities
- new housing:
  30% single detached
  35% townhouse and mid-rise
  35% high-rise
- most new housing in existing built-up areas

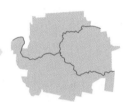

Spread Pattern of Growth

Housing Characteristics

- much lower residential densities
- new housing:
  70% single detached
  15% townhouse and mid-rise
  15% high-rise
- most new housing in subdivisions around existing built-up areas

new residential area

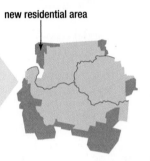

▲ **Figure 13–18** The two models shown here illustrate a pattern of growth for the London city area. No matter which model is selected, London will be a very different place in the future.

Viewpoint 1

Compact growth is good growth.

- The compact pattern of growth encourages the reuse of under-utilized lands. It also produces social and economic efficiencies with respect to energy and water consumption and public services, such as garbage collection, health care, and firefighting.

- The compact model would save more than 6400 hectares of Canada's best farmland from urban sprawl.

- The compact model would only cost $1.95 billion, versus $6.37 billion for the spread model.

- The spread model requires more infrastructure, such as roads, and is costlier in the long run.

- Building new residential areas inside the city helps to rejuvenate areas of the city that are in need of revitalization (Figure 13–19 on the next page).

- High-density neighbourhoods produce a larger customer base for businesses. This helps create a livelier downtown with more goods, products, and services for people to choose from. This also helps diversify the economic base of the city.

- High residential density allows for a more effective public transit system.

► **Figure 13–19** Here is one way in which land use intensification can be done. This condo development in Ottawa was based around a former church (the red brick structure on the left side of the building). It dramatically increased the intensity of use of this plot of land.

Viewpoint 2

Communities are much better spread out.

- Compact communities are good in theory, but they do not always work out the way we want them to. Under-utilized lands within the urban boundary are often limited, and redevelopment is very disruptive to existing neighbourhoods.

- Compact communities do not protect natural spaces within communities, such as yards, grass-lands, and woodlands. These spaces increase the liveability of an area, but, in a compact community, they are used for development.

- Compact communities can face opposition from people already living in an area. The spread model is less controversial, so it can be implemented more easily.

- Most people prefer lower-density living. Let the market determine where people will live.

- Intensification increases the demands on pre-existing infrastructure and services.

- The compact model increases traffic, congestion, noise, and air pollution in urban areas.

go online

What else does London, Ontario, have planned for the future? You can learn more about development proposals for London online. Will these plans increase liveability? How do they contribute to sustainability?

APPLY IT!

1. Can you add arguments to either viewpoint? Explain your arguments.

2. Which viewpoint do you support? Why?

3. Are compact communities an effective way to make cities more liveable and ultimately more sustainable? Evaluate this model by producing a PMI (pluses, minuses, and interesting) chart. Use examples in your local area to explain why compact growth is, or is not, an effective model.

4. Which model do you think would be more easily accepted by most people in London (and other parts of Canada)? Why?

©P

How Do We Build More Effective Transportation Systems?

Transportation systems, for moving people and goods, are features of the modern world. These systems exist at all scales—from how you get to the local movie theatre to how a kiwi fruit gets from New Zealand to your grocery store. Like many aspects of the modern world, the transportation systems we rely on are products of a complex pattern of decisions made by individuals, businesses, and governments.

An effective transportation system can add considerably to the liveability of a community. It meets the needs of all residents, regardless of age, income level, or physical ability (Figure 13–20). A poorly designed or overloaded system wastes time and money, increases stress, and is bad for the environment.

Changes in Transportation Technology

The size of a city at any time in history is directly related to transportation technology. Hundreds of years ago, when people had to walk or relied on horses, cities could not be very large. In the late 19th and early 20th centuries, streetcars allowed cities to get much bigger. Ownership of cars later in the 20th century dramatically increased people's ability to get around, and cities began to get bigger.

The increased mobility and freedom that cars give us comes with costs. Some of these costs are economic. We need to buy and maintain a car and pay for roads, for example. Other costs are social—in large Canadian cities, it is common for people to take an hour or more to commute to and from work. This reduces the time that people can spend with family or in leisure activities. There are also environmental costs. Cars are much less polluting than they used to be, but they still consume fossil fuels and generate enormous amounts of carbon emissions.

Local Connections

Think of your trip to school today. You may have walked, biked, taken a school or transit bus, or driven with someone. Each of these transportation methods has advantages and disadvantages, and each either contributes to or reduces liveability and sustainability.

Most local connections are made in private cars, often with only one person in a vehicle that might seat seven. This is not very efficient. People are spending longer on their daily commutes as traffic gets worse. Parking is becoming harder to find and more expensive. Fuel prices are rising, as are global temperatures. You probably could suggest a couple of ways to improve this situation. What would they be?

Geo Inquiry

Evaluate and Draw Conclusions

List all of the modes of transportation you can think of in your community. Rate them for liveability and sustainability.

You can investigate some of Canada's most important transportation connections on **GeoFlight 13.2**.

▼ Figure 13–20 How might a transit system that is accessible to all residents make a community more liveable?

THE 20-MINUTE NEIGHBOURHOOD

We can change existing transportation connections to make sure they work as well as possible, but there may be a better approach. Perhaps we should design our communities from the beginning to work at a more human scale. This means creating communities where people have easy access to jobs, schools, and goods and services. Instead of relying on cars, we can walk, bike, or take public transit. Key to this idea is designing compact communities with employment, housing of various types and costs, and urban services such as schools, stores, and restaurants. A community that has all these features in an area that is walkable or bikeable is often called a **20-minute neighbourhood** (Figure 13–21).

20-minute neighbourhood
a community in which important destinations (such as shops, jobs, schools, and parks) are within 1.6 kilometres, a distance that can be walked within 20 minutes at a brisk pace

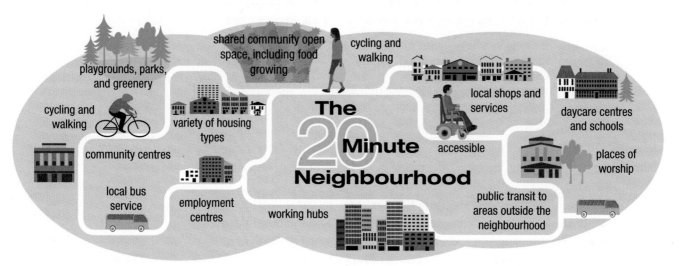

playgrounds, parks, and greenery

shared community open space, including food growing

cycling and walking

cycling and walking

variety of housing types

The 20 Minute Neighbourhood

local shops and services

daycare centres and schools

community centres

accessible

places of worship

local bus service

employment centres

working hubs

public transit to areas outside the neighbourhood

▲ **Figure 13–21** (OSSLT) In a 20-minute neighbourhood, as the name implies, you should be able reach all the features and services you need within 20 minutes. Would you like to live in such a community? Why are such communities so rare?

Regional Connections

The *Union Pearson Express* is a passenger rail line between Union Station in downtown Toronto and the Pearson International Airport, to be completed in 2015. While it is only 25 kilometres long, it is a critical regional (and even international) connection because it links Union Station, Canada's busiest surface transportation hub (subway, railway, and buses), with Canada's largest international airport.

Another example of a major regional connection is the new bridge being built between Windsor and Detroit. In 2012, $1 billion in trade passed between Canada and the United States over the Ambassador Bridge, which was built in 1929. *The New International Trade Crossing,* as the bridge is formally known, will help handle the huge number of trucks that cross the border there every day. A better connection will also help increase Canadian exports of manufactured goods, since transportation costs will be lower. Total construction costs for the bridge could be up to $4 billion. (The Canadian government will collect bridge tolls to pay for the American share of the bridge.)

©P

Global Connections

Effective transportation linkages between Canada and other parts of the world are important for both our export and import industries. They provide jobs and make imports cheaper and more available for Canadians. As a result, we have more choices of food, clothing, technology, cars, and many other imported items.

At present, Canada has three primary gateways, with another one likely in the future.

- The *Asia–Pacific gateway*, principally in the Vancouver area, links Asia to the interior of Canada via ship, rail, pipeline, and trucks.

- The *continental gateway* provides rail, truck, and pipeline links with the United States and eastern and western Canada.

- The *Atlantic gateway* connects Canada to the markets in Europe and Africa.

- Canada's *polar gateway* does not exist in any real sense yet, but it is an increasing possibility. Climate change is reducing ice coverage in the Arctic Ocean, which may allow freighters and tankers to pass through the Northwest Passage more reliably.

Geo ⚙ Inquiry

Interpret and Analyze

Using a map or globe, suggest the best "gateway" for trade from Ontario to different parts of the world.

APPLY IT!

1. Suggest three changes we could make that would reduce traffic congestion and help us move toward sustainability.

2. ■ **Patterns and Trends** Does a 20-minute neighbourhood exist where you live? If not, what components are missing? Would it be possible to add them?

3. Some Canadian cities are heavily dependent on bridges. Why? What particular problems does this cause?

4. a) How do effective local, regional, and global connections add to the liveability of our communities? How might these connections also be a threat to sustainability?

   b) How can we maximize liveability and sustainability when we plan and use our transportation connections (of all types)?

5. Research the impact on the liveability and sustainability of at least four of the following transportation-related innovations. Write a paragraph explaining what each is and what its impact would be.

   a) working from home

   b) car- and bicycle-sharing schemes

   c) self-driving cars

   d) parcel delivery by drones rather than trucks

   e) congestion charge zones

   f) pedestrian zones

   g) increased use of toll roads

   h) free public transit

   i) another innovation of your choice

6. What environmental risks are posed by use of the polar gateway? What might increased freighter traffic mean for the people living in the Acrtic?

Improving Ontario's Transportation

In the 2014 Ontario election, one of the most important issues was how to solve transportation problems. These problems exist at the local, regional, and provincial levels, and they have major implications for both liveability and sustainability in the province. People spend too much of their day in traffic or on crowded buses and trains. Resources are being wasted, and carbon emissions have increased as 30-minute journeys have become 60-minute journeys. These problems get worse as urban populations grow.

Each political party had its own vision of what needed to be done, how much it would cost, and how to pay for it. One plan from the provincial government was to spend $29 billion on transportation. This enormous sum indicates how serious the problems are and how expensive they are to fix.

The plan is composed of two parts. One plan is for what is known as the Greater Toronto and Hamilton Area (GTHA), which includes connections as far west as Kitchener-Cambridge-Waterloo, as far east as Peterborough, and toward Barrie (Figure 13–22). This part of the plan will cost the province $15 billion. The other $14 billion is to be spent in the rest of the province. The federal and local governments are also expected to make major contributions.

▲ **Figure 13–22** Major highways in central and northern Ontario need to be modernized and expanded. These two photographs show the same part of the highway. (a) Construction of Highway 69 began in 1936 and was finished in the early 1950s. Highway 69 was not designed to carry the heavy traffic that travels this section of the Trans-Canada Highway. (b) Highway 69 is gradually being "four-laned." This is a costly task. As Highway 69 becomes a four-lane highway, its number is being changed from 69 to 400. How does modernizing a highway increase liveability and sustainability in nearby communities?

©P

Transportation Improvements outside the GTHA

The regions outside of the GTHA involve most of the province's area and almost half of its population. There are enormous differences in the physical and human geography in the area. This means that there are very different transportation needs in different parts of the province. The major transportation improvements here include

- building the transportation infrastructure needed for the Ring of Fire mining development in northwestern Ontario
- building light rapid transit (LRT) lines in Ottawa (Figure 13–23) and Kitchener-Waterloo; LRT lines work in areas where the population density is not high enough to justify a subway line
- expanding the program of building four-lane sections of the Trans-Canada Highway (Highways 11, 17, and 69) in Ontario; more money will be spent on repairs to or replacements for highways and bridges

CONNECTING

You can review your knowledge of the Ring of Fire in **Chapter 7 (pages 158–159)**.

▼ **Figure 13–23** The first phase of the Ottawa LRT, from Lyon to Rideau stations, was under construction in 2014. This is the most difficult and costly part of the line, since it runs under the centre of the city near Parliament Hill. Away from downtown, the LRT will run above ground on its own right-of-way, so the trains will not be affected by road traffic.

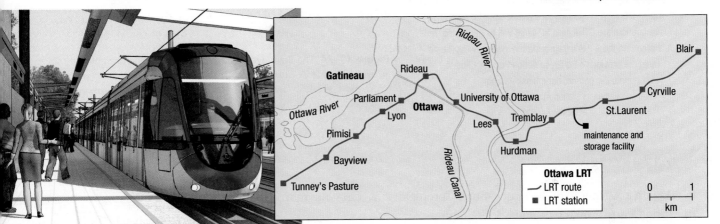

APPLY IT!

1. **a)** Which groups of people in our society most need effective public transit systems? Hint: Think about age, disabilities, and economic status.

   b) How do effective public transit systems add to the liveability and sustainability of cities for all residents, including those who drive?

2. Only two Canadian cities, Montréal and Toronto, have subway systems. Why are subways not found in cities like Vancouver and Ottawa? What is the best mass transit scheme for large cities in Canada that are smaller than Montréal and Toronto?

3. The transportation methods that are available in our communities are the result of the decisions made by individuals, companies, and governments. Give examples of how this works in your community.

The Big Move in Southern Ontario

Big Move a plan to dramatically improve transportation systems in the GTHA by 2035

25 YEARS FROM NOW...

The distance that people drive every day will drop by **one-third** compared to today. We will accommodate **50% more people** in the region with **less congestion** than we have today. On average, **one-third** of trips to work will be taken by transit and **one in five** will be taken by walking or cycling. **60%** of children will walk or cycle to school. There will be **six** times more bike lanes and trails than today. **All** transit vehicles will be accessible. Customer satisfaction with the transportation system will exceed **90%**. A single fare card will be used for **all** transit trips throughout the GTHA, and **all** fares will be integrated. By transforming the GTHA's transportation system, we will help meet the province's Go Green Action Plan for Climate Change. Per person, our emissions from passenger transportation will be **half** what they are today.

Source: Metrolinx

For many years, governments and people in the Greater Toronto and Hamilton Area ignored the issue of transportation. In the 1970s and 1980s, the region had effective highway and transit systems. Since then, the population of the region has risen dramatically, but little has been done to meet growing transportation demands. The **Big Move** is designed to play catch-up. It includes the provincial government's plan mentioned previously, but goes far beyond it in terms of length (it is expected to be a 25-year process) and cost ($50 billion in current dollars, which means even more with future inflation). Its aim is to generate faster and more efficient connections between and within the communities of the GTHA. Take a look at the goals of The Big Move (Figure 13–24).

◀ **Figure 13–24** The Big Move is a highly ambitious, long-term plan to provide the GTHA with an effective transportation system that will produce more liveability and sustainability, in spite of the fact that there will be three million more people in the GTHA than there are today.

APPLY IT!

Work with a partner to do these questions. Complete questions 1 and 2 on a base map of the region.

1. The Big Move is very complex and includes many individual projects. Use the weblink provided to start your research. On your map, summarize the following features of the plan and the existing regional transportation infrastructure.

   a) existing mass transit system, which includes TTC subways and GO Transit lines (rail and bus)

   b) transit improvements currently under construction, with their completion dates

   c) proposed transportation routes and whether they are high priority or lower priority

   d) the locations and purposes of mobility hubs

2. On your map, also summarize

   a) the various kinds of vehicles (subways, LRTs, buses, GO trains) that will be used, and the advantages and disadvantages of each

   b) parts of the Big Move that do not involve building transit routes but will still improve mobility

3. Look at Figure 13–24 again. Using specific examples, describe how the Big Move is designed to increase

   a) liveability   b) sustainability

go online

Learn more about the Big Move and Metrolinx, the Ontario government agency responsible for it. This page also has a very interesting trip planner that tells you how to go between any two points in the GTHA.

Better Choices Mean Better Communities

What choices can we make to create liveable and sustainable communities?

You saw, at the beginning of this chapter, how urban agriculture can improve liveability and sustainability. Urban farming comes about when people, companies, and governments cooperate to benefit their community, both now and in the future. Canadians, whether they live in large cities, smaller urban centres, or rural areas, all face their own particular set of liveability and sustainability challenges. We must all find the best way to work together to improve our communities.

1. **OSSLT** Use a concept web to summarize the ideas that you learned in this chapter. You might want to start with the concept of liveability, and show how it connects to sustainability. Use different colours to indicate which ideas you think fall under sustainability and which fall under liveability. Feel free to extend your web beyond the ideas in this chapter.

2. Why are decisions about residential density so important in determining both liveability and sustainability? What makes these decisions complex?

3. Private ownership of cars is an important part of modern life. It is also a major factor in many of the problems in our urban communities. Name four specific problems caused by too many cars.

Geo Inquiry

Interpret and Analyze

4. "The goals of liveability and sustainability should be seen as a journey, not a destination." What does this statement mean to you? Why might that be a useful way to look at these important goals?

Evaluate and Draw Conclusions

5. One of your roles as a Canadian is to be an informed and active citizen. Write a one-page letter to the mayor of your community. Describe one thing that could be done locally to improve liveability and sustainability. Explain why your idea is important and how it could be done at a reasonable cost.

Analyze an Issue

6. Think about issues related to urban growth that you have read about or that affect your every-day life. Pick one of these issues.

   a) Write a number of questions about the issue. Narrow your questions down to one clearly stated and important big question. Good questions raise more questions and start debate.

   b) What areas would you have to research in order to answer your big question? Find three or four resources and collect information to answer your question. Be sure to analyze the information and consider various viewpoints.

   c) Use your notes to take a position and answer your question. Support your answer with facts from your research.

   d) Create a product that communicates the answer to your question. This could be an opinion paper, a blog post, a poster, or a letter to the editor. Be creative!

Measuring Sustainability and Liveability

KEY TERMS

human development index (HDI)

ecological footprint (EF)

gross domestic product (GDP) per capita

gross national happiness (GNH)

environmental performance index (EPI)

happy planet index (HPI)

? **How might we be able to tell if we are creating more sustainable, liveable communities?**

Can We Combine a High Quality of Life with Environmental Sustainability?

By now, you know that we need to create communities that are both liveable and sustainable. But is there any way for us to measure how we are doing? The graph below shows us the relationship between the human development index (HDI) and the ecological footprint (EF). The HDI measures the quality of life for each country (grouped by geographic location in the graph), with respect to life expectancy, education, and income. The EF measures human demand on Earth's resources. In a way, the HDI represents liveability, while the EF represents sustainability.

biocapacity the average amount of land available to support each person

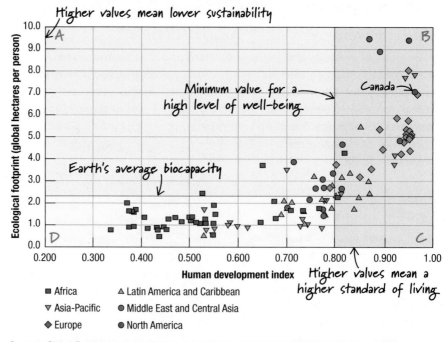

Sources: Global Footprint Network 2008 report (2005 data); UN Human Development Index 2005

THINKING CRITICALLY

Which part of the graph shows a high level of liveability (HDI ≥ 0.800)? Which part of the graph shows a sustainable level of resource use (EF ≤ 2.1)? Locate Canada on the graph. Describe our current levels of liveability and sustainability. Which section of the graph (A, B, C, or D) shows both high liveability and high sustainability? What must Canada do to move toward this part of the graph?

©P

Why Do We Need to Measure Liveability and Sustainability?

Collecting and measuring data is a vital element of most aspects of modern life. For example, golfers keep track of the trends in their weekly golf scores, while students are keen (or apprehensive!) to see their marks on the next report card (Figure 14–1). But what value is there in knowing golf scores and marks? There are really two related reasons why having good data matters. The first is to see if past decisions are working out as hoped. For example, did that extra study time result in a higher mark? The second reason is that accurate data make intelligent future planning easier.

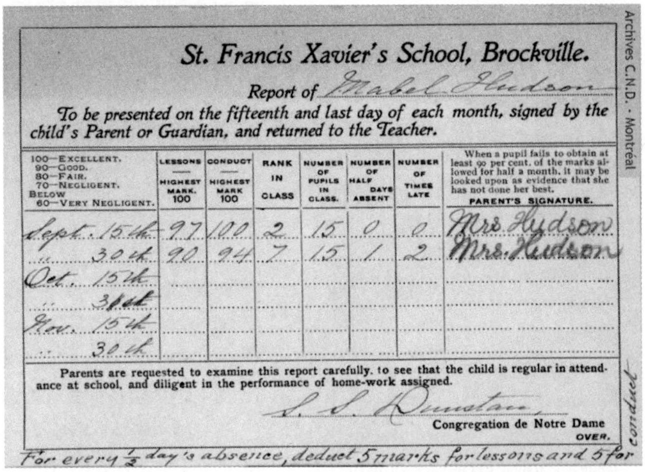

St. Francis Xavier's School, Brockville.

Report of Mabel Hudson

To be presented on the fifteenth and last day of each month, signed by the child's Parent or Guardian, and returned to the Teacher.

100—Excellent. 90—Good. 80—Fair. 70—Negligent. Below 60—Very Negligent.	Lessons — Highest Mark. 100	Conduct — Highest Mark 100	Rank in Class	Number of Pupils in Class.	Number of Half Days Absent	Number of Times Late	When a pupil fails to obtain at least 90 per cent. of the marks allowed for half a month, it may be looked upon as evidence that she has not done her best. Parent's Signature.
Sept. 15th	97	100	2	15	0	0	Mrs Hudson
" 30th	90	94	7	15	1	2	Mrs. Hudson
Oct. 15th							
" 31st							
Nov. 15th							
" 30th							

Parents are requested to examine this report carefully, to see that the child is regular in attendance at school, and diligent in the performance of home-work assigned.

S. S. Dunstan

Congregation de Notre Dame

OVER.

For every ½ day's absence, deduct 5 marks for lessons and 5 for conduct

Archives C.N.D. · Montréal

▲ **Figure 14–1** Report cards have changed dramatically since this one was used in Brockville, Ontario, just before 1900. Even though today's report cards look very different, their purpose is the same. This report card includes a request that parents look at their child's marks. How useful do you think this report card was in achieving its purpose?

Collecting and analyzing data also matters to those who are concerned about improving liveability and sustainability—including geographers, government officials, non-governmental organizations (NGOs), companies—and to you. People want and need to know about things such as how much the economy grew, whether the unemployment rate went down, whether commuting times are improving, and how much the average global temperature has changed. Their reasons for needing to know this information are the same as those of golfers and students. Without accurate data, decisions are made in ignorance, and that is never a good start for intelligent inquiry, planning, and decision making.

Things We Want to Measure

So far in this course, we have talked about many important aspects of modern life. These include

- managing our natural and human resources effectively
- improving the liveability of our communities
- ensuring that we have a strong and growing economy
- working toward increased global sustainability

There are many types of measures. Some measures require very complex calculations, while others are quite simple. All have been designed to be easily understood. Some measures focus on economic development. Others focus on environmental sustainability. Liveability is such a broad concept that it is very hard to measure. In its place, people have used a variety of related measures, such as happiness, prosperity (not just economic wealth), and well-being. In this chapter, you will have the opportunity to compare some of these measures.

Geo Inquiry

Gather and Organize

Brainstorm aspects of liveability and sustainability within the categories shown in the list on this page. Organize them in a chart, and then suggest ways that we might measure these aspects.

©P

How Do We Measure Liveability and Sustainability?

In this section, we will compare several ways to measure sustainability and liveability. At the end of this section, you will look at several selected measures in detail.

How something is described and then measured is critical in determining what the results will be. This is shown dramatically by four different measures of national happiness and well-being (Table 14–1). Note that in three of the measures, Canada, Norway, and Denmark are all grouped in the top 10 countries, with Costa Rica somewhere in the middle and Nigeria ranked near the bottom. The Happy Planet Index has entirely different rankings. This measure ranks, Costa Rica as the happiest country in the world (Figure 14–2). Canada and Norway are now somewhere in the upper middle range. What about Denmark? It is far down the list, not far above Nigeria.

GeoCareers

Wanted: Skills and Experience

What qualifications are needed for a career involving sustainability? In 2014, the Global Footprint Network (GFN), which is the world leader in EF studies, was looking for a Project Manager to analyze sustainable development projects in India.

They wanted someone with an advanced degree (master's level or higher) in a field related to international development. The person needed at least four years of experience with international development projects, specifically with numerical analysis. The GFN also wanted a person with experience in India and with excellent oral and written communication skills.

▲ **Figure 14–2** One reason why Costa Rica has such a high Happy Planet Index score is that the country has done an excellent job of protecting its rainforests. This has resulted in a strong eco-tourism industry, which strengthens the economy.

Table 14–1 Measures of national happiness and well-being

Country	World Happiness Report, 2013, 156 countries (UN Sustainable Development Solutions Network)	Legatum Prosperity Index, 2013, 142 countries (Legatum Institute)	Where to Be Born Index, 2013, 80 countries (Economist Intelligence Unit)	Happy Planet Index, 2012, 151 countries (The New Economics Institute)
Denmark	1	6	5	110
Norway	2	1	3	29
Canada	6	3	9	65
Costa Rica	12	31	30	1
Nigeria	82	123	80	125

Does this mean that the first three measures are right because they produce similar results, while the last one is wrong? Not necessarily. Instead, what we are seeing is the result of different data being chosen and the measure being calculated differently. This occurs because each study is based on a particular set of basic assumptions. When you research a measure, you must think about

- the assumptions that were made (and why they were made)
- the data that were chosen (and why other data were ignored)
- the formula that was used

Examples of Measures

HUMAN DEVELOPMENT INDEX

The **human development index (HDI)** is a measure of three key aspects of a country's standard of living: economy, health, and education. We must also consider differences within countries. For example, Canada is usually highly ranked for quality of life, but how might this apply to Aboriginal peoples in Canada? A 2004 United Nations report on human rights and Aboriginal people in Canada noted that Canada would rank 48th in the world if the country was judged on the quality of life experienced by First Nations people.

ECOLOGICAL FOOTPRINT

The **ecological footprint (EF)** is used to measure the demands that individuals place on the natural environment.

GROSS DOMESTIC PRODUCT PER CAPITA

Gross domestic product (GDP) per capita is the most commonly used measure of the health of a country's economy. It is very simple to describe — the value of all the goods and services produced in a country, divided by the country's population — but extremely complex to calculate. Governments have dozens of economists and statisticians who do the calculations each month.

GROSS NATIONAL HAPPINESS

The concept of **gross national happiness (GNH)** comes from the Kingdom of Bhutan, a tiny mountainous country between China and India. Bhutan has chosen to focus its efforts on creating increased happiness among its population rather than a higher GDP (see Figure 14–3 on the next page). A quote from 1729 shows that Bhutan has taken the pursuit of happiness seriously for a very long time: "If a government cannot create happiness for its people, there is no purpose for the government to exist."

go online

Find the most recent results of the measures described on this and the following page.

Geo ⚙ Inquiry

Evaluate and Draw Conclusions

Which of the measures shown here are used most often? Why?

human development index (HDI) a measure of overall quality of life that combines measures of wealth, health, and education. The HDI was developed by the United Nations.

ecological footprint (EF) a measure of resource use per person, expressed as the number of hectares of productive land that is needed to support a person

gross domestic product (GDP) per capita a measure of the size of an economy, in dollars, divided by the population

gross national happiness (GNH) a measure of the happiness of a population

The Four Pillars of GNH

1. Sustainable and Equitable Socio-Economic Development
2. Conservation of the Environment
3. Preservation and Promotion of Culture
4. Good Governance

▶ **Figure 14–3** (OSSLT) Students in Bhutan, such as these college students in Thimphu, are taught the "Four Pillars of GNH" in class. The pillars of GNH are described as a set of principles meant to guide the country toward a sustainable and equal society. Could all countries use this model? Why or why not?

ENVIRONMENTAL PERFORMANCE INDEX

environmental performance index (EPI) a UN–produced measure for evaluating performance in a wide range of environmental fields

The environmental performance index (EPI) is produced by the United Nations (as is the HDI). The EPI provides an overview of how successful countries are at solving many environmental problems, including disease control, water management, biodiversity protection, and carbon emissions reduction.

HAPPY PLANET INDEX

happy planet index (HPI) a measure that combines quality of life and sustainability

The happy planet index (HPI) focuses on identifying the extent to which countries provide their residents with long life expectancy and a high quality of life, combined with the country's long-term sustainability.

APPLY IT!

If you have used a jigsaw before, you already know that it is a simple and productive way to learn about several related things at once. The steps in this learning strategy are shown in Figure 14–4 and described below.

1. **a)** As a class, discuss the meanings of two similar terms: *liveability* and *standard of living*. In what ways are these terms similar in meaning? In what ways are they different?

   b) Get into your home group (Step 1 in the diagram). In this step, you get acquainted and make sure that everyone understands the process that follows.

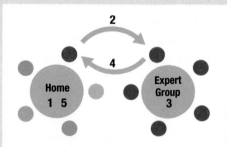

1. First meeting of home group
2. Breakout into expert groups
3. Expert group deliberations
4. Return to home group
5. Discussion in home group

▲ **Figure 14–4** Steps in the jigsaw strategy

©P

2. Each member of the home group moves to a different expert group (Step 2). Work together to research one of the measures described on pages 305 and 306. Write a summary as you answer the following questions (Step 3).

   a) What is the purpose of your measure? Does it focus on economic data, environmental data, social/well-being data, or some combination? Plot the measure on a graph (Figure 14–5).

   b) What kind of data were used in the calculation of the index? Why were these data selected?

   c) In general, how was the calculation done?

   d) Did you find the calculation easy to understand, or complex?

   e) How often is the measure calculated?

   f) How reliable and accurate does the measure appear to be?

3. Return to your home group (Step 4). Each person will do a short presentation to explain what he or she has learned about a measure. Graphs, data tables, or other graphics may be helpful in making the presentation clearer.

4. **OSSLT** The final stage is to discuss all of the measures and come up with a summary of what has been learned (Step 5).

   a) Create a summary of the purpose, methodology, strengths, and weaknesses of each measure. Do this based on the presentations of group members.

   b) Make a summary of how Canada ranks in each measure. What does this say about our liveability and sustainability?

c) As a group, choose which measure is best for showing liveability and which is best for showing sustainability.

d) After doing this analysis what conclusion can you now draw about the relative meanings of *liveability* and *standard of living*?

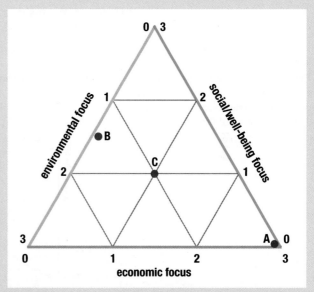

▲ **Figure 14–5** This graph shows ways of plotting different measures of sustainability and liveability. Measure A focuses entirely on economic aspects (economic = 3, environmental = 0, and social/well-being = 0). Measure B focuses equally on environmental and social/well-being (economic = 0, environmental = 1.5, and social/well-being = 1.5). What does Measure C show?

SKILL FOCUS

Long, detailed reports can slow down your research. Skim for main ideas by checking section headings and the first and last lines of paragraphs. Introductions and conclusions can also summarize main ideas.

CONNECTING

Check the definition of *liveability* in **Chapter 12 (page 258)**.

Liveability, Sustainability, and Canada's (and Your) Future

In the previous section, you learned how well Canada is doing on a number of sustainability, liveability, and combination measures. But why does this matter? Figure 14–6 describes what the problem is from the perspective of sustainability. We have now entered the beginning of a time of "overshoot." Humans, as a species, are living beyond Earth's carrying capacity. You will notice that the time scale does not show how many years these changes might take. The reason for this is quite simple—no one knows for sure. A rising population, and the increasing consumption of a population that is steadily getting richer, only shortens the time span. We are faced with a complex task in Canada. We need to do two things at the same time. We need to reduce our ecological footprint, while maintaining a high degree of liveability.

▶ **Figure 14–6** ■ **Interrelationships**
This graph shows the critical relationship between the carrying capacity of Earth and the environmental load that people place on it.

Earth's Carrying Capacity

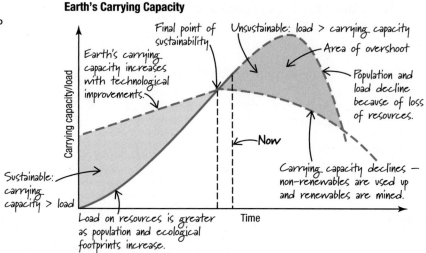

APPLY IT!

1. Think back to our definition of sustainability (Chapter 12, page 258) and look again at the graph on page 302. What connection is there between the EF of Canadians and the low HDI of many of the world's people?

2. Do you think richer countries treat their resources differently than poorer countries? Explain your reasoning.

3. **OSSLT** Ultimately, the world's ability to enjoy a good standard of liveability, while increasing sustainability, depends on the actions of billions of individuals over the next 50 to 100 years. How does this idea apply to each of the following?

   a) people in richer countries

   b) people in poorer countries

   c) government policies in various countries

   d) decisions taken by companies

   e) you

Is a Much Smaller Ecological Footprint Part of Canada's Future?

The Apply It! activity on pages 306 and 307 reveals several uncomfortable facts. Standards of living, as measured by the HDI, vary enormously. A few countries, including Canada, are ranked "Very High," but most countries fall below that. The inequality exists even though many countries have increased their use of resources and have EFs of more than 2.1 hectares per person. This makes the goal of sustainability difficult to achieve.

Two additional trends make sustainability even more challenging to achieve: the world population continues to grow, so, on a per capita basis, there are fewer resources to go around. This means that most of the world's people live in countries that are getting richer and use more resources, thereby increasing their EFs. What does this mean for Canadians in the years to come?

Viewpoint 1

Canadians have an obligation to reduce their EFs.

- It is clear that the world is not living in a sustainable manner. Canadians and residents of other rich countries are responsible for most of this problem.

- It is only fair that we reduce our EFs so that other countries can increase their standard of living.

- Most Canadians have access to modern technology, such as renewable energy, fuel-efficient cars, and effective recycling. This means that we can reduce our EFs while maintaining liveability.

Viewpoint 2

Canadians cannot avoid high EFs.

- Canada's physical geography means that we cannot avoid having high EFs.

- It is naive to think that people and nations make decisions based on what is fair. We should try to reduce our EFs, but only if this can be done without harming our standard of living.

- It is not our fault that we live in a country with so much productive land in relation to our population.

- It is premature to consider dramatically changing how we live. Much more research needs to be done to understand the situation.

CONNECTING

Review information about rethinking resource use in Canada in **Chapter 4 (pages 96–99)**.

APPLY IT!

1. ■ **Spatial Significance**
   What geographic features of Canada contribute to our high ecological footprint?

2. How could you reduce your EF without reducing your standard of living? Give specific examples in each of these aspects: housing, transportation, and food choices.

3. **OSSLT** Discuss the following statement: "While it may be possible for Canada to reduce its ecological footprint, it may not be politically practical to do so."

Measuring Sustainability and Liveability

? **How might we be able to tell if we are creating more sustainable, liveable communities?**

As you have seen in this chapter, there are many ways to measure sustainability and liveability. What can we learn from these measures to ensure both a good standard of living and sustainability for people around the world?

1. a) Would you like to live in a country that has the same goal as Bhutan? Explain.

b) Bhutan has chosen the pursuit of happiness rather than the pursuit of wealth as the key national goal. Would it make sense for Canada to do the same? Why or why not?

c) How do the Four Pillars of Gross National Happiness relate to sustainability? To liveability?

2. a) Compared to most countries, Canada ranks high on GDP, HDI, and happiness (on most measures), and ranks low on EF and HPI. Is this a situation of which we should be proud? Why?

b) As individuals, and through our governments, what could we do to improve Canada's rankings in EF and HPI? What should we do?

Geo ✿ Inquiry

Interpret and Analyze

3. Is it possible to have one index that measures all goals for sustainability and liveability (economic, environmental, and social)? Why might this be impossible?

Evaluate and Draw Conclusions

4. a) The measures or indexes you studied typically provide outcomes at a national level. Which ones could also be applied to smaller communities? Consider what data would be needed. Are such data available?

b) If you had to pick one index to apply to your own community, which would it be? Why?

Analyze an Issue

5. Think about issues related to sustainability or liveability that you have read about or that affect your everyday life. Pick one of these issues.

a) Write a number of questions about the issue. Narrow your questions down to one clearly stated and important big question. Good questions raise more questions and start debate.

b) What areas would you have to research in order to answer your big question? Find three or four resources and collect information to answer your question. Be sure to analyze the information and consider various viewpoints.

c) Use your notes to take a position and answer your question. Support your answer with facts from your research.

d) Create a product that communicates the answer to your question. This could be an opinion paper, a blog post, a poster, or a letter to the editor. Be creative!

©P

Where Is the "Best Place to Live" in Canada?

According to *MoneySense* magazine, in 2014, the best place to live in Canada was St. Albert, Alberta. What makes St. Albert, a small city on the fringe of Edmonton, the best place to live? The magazine suggests that there are a number of reasons. For example, unemployment is just above 4 percent (the national rate was close to 7 percent at this time), while incomes are among the highest in the country. St. Albert's crime rate is falling. It has sunny weather all year round. These are just four of the 34 factors that *MoneySense* uses in its annual survey to rank 201 cities in Canada.

In this unit, we have talked a great deal about the liveability of communities. In this performance task, you will consider what exactly is meant by *best place to live*. In what ways is it the same thing as *most liveable*? How might it be different? What is the best way to make such judgments?

> **go online**
>
> Find the most up to date *MoneySense* rankings. You will need the data for this activity.

ACTIVITY

Work with a partner to do this task. Your teacher will give you details on how you should present your findings.

1. The *MoneySense* analysis is a good starting point for your analysis. One problem is that the magazine provides so much information. (With 34 fields of data and 201 cities, there are 6834 individual pieces of data.) The 34 data fields can logically be put into categories. For example Population and Population Growth could be grouped in a category called Population Factors.

   a) Group the 34 fields into 10 or fewer logical categories. Give each category an appropriate title.

   b) Choose one field from each category that is representative of the category. Within each category, you may find that some factors seem critically important while others do not. Be sure to choose the most significant factors.

c) *MoneySense* compared 201 cities in Canada. Choose approximately 20 that are typical of all the regions in the country. Include St. Albert (or the current year's top choice) and either your community (if it is listed in *MoneySense*) or the listed city that is nearest to your community.

2. The *MoneySense* article only looked at communities with a population of at least 10 000. Is it possible to compare the liveability of cities that have over 1 million people with smaller towns and rural areas? Why or why not?

3. Use the *MoneySense* data to answer these questions.

   a) How do the data contribute to these cities having such different rankings?

   b) Identify two data fields that give you roughly the same information but in different ways.

c) Identify two data fields that should be looked at together to give a better picture of the situation.

d) Suggest at least two types of data that should be added to this analysis so that liveability is covered more completely.

e) Choose two or three important measures and try to identify characteristics of human and physical geography that contribute to these measures.

4. Now that you have your data, it is time to make your rankings. Begin by deciding whether all of your factors are equally important. If not, figure out a way to weight the importance of the various factors. For example, you might think one factor is three times as important as another. Explain why you have chosen your weightings, even if you chose to have equal weightings.

5. **a)** Use your data to choose the five most liveable Canadian cities. How are the concepts of *liveability* and *best place to live* related?

b) Write a paragraph to explain the method you used to make your choices.

c) What similarities do these cities have? What differences do they have?

d) How could these communities be made even more liveable?

e) Which of these factors will contribute to sustainability? How could we make these communities more sustainable?

Criteria for Success

In this activity, you will

❏ choose appropriate data for the analysis, and add at least one additional data set

❏ demonstrate a clear understanding of the role played by the data in answering the question

❏ use information from the unit in your analysis in an effective manner

❏ demonstrate a well-organized approach to answering the question

❏ communicate the method and conclusions of your analysis effectively

©P

Building a Better Canada: Target 2067

Some birthdays are just more special than others. July 1, 2067 will be a very special birthday for Canada and Canadians: the country will be 200 years old. Canada's 100th birthday, in 1967, was also very special. There were numerous special events. New schools, parks, arenas, and community centres were built to mark the occasion. There may even be one of these buildings in your community—just look for the word "centennial" in the name.

How should we mark Canada's bicentennial birthday? Perhaps there would be no better way than to help create a Canada that is as liveable and sustainable as possible. The year 2067 seems to be a long time in the future (How old will you be?), but this goal is complex and not easily reached. We will need at least 50 years to make the necessary changes.

WHAT'S INVOLVED IN THE TASK

To address issues about liveability and sustainability in Canada, we should acknowledge two critical things:

- While we do face significant social, economic, and environmental challenges, we are well placed now. Canada is continually ranked as one of the most liveable countries in the world. What we must do is maintain (and hopefully improve) our liveability, while at the same time increasing our contribution to global sustainability.

- During your study of issues in Canadian geography, you have acquired knowledge about certain challenges that will help you with this task (Figure CT–1).

GOAL

- to combine a high level of liveability with increased global sustainability

CHALLENGES

- managing demographic change
- providing effective management of renewable and non-renewable resources
- managing a changing economy so that it provides jobs and wealth
- being a responsible member of the world community
- reducing our environmental impact
- creating liveable communities across Canada

▲ **Figure CT–1** In this course, you have learned how each of these challenges is related to our overall goal. Now it's time to bring this knowledge together.

Let's see how this might work by looking at one aspect of the challenge: managing demographic change. Figure CT–2, on the next page, shows a range of projected populations for Canada to 2067. The graph suggests four questions you must answer as we work toward reaching our overall goal. (A similar set of questions can be applied to each challenge in Figure CT–1.)

1. What are the possible outcomes?
2. What is the most desirable outcome?
3. How do we achieve this?
4. How likely are we to succeed?

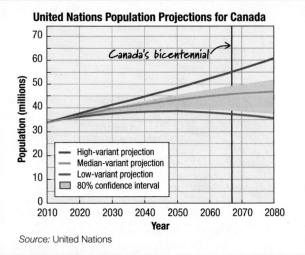

United Nations Population Projections for Canada

Canada's bicentennial

Population (millions) — vertical axis: 0, 10, 20, 30, 40, 50, 60, 70
Year — horizontal axis: 2010, 2020, 2030, 2040, 2050, 2060, 2070, 2080

— High-variant projection
— Median-variant projection
— Low-variant projection
▢ 80% confidence interval

Source: United Nations

▲ **Figure CT–2** According to the UN, there is an 80 percent certainty that Canada's future population will be in the shaded area of this graph.

THE ACTIVITY

Work in a group of three to six students. Each student will focus on one or two of the challenges in Figure CT–1 so that all six challenges will be covered. Your individual findings will be combined in a final presentation on how the goal will be reached.

1. Look at the six challenges listed in Figure CT–1. Brainstorm how Canadians might face these challenges in the future.

2. Formulate a big question that is related to your challenge and connected to the overall goal.

3. Start with the knowledge you already have. Consider existing patterns and trends that are related to your challenge and decide whether or not they are helpful.

4. Pursue additional research as needed. Focus on combining a high level of liveability with increased global sustainability.

5. Consider different views and beliefs about your challenge. (For example, Aboriginal peoples' beliefs about the natural environment.) You may need to resolve conflicting views.

6. Discuss your findings with other members of your group. The solution to one challenge should not make it impossible for another challenge to be met. For example, some economic plans would not be acceptable if they compromise environmental concerns.

7. Identify targets within the challenge that contribute to the overall goal of maximum liveability and sustainability.

8. Consider the four questions listed on page 313. What roles must individuals, governments, and companies play in finding solutions to these questions? What role could you take personally?

9. With other members of your group, consider how best to combine your individual findings and communicate your conclusions.

Criteria for Success

Your final presentation must

❏ show a clear understanding of the connections between the challenges and the overall goal

❏ include an effective big question to be answered

❏ demonstrate a fact-based analysis, using evidence you have gathered and organized

❏ suggest changes that would be practical over a 50-year period

❏ show how these actions would improve liveability and sustainability in Canada

❏ demonstrate an effective approach for communicating the results of the inquiry

©P

▶ SKILLS TOOL KIT

A good question can guide your inquiry by capturing your interest and focusing your attention on the information you need.

First Steps

If you are asked to develop an inquiry question, it probably isn't a closed question. Closed questions (What, Who, Where, When) elicit short, factual answers. They usually do not lead to deeper understanding of the topic.

Open questions are thinking questions. The best inquiry questions arise from your own curiosity about a subject. Your question may relate to an issue you feel strongly about, or perhaps a subject you would like to explore.

Types of Open Questions

Different types of open questions may help you dig deeper into an event or topic. Some of these are described below.

Causal Questions

These are questions designed to uncover the reasons for an event or situation. Why did something happen? What were the real reasons for a catastrophic event? Did one thing actually lead to another? For example, how did ice-age glaciation change Canada's human and physical geography?

Comparative Questions

These are questions that help increase your understanding of an event or situation by comparing it with another situation. Geographers, for example, might compare the popularity of public transport to car travel to determine which kinds of communities foster each mode of transport.

Evaluative Questions

These are questions that lead to an evaluation of a situation. They force you to examine all sides of an issue and support your final answer with evidence. "Does commercial production of oil from the Athabasca oil sands help or harm Canada?" is an example of an evaluative question.

▲ **Figure S–1** "What happened to Canadian-made jeans after the introduction of free trade?" is an example of a causal question.

Speculative Questions

These questions allow you to investigate how things might have turned out if a certain event had occurred or not occurred. "What if?" questions are speculative questions. For example, "What if Canada had not encouraged immigration? How would the country be different?"

APPLY IT!

Select an issue from this book, such as climate change, protecting the environment, or managing Canada's natural resources.

a) Develop four questions, one of each type, about the issue.

b) Which question would be most effective for exploring the issue? Explain why.

Research Steps

Follow these steps to gather and organize information.

Review the Question Review your research task or question to clarify exactly what information you need. Is there a specific time period, place, or focus to keep in mind?

Gather Information Use as many different sources as possible—books, print magazines and journals, web pages, online encyclopedias. Avoid material that is not important or relevant to your research.

Should you look for material that is ...

	Interesting	Not interesting
Important	yes	yes
Not important	no	no

Record Information Follow the tips below to ensure you take effective notes:

- For each source you use, record the title, the author's name, and the name of the publisher or the website. Recording these details will ensure that you can use the source in your bibliography.

- Make point-form notes in your own words. Read the source first, and then note the main ideas and supporting details.

- If you quote directly from the source, use quotation marks. Keep quotations short, and remember that plagiarism (passing off another person's work as your own) is dishonest and illegal.

- Use margins to highlight important terms and ideas, to ask questions that occur to you, or to make notes about the trustworthiness of the source.

Analyze Your Results Keep your research questions in mind. Are you answering these questions? Do you need to refine these questions or do more research? When you think you have enough information to begin writing up your results—or if the information is the same as information collected earlier—stop researching. You don't need to know everything about the topic of your research; you need just enough to complete the assignment you are working on.

Organize Your Information There are as many ways to organize information as there are students. Examples include index cards, graphic organizers (such as a pro-and-con chart or a cause-and-effect diagram), timelines, and web diagrams. Go online to find graphic organizers that might be useful to you. Find the ones that work for you and that fit the kind of information you are gathering.

APPLY IT!

Turn to page 154 and read the section called A Closer Look at Mining, which ends at the top of page 160. As you read, take notes and organize them into a format of your choice. Remember to examine the figures and read the captions, which often contain important information, and to take note of any new or unfamiliar terms.

When investigating geographic issues, geographers often use primary sources. Primary sources are sources of information that were created during an investigation or event, usually by a researcher but sometimes by a witness or participant.

▲ **Figure S–2** Although *The Glacier* by Arthur Lismer has its own style and point of view, it is still a primary source because it was created by an eyewitness.

Examples of Primary Sources

Primary sources in geography include

- raw data from field work, such as measurements, location data, observations of the environment, and observations of human behaviour

- eyewitness accounts, such as interview transcripts and diaries

- photographs and satellite images

- drawings or paintings (Figure S–2)

- official documents and statistics

- unedited sound or visual recordings

How do geographers evaluate their primary sources? They begin by asking questions about the nature of the source.

Relevance	What is the event or issue described in the primary source? Is the information geographic? (It should be.) For example, does it describe location, or the human or physical features of Earth? What conclusions can you draw about the event from this primary source?
Accuracy and completeness	Is the information accurate and complete? For example, if the source is a hand-drawn map, does it include a scale? If it is a description, does it include useful observations?
Reliability	Some primary sources are more trustworthy than others. For example, an official government source is often more trustworthy than a blog. Statistics Canada is an example of an agency that provides reliable demographic data useful to geographers.
Perspective	Does the primary source represent someone's viewpoint? How might point of view affect the usefulness of the information? How might this primary source differ if it had been created by someone else?

APPLY IT!

What do you think would be the best way to present information about a primary source? Would you write a paragraph, draw a poster, create a video? Would your selection depend on the source? Explain your response.

©P

Whether you are using your local library or the Internet, it is relatively easy to find information on just about any topic.

But Is It Accurate?

However, finding information does not guarantee that the information will be accurate. Here are some tips to help you critically assess the accuracy of your sources.

☐ **Authority**   Are the authors identified, and do they have qualified expertise in the subject area?

☐ **Accuracy**   Do the authors provide sources for their information? If not, how can you measure the accuracy of what they say? How does their information compare with that found in other sources?

☐ **Bias**   Are the authors arguing on behalf of a particular point of view? Is more than one point of view presented? Is the difference between facts and opinions clear?

☐ **Style**   Is the writing casual and/or full of grammatical errors, or does it seem thorough and well written?

☐ **Currency**   Is the information up to date? If the source is printed, check the date of publication. If the source is a website, check the copyright notice. Is the website current and active? A website that hasn't been updated in several years will not provide up-to-date information.

Another way to help you determine the reliability of a website is to assess what kind of site it is. Clues can be found in the domain names. (Note that these can vary from country to country.)

- .ca indicates a website based in Canada

- .com was once used to indicate a commercial site, but now has no special meaning

- .org indicates an organization, usually non-profit

- .edu indicates an educational institution

- .gov indicates a government agency (this can also be .gc in Canada)

If you find two or more sites on the same topic with conflicting information, use the clues above to help you determine which site is most reliable. Always record the website addresses of sites you visit. If you are still in doubt about the reliability of a website, ask your school librarian for assistance.

APPLY IT!

1. Wikipedia is a popular web-based encyclopedia. Investigate and evaluate it based on the tips in this section. In what ways is Wikipedia accurate? In what ways might the information on Wikipedia require verification?

2. Examine the Wikipedia collection of "Maps of Canada." You will find political, thematic, and topographic maps in this section. Clicking on a map should take you to its source information. What information is provided to indicate the authority, accuracy, and currency of the map?

Everybody has a bias. It is impossible to be human and not be biased. A bias is a way of looking at a situation or issue and judging it. Bias can be positive or negative. Positive bias creates a favourable impression of a situation or one side of an issue; negative bias creates an unfavourable impression.

While many writers try to avoid bias in their writing, it is almost impossible to remove it completely. Bias may be found in a wide variety of sources, including first-person accounts, newspaper articles and editorials, illustrations, cartoons, photographs, and paintings. It can also be found on social media sites such as Facebook and Twitter.

Detecting bias in material is another tool researchers use to assess the value of a source of information, especially a primary source (Figure S–3).

Detecting Bias

Here are three strategies you can use to detect bias:

1. Recognize fact versus opinion, and remember that fact and opinion can be present in the same document.

   • A fact can be verified with evidence from another source.

▲ **Figure S–3** Fracking is a relatively new way to release natural gas from Earth. Proponents of low-cost natural gas support fracking. Environmentalists think fracking could have long-term negative consequences. How might each side introduce bias when speaking or writing about this issue?

   • An opinion is based on a belief or point of view, and cannot be verified with evidence.

2. Recognize the language of bias. Biased accounts may use overly assertive language (positive or negative). Phrases such as "There is absolutely no doubt" or "It goes without saying" may be overly assertive. Extreme language (positive or negative—e.g., "Your children's lives are stake") is another hallmark of a biased account.

3. Identify the purpose of creating the source:

   • Who created the source?

   • Why was the source created?

   • For whom was it created?

A mistake many students make is to conclude that when they detect strong bias in a source, the source is no longer usable. This is not true. Biased sources lend insight into the events and people you are studying. They reveal what people think about certain issues, and why. Remember to examine as many sources as possible to gain a balanced view of a subject. For example, if you were gathering information about life on the Prairies, it would be best to locate accounts from different types of people, not just urban dwellers or farmers.

APPLY IT!

Examine different print articles, videos, or websites on all sides of an event or issue that your teacher has selected. In the sources that can be found in these selections, locate different examples of bias that have been discussed in the text above.

Statistics are numerical data—collections of numbers. The science of statistics refers to the gathering, presentation, and interpretation of these data. Sometimes statistics are presented as simple numbers or in tabular form (columns of numbers). Sometimes they are presented in graphic form (such as bar graphs and pie charts). Statistics help geographers in several ways.

Describing and Summarizing Data

A statistical table or graph can give geographers an instant picture of a situation or a trend, such as population size or land use in a specific area of a country.

Understanding a Situation

Why does one community experience population growth while another experiences a decline? Statistical information that is collected regularly, such as census data, encourages geographers to ask such questions. This leads to better understanding of human and natural environments and the relationship between the two.

Comparing Similar Types of Data

By comparing similar types of data across time periods, geographers can spot trends. For example, by comparing the top industries in a community

Canadian Population 65 Years and Over, by Region, Historical (2011) and Projected (2036)

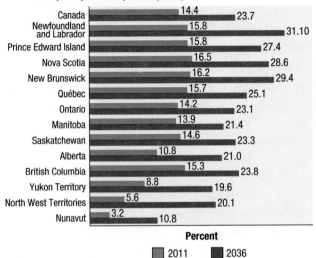

Source: HRSDC calculations based on Statistics Canada

▲ **Figure S–5** This graph shows the percentage of Canadians over 65, by region, projected to 2036.

30 years ago with the top industries today, it may be possible to draw conclusions about a community's economy or predict its future course.

Examine the two sets of statistics that describe some projected changes in Canada's population over the next few decades. Each set includes information that is useful to geographers. Then analyze the probable effects of this population shift using the Apply It! questions.

Canadian Population 65 Years and Over, Historical (1971–2011) and Projected (2012–2061)

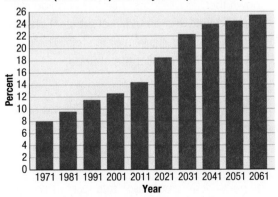

Source: HRSDC calculations based on Statistics Canada

▲ **Figure S–4** These statistics show the number of Canadians age 65 and over, as a percentage of the total population, from 1971 to 2061 (projected).

APPLY IT!

1. Examine Figure S–4. Provide possible reasons for the large increase in the percentage of people age 65 and older between 2011 and 2031.

2. Examine Figure S–5. Which region of Canada is likely to be *most* affected by a rise in the number of people age 65 and over?

3. How have statistics helped you understand a topic or an issue, or helped you explain it to another person? Describe your experience.

The purpose of graphs when studying geography is to show numerical data in a way that allows you to see and interpret patterns. Often, such patterns are not apparent when you look at the data in a list or table. Graphs are also an extremely effective way to present data when you are making a presentation to an audience. There are several types of graphs, each of which is best suited to particular types of data presentation.

Bar Graph

A bar graph is used to show data about a group of topics or items. There are two axes, and each one shows what is being measured. In the bar graph below, the amount of water being used for agriculture is measured over a period of time—from 1900 to its projected use in 2025.

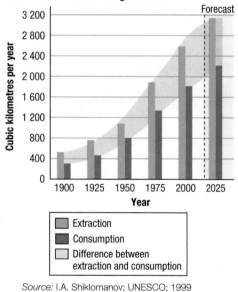

Source: I.A. Shiklomanov; UNESCO; 1999

▲ **Figure S–6**

Pie Graph

A pie graph is used to show relative sizes of numerical information about a topic. It is like looking at slices of one pie. These graphs are compact and easy to interpret, but unless specific amounts are given, you can only analyze relative proportions. The pie graph below illustrates where water exists on Earth.

When reading a pie graph, find the largest slice first, then the next largest, and so on, to get an overview of the topic being illustrated.

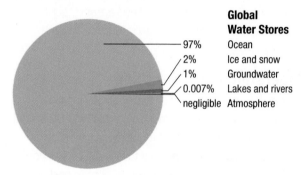

Source: U.S. Geological Survey (USGS)

▲ **Figure S–7**

Line Graph

A line graph shows information about a topic over time. The interval of time can be short (weeks or months) or long—even centuries. Every line graph has two axes—one marks off time periods, and the other shows the units being studied. When you read a line graph, identify the period(s) of greatest change by finding the steepest slope(s) of the line. The smaller the slope, the smaller the change.

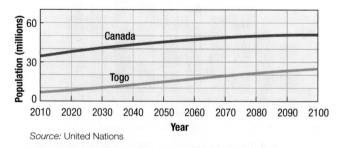

Source: United Nations

▲ **Figure S–8 United Nations population projections for Canada and Togo**

Multiple Graphs

More complex information can be presented in the form of a multiple graph. A *multiple line graph* uses lines to show change in many topics during the same period of time. A *multiple bar graph* can show different examples of corresponding information. A *compound bar graph* stacks different parts of a topic on top of one another. This is a good way to compare several parts of a topic at different times or at the same time.

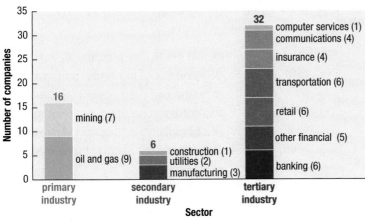

Source: Forbes Global 2000

◀ **Figure S–9 Compound bar graph.** In this compound bar graph, the sub-sectors of the main industry are stacked and shown in different shades of the same colour.

APPLY IT!

1. Which type of graph would be the most effective way to show the data in the table? Provide reasons for your answer.

2. Construct the graph you suggested in question 1. Be sure to add appropriate labels.

Indoor water conservation practices by province, 2009

	Had a low-volume toilet (% of all households)	Had a low-flow shower head (% of all households)
Canada	**42**	**63**
Newfoundland and Labrador	30	59
Prince Edward Island	31	60
Nova Scotia	39	66
New Brunswick	38	67
Québec	34	64
Ontario	48	65
Manitoba	39	49
Saskatchewan	42	51
Alberta	46	58
British Columbia	40	60

Source: Adapted from Statistics Canada, Environment Accounts and Statistics Division

Types of Maps

Different types of maps provide different kinds of information about places you are studying.

- **Political maps** show political borders and the names of important towns and cities.

- **Topographical maps** show the elevation of land and features such as lakes, rivers, and mountains. On flat maps, elevation is shown with lines. On 3-D maps or globes, elevation is shown as a raised surface.

- **Thematic maps** show information for a special purpose. They could show regions of natural vegetation, population distribution, temperature and precipitation patterns, or levels of pollution.

- **Historical maps** are a type of thematic map. They illustrate how things were in the past. They can show changes in borders, transportation networks, or the extent and type of agricultural activity.

Interpreting a Map

Examine a topographical map of Canada in an atlas. To begin interpreting this map, you need to ask questions such as the following:

- What area of the world is shown on this map?
- What type of information does it give me?
- What do the colours, symbols, and lines represent?
- What is the significance of the information in this map?

Locate the Prairies, the Rocky Mountains, the St. Lawrence lowlands, and the Arctic on this map.

Now examine the two maps below. Figure S–10 shows Canada's natural vegetation, and Figure S–11 shows Canada's population distribution. Answer the four questions above for each of these maps.

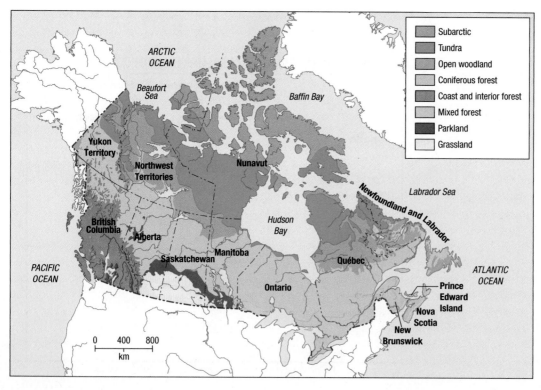

◀ **Figure S–10
Canada's natural
vegetation**

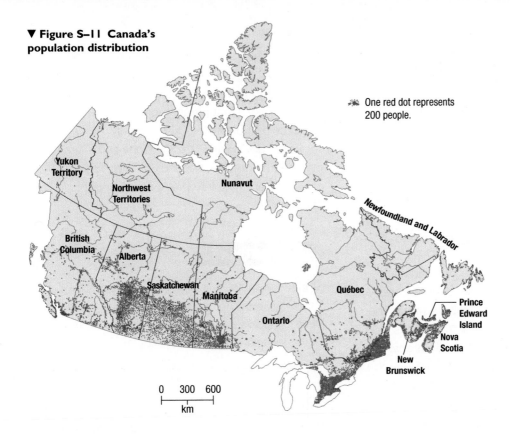

▼ **Figure S–11 Canada's population distribution**

* One red dot represents 200 people.

Yukon Territory

Northwest Territories

Nunavut

Newfoundland and Labrador

British Columbia

Alberta

Saskatchewan

Manitoba

Ontario

Québec

Prince Edward Island

Nova Scotia

New Brunswick

0   300   600
km

Comparing Maps

Once you have determined the kind of information a map provides, you can use that information to ask questions and draw conclusions about the region you are examining. Even if the maps are large-scale and do not include many details, you can still learn a great deal about the region.

APPLY IT!

Use the maps shown in Figures S–10 and S–11 to answer the following questions.

a) Which area(s) of Canada might be best suited for agriculture?

b) Which area(s) might be suitable for forestry activities?

c) Provide two reasons for the distribution of population in Canada. Why are so many areas of Canada relatively unpopulated?

"Our town is the smallest town in our area. Only one main road runs through it. It has no mall and we go by bus to school an hour away. The weather isn't the greatest— often too cold in the winter and too warm in the summer. In my opinion, this is the worst town ever. Last year, the district built a new school in another town, and I think it's not fair that we didn't get a new school, too. If we had more kids coming here, maybe there would be more places to hang out."

–Troya Shepard, Grade 10

In the paragraph above, there are both facts and opinions. The statements that the town has one road running through it and no mall are **facts**. The statements that the weather "isn't the greatest" and the town is the "worst ever" are **opinions**. Although Troya does not directly state a solution, the reader might suggest she has one—a new school, which might result in "more places to hang out." Suggesting what someone means when it is not stated outright is called making an **inference**.

Understanding the Terms

Fact

A fact is something that can be proven by hard evidence, and about which there is general agreement.

Opinion

Opinions are different viewpoints about the same event, situation, or issue. An author with an opinion may be trying to convince the reader to support his or her position on a subject.

Inference

An inference is a position or decision that you come to by concluding something about information presented to you. For example, Troya inferred that a new school might attract more young people, resulting in "more places to hang out."

Facts are always true. Opinions and inferences may be true or false, depending on one's point of view or ability to interpret a situation or piece of information.

APPLY IT!

Find the facts, opinions, and inferences in the following text about transporting goods to Canada's northern mines. You can read the full text in Chapter 7, page 164.

The plan is to build an all-weather, all-year highway from the mines to a new port on Bathurst Inlet.
Ice roads are an uncertain and expensive way to service the mines.
Two methods of transportation serve the mines.
The result would be cheaper, more reliable transportation and likely new life for the Jericho mine.
During the summer, freighters could bring large stockpiles of bulky goods to the beginning of the new highway.
Ice roads are just plowed sections of frozen lakes and rivers.
Conditions on them can be dangerous and difficult to predict.

A controversial issue is one about which different people hold widely divergent views. There is rarely common ground for agreement, and feelings may run high as positions are being explained or defended.

Controversial issues are usually complex; they do not have a straightforward answer. It may be hard to even discuss these issues rationally. Some controversial issues in geography are resource development, urban sprawl, climate change, illegal immigration, and consumerism (sometimes referred to as "the geography of stuff").

What can you do to assess various positions on a controversial issue?

▲ **Figure S–12** In Chapter 11, you considered the controversial issue of whether Canada should have a one-child policy—similar to China's policy shown in the poster above. What did you learn about investigating and discussing this issue that might help you approach other controversial issues?

Start with the Issue As with other investigations, it's best to start with the issue itself. What is the controversial issue you are examining? Try to describe it. What, exactly, is the controversy about? State it in your own words. You may find it useful to use the stem, "The issue is about whether _____ should ..."

Identify the Positions Try to identify the main groups speaking about the issue, and their viewpoints.

Identify the Facts What are the facts of the issue? (To determine whether a statement is a fact, see page 326.) Try to gather as many facts about the issue as possible.

Identify the Values One reason that issues become controversial is that people with differing views often have strong values. When assessing different perspectives on the issue, try to identify the values reflected in those views. Examples of values are materialism, equality, and self-sufficiency. You do not have to consider all values as equal. Racial inequality, for example, is not equivalent to fairness.

Identify the Arguments Finally, identify the arguments that are being made. You might find it helpful to use a pro-and-con chart for this purpose. Are the arguments supported with evidence? Do the arguments answer objections? Are the arguments being made by the people who stand to gain the most or lose the most? Which argument do you think is the most persuasive one? Why?

APPLY IT!

Select a controversial issue in geography to research. Assess two different positions on this issue using the steps described above.

Giving an effective presentation is a valuable skill you can use long after you leave school. Think about the last presentation you made. Were you prepared? Did you appear comfortable and confident? Did you have your audience's attention? What worked? What didn't work? Here are some tips to make your next presentation a success.

Establish Your Content

- Research your topic fully.

- Decide on the information you will present and the order of presentation. Think about a catchy introduction and an informative conclusion.

- Review your content when you have concluded your research. Will your audience understand what you are saying? If not, go back and adjust your content.

Use Multimedia

There are many types of multimedia that you can use to support your presentation.

- Use video or DVD material that is related to your topic. If your school has the capability, you can use video clips from the Internet.

- Design a webpage on your topic, including a homepage, links to useful sites, text, photographs, and sound or video clips. If possible, project your webpage during your presentation.

- Look for programs and apps designed to assist in effective presentations, such as PowerPoint, Keynote, and Prezi. They can be used to create strong visual effects.

Prepare

- Write an outline of your presentation. Include cues to multimedia elements. If you make changes, they should be clean and easy to read.

- Rehearse your presentation—not once, but several times.

◄ **Figure S–13**
Multimedia technology can support your presentation and make it more visually interesting.

- If you are using any sort of audiovisual or computer equipment, make sure that it works—before your presentation!

Presentation Dos and Don'ts

- **DO** make eye contact with your audience.

- **DO** use a hook—an interesting image, story, or question at the beginning of your presentation that catches the attention of your audience.

- **DO** speak clearly and loudly, so everyone can hear you. Speak at a medium pace, neither too fast nor too slow.

- **DON'T** read your presentation with your face buried in your notes. You are speaking to your audience, not yourself.

- **DON'T** sit or lean on a desk. Stand and face your audience.

APPLY IT!

Look back at presentations you have made recently.

a) What were your strengths? What were your weaknesses?

b) What strategies could you use to capitalize on your strengths and improve your weaknesses?

Glossary

Note: Glossary terms in **blue** are Key Terms.

20-minute neighbourhood a community in which important destinations (such as shops, jobs, schools, and parks) are within 1.6 kilometres, a distance that can be walked within 20 minutes at a brisk pace

A

absolute location where something is located in terms of latitude and longitude

absolute measure a quantity of something using simple units, such as kilometres, dollars, or number of people

annual temperature range temperature of the warmest month minus the temperature of the coldest month

aquaculture fish farming

aridity index a value used to show water availability. It combines measures of supply and natural demand.

B

banks shallow parts of the continental shelf that are good for fishing

basic job a job that brings money into an economy from somewhere else

Big Move a plan to dramatically improve transportation systems in the GTHA and Ottawa areas by 2035

biocapacity the average amount of land available to support each person

bioenergy electricity generated from burning *biomass* (wood products, plant products, or even garbage) or *biogas* (gas produced in landfills and sewage treatment plants)

birth rate the number of births in a population per year per 1000 people

bulk water exports according to NAFTA rules, any water exports in quantities larger than 20 litre containers

C

carrying capacity the ability of the environment to support a population without environmental damage

census metropolitan area (CMA) an urban area in Canada with a population over 100 000. A CMA is centred around a city and generally extends beyond the borders of the city.

climate graph (also called a *climograph*) a graph that summarizes climate data for a particular location

community a group of people who share common characteristics, such as their history, culture, beliefs, or simply the space where they live. You belong to more than one community (e.g., your neighbourhood, town, ethnic group, school, country, or even the world).

concentrated population a population focused in patches with specific resource industries, such as mines or paper mills

conservation the wise use of resources

consumption the process of taking water from a store to be used, but it is not returned to the store after the use (e.g., it evaporates). It cannot be reused.

continental climate climate in areas far from an ocean. The annual temperature range is large and precipitation is low.

continental shelf the part of the ocean that is next to continents and is typically less than 200 metres deep

continuous ecumene the part of the country where there is continuous, permanent settlement

D

death rate the number of deaths in a population per year per 1000 people

demographic transition model a model used to describe the change from a high birth rate and high death rate demographic pattern to a low birth rate and low death rate pattern

demographic trap the situation in which a country's population growth rate is so high that the country is not able to develop economically and socially

demography the study of human populations

dependency load the percentage of the population that is non-working. It is conventionally defined as including people younger than age 15 and older than age 65.

deposition the building up of eroded materials in a new location

discontinuous ecumene the part of the country where there are significant patches of settlement

dispersed population a population spread evenly across the land; common in agricultural areas

doubling time the length of time for a country's population to double at a particular population growth rate

drainage basin the area of land in which all of the water flows (drains) to the same body of water (river, lake, ocean, etc.)

dry-climate soils soils that develop where calcification is the dominant soil-forming process

E

ecological footprint (EF) a measure of resource use per person, expressed as the number of hectares of productive land that is needed to support a person

ecosystem a community of living things and the physical environment in which they live

©P

emigrant a person who leaves one country to move to another country

emigration rate the number of emigrants moving from a country per year per 1000 people

environmental performance index (EPI) a UN–produced measure for evaluating performance in a wide range of environmental fields

erosion the moving of broken-up pieces of rock

extraction the process of taking water from a store (e.g., groundwater or a river) to be used. After the use, it is returned to the store, where it is available to be used again.

F

feedback loop a cycle in which the output of a process becomes an input back into the process

flow resources resources that are replaced by natural actions and must be used when and where they occur or be lost

flows mechanisms by which stores move from one reserve to another

fracking a variety of techniques used to break up shale layers far below the surface in order to liberate natural gas and/or oil that has been trapped. Injecting a mixture of water, sand, and dozens of chemicals into a well usually breaks up the rock.

fragile state a poor country that is not able to respond to crises that might occur in its food supply, health care, or other critical systems

G

geographic inquiry an active, questioning approach to learning about the world from a geographic perspective

geographic perspective a way of looking at the world that includes environmental, political, and social implications

georeferencing linking geographic data to a particular location

geotechnology the use of advanced technology in the study of geography and in everyday use

GIS (Geographic Information System) computer system that manages and analyzes geographic information

glaciation the process of ice advancing and covering large areas of land

GPS (Global Positioning System) a satellite-based system that provides location data

greenbelt an area of rural land around a city that cannot be built on

gross domestic product (GDP) per capita a measure of the size of an economy, in dollars, divided by the population

gross national happiness (GNH) a measure of the happiness of a population

groundwater water held underground in tiny spaces in the soil or some types of rocks

H

happy planet index (HPI) a measure that combines quality of life and sustainability

higher-order goods and services goods and services that are needed infrequently. These goods and services tend to be quite specialized and often costly.

high-rise a building 35 metres to 100 metres tall

human development index (HDI) a measure of overall quality of life that combines measures of wealth, health, and education. The HDI was developed by the United Nations.

human resources the people who work for a business or other organization. Their skills and efforts are a significant asset.

I

immigrant a person who moves to one country from another country

immigration rate the number of immigrants moving to a country per year per 1000 people

index value a value without units, usually calculated in comparison to a common base number

inshore fishery commercial fishing carried out close to shore in small, independently owned boats

interrelationship a relationship that exists between different patterns and trends

J

just-in-time (JIT) delivery system in which parts used in manufacturing are delivered to the factory just in time to be taken directly to the assembly line rather than being put into storage

L

land use intensification a process in which development is focused on filling vacant lots (residential infill), bringing disused buildings back into use, and replacing low-density dwellings with higher-density buildings

land use the various functions of land in an urban or rural area

land-use conflict a situation that exists when adjacent land uses interfere with each other in some way. The interference could include noise, smell, dust, traffic, or air or water pollution.

linear population a population settled along a line, such as a coastline, river, or highway

liveability all the characteristics of a community that contribute to the quality of life of the people who live there

lower-order goods and services goods and services that are purchased frequently. Generally these goods and services are relatively inexpensive.

©P

M

maritime climate climate in areas near an ocean. The annual temperature range (summer to winter) is small and precipitation is high.

metallic mineral a mineral that yields a metal (e.g., iron, gold, copper, uranium, zinc, silver, lead) when melted. It typically comes from igneous and metamorphic rocks.

mid-ocean ridge a feature created by the spreading of the sea floor where two plates are diverging. The best-known example runs through the Atlantic Ocean from north to south.

mineral reserve a mineral deposit that can be mined profitably

mining the resource exploiting a renewable resource in an unsustainable way

model a simplified description of a complex process or system

multiplier effect the increase in total wealth or income that occurs when new money is injected into an economy

N

natural increase rate the birth rate minus the death rate

natural resources things found in the total stock that people find useful

natural vegetation the plants that would grow in an area with no human interference

net migration rate the immigration rate minus the emigration rate

NGO (non-governmental organization) a private, not-for-profit organization that works to achieve particular social, environmental, or political goals

non-basic job a job that circulates money within an economy

non-metallic mineral a mineral that does not change its form when melted (e.g., potash, sand, gravel, diamonds, salt, limestone, building stone). It most commonly comes from sedimentary rocks.

non-renewable resources resources that are limited and cannot be replaced once they are used up

O

official plan an important document that all municipalities must have that lays out the general policies to be followed to achieve long-term planning goals

offshore fishery commercial fishing carried out farther from shore in larger company-owned boats

oil sands/tar sands deposits of sand containing a heavy form of crude oil called bitumen

old-growth forest a forest that has never been logged

ore a rock that contains enough of a valuable metallic mineral to make mining profitable

other resources resources that do not fit into the other three categories (renewable, non-renewable, and flow resources)

outsourcing when a company moves part of its operation (e.g., manufacturing or IT support) to another country to take advantage of cheaper labour costs and less stringent labour and environmental controls

P

pattern the arrangement of objects on Earth's surface in relationship to each other

plate tectonics the theory that Earth's outer shell is made up of individual plates that move, causing earthquakes, volcanoes, mountains, and the formation and destruction of areas of the crust

population density the average number of people living in a particular place. It is calculated by dividing the population of a place (e.g., country, province, or city) by the area of the place.

population growth rate the natural increase rate plus the net migration rate

population implosion a dramatic decline in population; the opposite of a population explosion

population pyramid a type of graph that shows population distribution by age and gender

potential evapotranspiration the natural demand for water in a particular environment, including evaporation from the land surface and transpiration by plants

precipitation water from the atmosphere that falls to Earth, including rain, snow, hail, and sleet

primary industry (also called *extractive industry*) an industry that focuses on producing or extracting natural resources. This sector includes forest industries, agriculture, mining, and fishing.

production how much of a resource is being taken from the ground each year

pull factor a reason that makes a particular country seem attractive to potential immigrants

push factor a reason that encourages people to move away from their current country

R

R/P ratio the number of years that the reserves of a non-renewable resource will last at current rates of production

refugee someone who moves to another country because of fear of cruel or inhumane treatment (even death) in her or his home country as a result of race, religion, sexual orientation, nationality, political opinion, or membership in a particular social group

relative location where something is located in relation to other geographic features

relative measure a quantity of something compared to the quantity of something else, using units such as percentages and ratios (e.g., people per square kilometre)

remote sensing seeing or measuring something from a considerable distance, often from a satellite

renewable resources resources that can be regenerated if used carefully

replacement rate (RR) the TFR (total fertility rate) that will result in a stable population. The RR is usually considered to be 2.1 children per woman.

reserves how much of a resource is thought to be in the ground, based on exploration to date

residential density a measure of the number of housing units per hectare

resource anything that can be used to produce goods and services, such as raw materials, workers, money, and land

rule of 70 a simple calculation to estimate doubling time (70 ÷ population growth rate)

S

secondary industry an industry that focuses on making things using the products of primary industries. This sector includes manufacturing, construction, and utilities (the provision and distribution of electricity, water, natural gas, etc.).

skyscraper a building more than 100 metres tall

soil profile the three different layers that exist in the soil beneath the surface of the ground. Each layer has a particular combination of physical, biological, and chemical characteristics.

spatial significance the importance of a particular location in geography

stores places in the world where water is stored

subduction the process in which one plate slides underneath another. The subducted plate moves into Earth's interior and is "recycled" (it melts).

subsistence farming farming done with the primary goal of feeding one's family rather than selling agricultural products for income

survey system a grid system used to locate and identify parcels of land and roads

sustainability improving the quality of human life while living within the carrying capacity of supporting ecosystems

sustained yield management the process of managing a renewable resource to ensure that the amount harvested does not cause long-term depletion of the resource. The harvest is equal to or less than the amount replenished each year.

T

telematics any technology that involves the long-distance transmission of digital information

tertiary industry (also called *service* or *services-providing industry*) an industry that focuses on providing services. This sector includes "everything else" that is not included in the primary and secondary industries.

total fertility rate (TFR) the average number of children born to a woman in her lifetime

total stock all parts of the natural environment including energy, living organisms, and non-living materials. For example, sunlight, trees, and water are all part of the total stock.

trend a noticeable change in a pattern over time

tsunami a set of large ocean waves caused by an earthquake or other powerful disturbance under the sea. A tsunami can cause great destruction when it reaches land.

U

urban growth growth in the number of people who live in cities and towns

urban sprawl largely uncontrolled expansion of cities onto adjacent rural lands

urbanization growth in the percentage of a country's population that lives in cities and towns

W

waste diversion processes that reduce the amount of waste that ends up going to landfills. These include source reduction (producing less waste in the first place), recycling, and reusing.

weathering the breaking down of rocks

wet-climate soils soils that develop where leaching is the dominant soil-forming process

Z

zoning the result of a detailed planning process that specifies exactly what land uses are allowed in each part of a municipality

©P

Index

©P

©P

©P

©P

Credits

Photo Credits

Cover: (top) © John Greim/First Light; (bottom) © Con Tanasiuk/First Light.

Exploring Geography: 1 Courtesy of the University of Northern British Columbia; **2** (from top clockwise) © jack thomas/Alamy; John Mahler/Toronto/GetStock.com; Chuck Savage/Lithium/First Light; CP Photo/Jonathan Hayward; © Gaertner/Alamy; © Stefano Ginella/Alamy; **5** (top) © Christi Belcourt; (bottom) AP Photo/The Canadian Press, Adrian Wyld; **6** (top right) Doug Barber/ArcticNet; (bottom) tbkmedia.de/Alamy; **7** Courtesy of Jillian Schlesinger. © A Wild Shot Films Production; **10** (top left) imagesandstories/Blickwinkel/First Light; (top right) Jenifoto/fotolia.com; (bottom) Fotofermer/fotolia.com; (centre left) Sommai/fotolia.com; (centre right) © Mike Booth/Alamy; **11** (top left) Bill/fotolia.com; (top right) Jet Sky/fotolia.com; (bottom) Lana Langlois/fotolia.com; **12** Oleksiy Maksymenko/Alamy; **13** AP Photo/Stephan Kogelman; **14** (left) NOAA/JMA; (right) RADARSAT-2 Data and Products © MacDONALD, DETTWILER AND ASSOCIATES LTD. 2008 – All Rights Reserved. RADARSAT is an official mark of the Canadian Space Agency; **15** Earth Science and Remote Sensing Unit, NASA-Johnson Space Center, The Gateway to Astronaut Photography of Earth; **16** © Caryn Becker/Alamy.

Interactions with the Physical Environment: 17 Dan Barnes/Getty Images.

Chapter 1: 18 Canadian Tourism Commission; **19** Courtesy of Amy Snowden; **23** © imageBROKER/Alamy; **25** Scott Steeves/AsphaltPlanet.ca; **26** © Gaertner/Alamy; **28** (left) © Design Pics Inc./Alamy; (right) © jake wyman/Alamy; **29** Natural Resources Canada.

Chapter 2: 32 (top) © Jackie Kloosterboer; (bottom) Dan Breckwoldt/Shutterstock; **33** AP Photo/Damian Dovarganes/CP Images; **34** (top) © Sunshine Pics/fotolia.com; (bottom) © Bill Brooks/Alamy; **37** © Jan Krogh; **38** Michael Interisano/Design Pics/First Light; **40** © sciencephotos/Alamy; **41** © The Natural History Museum/Alamy; **42** Dirk Wiersma/Science Source; **45** Image Courtesy SRTM Team NASA/JPL/NIMA; **46** (A) Mike Grandmaison/All Canada Photos; (B) Imfoto/Shutterstock; (C) © Bill Brooks/Alamy; (D) LesPalenik/Shutterstock; (E) Michael P. Gadomski/Science Source; (F) Reproduced with the permission of the Minister of Agriculture and Agri-Food Canada; **47** *White Pine* by A.J. Casson. Gift of the Founders, Robert and Signe McMichael, McMichael Art Collection 1966.16.119; **48** (top) *Lake Alphonse* by William Goodridge Roberts1942 oil on canvas 48.5 x 74.0 cm, purchased 1984 McMichael Art Collection 1984.20; (bottom) *The Glacier* by Arthur Lismer, 1928, oil on canvas, Art Gallery of Hamilton, Gift of the Women's Committee, 1960 © Mrs. Phillip N. Bridges and Marjorie Bridges; **49** (top) *No Grass Grows on the Beaten Path* by William Kurelek, courtesy of the Estate of William Kurelek and the Isaacs Gallery, Toronto; (bottom) Tyler Olson/fotolia; **51** (top) Mike Grandmaison/All Canada Photos; (bottom left) © Visual&Written SL/Alamy; (bottom centre) metalstock/Shutterstock; (bottom right) © Dawns Images Nature Photography/Alamy; **52** (left) John E Marriott/All Canada Photos; (centre) Ron Erwin/All Canada Photos; (right) Alexandra Kobalenko/All Canada Photos; **54** © Sue Thomas, http://suethomas.ca.

Chapter 3: 55 Photo by Peter Power/The Globe and Mail; **66** (left) Dave Reede/All Canada Photos; (right) Keith Levit/Design Pics/First Light; **67** Agriculture and Agri-Food Canada. Reproduced with the permission of the Minister of Agriculture and Agri-Food Canada, 2014; **69** Courtesy of Kara Webster; **70** (top) © Accent Alaska.com/Alamy; (bottom) Agriculture and Agri-Food Canada. Reproduced with the permission of the Minister of Agriculture and Agri-Food Canada, 2014; **73** First Light/All Canada Photos; **74** Ron Erwin/All Canada Photos; **75** (top) Kitchin and Hurst/All Canada Photos; (bottom) Don Johnston/Alamy; **76** (top) Ryan Creary/All Canada Photos; (bottom) Curt Teich Postcard Archives/Heritage Images/Glow Images.

Resources and Industries: 81 Larry Macdougal/First Light.

Chapter 4: 82 Stephen Barnes/Transport/Alamy; **83** PHILIPPE PSAILA/SCIENCE PHOTO LIBRARY; 84 Oil Museum of Canada, Oil Springs, ON; **85** Ontario Power Generation; **86** Peter Power/The Globe and Mail; **87** City of Mississauga; **88** ImageBROKER/Superstock; **89** © Eye-Stock/Alamy; © Libby Welch/Alamy; © Louise Heusinkveld/Alamy; © Realimage/Alamy; **90** © ZUMA Press, Inc/Alamy; **92** © 2010 Green Hotels Association; **93** (inset) © Yiyi Shangguan; Bill Ivy/Ivy Images; **94** (left) rSnapshotPhotos/Shutterstock; (right) Brian Summers/First Light; **95** (left) © DWImages Motoring/Alamy; (right) AP Photo/Paul Sancya, File; **97** Tree Canada, www.treecanada.ca.

Chapter 5: 101 © ZUMA Press, Inc/Alamy; **103** Andrew McLachlan/All Canada Photos; **104** (left) © Stephen Datnoff/DanitaDelimont.com; (right) Pacific Stock/All Canada Photos; **108** Thomas Kokta/Getty Images; **109** (left) Bill Brooks/Alamy; (right) Designpics/All Canada Photos; **110** Glenbow Archives/NA-4722-18; **112** (left) Library and Archives Canada; (right) Brian Davies/The Register-Guard/Associated Press; **116** (top) © LOOK Die Bildagentur der Fotografen GmbH/Alamy; (bottom) Algonquin Forest Authority; **120** (left) © Gunter Marx/IN/Alamy; (right) Arne Bramsen/Shutterstock; **123** © Marine Stewardship Council, www.msc.org.

Chapter 6: 126 CP PHOTO/ Thunder Bay Chronicle-Journal/Brent Linton; **128** © Carmela Marshall; **130** © Cameron Davidson/Corbis; **133** © Bill Brooks/Alamy; **137** © Peter Dudley; **140** (left) Barrett & MacKay/All Canada Photos; (right) ANDY Clark/Reuters/Landov.

Chapter 7: 142 (left) © Bayne Stanley/Alamy; (right) © Design Pics Inc./Alamy; **143** (top) Ken M. Johns/Science Source; (bottom) © ATI; **146** © David Lyons; **149** © Hayley Dunning; **153** THE CANADIAN PRESS IMAGES/Graham Hughes; **154** Saskatchewan Mining Association; **155** © RF Company/Alamy; **156** (left) © Ashley Cooper/Alamy; (right) Chris Harris/All Canada Photos; **157** Monty Rakusen/Glow Images; **162** Photo Courtesy of The Diavik Diamond Mine; **164** Jason Pineau/All Canada Photos; (inset) Photo Courtesy of The Diavik Diamond Mine.

©P

Chapter 8: 169 THE CANADIAN PRESS/Aaron Vincent Elkaim; © GIPhotoStock X/Alamy; © Alex Segre/Alamy; © Beaconstox/Alamy; © GIPhotoStock X/Alamy; © GIPhotoStock Z/Alamy; © luciopix/Alamy; © Q-Images/Alamy; © Tetra Images/Alamy; © Yankee/Alamy; © Lux Igitur/Alamy; © Independent Picture Service/Alamy; © Alpha and Omega Collection/Alamy; © Carolyn Jenkins/Alamy; © MARKA/Alamy; © Carolyn Jenkins/Alamy; The Canadian Press Images/Lee Brown; © openwater/fotolia.com; John Kwan/fotolia.com; roberaten/fotolia.com; 170 (top) © Greg Taylor/Alamy; (right) Fred Thornhill/Reuters/Landov; (left) © Hero Images Inc./Alamy; 172 © Ileen MacDonald/Alamy; 173 © Lloyd Sutton/Alamy; 174 Masterfile; 177 Jeff Goode/GetStock.com; 178 Courtesy of Rio Tinto; 181 The Canadian Press Images/Stephen C. Host; 182 (top) Copyright © 2014 Town of Smiths Falls; (bottom) Courtesy of Heritage House Museum, Smiths Falls; 184 © RubberBall/Alamy; 188 Manitobah Mukluks; 189 Michael Stuparyk/Toronto Star via Getty Images; 190 © Ingrid Rice.

Chapter 9: 194 (left) MATT CROSSICK/PA Photos/Landov; (right) JOEL PHILIPPON/Maxppp/Landov; 196 Courtesy of Kenneth Pong; 202 (top) Courtesy of Newcastle Home Décor; (bottom) © James Smedley Outdoors; 203 Ernest Doroszuk/Toronto Sun/QMI Agency; 204 (left) Copyright 2007 Pierre Bouchard; (right) Don Johnston/All Canada Photos; 206 Courtesy of Cowater International.

Changing Populations: 211 RonTech2000/Getty Images.

Chapter 10: 215 Marco WEBER/PONOPRESSE/Gamma-Rapho via Getty Images; 218 (left) ROBERTO SALOMONE/AFP/Getty Images; (right) HECTOR MATA/AFP/Getty Images; 220 Glenbow Archives/NA-984-2; 221 Photo by D'Arcy Glionna; 223 (left) Tristram Kenton/Lebrecht Music & Arts; (right) © canadabrian/Alamy; 224 (top) MACLEAN'S PHOTO/Bayne Stanley; (bottom) Photo by Ed Giles/Getty Images; 226 © Screen Media Films/courtesy Everett Collection; 227 © Susan Niazi; 228 THE CANADIAN PRESS/Darryl Dyck; 229 Photo by Matthew Staver/Bloomberg via Getty Images; 231 Henri Georgi/All Canada Photos/Getty Images; 232 Ontario Federation of Indigenous Friendship Centres; 234 (left) Giacomo Pirozzi/Panos Pictures; (right) Yuriko Nakao/Bloomberg via Getty Images.

Chapter 11: 237 © Barry Lewis/Alamy; 238 © Arochau/fotolia.com; 240 © Chris Howes/Wild Places Photography/Alamy; 241 © Kevin Landwer-Johan/Alamy; 242 (top) Dinodia/Getty Images; (bottom) © Jaren Wicklund/fotolia.com; 244 Juniors Bildarchiv/Glow Images; 248 (top right) Courtesy of Bruce Clarke; (bottom right) © Google Earth; 249 Photo by Ray Tang/REX Feature/The Canadian Press; 250 (top left) © Bert Hoferichter/Alamy; (top right) Tim Graham/Robert Harding/Newscom; (bottom left) The State of the World's Children 2013, © UNICEF. Reproduced with permission of UNICEF Canada; (bottom right) Matthias Schrader Deutsche Presse-Agentur/Newscom; 254 © gpointstudio/fotolia.com.

Liveable Communities: 255 (left) © Fred Ingram; (right) Ashley Coombs Photography.

Chapter 12: 256 Lucas Oleniuk/GetStock.com; 258 THE CANADIAN PRESS/Darryl Dyck; 260 Image © 2014 DigitalGlobe; 261 © Islemount Images/Alamy; 262 © Google Earth; 264 (top left) V. J. Matthew/Shutterstock; Mary Beth MacLean; (centre) © Volodymyr Kyrylyuk/fotolia.com; (bottom) © labalajadia/fotolia.com; 265 Fred Lum/The Globe and Mail; 266 Angeles Antolin/ Moment/ Getty Images; 268 (left) © National Geographic Image Collection/Alamy; (right) Todd Korol/Aurora/Getty Images; 269 Fred Lum/The Globe and Mail/CP Images; 270 (left) © Robert Fried/Alamy; (right) Rolf Hicker/All Canada Photos; (inset) Courtesy of Bruce Clarke; 272 (top) © RICK WILKING/Reuters/Corbis; (bottom) © Andreas von Einsiedel/Alamy; 273 (left) © Radius Images/Alamy; (right) Copyright © Cosette Schulz; 275 Rick Madonik/GetStock.com.

Chapter 13: 277 © Canadian Broadcasting Corporation; 279 © Sue Cunningham Photographic/Alamy; 280 (top) Virginie Blanquart/Moment/Getty Images; (bottom) © dbimages/Alamy; 281 Photo by Bongani Mnguni/City Press/Gallo Images/Getty Images; 284 THOMAS MUKOYA/Reuters/Landov; 285 © Bill Brooks/Alamy; 286 Ethan Meleg/All Canada Photos; 290 (top) © Sean O'Neill/Alamy; (bottom) THE CANADIAN PRESS IMAGES/Don Denton; 291 Carmanah Technologies; 292 Fernando Morales/The Globe and Mail; 294 © All rights reserved by Mikey G Ottawa; 295 Kristen Thompson/MetroNews Vancouver; 298 Scott Steeves/AsphaltPlanet.ca; 299 © 2014 City of Ottawa. All rights reserved.

Chapter 14: 303 Archives Congrégation de Notre-Dame; 304 © Martin Shields/Alamy; (inset) © Gstudio Group/fotolia.com; 306 John Warburton-Lee/Alamy.

Skills Tool Kit: 316 © RubberBall/Alamy; 318 The Glacier by Arthur Lismer, 1928, oil on canvas, Art Gallery of Hamilton, Gift of the Women's Committee, 1960 © Mrs. Phillip N. Bridges and Marjorie Bridges; 320 © Hayley Dunning; 327 Canadian Tourism Commission; 328 Pearson Canada.

Literary Credits

Chapter 1: 19 Population Division of the Department of Economic and Social Affairs of the United Nations Secretariat, World Population Prospects: The 2012 Revision, http://esa.un.org/unpd/wpp/index.htm; 20 ©Mapping Worlds 2004-2014; 21 © University of British Columbia; 24 Statistics Canada, Statistics Canada, CANSIM, table 051-0056. Reproduced and distributed on an "as is" basis with the permission of Statistics Canada; 26 Statistics Canada, 2011 Census. Reproduced and distributed on an "as is" basis with the permission of Statistics Canada.

Chapter 2: 31 Canada Land Inventory: Soil Capability for Agriculture (cartography by the Soil Research Institute, Research Branch), Agriculture and Agri-Food Canada, 1968. Reproduced with the permission of the Minister of Agriculture and Agri-Food Canada, 2014.

Chapter 3: 57 NOAA; 62-63 Environment Canada, 1981-2010 Climate Normals & Averages; 71 From Remarks by Sheila Watt-Cloutier, Chair of the Inuit Circumpolar Conference, at the Award Ceremony for the 2005 Sophie Prize.

Chapter 4: 84 Based on data from National Energy Board. Reproduced with permission from the National Energy Board Canada.

Chapter 5: 116 A Royal Commission for Forest Preservation and National Park, 1892 Ontario Legislative Assembly, Sessional Papers, Volume 25, Part 8.

Chapter 6: 126 Courtesy of Mattawa/North Bay Algonquin First Nation; **135** Environment Canada, 1981-2010 Climate Normals & Averages.

Chapter 7: 144 US Geological Survey; **147** National Energy Board Library; **165** Adapted from Earth Science Australia.

Chapter 8: 177 © Magna International; **187** Statistics Canada, Canada's International Trade in Goods, 2013. Reproduced and distributed on an "as is" basis with the permission of Statistics Canada; **189** Statistics Canada, Manufacturing output rises in January. Reproduced and distributed on an "as is" basis with the permission of Statistics Canada; **190** Board of Governors of the Federal Reserve System; **191** Statistics Canada, Chinese Imports into Canada, 1990-2013. Reproduced and distributed on an "as is" basis with the permission of Statistics Canada.

Chapter 9: 195, 196 Forbes Global 2000; **197** Statistics Canada, Kapuskasing, T, Ontario (Code 3556066) (table). National Household Survey (NHS) Profile. 2011 National Household Survey. Statistics Canada Catalogue no. 99-004-XWE. Ottawa. Released September 11, 2013. Reproduced and distributed on an "as is" basis with the permission of Statistics Canada; **198** Statistics Canada, Employmentby industry. CANSIM, table 282-0008. Last modified: 2014-01-10. Reproduced and distributed on an "as is" basis with the permission of Statistics Canada; **199** Statistics Canada, Job distribution in Canada, 2013. Reproduced and distributed on an "as is" basis with the permission of Statistics Canada.

Chapter 10: 227 Susan Niaizi.

Chapter 11: 239 Population Division of the Department of Economic and Social Affairs of the United Nations Secretariat, World Population Prospects: The 2012 Revision, http://esa.un.org/unpd/wpp/index.htm; **245** Global Poverty is Declining Sharply Except in Fragile States, © OECD, 2013, http://www.oecd.org/media/oecdorg/directorates/developmentco-operationdirectoratedcd-dac/incaf/DECLINING%20POVERTY_705.jpg; **247** Where Will the Global Poor Be in 2015? From Fragile States 2013: Resource Flows and Trends in a Shifting World, 2013. © OECD; 247 Based on data from OECD, Compare your country – Official Development Assistance 2013 http://www.compareyourcountry.org/?cr=o-ecd&lg=en, accessed on Nov 2, 2014; **253** Average Number of persons living in Canadian households, 1961-2011. Reproduced and distributed on an "as is" basis with the permission of Statistics Canada.

Chapter 12: 260 Centre for Urban and Community Studies, University of Toronto; **265** © Royal Bank of Canada.

Skills Tool Kit: 302 Data sourced from Global Footprint Network 2008 report (2005 data) UN Human Development Index 2005.

Art Credits

Endpaper Maps Dave McKay © Pearson Canada Inc.; **102** Dave Whamond © Pearson Canada Inc.; **All Other Art** ArtPlus Ltd. © Pearson Canada Inc.

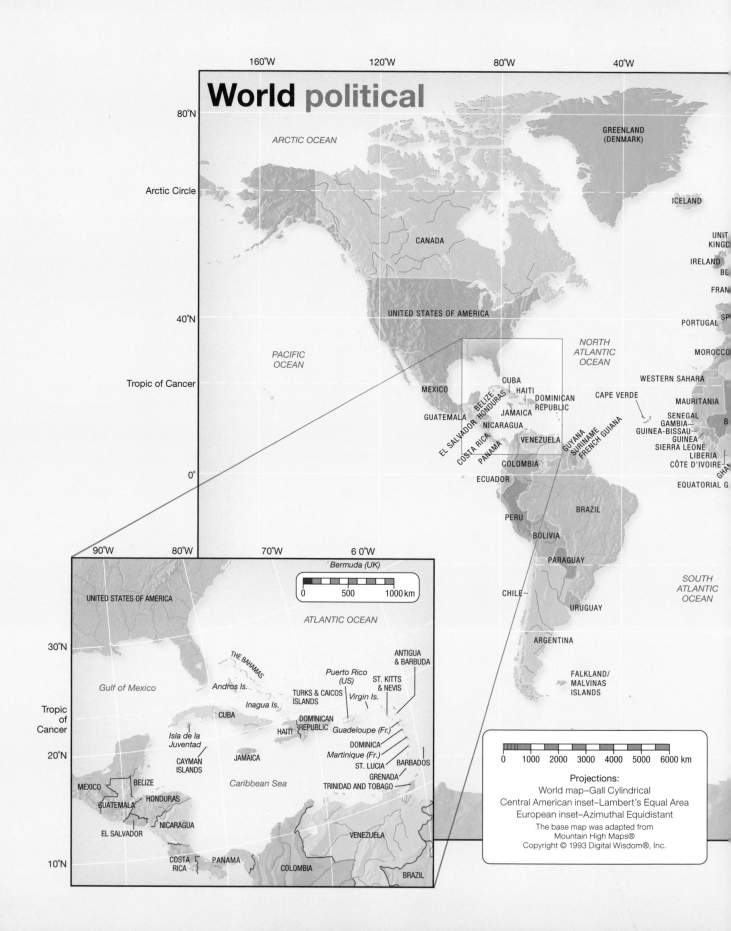

World political

160°W   120°W   80°W   40°W

80°N

ARCTIC OCEAN

GREENLAND
(DENMARK)

Arctic Circle

ICELAND

CANADA

UNIT
KINGD

IRELAND

BE

40°N

FRAN

UNITED STATES OF AMERICA

PORTUGAL   SP

NORTH
ATLANTIC
OCEAN

MOROCCO

PACIFIC
OCEAN

WESTERN SAHARA

Tropic of Cancer

CUBA

CAPE VERDE

MAURITANIA

MEXICO

BELIZE
HAITI

DOMINICAN
REPUBLIC

HONDURAS

JAMAICA

SENEGAL
GAMBIA

GUATEMALA

NICARAGUA

GUINEA-BISSAU
GUINEA

EL SALVADOR

VENEZUELA

GUYANA
SURINAME
FRENCH GUIANA

SIERRA LEONE
LIBERIA

B

COSTA RICA
PANAMA

CÔTE D'IVOIRE

0°

COLOMBIA

GHA

ECUADOR

EQUATORIAL G

BRAZIL

PERU

BOLIVIA

SOUTH
ATLANTIC
OCEAN

PARAGUAY

CHILE

URUGUAY

90°W   80°W   70°W   6 0°W

Bermuda (UK)

ARGENTINA

0   500   1000 km

FALKLAND/
MALVINAS
ISLANDS

UNITED STATES OF AMERICA

30°N

ATLANTIC OCEAN

Gulf of Mexico

THE BAHAMAS

ANTIGUA
& BARBUDA

Puerto Rico
(US)

ST. KITTS
& NEVIS

Andros Is.

TURKS & CAICOS
ISLANDS

Inagua Is.

Virgin Is.

CUBA

Tropic
of
Cancer

DOMINICAN
REPUBLIC

Guadeloupe (Fr.)

Isla de la
Juventad

HAITI

DOMINICA

20°N

CAYMAN
ISLANDS

Martinique (Fr.)

JAMAICA

ST. LUCIA

BARBADOS

MEXICO

BELIZE

Caribbean Sea

GRENADA

GUATEMALA

HONDURAS

TRINIDAD AND TOBAGO

EL SALVADOR

NICARAGUA

0   1000   2000   3000   4000   5000   6000 km

VENEZUELA

Projections:
World map–Gall Cylindrical
Central American inset–Lambert's Equal Area
European inset–Azimuthal Equidistant

COSTA
RICA

PANAMA

10°N

COLOMBIA

The base map was adapted from
Mountain High Maps®
Copyright © 1993 Digital Wisdom®, Inc.

BRAZIL